MAN UPON THE SEA:

OR, A HISTORY OF

MARITIME ADVENTURE, EXPLORATION AND DISCOVERY,

From the Earliest Ages to the Present Time.

COMPRISING A DETAILED ACCOUNT OF

REMARKABLE VOYAGES,

ANCIENT AS WELL AS MODERN.

BY

FRANK B. GOODRICH,

AUTHOR OF "THE LETTERS OF DICK TINTO," "THE COURT OF NAPOLEON," ETC.

WITH NUMEROUS ILLUSTRATIONS,

By Van Ingen and Snyder.

PHILADELPHIA:
J. B. LIPPINCOTT & CO.
1858.

CONTENTS.

SECTION I.

FROM THE EARLIEST TIMES TO THE COMMENCEMENT OF THE CHRISTIAN ERA.

SECTION II.

FROM THE COMMENCEMENT OF THE CHRISTIAN ERA TO THE APPLICATION OF THE MAGNETIC NEEDLE TO EUROPEAN NAVIGATION, A.D. 1300.

SECTION III.

FROM THE APPLICATION OF THE MAGNETIC NEEDLE TO EUROPEAN NAVIGATION TO THE FIRST VOYAGE ROUND THE WORLD UNDER MAGELLAN: 1300–1519.

SECTION IV.

FROM THE FIRST VOYAGE ROUND THE WORLD TO THE DISCOVERY OF CAPE HORN: 1519–1616.

SECTION V.

FROM THE DISCOVERY OF CAPE HORN TO THE APPLICATION OF STEAM TO NAVIGATION: 1616–1807.

SECTION VI.

FROM THE APPLICATION OF STEAM TO NAVIGATION TO THE LAYING OF THE ATLANTIC CABLE: 1807-1858.

LIST OF SEPARATE ILLUSTRATIONS.

THE HAND OF SATAN UPON THE SEA OF DARKNESS.

MAN UPON THE SEA.

Section I.

FROM THE EARLIEST TIMES TO THE COMMENCEMENT OF THE CHRISTIAN ERA.

CHAPTER I.

THE PURPOSE OF THIS WORK—THE OCEAN IN THE SCRIPTURAL PERIOD—THE MARVELS OF THE SEA—THE CLASSIC LEGENDS—THE FANTASTIC NOTIONS ENTERTAINED OF THE NORTH AND THE EQUATOR—THE GIANT OF THE CANARIES—THE SEA OF SEA-WEED—THE SPECTRE OF THE CAPE—THE GRADUAL SURRENDER OF THE SECRETS OF THE SEA—IT BECOMES THE HIGHWAY OF NATIONS—ITS PRESENT ASPECT—ITS POETICAL SIGNIFICANCE—ITS MORAL LESSONS.

A HISTORY of the ocean from the Flood to the Atlantic Telegraph, with a parallel sketch of shipbuilding from the Ark to the Leviathan; a narrative of the rise of commerce, from the days when Solomon's ships traded with Ophir, to the time when an American squadron forced the gates of Japan; a consecutive chronicle of the progress of navigation, from the day when the timid mariner hugged the coast by day and prudently cast anchor by night, to the time when the steamship, apparently endowed with reason, or at least guided by instinct, seems almost to dispense with the aid of man,—such a theme seems to offer topics of interest which it would be difficult to find in any other subject. The reader will readily perceive its scope when we have briefly rehearsed what the sea once was to man, and what it now is,—the purpose of the work being to narrate how from the one it has become the other.

In early times, in the scriptural and classic periods, the great oceans were unknown. Mankind—at least that portion whose history has descended to us—dwelt upon the borders of an inland, mediterranean sea. They had never heard of such an expanse of water as the Atlantic, and certainly had never seen it. The land-locked sheet which lay spread out at their feet was at all times full of mystery, and often even of dread and secret misgiving. Those who ventured forth upon its bosom came home and told marvellous tales of the sights they had seen and the perils they had endured. Homer's heroes returned to Ithaca with the music of the sirens in their ears and the cruelties of the giants upon their lips. The Argonauts saw whirling rocks implanted in the sea, to warn and repel the approaching navigator; and, as if the mystery of the waters had tinged with fable even the dry land beyond it, they filled the Caucasus with wild stories of enchantresses, of bulls that breathed fire, and of a race of men that sprang, like a ripened harvest, from the prolific soil. If the ancients were ignorant of the shape of the earth, it was for the very reason that they were ignorant of the ocean. Their geographers and philosophers, whose observations were confined to fragments of Europe, Asia, and Africa, alternately made the world a cylinder, a flat surface begirt by water, a drum, a boat, a disk. The legends that sprang from these confused and contradictory notions made the land a scene of marvels and the water an abode of terrors.

At a later period, when, with the progress of time, the love of adventure or the needs of commerce had drawn the navigator from the Mediterranean through the Pillars of Hercules into the Atlantic, and when some conception of the immensity of the waters had forced itself upon minds dwarfed by the contracted limits of the inland sea, then the ocean became in good earnest a receptacle of gloomy and appalling horrors, and the marvels narrated by those fortunate enough to return told how deeply the imagination had been stirred by the new scenes opened to their vision. Pytheas, who coasted from Marseilles to the Shetland Isles, and who there obtained a glance at the bleak and wintry desolation of the North Sea, declared, on reaching home, that his further progress was barred by an immense black mollusk, which hung suspended in the air, and in which a ship would be inextricably involved, and where no man could breathe. The menaces of the South were even more appalling than the perils of the North; for he who should venture, it was said, across the equator into the regions of the Sun, would be changed into a negro for his rashness: besides, in the popular belief, the waters there were not navigable. Upon the quaint charts of the Middle Ages, a giant located upon the Canary Islands forbade all farther venture westward, by brandishing his formidable club in the path of all vessels coming from the east. Upon these singular maps the concealed and treacherous horrors of the deep were displayed in the grotesque shapes of sea-monsters and distorted water-unicorns, which were represented as careering through space and waylaying the navigator. Even in the time of Columbus, and when the introduction of the compass into European ships should have somewhat diminished the fantastic terrors of the sea, we find that the Arabians, the best geographers of the time, represented the bony and gnarled hand of Satan as rising from the waves of the Sea of Darkness,—as the Atlantic was then called,—ready to seize and engulf the presumptuous mariner. The sailors of Columbus, on reaching the Sargasso Sea, where the collected weeds offered an impediment to their progress, thought they had arrived at the limit of navigation and the end of the world. Five years later, the crew of da Gama, on doubling the Cape of Good Hope, imagined they saw, in the threatening clouds that gathered about Table Rock, the form of a spectre waving off their vessel and crying woe to all who should thus invade his dread dominion. The Neptune of the classics, in short, who disported himself in the narrow waters of the Mediterranean, and of whose wrath we have read the famous mythologic accounts, was a deity altogether bland and debonnaire compared to the gloomy and revengeful monopolist of the seas, such as the historians and geographers of the Middle Ages painted him.

And now Columbus had discovered the Western Continent, da Gama had found an ocean route to the Indies, and Magellan, sailing around the world, had proved its sphericity and approached the Spice Islands from the east. For centuries, now, the two great oceans were the scenes of grand and useful maritime expeditions. The tropical islands of the Pacific arose, one by one, from the bosom of the sea, to reward the navigator or relieve the outcast. The Spanish, by dint of cruelty and rapacity, filled their famous Manilla galleons and Acapulco treasure-ships with the spoils of warfare and the legitimate fruits of trade. The English, seeking to annoy a nation with whom, though not at war, they were certainly not at peace, sent against their golden fleets the piratical squadrons of Anson, Drake, and Hawkins. For years property was not safe upon the sea, and trading-ships went armed, while the armed vessels of nations turned buccaneers. The Portuguese and Dutch colonized the coasts and islands of India, Spain sent Cortez and Pizarro to Mexico and Peru, and England drove the Puritans across a stormy sea to Plymouth. Commerce was spread over the world, and Civilization and Christianity were introduced into the desert and the wilderness. Two centuries more, and steam

THE SPECTRE OF THE CAPE.

PHILADELPHIA:
J. B. LIPPINCOTT & CO.
1858.

made the Atlantic Ocean a ferry-transit, and the electric telegraph has now made its three thousand miles of salt water but as one link in that girdle which Shakspeare foresaw and which Puck promised to perform. The cable is complete and in working-order from New Orleans to Sebastopol.

Having thus rapidly described what the ocean once was in man's estimation, and having cursorily traced the steps by which it has taken its place in the world's economy, it remains for us to say what the ocean now is, and what place it now holds. It is the peaceful Highway of Nations,—a highway without tax or toll. Were the noble idea of the late Secretary Marcy adopted by all nations, private property upon the sea would be sacred even in time of war. If the distances be considered, the sea is the safest and most commodious route from spot to spot, whether for merchandise or man. It has given up its secrets, with perhaps the single exception of its depth, and, like the lightning and the thunderbolt, has submitted to the yoke. Though still sublime in its immensity and its power, it has lost those features of character which once made it mysterious and fantastic, and has become the sober and humdrum pathway of traffic. Mail-routes are as distinctly marked upon its surface as the equator, or the meridian of Greenwich: steamships leave their docks punctually at the stroke of noon. The monsters that plough its waters have been hunted by man till the race is well nigh exhausted; for the leviathan which frightened the ancients is the whale which has illuminated the moderns. The chant of the sirens is hushed, and in its place are heard the clatter of rushing paddle-wheels, the fog-whistle on the banks, the song of the forecastle, the yo-ho of sailors toiling at the ropes, the salute in mid-ocean,—sometimes—alas!—the minute-gun at sea. The romance and fable that once had here their chosen home, have fled to the caves and taken refuge amid the grottos; and the legends that were lately told of the ocean would now be out of place even in a graveyard or a haunted house.

The sailor, to whom once the route was trackless and untrodden, now consults a volume of charts which he has obtained from the National Observatory, and finds his course laid out upon data derived from analogy and oft-repeated experience. He takes this or that direction in accordance with known facts of the prevalence of winds or the motion of currents. He keeps a record of his own experience, that in its turn it may be useful to others. He has plans and surveys which give him the bearings of every port, the indentations of every coast, the soundings of every pass. Beacons warn him of reefs and sunken rocks, and buoys mark out his course through the shallows of sounds and straits. A modern light-house costs a million dollars, and a breakwater involves the finances of a state. If a new light-house is erected, or is the warning lamp for any reason discontinued, upon any coast, the fact is made known to the commerce of all nations by a "Notice to Mariners," inserted in the marine department of the newspapers most likely to meet their eye. A vessel at sea is safer from spoliation than is the traveller upon the high road or the sojourner in a city; for there are robbers and depredators everywhere upon the land, while there is not a pirate on the ocean. There are well-laden treasure-ships in the Panama and California waters, as in the times of Drake and Anson; but the world is much older than it was, and buccaneers and flibustiers now only infest the land.

In short, the ocean, once a formidable and repellant element, now furnishes Christian food and healthful employment to millions. Instead of serving to affright and appall the dwellers upon the continents which it surrounds, it renders their atmosphere more respirable, it affords them safe conveyance, and raises for them a school of heroes. The ocean, then, has a history: it has a past worth narrating, adventures worth telling, and it has played a part in the advancement of science, in the extension of geographical knowledge, in the spread of civilization and the progress of discovery, which it is eminently worth our while to ponder and digest. Its gradual submission to invasion from the land, its successive surrender of the islands in the tropics and the ice-mountains at the poles, its slow but certain release of its secrets, its final abandonment of its exclusiveness, form—with a multitude of attendant incidents, accidents, battles, disasters, shipwrecks, famines, robberies, mutinies, piracies—the theme and purpose of these pages.

Although the ocean has lost its terrors and has given up its dominion of dread over the mind of man, it is still poetic, and has been often made to assume a profound moral significance and furnish apt religious illustrations. In this connection, we cannot do better than to quote, from Dr. Greenwood's "Poetry and Mystery of the Sea," a passage which strongly and beautifully enforces this view:—

"'The sea is his, and He made it,' cries the Psalmist of Israel, in one of those bursts of enthusiasm in which he so often expresses the whole of a vast subject by a few simple words. Whose else, indeed, could it be, and by whom else could it have been made? Who else can heave its tides and appoint its bounds? Who else can urge its mighty waves to madness with the breath and wings of the tempest, and then speak to it again in a master's accents and bid it be still? Who else could have peopled it with its countless inhabitants, and caused it to bring forth its various productions, and filled it from its deepest bed to its expanded surface, filled it from its centre to its remotest shores, filled it to the brim with beauty and mystery and power? Majestic Ocean! Glorious Sea! No created being rules thee or made thee.

"What is there more sublime than the trackless, desert, all-surrounding, unfathomable sea? What is there more peacefully sublime than the calm, gently-heaving, silent sea? What is there more terribly sublime than the angry, dashing, foaming sea? Power—resistless, overwhelming power—is its attribute and its expression, whether in the careless, conscious grandeur of its deep rest, or the wild tumult of its excited wrath. It is awful when its crested waves rise up to make a compact with the black clouds and the howling winds, and the thunder and the thunderbolt, and they sweep on, in the joy of their dread alliance, to do the Almighty's bidding. And it is awful, too, when it stretches its broad level out to meet in quiet union the bended sky, and show in the line of meeting the vast rotundity of the world. There is majesty in its wide expanse, separating and enclosing the great continents of the earth, occupying two-thirds of the whole surface of the globe, penetrating the land with its bays and secondary seas, and receiving the constantly-pouring tribute of every river, of every shore. There is majesty in its fulness, never diminishing and never increasing. There is majesty in its integrity,—for its whole vast substance is uniform in its local unity, for there is but one ocean, and the inhabitants of any one maritime spot may visit the inhabitants of any other in the wide world. Its depth is sublime: who can sound it? Its strength is sublime: what fabric of man can resist it? Its voice is sublime, whether in the prolonged song of its ripple or the stern music of its roar,—whether it utters its hollow and melancholy tones within a labyrinth of wave-worn caves, or thunders at the base of some huge promontory, or beats against a toiling vessel's sides, lulling the voyager to rest with the strains of its wild monotony, or dies away, with the calm and fading twilight, in gentle murmurs on some sheltered shore.

"The sea possesses beauty, in richness, of its own; it borrows it from earth, and air, and heaven. The clouds lend it the various dyes of their wardrobe, and throw down upon it the broad masses of their shadows as they go sailing and sweeping by. The rainbow laves in it its many-colored feet. The sun loves to visit it, and the moon and the glittering brotherhood of planets and stars, for they delight themselves in its beauty. The sunbeams return from it in showers of diamonds and glances of fire; the moonbeams find in it a pathway of silver, where they dance to and fro, with the breezes and the waves, through the livelong night. It has a light, too, of its own,—a soft and sparkling light, rivaling the stars; and often does the ship which cuts its surface leave streaming behind a Milky Way of dim and uncertain lustre, like that which is shining dimly above. It harmonizes in its forms and sounds both with the night and the day. It cheerfully reflects the light, and it unites solemnly with the darkness. It imparts sweetness to the music of men, and grandeur to the thunder of heaven. What landscape is so beautiful as one upon the borders of the sea? The spirit of its loveliness is from the waters where it dwells and rests, singing its spells and scattering its charms on all the coasts. What rocks and cliffs are so glorious as those which are washed by the chafing sea? What groves and fields and dwellings are so enchanting as those which stand by the reflecting sea?

"If we could see the great ocean as it can be seen by no mortal eye, beholding at one view what we are now obliged to visit in detail and spot by spot,—if we could, from a flight far higher than the eagle's, view the immense surface of the deep all spread out beneath us like a universal chart,—what an infinite variety such a scene would display! Here a storm would be raging, the thunder bursting, the waters boiling, and rain and foam and fire all mingling together; and here, next to this scene of magnificent confusion, we should see the bright blue waves glittering in the sun and clapping their hands for very gladness. Here we should see a cluster of green islands set like jewels in the bosom of the sea; and there we should see broad shoals and gray rocks, fretting the billows and threatening the mariner. Here we should discern a ship propelled by the steady wind of the tropics, and inhaling the almost visible odors which diffuse themselves around the Spice Islands of the East; there we should behold a vessel piercing the cold barrier of the North, struggling among hills and fields of ice, and contending with Winter in his own everlasting dominion. Nor are the ships of man the only travellers we shall perceive upon this mighty map of the ocean. Flocks of sea-birds are passing and repassing, diving for their food or for pastime, migrating from shore to shore with unwearied wing and undeviating instinct, or wheeling and swarming around the rocks which they make alive and vocal by their numbers and their clanging cries.

"We shall behold new wonders and riches when we investigate the sea-shore. We shall find both beauty for the eye and food for the body, in the varieties of shell-fish which adhere in myriads to the rocks or form their close dark burrows in the sands. In some parts of the world we shall see those houses of stone which the little coral-insect rears up with patient industry from the bottom of the waters, till they grow into formidable rocks and broad forests whose branches never wave and whose leaves never fall. In other parts we shall see those pale, glistening pearls which adorn the crowns of princes and are woven in the hair of beauty, extorted by the relentless grasp of man from the hidden stores of ocean. And spread round every coast there are beds of flowers and thickets of plants, which the dew does not nourish, and which man has not sown, nor cultivated, nor reaped, but which seem to belong to the floods alone and the denizens of the floods, until they are thrown up by the surges, and we discover that even the dead spoils of the fields of ocean may fertilize and enrich the fields of earth. They have a life, and a nourishment, and an economy of their own; and we know little of them, except that they are there, in their briny nurseries, reared up into luxuriance by what would kill, like a mortal poison, the vegetation of the land.

"There is mystery in the sea. There is mystery in its depths. It is unfathomed, and, perhaps, unfathomable. Who can tell, who shall know, how near its pits run down to the central core of the world? Who can tell what wells, what fountains, are there, to which the fountains of the earth are but drops? Who shall say whence the ocean derives those inexhaustible supplies of salt which so impregnate its waters that all the rivers of the earth, pouring into it from the time of the creation, have not been able to freshen them? What undescribed monsters, what unimaginable shapes, may be roving in the profoundest places of the sea, never seeking—and perhaps, from their nature, never able to seek—the upper waters and expose themselves to the gaze of man! What glittering riches, what heaps of gold, what stores of gems, there must be scattered in lavish profusion in the ocean's lowest bed! What spoils from all climates, what works of art from all lands, have been engulfed by the insatiable and reckless waves! Who shall go down to examine and reclaim this uncounted and idle wealth? Who bears the keys of the deep?

"And oh! yet more affecting to the heart and mysterious to the mind, what companies of human beings are locked up in that wide, weltering, unsearchable grave of the sea! Where are the bodies of those lost ones over whom the melancholy waves alone have been chanting requiem? What shrouds were wrapped round the limbs of beauty, and of manhood, and of placid infancy, when they were laid on the dark floor of that secret tomb? Where are the bones, the relics, of the brave and the timid, the good and the bad, the parent, the child, the wife, the husband, the brother, the sister, the lover, which have been tossed and scattered and buried by the washing, wasting, wandering sea? The journeying winds may sigh as year after year they pass over their beds. The solitary rain-cloud may weep in darkness over the mingled remains which lie strewed in that unwonted cemetery. But who shall tell the bereaved to what spot their affections may cling? And where shall human tears be shed throughout that solemn sepulchre? It is mystery all. When shall it be resolved? Who shall find it out? Who but He to whom the wildest waves listen reverently, and to whom all nature bows; He who shall one day speak, and be heard in ocean's profoundest caves; to whom the deep, even the lowest deep, shall give up its dead, when the sun shall sicken, and the earth and the isles shall languish, and the heavens be rolled together like a scroll, and there shall be NO MORE SEA!"

It now remains for us to investigate the origin of navigation, as preliminary to our subject, and then to commence the task before us with the history of Noah, the first seaman, and the Ark, the vessel he commanded.

THE FIRST NAVIGATOR.

CHAPTER II.

THE ORIGIN OF NAVIGATION—THE NAUTILUS—THE SPLIT REED AND BEETLE—THE BEAVER FLOATING UPON A LOG—THE HOLLOW TREE—THE FIRST CANOE—THE FLOATING NUTSHELL—THE OAR—THE RUDDER—THE SAIL—THE TRADITION OF THE FIRST SAIL-BOAT.

THE origin of navigation is unknown. It has baffled the research of antiquaries, for the simple reason that men sailed upon the sea before they committed the records of their history to paper, or that such records, if any existed, were swept away and lost in the periods of anarchy which succeeded. Imagination has suggested that the nautilus, or Portuguese man-of-war, raising its tiny sail and floating off before the breeze, first pointed out to man the use which might be made of the wind as a propelling force; that a split reed, following the current of some tranquil stream and transporting a beetle over its glassy surface, was the first canoe, while the beetle was the first sailor. Mythology represents Hercules as sailing in a boat formed of the hide of a lion, and translates ships to the skies, where they still figure among the constellations. Fable makes Atlas claim the invention of the oar, and gives to Tiphys, the pilot of the Argo, the invention of the rudder. The attributing of these discoveries and improvements to particular individuals doubtless afforded pastime to poets in ages when poetry was more popular than history. Instead of trusting to these fanciful authorities, we may form a very rational theory upon the matter in the following manner:—

Whether it was an insect that floated on a leaf across a rivulet and was stranded on the bank, or a beaver carried down a river upon a log, or a bear borne away upon an iceberg, that first awakened man to the conception of trusting himself fearlessly upon the water, it is highly probable that he learned from animals, whose natural element it is, the manner of supporting his body upon it and of forcing his way through it. A frog darting away from the rim of a pond and striking out with his fore-legs may have suggested swimming, and the beaver floating on a log may have suggested following his example. The log may not have been sufficiently buoyant, and the adventurer may have added to its buoyancy by using his arms and legs. Even to this day the Indians of our own country cross a rapid stream by clasping the trunk of a tree with the left leg and arm and propelling themselves with the right. Thus the first step was taken; and the second was either to place several logs together, thus forming a raft, and raising its sides, or to make use of a tree hollowed out by nature. Many trees grow hollow naturally, such as oaks, limes, beeches, and willows; and it would not require a degree of adaptation beyond the capacity of a savage, to fit them to float and move upon the water. The next step was probably to hollow out by art a sound log, thus imitating the trunk which had been eroded by time and decay. And, in making this step from the sound to the hollow log, the primitive mariners may have been assisted by observing how an empty nut-shell or an inverted tortoise-shell floated upon the water, preserving their inner surface dry and protecting such objects as their size enabled them to carry. It has been aptly remarked that this first step was the greatest of all,—"for the transition from the hollow tree to the ship-of-the-line is not so difficult as the transition from nonentity to the hollow tree."

The first object for obtaining motion upon the water must evidently have been to enable the navigator to cross a river,—not to ascend or descend it; as it is apparent he would not seek the means of following or stemming its current while the same purpose could be more easily served by walking along the shore. It is not difficult to suppose that the oar was suggested by the legs of a frog or the fins of a fish. The early navigator, seated in his hollow tree, might at first seek to propel himself with his hands, and might then artificially lengthen them by a piece of wood fashioned in imitation of the hand and arm,—a long pole terminating in a thin flat blade. Here was the origin of the modern row-boat, one of the most graceful inventions of man.

From the oar to the rudder the transition was easy, for the oar is in itself a rudder, and was for a long time used as one. It must have been observed at an early day that a canoe in motion was diverted from its direct course by plunging an oar into the water and suffering it to remain there. It must have been observed, too, that an oar in or towards the stern was more effective in giving a new direction to the canoe than an oar in any other place. It was a natural suggestion of prudence, then, to assign this duty to one particular oarsman, and to place him altogether at the stern.

The sail is not so easily accounted for. An ancient tradition relates that a fisherman and his sweetheart, allured from the shore in the hope of discovering an island, and surprised by a tempest, were in imminent danger of destruction. Their only oar was wrenched from the grasp of the fisherman, and the frail bark was thus left to the mercy of the waves. The maiden raised her white veil to protect herself and her lover from the storm; the wind, inflating this fragile garment, impelled them slowly but surely towards the coast. Their aged sire, the tradition continues, suddenly seized with prophetic inspiration, exclaimed, "The future is unfolded to my view! Art is advancing to perfection! My children, you have discovered a powerful agent in navigation. All nations will cover the ocean with their fleets and wander to distant regions. Men, differing in their manners and separated by seas, will disembark upon peaceful shores, and import thence foreign science, superfluities, and art. Then shall the mariner fearlessly cruise over the immense abyss and discover new lands and unknown seas!" Though we may admire the foresight of this patriarch, we cannot applaud him for choosing a moment so inopportune for exercising his peculiar gift: it would certainly have been more natural to afford some comfort to his weather-beaten children. The legend even goes on to state that he at once fixed a pole in the middle of the canoe, and, attaching to it a piece of cloth, invented the first sail-boat. Mythology assigns a different, though similar, origin to the invention:—Iris, seeking her son in a bark which she impelled by oars, perceived that the wind inflated her garments and gently forced her in the direction in which she was going.

No research would bring the investigator to conclusions more satisfactory than these. The fact would still remain, that the first mention in profane history of constructions moving upon the water, is many centuries subsequent to the period in which the idea of building such constructions must be presumed to have been first conceived. It would consequently be idle to devote more space to this subject; and we proceed at once, therefore, to the first of recorded ventures upon the sea.

THE DELUGE AND THE ARK.

CHAPTER III.

THE FLOOD AND THE BUILDING OF THE ARK—THE ARGUMENTS OF INFIDELITY AGAINST A UNIVERSAL DELUGE—THE MATERIAL OF WHICH THE ARK WAS BUILT—ITS CAPACITY, DIMENSIONS, AND FORM—ITS PROPORTIONS COPIED IN MODERN OCEAN STEAMERS.

THE earliest mention of the sea made in history occurs in the first chapter of Genesis. During the period of chaos, and before the creation of light, darkness was upon the face of the deep, and the Spirit of God moved upon the face of the waters. Upon the third day the waters under the heavens were gathered together in one place and were called Seas; the dry land appeared and was called Earth. The waters were commanded to bring forth abundantly the moving creature that hath life; and, upon the creation of man in the image of God, dominion was given him over the fish of the sea, the fowl of the air, and every creeping thing that creepeth upon the earth.

In the year of the world 1556—according to the generally accepted computation—God determined to destroy man and all creeping things and the fowls of the air, for He said, "It repenteth me that I have made them." Noah alone found grace in the eyes of the Lord, and was instructed to build him an ark of gopher-wood three hundred cubits in length, fifty in breadth, and thirty in height. It was to consist of three stories, divided into rooms, to contain one door and one window, and was to be smeared within and without with pitch. Noah was engaged one hundred years in constructing the ark,—from the age of five hundred to that of six hundred years,—and when it was fully completed he gathered his family into it, with pairs of all living creatures. Then were the fountains of the great deep broken up and the windows of heaven opened. The rains descended during forty days and forty nights. The waters arose and lifted up the ark from the earth. The mountains were covered to a depth of twenty-two feet, and all flesh died that moved upon the earth: Noah alone remained alive, and they that were with him in the ark.

The flood commenced in the second month of Noah's six hundredth year. During five months the waters prevailed; in the seventh the ark rested upon the summit of Mount Ararat. In the tenth month the tops of the mountains were seen; in the eleventh Noah sent forth a dove, which speedily returned, having found no rest for the sole of her foot; on the seventeenth day he again sent forth the dove, which returned, bringing an olive-leaf in her bill, and, being again sent forth, returned no more. On the first day of the first month of his six hundred and first year, Noah removed the covering of the ark and saw that the face of the ground was dry. Toward the close of the second month the earth was dried, and Noah went forth with his sons, his wife, and his sons' wives. He built an altar and offered burnt-offerings of every beast and fowl to the Lord. God then made a promise to Noah that he would no more destroy the earth by flood, and stretched the rainbow in the clouds in token of this solemn covenant between himself and the children of men.

Such is the scriptural history of the Deluge,—the first great chronological event in the annals of the world after the Creation. The investigations of philosophy and of infidelity into the accuracy of the Mosaic account have resulted in furnishing confirmation of the most direct and positive kind. The principal objections of cavillers turn upon three points: 1st, the absence of any concurrent testimony by the profane writers of antiquity; 2d, the apparent impossibility of accounting for the quantity of water necessary to overflow the whole earth to the depth stated; and, 3d, the needlessness of a universal deluge, as the same purpose might have been answered by a partial one. These objections may be briefly considered here.

1. The absence of positive testimony from profane historians. However true it may be that there is no consecutive account of the Deluge except that given in the Bible, it is certain that records relating to the ark had been preserved among the early nations of the world and in the general system of Gentile mythology. Plutarch mentions the dove that was sent forth from the ark. The Greek fable of Deucalion and Pyrrha is absolutely the same as the scriptural narrative of Noah and his wife. The Egyptians carried their deity, upon occasions of solemnity, in an ark or boat, and this ark was called "Baris," from the name of a mountain upon which, doubtless, in their own legend, the Egyptian ark had rested, as did the scriptural ark upon Mount Ararat. The Temple of Sesostris was fashioned after the model of the ark, and was consecrated to Osiris at Theba. This name of Theba given to a city is an important point, for Theba was the appellation of the ark itself. The same name was borne by numerous cities in Bœotia, Attica, Ionia, Syria, and Italy; and the city of Apamea, in Phrygia, was originally called Kibotos, or Ark, in memory of the Deluge. This fact shows that the tradition of the Deluge was preserved in Asia Minor from a very remote antiquity. In India, ancient mythological books have been shown to contain fragmentary accounts of some great overflow corresponding in a remarkable degree with that given by Moses. The Africans, the Chinese, and the American Indians even, have traditions of a flood in the early annals of the world, and of the preservation of the human race and of animated nature by means of an ark. It is impossible to account for the universality of this legend, unless the fact of the Deluge be admitted.

2. The apparent material impossibility of producing water in sufficient quantity to overflow the earth. The means by

which the flood was produced are stated in the Mosaic narrative: the fountains of the great deep were broken up, and the windows of heaven were opened; that is, the water rushed out from the bowels of the earth, where it had been confined, and the clouds poured forth their rains. This would seem to be a sufficient explanation, if any explanation of an event clearly miraculous and supernatural be necessary at all. It has been discovered, however, that the Deluge might have been caused, and might at any time be repeated, by a very simple process. It has been demonstrated that the various seas and oceans which invest the two principal hemispheres, contain water enough to overflow the land and cover the highest mountains to the depth of twenty-two feet, were their temperature merely raised to a degree equal to that of the shallow tropical seas!. Were the Atlantic and Pacific Oceans suddenly warmed to a point perfectly compatible with the maintenance of animal life, they would expand sufficiently to overflow the Cordilleras and the Alps.

3. The needlessness of a universal deluge, as a partial one would have answered all purposes. That the Deluge was universal is distinctly stated by Scripture. Had not God intended it to be so, he would hardly have instructed Noah to spend a hundred years in the construction of an ark: a spot of the earth yet uninhabited by man might have been designated, where Noah could have gathered his family; there would have been no necessity for shutting up pairs of all animals in the ark with which to re-stock the earth, for they could have been easily brought from the parts of the earth not overflowed into those that were. Then we are told that the water ascended twenty-two feet above the highest mountains,—a distinct physical proof that the whole earth was inundated, for water then, as now, would seek its level, and must, by the laws of gravity, spread itself over the rest of the earth, unless, indeed, it were retained there by a miracle; and in this case Moses would certainly have mentioned it, as he did the suspen-

sion of the laws of nature in the case of the waters of the Red Sea. Then, again, had the Deluge been partial and confined to the neighborhood of the Euphrates and Tigris, it would be impossible to account for the fact that in remote countries—in Italy, France, Germany, England, the United States—there have been found, in places far from the sea, and upon the tops of high mountains, the teeth and bones of animals, fishes in an entire condition, sea-shells, ears of corn, &c., petrified. The explanation of this has always been derived from the circumstance of a universal deluge. The fact, too, already mentioned, that the Chinese, the Greeks, and the Indians have traditions of a deluge, seems to be conclusive evidence that that terrible dispensation was not confined to the district which was at that period scriptural ground, but visited alike Palestine and Peru, Canaan and Connecticut.

We now return to the ark, the period of whose completion we have already given,—the year of the world 1656, or the year before Christ 2348. Three points are now to be considered:—the material of which it was built, its capacity and dimensions, and its form.

1. *The Material of which it was built.* The Mosaic account says expressly that it was built of gopher-wood; but it has never been satisfactorily determined what wood is meant by the term "gopher." Numerous interpretations have been placed upon it: by one authority it is rendered "timber squared by the workman;" by another, "timber made from trees which shoot out quadrangular branches in the same horizontal line," such as cedar and fir; by another, "smoothed or planed timber;" by another, "wood that does not readily decay," such as boxwood or cedar; by another, "the wood of such trees as abound with resinous, inflammable juices," as the cedar, fir, cypress, pine, &c. That the ark was built of cedar would seem to be probable, from the fact that this wood corresponds more than any other with the numerous significations given to the term "gopher," as

it is quadrangular in its branches, durable, almost incorruptible, resinous, and highly inflammable; from the fact, too, that it is abundant in Asia, and known to have been employed by the Assyrians and Egyptians in the construction of ships. One or two authorities, however, maintain that the ark was made of the wood of the cypress, their grounds being that the cypress was considered by the ancients the most durable wood against rot and worms; that it abounded in Assyria, where the ark was probably built; and that it was frequently employed in the construction of ships, especially by Alexander, who built a whole fleet from the cypress groves in the neighborhood of Babylon.

2. *Its Capacity and Dimensions.* The proportions of the ark, as given in the sacred volume, have been examined and compared with the greatest precision by the most learned and accurate calculators; and, assuming the cubit to have been of the value of eighteen inches of the present day, it follows that the ark was four hundred and fifty feet long, by seventy-five wide, by forty-five high. From these data its burden has been deduced, and is now understood to have been forty-two thousand four hundred and thirteen tons. Such a construction would have allowed ample room for the eight persons who were to inhabit it;—Noah and his wife, Shem, Ham, and Japheth, and their wives,—about two hundred and fifty pair of four-footed beasts, the fowls of the air, such reptiles and insects as could not live under water, together with the food necessary for their subsistence for a twelvemonth. It has been doubted whether Noah took with him into the ark specimens of all living creatures. It is reasonable to suppose that, as the world was nearly seventeen centuries old, the animal creation had spread itself over a large portion of the antediluvian earth, and that certain species had consequently become indigenous in certain climates. It is therefore probable that many species were not to be found in the country where Noah dwelt and where he built the ark. We are not told in the Bible that any

kind of animals were brought from a distance,—a fact which renders it probable that Noah only saved pairs of the species which had become natives of the territory which he inhabited. This would be to suppose that many species perished in the flood and were consequently never renewed,—a supposition which derives strong support from the numerous discoveries made in modern times of the exuviæ of animals which no longer exist, and whose destruction is attributed to the Deluge. A list of such extinct species was drawn up by Cuvier.

The presumptive evidence which may be adduced in support of the scriptural history of the preparation of the ark is very strong; it is, indeed, the only solution of an otherwise insuperable difficulty. The early records of the whole Gentile world, as has been stated, concur in declaring the fact of a universal deluge; and yet the human race and all the more useful and important species of animals survived it. Now, the people of those times had no ships and were totally unacquainted with navigation: it is evident, therefore, that they were not saved by vessels in ordinary use. Even though we were to suppose them possessed of shipping, it is impossible to believe that they would or could have provisioned them for a year's cruise, unless we suppose them to have been forewarned precisely as Moses relates; and it is certainly as easy to believe the whole of the Bible narrative as a portion. Such a structure as the ark, for the preservation and sustenance of the human race and of the animal kingdom, seems, then, to have been absolutely indispensable.

3. *Its Form.* From the dimensions given in the sixth chapter of Genesis, it is evident that the ark had the shape of an oblong square, with a sloping roof and a flat bottom; that it was furnished with neither helm, mast, nor oars; that it was intended to lie upon the water without rolling, and formed to float rather than to sail. Its proportions, it has been remarked, nearly agree with those of the human figure,—three hundred cubits in length being six times its breadth, fifty cubits, and the average

length of the human frame being to its width as six is to one. Now, the body of a man lying in the water flat on his back will float with little or no exertion. It would appear, therefore, that similar proportions would suit a vessel whose purpose was floating only. It is not necessary to suppose that the ark had to contend with either storm or wind. The waves of water lying to the depth of a few fathoms upon a submerged continent could not, at any rate, be compared in violence to those of the ocean. The gathering of the flood lasted but forty days, and although the ark floated for a year, nearly eleven months were occupied in the subsidence of the water. It is probable that the ark was gradually and slowly surrounded by the advancing tide, was quietly lifted up upon its surface, that it hovered about the spot where it was constructed, and finally, upon the disappearance of the water, settled as quietly back upon its broad basis and projecting supports.

It is a curious fact that many minds which have refused to accept the evidences of a communication between God and man in the instances of Moses and of our Savior, admit the strong probability of a communication having passed from God to Noah. The chain of argument is indeed exceedingly strong. Mr. Taylor thus seeks to establish the fact that the Deity did, in the case of Noah, condescend to make known his intentions to man. "Was the Deluge," he asks, "a real occurrence? All mankind acknowledge it. Wherever tradition has been maintained, wherever written records are preserved, wherever commemorative rites have been instituted, what has been their subject? The Deluge:—deliverance from destruction by a flood. The savage and the sage agree in this: North and South, East and West, relate the danger of their great ancestor from overwhelming waters. But he was saved: and how? By personal exertion? By long-continued swimming? By concealment in the highest mountains? No: but by enclosure in a large floating edifice of his own construction. But this labor was long:

it was not the work of a day: he must have foreseen so astonishing an event a considerable time previous to its actual occurrence. Whence did he receive this foreknowledge? Did the earth inform him that at twenty, thirty, forty years' distance it would disgorge a flood? Surely not. Did the stars announce that they would dissolve the terrestrial atmosphere in terrific rains? Surely not. Whence, then, had Noah his foreknowledge? Did he begin to build when the first showers descended? It was too late. Had he been accustomed to rains, formerly? Why think them now of importance? Had he never seen rain? What could induce him to provide against it? Why this year more than last year? Why last year more than the year before? These inquiries are direct: we cannot flinch from the fact. Erase it from the Mosaic records, still it is recorded in Greece, in Egypt, in India, in Britain; it is registered in the very *sacra* of the pagan world. Go, infidel, take your choice of difficulties: either disparage all mankind as fools, as willing dupes to superstitious commemoration, or allow that this fact, this one fact, is established by testimony abundantly sufficient; but remember that if it be established, it implies a *communication from God to man.* Who could inform Noah? Why did not that great patriarch provide against fire? against earthquakes? against explosions? Why against water? why against a deluge? Away with subterfuge! confess frankly it was the dictation of Deity. Say that He only who made the world could predict the time and causes of this devastation, that He only could excite the hope of restoration, or suggest a method of deliverance."

It is a remarkable fact, and one which goes far to support the argument often urged to combat the opinions of atheists, that the ark could not have been built by man, unassisted by the divine intelligence, at that age of the world,—that the ark, the first and largest ship ever built, had precisely the same proportions as the ocean steamers of our own day. Its dimensions were, as we have said, three hundred cubits, by fifty, by thirty. Those of several of the fleetest Atlantic mail steamers are three hundred feet in length, fifty feet in breadth of beam, and twenty-eight and a half in depth. They have, like the ark, upper, lower, and middle stories. It is, to say the least, singular, that the ship-builders of the present day, neglecting the experience acquired by man from forty-two centuries spent more or less upon the sea, should so directly and unreservedly return to the model of the vessel constructed to outride the Flood. It was therefore with obvious propriety that, at one of the late convivial meetings in England during the preparations for laying the telegraphic cable, after due honor had been paid to the celebrities of the occasion and the moment, after the health of the Queen and the memory of Columbus had been pledged and drunk, a toast was offered to our great ancestor Noah. Though the proposition was received with hilarity and the idea seemed to savor somewhat of a jest, yet the patriarch's claims, as the first admiral on record, to being the father of seamen and the great originator of navigation, were willingly and vociferously acknowledged. After this recognition—which must, from the circumstances, be regarded as in some measure official and conclusive—we could not consistently have ventured to withhold from him the first place in this record of the achievements of "Man upon the Sea."

CHAPTER IV.

THE SHIPS, COMMERCE, AND NAVIGATION OF THE PHŒNICIANS—THEIR TRADE WITH OPHIR—SIDON AND TYRE—THEIR VOYAGE ROUND AFRICA—NEW TYRE—A PATRIOTIC PHŒNICIAN CAPTAIN—THE EGYPTIANS AS A MARITIME PEOPLE—THEIR SHIPS AND COMMERCE—THE JEWS—THEIR GEOGRAPHY—IDEAS UPON THE SHAPE OF THE EARTH—THE WORLD AS KNOWN TO THE HEBREWS.

It is upon the shores of the Mediterranean, alike the sea of the Bible and of mythology, of Mount Ararat and Mount Olympus,—among the Phœnicians, the Egyptians, and the Hebrews,—that we must look for the earliest traces of navigation and commerce. The most cursory inspection of a map of Palestine, Phœnicia, and Egypt will show how admirably these countries were situated for trade both by land and sea. The Phœnicians, though confined to the narrow slip of land between Mount Lebanon and the Mediterranean, possessed a safe coast and the admirable harbor of Sidon, while their mountains furnished them an abundant supply of the best woods for shipbuilding. The confined limits of their own territory prevented them from being themselves producers or manufacturers,—a circumstance which naturally led them to be the carriers of producing and manufacturing nations whose maritime advantages were inferior to their own. The fact, also, that the Jews were prevented by their government, laws, and religion from engaging extensively in commerce, and that the Egyptians were characteristically averse to the sea, augmented the commercial supremacy of the Phœnicians,—a supremacy recognised both in the sacred writings and in profane records.

It is now generally conceded that the date of the maritime enterprises which rendered the Phœnicians famous in antiquity must be fixed between the years 1700 and 1100 before Christ. The renowned city of Sidon was the centre from which their expeditions were sent forth. What was the specific object of these excursions, or in what order of time they took place, is but imperfectly known: it would appear, however, that their adventurers traded at first with Cyprus and Rhodes, then with Greece, Sardinia, Sicily, Gaul, and the coast of Spain upon the Mediterranean. About 1250 B.C., their ships ventured cautiously beyond the Straits of Gibraltar, and founded Cadiz upon a coast washed by the Atlantic. A little later they founded establishments upon the western coast of Africa. Homer asserts that at the Trojan War, 1194 B.C., the Phœnicians furnished the belligerents with many articles of luxury and convenience; and we are told by Scripture that their ships brought gold to Solomon from Ophir, in 1000 B.C. Tyre seems now to have superseded Sidon, though at what period is not known. It had become a flourishing mart before 600 B.C.; for Ezekiel, who lived at that time, has left a glowing and picturesque description of its wealth, which must have proceeded from a long-established commerce. He enumerates, among the articles used in building the Tyrian ships, the fir-trees of Senir, the cedars of Lebanon, the oaks of Bashan, the ivory of the Indies, the linen of Egypt, and the purple of the Isles of Elishah. He mentions, as brought to the great emporium from Syria, Damascus, Greece, and Arabia, silver, tin, lead, and vessels of brass; slaves, horses, mules; carpets, ebony, ivory, pearls, and silk; wheat, balm, honey, oil, and gum; wine, wool, and iron.

It is about this period—600 B.C.—that the Phœnicians, though under Egyptian commanders, appear to have performed a voyage which, if authentic, may justly be regarded as the most important in their annals,—a circumnavigation of Africa. The extent of this unknown region, and the peculiar aspects of man and nature there, had already drawn toward it in a particular degree the attention of the ancient world. The manner in which its coasts converged, south of the Mediterranean and the Red Sea, suggested the idea of a peninsula, the circumnavigation of which might be effected even by the limited resources of the early naval powers. The first attempt in this direction originated in a quarter which had been accustomed, from its agricultural avocations, to hold itself aloof from every species of maritime enterprise. It was undertaken by order of Necho, king of Egypt,—the Pharaoh Necho of the Scriptures,—and is recorded by Herodotus as follows:

"When Necho had desisted from his attempts to join the Red Sea with the Mediterranean by means of a canal at the Isthmus of Suez, he despatched some vessels, under the guidance of Phœnician pilots, with orders to sail down the Red Sea and follow the coast of Africa: they were to return to Egypt by the Pillars of Hercules and the Mediterranean. The Phœnicians, therefore, taking their course by way of the Red Sea, sailed onward to the Southern Ocean. Upon the approach of autumn they landed in Libya and planted corn in the place where they first went ashore. When this was ripe they cut it down and set sail again. Having in this manner consumed two years, in the third they passed the Pillars of Hercules and returned to Egypt. This story may be believed by others, but to me it appears incredible, for they affirm that when they sailed round Libya they had the sun on their right hand."

In the time of Herodotus, the Greeks were unacquainted with the phenomenon of a shadow falling to the south,—one which the Phœnicians would naturally have witnessed had they actually passed the Cape of Good Hope, for the sun would have been on their right hand, or in the north, and would thus have projected shadows to the south. As this story was not one likely to have been invented in the time of Necho, it is the strongest proof that could be adduced of the reality of the voyage. Doubts have been raised in modern times upon the accuracy of the narrative; but the objections are considered as having been refuted by Rennell and Heeren. Bartholomew Diaz has the credit of having discovered and having been the first to double the Cape of Good Hope, in 1486: it is clear that, if the claims of the Phœnician pilots are to be regarded, Diaz was preceded in this path at least twenty centuries.

Soon after the date of this voyage, Tyre was besieged and destroyed by Nebuchadnezzar. The inhabitants succeeded in escaping with their property to an island near the shore, where they founded New Tyre, which soon surpassed, both in commerce and shipping, the city they had abandoned. The Phœnicians seem now to have advanced with their system of colonization farther to the south upon the coast of Africa, and farther to the north upon the coast of Spain. They discovered the Cassiterides—now the Scilly Islands—upon the coast of Cornwall, and retained the monopoly of the trade in the tin which they found there. They carried spices and perfumes, obtained from Arabia, to Greece, where they were employed for sacrifice and incense. They also sold there the manufactures, purple, and jewels of Tyre and Sidon. From Spain they obtained silver, corn, wine, oil, wax, wool, and fruits. They procured amber in some place which they visited in the North,—doubtless the shores of the Baltic. As the value of this article was equal to that of gold, they desired to retain the monopoly of the trade and to keep all knowledge of the regions yielding it from their commercial rivals. Hence the secret was most carefully hoarded.

A remarkable circumstance connected with the maritime history of the Phœnicians was their jealousy of the influence of foreigners. When a strange ship was observed to keep them company at sea, they would either outsail her, or at night change their course and disappear. On one occasion a Phœnician captain, finding himself pursued by a Roman vessel, ran his ship aground and wrecked her, rather than lose the secret which a capture would have revealed. This act was deemed so patriotic that the government rewarded him, and compensated him for the loss of his vessel. New Tyre was destroyed by Alexander the Great, 324 B.C. The inhabitants were either put to death or sold as slaves, and thus the maritime glory of the Phœnicians came to an untimely end.

Little is known of the construction and equipment of Phœnician ships. All that can be said with certainty is, that there were two kinds,—those employed in commerce and those used for war,—a distinction, indeed, which all nations, both ancient and modern, have found it convenient to make. The hulls of the trading-vessels were round, that they might carry more goods, while the fighting-ships were longer and sharp at the bottom. In other respects they probably resembled the vessels of Greece and Rome, for which they undoubtedly furnished models. Of these fuller details have reached us, and we shall speak of them in their place. The Phœnicians were better astronomers than the unskilful navigators who had preceded them; for, while these attempted to guide their course by the imperfect aid of the constellation known as the Great Bear,—some of whose stars are forty degrees from the pole,—the Phœnicians were the first to apply to maritime purposes the Lesser Bear,—the group which has furnished to more modern navigation the North or Polar Star. It is not probable that they fixed upon this particular star, for at that period—1250 years B.C.—it was eighteen degrees from the pole, too distant to serve any positive astronomical purpose.

We come now to the Egyptians as a maritime people in the earliest historical periods, of whom we have incidentally said that they were characteristically disinclined to enter with spirit into any maritime enterprises, whether for commerce or war. This may have been owing to the want of proper timber, to the insalubrity of the sea-coasts, and to the absence of good harbors; while the advantages presented by the Nile for intercourse and traffic with the interior precluded the necessity of resorting to commerce by sea. Sesostris, who lived about 1650 years before Christ, is supposed to have been the first king who overcame the dislike of the Egyptians to the water. Herodotus assigns him a large fleet in the Red Sea, and other historians attribute to him fleets upon the Mediterranean. Upon his death, his subjects relapsed into their former aversion for commerce. Bocchoris, 700 B.C., imitated and revived his legislation upon the subject; and during the reign of Psammeticus the ports of Egypt were first opened to foreign ships, and intercourse with the Greeks was for the first time encouraged. It was Necho, the successor of Psammeticus, who employed, 600 B.C., the Phœnicians in the voyage around Africa of which we have spoken; and this enterprise bespeaks a monarch bent on maritime discovery. Apries, the grandson of Necho, took the city of Sidon by storm and defeated the Phœnicians in a sea-fight. It is probable that the Egyptians, had they continued independent, would have become distinguished as a commercial people; but seventy years afterwards they were conquered by the Persians, and became successively subject to the Macedonians and Romans.

We possess but little knowledge of the construction and equipment of the Egyptian ships. According to Herodotus, they were built of planks of the thorn-tree, fastened together, like tiles, with a great number of wooden pins, and were entirely without ribs. On the inside papyrus was used for stopping the crevices. The sails were made of the papyrus, or of twisted rushes. These vessels were always towed up the Nile, while they descended the stream in the following manner. The current not acting with sufficient force upon their flat bottoms, the sailors hung a bundle of tamarisk over the prow and let it down under the keel by a rope: the stream, bearing upon this bundle, carried the boat along with great celerity.

The Jews, whose country was ill situated for commerce by

sea, were even more averse than the Egyptians to intercourse with foreigners and to maritime occupations. Joppa was the only seaport of Judea and Jerusalem, and into it many of the articles used by Solomon in the construction of the Temple were imported. During Solomon's reign, he employed the ships of his ally, Hiram, King of Tyre, in commercial avocations, for which his own people were not fitted. It is among the Jews, whose history is given in the Scripture with so much detail, that we should naturally look for the earliest geographical records. The sacred writers, however, seem to have entertained no idea of any system of geography, having been occupied with the affairs of the world to come, to the total exclusion of the concerns of the mundane earth. They do not even allude to any such branch of learning as being then in existence. It is clear that the Hebrews never attempted to form any theory upon the structure and shape of the globe. Their ideas with regard to the boundaries of the known world may be vaguely inferred from the tenth chapter of Genesis, from the chapters treating of the commerce of Tyre, and from various detached allusions in the prophets.

The idea, common to all uninstructed people, that the earth is a flat surface and the heaven a firmament or curtain spread over it, prevails throughout the Bible. The abode of darkness and of the shadow of death was conceived to be a deep pit beneath it. One sacred writer speaks of the earth as being "hung upon nothing;" another speaks of the "pillars of the earth," and another of the "pillars of heaven." These allusions show sufficiently that, though the writers of those days were impressed by the external view of the grand scenes of nature, they did not endeavor to group them into any regular system.

The localities always alluded to as being at the farthest bounds of their geographical knowledge are Tarshish, Ophir, the Isles, Sheba, Dedan, The River, Gog, Magog, and the North. The first has given rise to infinite discussion. The best theory makes it the name of Carthage, and gives it, by extension, to the whole continent of Africa. Ophir is probably Sofala, on the eastern coast of Africa. The Isles are thought to have been the southern coasts and promontories of Europe, Greece, Italy, &c., which were supposed at that period to be insular. Sheba was Sabæa, or Arabia Felix. Dedan is supposed to have been a port in the Persian Gulf. The River was the Euphrates, beyond which were tracts indefinitely known as Elam and Media, and still beyond a region known as "The Ends of the Earth." Gog, Magog, and the North have been usually supposed to refer to the inhabitants of Scythia and Sarmatia, and the hyperborean nations in general, though a later and more natural theory makes them refer to the migratory shepherds and warriors of Cappadocia, Phrygia, and Galatia. It thus appears that the primitive Israelites knew little beyond the limits of their own country, Egypt, and the regions lying between the Mediterranean, or the Sea, and the Euphrates. A knowledge of the water, we have already remarked, is essential to the formation of any correct and adequate idea of the shape and extent of the land. The Jews had never ventured forth upon the sea for the discovery of new regions, and were, in consequence, ignorant even of that in which they dwelt. We shall find that the Greeks and Romans, whose maritime history we shall now briefly narrate, approached the truth in regard to the form and extent of the world, precisely as their commerce expanded and their ambition for conquest and colonization augmented.

SUPPOSED FORM OF THE SHIP ARGO, (FROM AN ANCIENT BAS-RELIEF.)

CHAPTER V.

THE EARLY MARITIME HISTORY OF THE GREEKS—THE EXPEDITION OF THE ARGONAUTS—THE VESSELS USED IN THE TROJAN WAR—SHIP-BUILDING IN THE TIME OF HOMER—THE POETIC GEOGRAPHY OF THE GREEKS—THE PALACE OF THE SUN—THE MARVELS OF A VOYAGE OUT OF SIGHT OF LAND—THE GEOGRAPHY OF HESIOD—OF ANAXIMANDER—OF THALES, HERODOTUS, SOCRATES, AND ERATOSTHENES—THE GREAT OCEAN IS NAMED THE ATLANTIC.

At what period the Greeks began to build vessels and to venture upon the waters washing their coasts and girding their numerous archipelagoes, is not known: it is certain, at any rate, that the commencement of navigation with them, as with all other nations, must be referred to a time much anterior to the ages of which we have any record. Long voyages are mentioned as having taken place at periods so early that they must be considered mythical. The first maritime adventure which lays any claim to authenticity, and the most celebrated in ancient times, is the expedition of the Argonauts to Colchis. Though this enterprise is by many learned authorities deemed fabulous, we shall nevertheless consider three points connected with it,—the probable era of the voyage, its supposed object, and the various routes by which the adventurers are said to have returned.

The date of the expedition, if it took place at all, may be

safely fixed at the year 1250 B.C. A theory propounded by Sir Isaac Newton would connect it with the year 937; but this is regarded with less favor than the earlier date. Its alleged object was the Golden Fleece; but what this was can only be conjectured. It is hardly likely that the people of that age would have been tempted by the prospect of commercial advantages by opening a trade with the Euxine Sea. It is quite as unlikely that they would have undertaken so dangerous a voyage for the purpose of plunder, better opportunities for which existed much nearer home. The supposition that the Golden Fleece was a parchment containing the secret of transmuting the baser metals into gold, and the opinion that the Argonauts went in quest of skins and rich furs, hardly require discussion. There seems, indeed, no adequate motive but a desire to obtain the precious metals, which were believed to be furnished in abundance by the mines near the Black Sea. Why these mines were symbolized under the appellation of a golden fleece it is not easy to say, and no satisfactory reason has ever been suggested. The most probable is that the gold dust was supposed to be washed down the sides of the Caucasus Mountains by torrents, and caught by fleeces of wool placed among the rocks by the inhabitants.

Jason, the son of the King of Thessaly, being deprived of his inheritance, and having resolved to seek his fortune by some remote and hazardous expedition, was induced to go in quest of the Golden Fleece in Colchis. He enlisted fifty men, and employed a person named Argus to build him a ship, which from him was called Argo, the adventurers being named Argonauts. The Argo is described as a pentecontoros,—that is, a vessel with fifty oars. The number of the Argonauts is usually stated at fifty, though one authority asserts that they numbered one hundred. They started from Iolcos in Thessaly, and with a south wind sailed east by north. The narrative of the expedition is full of wonders. They landed at the island of Lemnos, where they found that the women had just murdered their husbands and fathers.

The Argonauts supplied the place of the assassinated relatives, and Jason had two sons by one of the bereaved Lemnians. When the vessel arrived at the entrance to the Euxine,—the narrow strait now called the Bosphorus,—they built a temple, and implored the protection of the gods against the Symplegades, or Whirling Rocks, which guarded the passage. A seer named Phineas was consulted upon the probability of their sailing through unharmed. The rocks were imagined to float upon the waves, and, when any thing attempted to pass through, to seize and crush it. According to Homer,—

"No bird of air, no dove of swiftest wing,
That bears ambrosia to th' ethereal king,
Shuns the dire rocks: in vain she cuts the skies:
The dire rocks meet, and crush her as she flies."

Phineas advised them to loose a dove, to mark its flight, and to judge from its fate of the destiny reserved for them. They did so, determined to push boldly on if the bird got through in safety. The pigeon escaped with the loss of some of its tail-feathers. The Argo dashed onward, and cleared the formidable rocks with the loss of a few of its stern ornaments. From this time forward, the legend adds, the Symplegades remained fixed, and were no longer a terror to navigators.

The Argonauts, after entering the Black Sea, sailed due east, to the mouth of the river Phasis, now the Rione. Æetes, the king, promised to give Jason the fleece upon certain conditions. These he was enabled to fulfil by the aid of Medea, a sorceress, and daughter of Æetes. They then fled together to Greece. The route followed by the Argonauts upon their return is differently given by the various poets who have told the story and the commentators who have illustrated it. By one they are represented as sailing up some river across the continent to the Baltic, and thence homeward along the coasts of France and Spain, and through the Straits of Gibraltar. It is needless to say that there is no river which flows between the Euxine and the Baltic. Other tracks laid down are equally preposterous in the eyes of modern geography. Herodotus adopts the tradition that they returned by the same way they went,—the only way, indeed, they could have returned,—by water. The reader, in view of the romantic embellishments with which this story is loaded, and of the strong doubts resting upon it as an historical event, must choose, from among the various theories we have given, the one he deems the most satisfactory.

One generation after the date we have assigned to this expedition occurred the Trojan War. In the year 1194 B.C., all the Greek states, with Agamemnon at their head, united to revenge the insult offered to Menelaus, King of Sparta, by the Trojan prince Paris, who had carried off the king's wife Helen. During the interval the Greeks, if the Homeric account is to be believed, had made great advances in the arts of ship-building and navigation; for in a very short time eleven hundred and fifty ships were collected at Aulis, the general rendezvous. The Bœotians furnished fifty, and the other states contributed in proportion. Each of them contained one hundred and twenty warriors; they must therefore have been vessels of considerable magnitude. All the ships are described as having masts which could be taken down as occasion required. The sail could only be used when the wind was directly astern. The delicate art of sailing in the wind's eye, or of making to the north with a north wind, was not yet understood. The principal propelling power lay in the oars, which turned in leathern thongs as a key in its hole. Homer represents the ships to have been black, from the color of the pitch with which they were smeared. The sides near the prow were often painted red, whence vessels are sometimes called by the poets red-cheeked. On their arrival upon the Trojan coast, the Greeks drew their fleet up on the land and anchored them by means of large stones. They then surrounded them with fortifications, to protect them from the enemy.

Homer, who lived two centuries later,—1000 B.C.,—has left us a tolerably full account of the ship-building, navigation, and geography of his time. The following passage from the Odyssey, as rendered into English by Cowper, is regarded by antiquaries as important, showing, as it does, the point at which the art of ship-building had now arrived. Ulysses, having been wrecked upon an island, is enabled to build a ship by the aid of the nymph Calypso.

> "She gave him, fitted to the grasp, an axe
> Of iron, ponderous, double-edged, with haft
> Of olive-wood inserted firm, and wrought
> With curious art. Then, placing in his hand
> A polish'd adze, she led herself the way
> To her isle's utmost verge, where loftiest stood
> The alder, poplar, and cloud-piercing fir,
> Though sapless, sound, and fitted for his use
> As buoyant most. To that once verdant grove
> His steps the beauteous nymph Calypso led,
> And sought her home again. Then slept not he,
> But, swinging with both hands the axe, his task
> Soon finish'd: trees full twenty to the ground
> He cast, which dextrous with his adze he smoothed,
> The knotted surface chipping by a line.
> Meantime the lovely goddess to his aid
> Sharp augers brought, with which he bored the beams,
> Then placed them side by side, adapting each
> To other, and the seams with wadding closed.
> Broad as an artist skill'd in naval works
> The bottom of a ship of burthen spreads,
> Such breadth Ulysses to his raft assign'd.
> He decked her over with long planks, upborne
> On massy beams: he made the mast, to which
> He added, suitable, the yard: he framed
> Rudder and helm to regulate her course:
> With wickerwork he border'd all the length
> For safety, and much ballast stow'd within.
> Meantime Calypso brought him, for a sail,
> Fittest materials, which he also shaped,
> And to it all due furniture annex'd
> Of cordage strong, foot-ropes, and ropes aloft;
> Then heaved her down with levers to the deep."

Besides the facts contained in this passage, it is worth remarking that Homer seems to regard ship-builders with no little consideration, inasmuch as he calls them "artists."

The Greeks, like the Hebrews, were ignorant of the real figure of the earth. It is in Homer that we find the first written trace of the widely prevalent idea that the earth is a flat surface begirt on every side by the ocean. This was a natural belief in a region almost insular, like Greece, where the visible horizon and an enveloping sea suggested the idea of a flat circle. Homer took the lead among the poetic geographers of Greece, and his authority gave to the subject a fanciful cast, the traces of which are not yet obliterated. Beneath the earth he placed the fabled regions of Elysium and Tartarus: above the whole rose the grand arch of the heavens, which were supposed to rest on the summits of the highest mountains. The sun, moon, and stars were believed to rise from the waves of the sea, and to sink again beneath them on their return from the skies.

Homer's distribution of the land was even more fantastic. Beyond the limits of Greece and the western coasts of Asia Minor his knowledge was uncertain and obscure. He had heard vaguely of Thebes, the mighty capital of Egypt, and in his verse sang of its hundred gates and of the countless hosts it sent forth to battle. The Ethiopians, who lived beyond, were deemed to be the most remote dwellers upon the habitable earth. Towards the centre of Africa were the stupendous ridges of the Atlas Mountains: Homer deified the highest peak, and made it a giant supporting upon his shoulders the outspreading canopy of the heavens. The narrow passage leading from the Mediterranean to the Atlantic, and now known as the Straits of Gibraltar, was believed to have been discovered by Hercules, and the mountains on either side—Gibraltar and Ceuta—were, from him, called the Pillars of Hercules.

Colchos, upon the Black Sea, was believed to be an ocean-city, and here Greek fancy located the Palace of the Sun. It was here that the charioteer of the skies gave rest to his coursers during the night, and from whence in the morning he drove them forth again. Colchos, therefore, was Homer's eastern confine of the globe. On the north, Rhodope, or the Riphean Mountains, were supposed to enclose the hyperborean limits of the world. Beyond them dwelt a fabled race, seated in the recesses of their valleys and sheltered from the contests of the elements. They were represented as exempt from all ills, physical and moral, from sickness, the changes of the seasons, and even from death. A race directly the converse of the ideal hyperboreans were the Cimmerians, located at the mouth of the Sea of Azof, who are described by Homer as dwelling in perpetual darkness and never visited by the sun. He imagined the existence of numerous other nations, who long continued to hold a place in ancient geography. The Cyclops, who had but one eye, were placed in Sicily; the Arimaspians, similarly afflicted, inhabited the frontiers of India; the Pigmies, or Dwarfs, who fought pitched battles with the cranes, were supposed to dwell in Africa, in India, and, in fact, to occupy the whole southern border of the Earth.

In the time of Homer, all voyages in which the mariner lost sight of land were considered as fraught with the extremest peril. No navigator ever visited Africa or Sicily from choice, but only when driven there by tempest and typhoon, and then his woes usually terminated in shipwreck: a return was not merely a marvel, but a miracle. Homer made Sicily the principal scene of the lamentable adventures of Ulysses, and sufficient traces are furnished by the Odyssey of the distorted and exaggerated notions entertained in the poet's time of the character of places reached by a voyage at sea. The existence of monsters of frightful form and size, such as Polyphemus, who watched for the destruction of the mariner and even roasted and devoured his quivering limbs; of treacherous enchantresses, such as Circe, who lured but to ensnare; of amiable goddesses, like Calypso, who offered immortality in exchange for love,—was doubtless believed by Homer, though we must make some allowance for poetical license. At any rate, the invention of these fables is not to be attributed to Homer, who, at the most, gave a highly-colored repetition of the terrific reports brought back from those formidable coasts by the few who had been fortunate enough to return. It was thus that an ideal and poetic character was communicated to the science of geography by the fables with which Homer tinged his narrative. In the early ages of the world, science and poetry were twin sisters: every poet was a savant, and every savant was a poet.

As far as his ideas can be reduced to a system, the earth was a flat disk, around which flowed the river Ocean. The

THE WORLD ACCORDING TO HOMER.

accompanying plan will enable the reader to form an adequate conception of the Homeric geography. The radius of the territories described by Homer with any degree of precision was hardly three hundred miles in length.

Hesiod, who lived a century after Homer, thus states the scientific attainments of his time:—"The space between the heavens and the earth is exactly the same as that between the earth and Tartarus beneath it. A brazen anvil, if tossed from heaven, would fall during nine days and nine nights, and would reach the earth upon the tenth day. Were it to continue its course towards the abode of darkness, it would be nine days and nine nights more in accomplishing the distance." It is worth while remarking that this statement is at variance with that of Homer, who makes Vulcan, when precipitated from heaven by Jupiter, land at Lemnos in a single day: he had travelled, therefore, nearly twenty times faster than one of his own anvils. Hesiod intended to convey, by this illustration, an imposing idea of the loftiness of the heavens. In the eyes of modern astronomy, nothing can be more paltry. The time that an anvil thrown from Halcyon, the brightest star of the Pleiades, towards our globe, would require to reach it, may perhaps be imagined from the fact that the rays of light emitted by Halcyon travel five centuries before they strike the earth! It is thus that the positive revelations of modern science surpass in marvels the most daring inventions of ancient fable.

THE EARTH ACCORDING TO ANAXIMANDER.

Anaximander, four hundred years after Homer, held that the earth, instead of being flat, was in the form of a cylinder, convex upon its upper surface. Its diameter was three times greater than its height; and its form was round, as if it had been shaped by a turner's lathe. The Oracle of Delphi was the centre of his system.

Somewhat later, Thales, one of the Seven Sages, declared his belief that the earth was spherical, and remained suspended in mid air without support of any kind. This frightful doctrine made few proselytes: it was not likely, indeed, that any one but a sage would adopt a theory which made him the inhabitant of a globe abandoned and isolated in the midst of space.

In the fifth century before Christ, Herodotus, the most celebrated traveller of antiquity, and consequently capable of forming rational ideas upon the subject of geography, rectified many errors which had crept into the popular belief, though Homer was still considered infallible by the masses of the people. "I know of no such river as the ocean," he says, ironically: "this denomination seems to be a pure invention of Homer and the old poets. I cannot help laughing when I hear of the river Ocean, and of the spherical form of the earth, as if it were the work of a turner." He displaced the centre of the inhabited surface, which the Greeks had at first made Mount Olympus and afterwards Delphi, making Rhodes the fortunate possessor of the privilege. Socrates, a century later, (400 B.C.,) asserted that the earth was in the form of a globe, sustained in the middle of the heavens by its own equilibrium.

About the year 230 B.C., Eratosthenes, a Greek of Cyrene, succeeded in reducing geography to a system, under the patronage of the Ptolemies of Egypt, which gave him access to the immense mass of materials gathered by Alexander and his successors and accumulated at the Alexandrian Library. The spherical form of the earth was now quite generally considered by scientific men to be the correct theory, though it could never be substantiated till some navigator, sailing to the east, should return by the west. Eratosthenes, proceeding upon this principle, made it his study to adjust to it all the known features of the globe. The great ocean of Homer and Herodotus, surrounding the world, still remained in his system. He compared, however, the magnitude of the regions known in his time with what he conceived to be the whole circumference, and became convinced that only a third part of the space was filled up. He conjectured that the remaining space might consist of one great ocean, which he called the Atlantic, from Mount Atlas, which was fancifully believed to support the globe. He supposed, too, that lands and islands might be discovered in it by sailing towards the west.

We shall now proceed to give such a description of the vessels used by the Greeks after the time of Homer, as the confused and incomplete data which have reached us will enable us to furnish.

A GREEK VESSEL OF THE SIXTH CENTURY B.C.

CHAPTER VI.

CONSTRUCTION OF GREEK VESSELS—THE PROW, POOP, RUDDER, OARS, MASTS, SAILS, CORDAGE, BULWARKS, ANCHORS—BIREMES, TRIREMES, QUADRIREMES, QUINQUEREMES—THE GRAND GALLEY OF PTOLEMY PHILOPATOR—ROMAN VESSELS—THEIR NAVY—MIMIC SEA-FIGHTS—THE FIVE VOYAGES OF ANTIQUITY.

THE PROW or foredeck of Greek vessels was ornamented on both sides by figures in mosaic or painted. An eye on each side of the cutwater, as is represented above, was a very common embellishment. A projection from the head of the prow, pointed or covered with brass, and intended to damage an enemy upon collision, was often in the shape of a wild beast, or helmet, or even the neck of a swan. Below this was the rostrum or beak, which consisted of a beam armed with sharp and solid irons. They were at first above the water; but their efficiency was afterwards increased by putting them below the water-line and rendering them invisible. The commanding officer of the prow was next in rank to the helmsman, and had charge of the rigging and the control of the rowers.

The DECK proper, or middle deck, appears to have been raised above the bulwark, or at least upon a line with its upper edge, thus enabling the soldiers to see far around them and hurl their darts at the enemy from a commanding position.

The POOP, or stern, was usually higher than the rest of the vessel, and upon it the helmsman had his elevated seat. It was rounder than the prow, though its extremity was likewise sharp. It was embellished in various ways, but especially with the figure of the tutelary goddess or deity of the vessel. Over the helmsman was a roof, and above that an elegant ornament, rising from the stern and bending gracefully over him. In consequence of its conspicuous place and beautiful form, this ornament, named an aplustre, was considered emblematic of the sea, and was carried off by the victor in a naval engagement, as a standard or a scalp in more modern times.

The RUDDER was a singular contrivance. The origin of this very useful invention is attributed by Pliny, as we have said, to Tiphys, of the Argo,—a doubtful pilot of a doubtful vessel. Previous to this, vessels must have been guided by the same oars which propelled them. The Grecian rudder was a long oar with a very broad blade, inserted, not at the extremity of the stern, but at either side where it begins to curve; and a ship usually had two, both being managed by the same man. In large ships they were connected by a pole which kept them parallel and gave to both the position in which either was turned. The rudder seems to have been considered an emblem, as it frequently occurs on gems, coins, and cameos. Thus a Triton is found represented as blowing a shell and holding a rudder over his shoulder. A tiller and cornucopia are frequently seen in juxtaposition. A cameo, still preserved, shows a Venus Anadyomene leaning with her left arm upon a rudder the same height as herself, and thereby indicating, as is supposed, her own maritime origin.

The OARS, bearing a name which at first signified only the blade, but was afterwards applied to all oars except the rudder, varied in size as they were used by a higher or lower rank of rowers. A trireme may be said to have had one hundred and seventy oars, a quinquereme three hundred, and even four hundred. The lower part of the holes through which the oars passed appears to have been covered with leather, which also extended a little way outside the hole. In vessels mounting five ranks of oars, the upper ones were of course much larger than the lower ones, and we therefore find it stated by Greek authors that the lower rank of rowers, having the shortest oars and consequently the easiest work, received the smallest salary, while those who had the largest oars and the heaviest work received the largest salary. They sat upon benches attached to the ribs of the vessel, each oar being managed by one man.

The MASTS of Grecian vessels, of which there were one, two, and three, were usually made of the fir-tree. A vessel with thirty rowers had two masts, the smaller being near the prow. In three-masted vessels the largest mast was nearest the stern. The part of the mast immediately above the yard formed a structure similar to a drinking-cup, and the sailors ascended into it in order to manage the sails, to obtain a wider view, and to discharge missiles. In large ships these were made of bronze and would hold three men: they were furnished with pulleys for hoisting stones and projectiles from below. The portion of the mast above the cup, or *carchesium*, was called the distaff, and corresponded to the modern topmast. The sail was hoisted, as at present, by means of pulleys and a hoop sliding up and down the mast.

The SAILS were usually square. It was not common to furnish more than one sail to one ship, and it was then attached with the yard to the great mast. Sometimes each of the two masts of a trireme had two sails, which were spread the one over the other, those of the foremast being used only on occasions when great speed was required. It does not appear that the triangular or lateen sail, so prevalent afterwards among the Romans, was ever used by the Greeks. In Homer's time, sails were of linen. Subsequently, sail-cloth was made of hemp, rushes, and leather. Originally white, the sails of the ancients were afterwards dyed of various colors. Those of Alexander's

Indus fleet, of which we shall hereafter speak more particularly, were blue, white, and yellow. Those of pirates were sea-green, and those of Cleopatra, at the battle of Actium, were purple.

The CORDAGE used was of various sizes and strength. In the first place, thick and broad ropes ran in a horizontal direction around the ship from stem to stern, for the purpose of binding the whole fabric strongly together. They ran around in several circles and at fixed distances from each other. Their number varied according to the size of the ship, a trireme usually requiring four, and six in case they were intended for very boisterous weather. These ropes were always held in readiness in the Attic arsenals. A second-sized rope was used for the anchors, while those attached to the masts, sails, and yards were altogether lighter and made with greater care. One of these ran from the top of the mainmast to the prow, corresponding to the modern mainstay.

The BULWARKS were artificially elevated beyond the height intended by the builder of the frame by means of a wickerwork covered with skins. These served as a protection from high waves, and also as a breastwork against the enemy. They appear to have been fixed upon the upper edge of the wooden bulwark, and to have been removed when not wanted. Each galley had four, two of which were "white," and two "made of hair." What these distinctions were is quite unknown.

The ANCHORS of Greek vessels, in the earlier periods, were stones or crates of sand, but soon came to be made of iron, and to be formed with teeth or flukes. The Greeks used the several expressions of lowering, casting, and weighing anchor precisely as we do, and the elliptical phrase "to weigh" meant then, as now, to "set sail." Each ship had several anchors: we learn, from the twenty-seventh chapter of Acts, that the vessel of St. Paul had four. The last and heaviest anchor was considered "sacred," in the same way as it is now regarded as "a last hope." The sailors, in casting it, recommended themselves to the protection of the gods; and it was rather a pretext for resorting to prayer than an instrument reliable from its strength and weight. "In our day," says an eminent writer upon the art of ship-building, "when every thing is calculated and weighed, and, even in this most poetic of professions, tends to the driest and most prosaic materialism, instead of the sacred anchor, cast in the midst of prayer and sacrifice, we have the anchor of eight thousand pounds." With all proper deference to the religious spirit of this learned commentator, we may remark, without irreverence, that even the most "poetic" of mariners would prefer a single modern best bower to a dozen of the sacred anchors of the Greeks; and it can hardly be doubted that, if the latter themselves had been acquainted with the "anchor of eight thousand pounds," they would have dispensed with both prayer and sacrifice. Heaven helps those who help themselves.

Every Greek vessel had a distinctive name, which was usually of the feminine gender, and often that of some popular heroine. In many cases, the name of the builder was added.

After the Trojan War, the establishment of Greek colonies upon foreign coasts, the commercial intercourse with these colonies, and the very prevalent practice of piracy, contributed largely to the improvement of ships and of navigation. For many years no innovation was made upon the custom of employing ships with one rank of rowers on each side. The Erythræan Greeks are supposed to have invented the biremes, with two ranks, and the Corinthians the triremes, with three. Themistocles, in the fifth century B.C., persuaded the Athenians to build two hundred triremes, for the purpose of attacking Ægina. Even at this period, vessels were not provided with complete decks, some having partial decks, and some none at all, the only protection for the men consisting in the bulwark. The invention of decked ships is ascribed to the Thasians. After Alexander the Great, the Rhodians became the greatest maritime power in Greece. The Colossus of Rhodes, a brazen statue of Apollo, one hundred feet high, seems to have been erected in assertion of their commercial supremacy, for the legend is that it stood across the mouth of the harbor, and that vessels passed between its legs.

Navigation still remained what it had been before, the Greeks seldom venturing into the open sea, and considering it necessary to remain in sight of the coast by day and to observe the rising and setting of the stars by night, in order to replace the landmarks no longer visible in the darkness. In winter, navigation was suspended altogether. Rather than double a cape, they would drag their vessel across a neck of land from one sea to another, by machines contrived for the purpose. This was frequently done across the Isthmus of Corinth. The ordinary size of a war-galley or trireme may be inferred from the fact that its complement of men was two hundred and thirty; and its speed in smooth water and with a favorable wind may be stated as very nearly that of a modern steamboat.

Dionysius of Syracuse (405 B.C.) is said to have built the first quadrireme and quinquereme in Greece,—inventions which he probably obtained from the Carthaginians and Salaminians. Alexander the Great built ships with twelve and thirty ranks of oars. Ptolemy Philopator, of Egypt, is said to have constructed one of forty, after a Greek model. Callixenus has left a description of this vessel; and this, having been transcribed by Plutarch and Athenæus, was, until very lately, thus supported by competent authority, regarded as quite authentic. Late investigations have shown conclusively that the vessel, with the proportions given, never could have existed. She was said to have had forty tiers of oars, one above the other. It is clear that the uppermost tiers must have been of enormous length to reach the water, and we find their length stated, in consequence, at seventy feet. Sixty feet of this length must naturally have been without the vessel, leaving ten feet of handle within. As the strength of no one man would be sufficient to manage an oar thus unequally poised, the fabulists assert that the handles were made of lead, that the equilibrium might be restored. What the story thus gains in weight, however, it certainly loses in credibility. Oars of seventy feet were out of the question, even in the heroic ages. Their number was equally extraordinary, for they counted no less than four thousand, and were managed by four thousand men. Besides these, there were two thousand eight hundred and fifty combatants collected in castles and behind her bulwarks. She had four rudders, each forty-five feet long, and a double prow. This last feature would have been an impediment instead of an advantage, as the re-entering angles of the two prows would have presented a very violent resistance to the water, which, in its turn, would have exerted a great power to separate them. Her stern was said to have been decorated with resplendent paintings of terrible and fantastic animals, her oars to have protruded through masses of foliage, and, as if she was not already overladen, her hold was declared to have contained huge quantities of grain. A critical comparison has shown that this famous galley could not have turned her head from west to east without describing an enormous orbit and occupying a full hour in the manœuvre. Indeed, had the Egyptians been foolish enough to build such a ship, they would not have been fortunate enough to navigate her.

Nevertheless, as it is quite clear that Ptolemy did construct a galley of unusual size and capacity, modern commentators have earnestly sought to explain away the glaring exaggerations and impossibilities of the description given by Callixenus. The chief difficulty lay in the forty tiers of oars and in the four thousand oarsmen. The engraving upon the opposite page gives a representation of the Ptolemy, as she may reasonably be supposed to have appeared. Instead of forty *tiers*, she has, when thus restored, forty *groups* of oars: with this substitution, and a liberal diminution in the aggregate number, it is not impro-

THE PTOLEMY PHILOPATOR.

bable that she may have existed, and floated even. It is not, however, pretended by Callixenus that she was ever useful in war: she seems to have been regarded as a curiosity and a spectacle. She was, in fact, the Leviathan of antiquity,—the original "Triton among the minnows."

The Romans obtained the models of their vessels from the Greeks, though they remained almost entirely unacquainted with the sea till the third century before Christ. They then had no fleet, and few or no ships for any peaceful or commercial use. Livy mentions the appointment of naval decemvirs about the year 300 B.C. But it was not till 260 B.C. that Rome became a maritime power. It was now seen that she could not maintain herself against Carthage without a navy, and the senate ordered the immediate construction of a fleet. Triremes would have been of little avail against the high-bulwarked quinqueremes of the Carthaginians. It so happened, very fortunately for them, that a vessel of the largest class, belonging to Carthage, was wrecked upon the coast of Bruttium, and thus furnished them a model. They built, after this design, over one hundred vessels, the greater part of them quinqueremes, the whole being completed in sixty days after the trees were cut down. Thus built of green timber, they were unsound and clumsy. Still, to their own astonishment, they achieved a naval victory, capturing fifty of the enemy's vessels. Seventeen of their own were taken and destroyed by the Carthaginians off Messina. It was not long before the Romans completely crippled the maritime power of their African foe. From this time forward they continued to maintain a powerful navy, and built vessels with six and even ten ranks of oars. The construction of their vessels differed little from that of the Greeks, with the exception of the destructive engines of war and the towers and platforms with which they furnished them.

During the Imperial period, the Romans took great delight in witnessing representations of fights at sea, and their emperors were equally fond of exhibiting them. The first spectacle of this kind, or *naumachia*, was given by Julius Cæsar upon a lake dug for the purpose in the Campus Martius. Augustus caused a lake or "stagnum" to be made for a similar use. This remained as the permanent scene of such exhibitions. The combatants in these fights were usually captives or criminals condemned to death, who fought as in gladiatorial combats, until one side was exterminated or spared by imperial clemency. In a naumachia given by Nero, there were sea-monsters swimming about in the artificial lake. Claudius ordered a naval battle upon Lake Fucinus, in which one hundred ships and nineteen thousand combatants were engaged. Troops of nereids were seen swimming about, and the signal for attack was given by a silver Triton, who was made, by means of machinery, to blow the alarum upon a trumpet.

We now proceed to narrate, in chronological order, the very few voyages of discovery made previous to the Christian era. These were those of Hanno to Sierra Leone, of Sataspes to Sahara, of Nearchus from the Indus to the Tigris, of Pytheas from Massilia to Shetland, and of Eudoxus from Cadiz to the Equator.

CHAPTER VII.

THE VOYAGE OF HANNO THE CARTHAGINIAN—HE SEES CROCODILES, APES, AND VOLCANOES—THE VOYAGE OF HIMILCON TO AL-BION—THE VOYAGE AND IGNOMINIOUS FATE OF SATASPES THE PERSIAN—THE VOYAGE OF PYTHEAS THE PHOCIAN—THE SACRED PROMONTORY—A NEW ATMOSPHERE—AMBER—RETURN HOME—THE VERACITY OF PYTHEAS' NARRATIVE—THE EXPEDITION OF NEARCHUS THE MACEDONIAN—STRANGE PHENOMENA IN THE HEAVENS—THE ICTHYOPHAGI—HOUSES BUILT OF THE BONES OF WHALES—FISH FLOUR—A BATTLE WITH WHALES—AN UNEXPECTED MEETING—THE DISTANCE TRAVERSED BY NEARCHUS—THE VOYAGE OF EUDOXUS ALONG THE AFRICAN COAST—STATE OF NAVIGATION AT THE OPENING OF THE CHRISTIAN ERA.

AT a period which it is no longer possible to settle with precision, but certainly anterior to the fifth century B.C., the Carthaginians, then in the height of their maritime and commercial prosperity, ordered a navigator by the name of Hanno to make a voyage beyond the Pillars of Hercules, and to found cities along the western shore of Africa. He set sail with a fleet of sixty vessels, each of which was impelled by fifty oars. He carried with him thirty thousand men and women, with abundant supplies and provisions. Within a week after passing the straits, they founded a city and erected a temple to Neptune; they also established five trading stations along the coast. They saw a race of people called Lixitæ, with whom they formed ties of friendship, and by whom they were furnished with interpreters. Continuing their course, they found another race dressed in the skins of wild beasts, who repelled them from the shore with stones and other missiles. They next came to the mouth of a river which was filled with crocodiles and hippopotami. They soon arrived at a coast edged with high mountains covered with trees, the wood of which was odoriferous and variously tinted. Beyond was an immense opening of the sea, bordered by plains on which they saw many blazing fires. Then they came to a large bay, in which was an island enclosing a salt-water lake, in which, again, was another island. Entering this lake in the night, they saw huge fires burning and heard the sounds of musical instruments and the cries of innumerable human beings. They next reached the fiery region of Thymiamata, whence torrents of flame poured down into the sea. Here the heat of the earth was such that the foot could not rest upon it. After four days' farther sail, they again found the land at night enveloped in flames. In the midst of these fires appeared one much more lofty than the rest: this, when seen by daylight, proved to be a very tall mountain, called the Chariot of the Gods. They soon met with a rude description of people, who had rough skins, and among whom the females were much more numerous than the males: the interpreters called them *Gorillæ*. They endeavored to catch some of them, but only succeeded in capturing three females, who made so violent a resistance, that they were obliged to kill them and strip off their skins, which they carried back to Carthage. Being out of provisions at this point, they were unable to pursue their voyage, and returned home.

This narrative, as given by Hanno himself, hardly fills two octavo pages: volumes of commentaries have been written upon it by geographers and antiquaries. The most probable of the various hypotheses formed upon it, is, that Hanno's voyage extended to Sherbro Sound, a little south of Sierra Leone. The features of man and nature, as described by Hanno, are to be found in Tropical Africa only: Ethiopians or negroes; Gorillæ, who are clearly apes, or orang-outangs; rivers so large as to contain crocodiles and river-horses. The great conflagrations of the grass, too, and the music and dancing prolonged through the night, are phenomena which have been observed only in the negro territories. But this hypothesis is not accepted by all geographers, one of whom gives to Hanno's course an extent of three thousand miles, while another limits it to less than seven hundred.

While Hanno was thus exploring the western coast of Africa, another Carthaginian, named Himilcon, was sent by his countrymen to the North of Europe. From a very vague description of his voyage given in a Latin poem entitled *Ora Maritima*, it is plain that he crossed the Bay of Biscay, and found, upon islands, as is asserted, but probably upon the mainland, a race of athletic people who went fearlessly to sea in barks made of skins sewed together. They crossed, in the space of two days, to a place called the Sacred Island, (Ireland,) which was not far from another island, named Al-Bion, (England.) No further details of this expedition have been preserved.

Upon the establishment of the Persian sway over the eastern coasts of the Mediterranean, towards the close of the fifth century B.C., the exploration of Africa became the peculiar province of the Persian monarchs. But this nation labored under an unconquerable aversion for the sea, and the only maritime effort of theirs on record was entirely casual in its origin, and futile in its results. It was as follows, as recorded by Herodotus:

Sataspes, a Persian nobleman, having committed a crime punishable with death, was condemned by Xerxes to be crucified. One of his friends persuaded the monarch to commute the sentence into a voyage around Africa, which, he said, was much more severe, and might result advantageously to the nation. Sataspes obtained a vessel and recruited a crew in Egypt, and, sailing through the Pillars of Hercules, bent his course southward. He is represented as having beat about for many weeks, and probably reached the shores of the Great Saharan Desert. The aspect of this formidable and tempest-lashed coast might well appall an amateur navigator accustomed to the luxurious indolence of a Persian court. He seems to have preferred crucifixion to circumnavigation, for he at once measured back his course to the Straits. He gave an incoherent account of his adventures to Xerxes, attributing his failure to the interference of an insurmountable obstacle, the nature of which he was unable to explain. Xerxes would listen to no excuse, and ordered the original sentence to be executed forthwith. Authorities differ as to the fate of Sataspes,—one asserting that he suffered the ignominious death to which he was condemned, and another alleging that he made his escape to the island of Samos.

THE SACRED PROMONTORY.

A colony which had been established at Massilia—now Marseilles—about six hundred years before Christ, by the Phocians, was, in the year 340 B.C., at the height of its commercial prosperity. The citizens, being desirous of extending their maritime relations, sent, at this period, upon an expedition to the North of

Europe, through the Pillars of Hercules, a learned geographer and astronomer by the name of Pytheas. He started with a single ship, the finances of the city not permitting a larger outlay of means.

He passed the Pillars on the sixteenth day from Massilia; and on the twentieth he arrived at the Sacred Promontory, the extreme western point of Iberia or Spain. A temple to Hercules had been erected at this spot. The inhabitants of the promontory declared, during the time of Pytheas, and, indeed, for two hundred years afterwards, that as the sun plunged at evening into the sea, they heard a hissing like that of a red-hot body suddenly dropped into water.

Following the coasts of Iberia and of Celtica, he came to the point of land now known as Finisterre, in France, and the promontory Calbium. Turning to the east, he was surprised to

PLAN OF PYTHEAS' VOYAGE.

find himself in a wide gulf, with Celtica on his right, and an immense island on his left. The gulf was the British Channel, and the island the Al-Bion that Himilcon had vaguely discerned some centuries before. It was at this point that Pytheas may be said to have begun his career; and the discovery of Great Britain may safely be attributed to him.

He described the island as having the form of an isosceles triangle, as may be seen upon the foregoing plan. Three promontories formed the three angles,—Belerium being now Land's

End, Cantium Cape Pepperness, and Orcas Duncansby Head. He found the inhabitants of the southern coast industrious and sociable, peaceable, honest, and sober. They raised wheat and worked rich mines of tin. As he sailed northward, along the eastern coast, he noticed that the days grew sensibly longer; and at Point Orcas, nineteen hours elapsed between the rising and the setting of the sun. He sailed still northward, and six days after leaving Orcas he came to an island, or a continent,—he knew not which,—which he called Thule. As he found he could go no farther to the north, he spoke of this spot as *Ultima Thule*, an expression which has passed into the figurative language of all modern nations as one denoting any remote point. Thule is generally considered to have been Shetland, although theories have been ardently advocated making it respectively Iceland, Sweden, and Jutland.

The narrative of Pytheas, which has been thus far clear and reliable, assumes at this point a very fabulous aspect. He declares that north of Thule there was neither earth, nor sea, nor air. A sort of dense concretion of all the elements occupied space and enveloped the world. He compared it to the thick, viscid animal substance called *pulmo marinus*, a sort of mollusk or medusa. He said that this substance was the basis of the universe, and that in it earth, air, and sky hung, as it were, suspended. This illusion has been explained by the dreary spectacle of fogs, mists, rains, and tempests which at this point of his voyage must have met the gaze of the daring navigator. It would have been difficult for any mind, in those early ages, to have been on its guard against the sinister impressions likely to result from the contemplation of a scene so appalling. It must be remembered that Pytheas was accustomed to the pure and transparent atmosphere, the dazzling sky, and the phosphorescent waters of the Mediterranean. It would have been astonishing if a man educated among the splendors of an almost tropical climate had not been oppressed by influences so gloomy. It was the belief of all early navigators that a point would be found somewhere without the Pillars of Hercules beyond which it would be impossible to penetrate. While timid adventurers declared they had arrived at this point hardly a week's sail from the Straits, and declared that an atmosphere of mist, darkness, and gigantic sea-weed barred their passage, Pytheas did not allow his imagination to be affected or his courage to be shaken till he found himself in presence of the sombre and formidable scenery of what, with true geographical propriety, he denominated "Thule and her utmost isles."

Leaving his animal atmosphere behind him, Pytheas returned to Orcas and from thence to Cantium. Instead of following his former track through the British Channel homeward, he turned to the eastward, and arrived, in a few days' sail, at the mouth of the Rhine. He found the country here inhabited by a race of fierce barbarians. Upon the shores of a vast gulf, beyond, dwelt the Teutons and the Guttones. In this gulf was an island named Abalcia, upon whose shores the waves deposited, in spring, immense quantities of yellow amber, which the inhabitants burned instead of wood, or sold for fuel to their neighbors the Teutons. Pytheas pursued his voyage as far as a river named Tanais, now supposed to be either the Elbe or the Oder. He considered this stream to be the eastern boundary of Celtica, in which he included Germania. He now turned his face homeward, and, coasting along the shores of Celtica and Iberia, arrived without accident or adventure at Massilia. He had sailed one hundred and eighty-six thousand stadia, or eleven thousand miles: the duration of the expedition was less than a year.

Geographers subsequent to Pytheas strove zealously to discredit his assertions. One denied the voyage altogether; another questioned the veracity of the narrative. Strabo was particularly hostile to Pytheas, whom he said he would prove "a liar of the first magnitude." He was thus led to make long quotations from his descriptions for the purpose of refuting them. As the original account given by Pytheas is not extant, the world is indebted to the skepticism of Strabo for all that it knows of one of the most interesting and daring maritime enterprises of antiquity.

In the year 326 before Christ, Alexander of Macedon, having accomplished the conquest of Persia, and having invaded Hindostan by the north, found himself compelled, by a mutiny of his troops, to arrest his course upon the eastern bank of the river Indus. He was here seized with a desire to explore the lower course of that river, and afterwards the southern shores of Asia, a tract of coast with which the Greeks were entirely unacquainted. The object of the expedition was partly exploration, and partly to convey a portion of the army back to Babylon upon the river Euphrates. The dangers of the enterprise and the improbability of success deterred the greater part of the naval officers from attempting it, as neither the Arabian Sea nor the Persian Gulf had ever been traversed before. Nearchus, the admiral of the fleet, proposed several candidates for the perilous honor, who variously excused themselves. Nearchus at last proffered his own services, which, after some hesitation, were accepted. This selection of a commander tranquillized the soldiers and sailors intended for the expedition; for they felt that Alexander would not have sent his intimate friend upon a voyage from which he would not be likely to return. The splendor of the preparations, the beauty of the vessels, the confidence of the officers, also went far towards dissipating their fears. At the word of Alexander, says a modern poet,—

"The pines descend; the thronging masts aspire;
The novel sails swell beauteous o'er the curves
Of Indus: to the moderator's song
The oars keep time, while bold Nearchus guides
Aloft the gallies. On the foremost prow

> The monarch from his golden goblet pours
> A full libation to the gods, and calls
> By name the mighty rivers through whose course
> He seeks the sea."

Alexander accompanied his fleet to the delta of the Indus, from whence he obtained a view of the gulf. He then returned to lead his men across Gedrosia, Caramania, and Persis to Babylon. Nearchus then set sail, after offering sacrifices to Neptune and Jupiter Salvator, and ordering a series of games and gymnastic exercises. The voyage thus undertaken was an event of real importance in the history of navigation: it opened a route between Europe and the extremities of Asia. It was the source of the discoveries made in later times by the Portuguese, and the primary, though remote, cause of the successful establishment of the British in India.

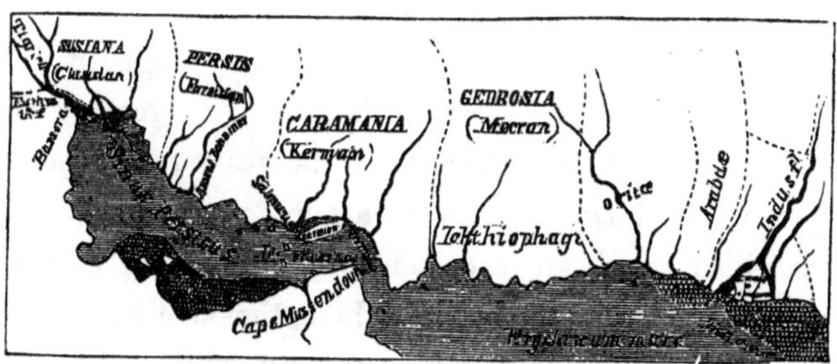

PLAN OF THE VOYAGE OF NEARCHUS.

At the very mouth of the river they met a formidable obstacle,—a rocky bar over which the waves broke with extreme violence. Through this bar, in its softest parts, they cut a canal one-third of a mile in length, and at high tide passed through it with the fleet. They had hardly reached the open ocean before a heavy gale drove them into an indentation of land protected by an island: to this natural harbor Nearchus gave the name of Alexander. Here he caused a camp to be laid out and entrenched, and remained for twenty-four days, the soldiers subsisting chiefly on shell-fish. When the gale abated they again embarked, meeting with constant adventures and difficulties upon their way. One day they would pass through huge menacing rocks, so near that they touched them with their oars on either side. On another they would be compelled, on landing for water, to ascend for miles into the interior before finding fresh-water sources. A storm caused two galleys and a vessel to founder, the crews of which, however, succeeded in swimming to shore. Nearchus caused his whole army to land at this point, for they needed repose, and his shattered fleet required repairs. He met with Leonatus, whom Alexander had detached from the main body of the army to follow the coasts and keep up a communication with Nearchus. Wheat was also sent to this spot by Alexander for the fleet, and each vessel took a supply sufficient for ten days. Nearchus exchanged such sailors and soldiers as had proved inefficient, for fresh men selected from the division of Leonatus.

At this point the narrative becomes strongly tinged with the usual exaggerations of the early navigators. Nearchus asserts that he observed strange phenomena in the heavens. When the sun was in the meridian, he says, no shadow was projected, and the stars which they were accustomed to see above them were now crouching close to the horizon; others, that had never before disappeared from the sky, now rose and set at intervals. The assertion in regard to shadows at noon is evidently a fabrication. Enough was known of astronomy and the motions of the heavenly bodies, in the time of Nearchus, to convince the learned that there must be a point where no shadow would be cast by a body directly beneath the sun at the summer solstice; and Nearchus, with a vanity quite usual in the conquerors and adventurers of those times, chose to assert, and he perhaps believed, that he had seen this singular phenomenon. Two circumstances will show the inaccuracy of his statement. The alleged appearance took place in the middle of the month of November, and twenty-five degrees north of the equator. Even had Nearchus been at this spot in midsummer, he would have seen shadows of very respectable length. Upon the coast of Gedrosia he found a people called Icthyophagi, or Fish-eaters. The mutton here tasted of fish, and Nearchus discovered that the sheep eat fish as well as the inhabitants, for the land yielded no pasturage.

In one of the villages of the Fish-eaters Nearchus engaged a pilot who undertook to guide him as far as Caramania. The aspect of the coast now became less repulsive, and palm-trees, myrtles, and flowers grew wild upon the hill-sides. Such was the delight of the Macedonians at this sight, that they landed and wove garlands and wreaths of the foliage for the wives and daughters of the natives. Farther on, at a spot where the inhabitants made them presents of roasted tunny-fish—the first cooked fish they had yet received from the Icthyophagi—and where they noticed wheat-fields, they landed, and, after taking possession of the village, demanded the surrender of all their wheat. The people made a feeble resistance, and then gave up all the flour they possessed,—not wheat flour, but fish flour,—flour made by reducing fish to powder, as we make flour by pulverizing the kernels of wheat.

The coast again becoming almost desert, the crew were obliged to eat the tender buds of palm-trees, and on one occasion were glad to devour seven camels which they were fortunate enough to encounter. Besides the dangers of famine, Nearchus had to contend with legions of whales, many of them one hundred and fifty feet long,—a prodigious size for inland seas like the Persian Gulf. One day he noticed a jet of water of great height and violence, and soon the air was filled with spray tossed up by a sportive herd of these monsters. The frightened sailors let drop their oars: but Nearchus encouraged them and dissipated their fears. He placed the vessels of the fleet abreast in a single line, and ordered them to advance simultaneously at full speed, as in a naval combat, and, upon approaching the whales, to terrify them by shouts and the din of trumpets. At a given signal, the vessels started and dashed forward upon the cetaceous army: the whales plunged into the abysses of the water, and, reappearing at the sterns of the fleet, sent up a shower of spirts in derision of their timorous enemy. Nearchus found these fish so abundant that large numbers of them were stranded in every storm: the inhabitants built houses of their bones, using the larger bones for posts, planks, and doors; the jaw-bones furnished an excellent thatch, or roofing material. He also saw huts constructed of the back-bones of smaller fish.

The fleet now reached the coast of Caramania, after passing an island supposed to be inhabited by an enchantress very much like the Circe of the Greek fable, who was said to seduce navigators by the promise of voluptuous pleasures and then change them into fish. Nearchus now found his distresses nearly at an end, as the soil was productive of grain and fruit, and as the streams yielded an abundance of water. He soon came in view of a vast promontory on the Arabian side, (Cape Mussendoun,) which seemed completely to close the entrance to the Persian Gulf. The sailors, weary of their long voyage, earnestly besought Nearchus to land here and to march across the country to Babylon. Nearchus insisted that this would not be fulfilling the intentions of Alexander, whose command it was to survey every portion of the coast from the Indus to the Euphrates. They doubled the cape, therefore, and entered the Persian Gulf. Keeping close to the northern shore, they came at last to a tract of territory inhabited by friendly races and yielding an abundance of every fruit except the olive. They landed at the mouth of the Anamis,—the modern Minab,—and refreshed themselves after their long hardships. They reposed under the shade of palms, and conversed gayly of the dangers they had escaped and the wonders they had seen. A party wandered from the coast towards the interior, and, to their surprise and joy, met a man clothed in the Greek chlamys and speaking the Greek language. They asked him who he was and what country he was from. He replied that he belonged to the army of Alexander, and that the camp was not far off. Transported with delight, they took the stranger to Nearchus, whom he told that Alexander was at five days' journey from the sea.

Nearchus, upon receiving this intelligence, caused his ships to be drawn on shore, a rampart to be built round them, and repairs to be commenced upon them, while he, Archius, a lieutenant, and six sailors should set out to find the camp of the king. As they approached the outposts, soldiers sent forward to meet them by Alexander, who had been informed of their coming, did not recognise them, on account of their changed dress and haggard aspect. Alexander received them with kindness, but in deep sorrow, for he had conceived the idea that the eight persons before him were all that had survived the perils of the sea. "You two have returned," he said, "you and Archius, safe and sound, and this alone renders the loss of my fleet endurable: tell me in what manner perished my vessels and my army." Upon learning the safety of the entire expedition, he is said to have burst into a flood of tears, and to have sworn that he derived more pleasure from this event than from the entire conquest of Asia. He offered sacrifices to Jupiter, Hercules, Apollo, and Neptune. He then proposed that Nearchus should repose from his trials, and that another should conduct the fleet to Susa, the capital of Susiana. Nearchus thought it unjust, however, that the glory of completing a task which he had so successfully begun should be taken from him, and retained the command. He was obliged to fight his way back to the sea through warlike and hostile tribes.

The rest of the voyage, along the coasts of Caramania and Persis,—the modern Fars,—was comparatively easy, orders having been given by Alexander that Nearchus should find at intervals supplies of every species of provisions. On the 24th of February, in the year 325 B.C., the fleet arrived at the mouth of the Euphrates. Nearchus learned that Alexander had already reached Susa, which was situated some forty miles towards the interior upon the borders of the Tigris. He therefore ascended that river, and, at a bridge newly thrown over it for the passage of Alexander's army, the junction of the long-separated naval and land forces took place. Nearchus received a crown of gold for his success in the expedition; the pilot was rewarded with a crown of smaller size, and the debts of the army were discharged by Alexander.

The voyage had occupied nearly five months, and the distance sailed was not far from fifteen hundred miles, if the sinuosities and indentations of the coast are included, and twelve hundred in a straight line. Half of this period of five months must be considered to have been spent upon the land, in surveys of the coast, in repairs of the vessels, and in forays in search of food and water. The same route is now usually traversed by merchant vessels in the space of three weeks. Nothing can give a better idea of the immense service Nearchus was thought to have rendered the state, than the fact that it was in the convivialities of a banquet in his honor, a year later, that Alexander abandoned himself to the excesses which resulted in his death.

Eudoxus, the next navigator in chronological order, was a native of Cyzicus, in Mysia, and was sent by its citizens, in the third century B.C., upon a mission connected with the promotion of geographical science, to Alexandria, then the seat of maritime enterprise. He became strongly imbued with the spirit of exploration and investigation which reigned there, and succeeded in inducing Ptolemy Euergetes, the reigning king, to fit out a naval armament, and to send it under his command upon an expedition down the Arabian Gulf or Red Sea. He appears to have made a successful voyage, for he returned with a cargo of aromatics and precious stones. It is supposed that he sailed down the Red Sea, and, passing out by the Straits of Babelmandel, followed the southern coast of Arabia as far as the Persian Gulf: it is altogether unlikely that he reached the shores of India. Euergetes plundered him of his wealth upon his return, but died soon after, leaving the throne to his widow Cleopatra.

The queen took Eudoxus into favor, and sent him upon a fresh voyage. He seems to have been driven by unfavorable winds upon the coast of Abyssinia, where he made advantageous bargains with the inhabitants. He rescued from the water a fragment of a wreck,—the prow of a vessel which, from a sculpture representing the figure of a horse, seemed to have come from the West. This prow was exhibited by Eudoxus in the harbor of Alexandria, and was declared by some mariners from Cadiz to be of the precise form peculiar to large vessels which went from that port to fish upon the coast of Mauritania, or Morocco. It was evident, therefore, to the ardent mind of Eudoxus, that this fragment of a wrecked vessel, left to the mercy of the waves, had performed the grand maritime problem of antiquity, —the circuit of Africa. He abandoned himself with enthusiastic credulity to the enticing hope that he might himself succeed in achieving this darling object of the ambition of princes, kings, and states.

He determined to renounce the deceitful patronage of courts, and to start with a new expedition from Cadiz. He went thither by way of Massilia and other trading settlements, and urged all who were animated by the spirit of progress to follow him. He thus succeeded in equipping an armada, consisting of one ship and two large boats, on board of which were not only goods and provisions and the necessary crews, but artisans, scientific men, and musicians. The very ardor and extravagance of their hopes, and perhaps, too, the undue gayety in which they took their departure, unfitted them to encounter the dangers and hardships of African discovery. The crew were frightened at the swell of the open sea through which Eudoxus wished to make his way, and insisted upon following the shore, according to the usual cautious method of those days. The consequence was that the ship was stranded, and the cargo was with difficulty saved. Eudoxus prosecuted the voyage in a single ship of lighter construction, till he came to a race of people who spoke, as he thought, the same language as those he had met on the opposite side of the continent. Thinking this discovery enough for the expedition in its now enfeebled state, he returned to Spain and equipped another small fleet, better fitted to buffet the waves of the open sea.

He again set forth; but the narrative, as handed down by Strabo, breaks off at this point, and we are without information upon the results of the enterprise. It is true that rumor and fable have supplied the place of authentic facts, and that Eudoxus is described by one version as having actually circumnavigated Africa; by another, as having come to a race of people who were born dumb; and by another, as having fallen in with a nation who had no mouths, but received their food through an orifice in the nose. These exaggerations are unworthy of notice; and they do not seem to have thrown discredit upon the account of the earlier experience of Eudoxus, which ranks among the most esteemed narratives of ancient maritime adventure.

We have thus given, in some detail, descriptions of all the noteworthy experiments in navigation previous to the birth of Christ. Two features, it will be at once remarked, characterized all these efforts:—1st, The only reliable propelling force continued to lie in the oars; and, 2d, no sailor ventured out of sight of land, unless, as when crossing the Mediterranean, he knew that other lands lay beyond the visible horizon. We close this division of the subject with the general observation, that the opening of the Christian era found the world almost entirely under Roman dominion,—one which preferred extending its sway by land to prosecuting discovery by sea. The Mediterranean was, thus far, the only seat of commerce and the exclusive scene of navigation. Though Hanno and Eudoxus had indeed passed the Pillars of Hercules, and had coasted along the African shore as far as the negro territories, and though Pytheas, proceeding to the north, had visited—still hugging the land—the Baltic and the British Channel, their expeditions must be considered as at once venturesome and futile, for the age was not able to repeat them, and totally failed to make them useful either to geography or commerce. As long as the centre of power, of luxury, of wealth, remains within the Mediterranean, as long as Tyre, Sidon, Rome, Carthage, successively control the destinies of the world, so long shall we find mankind lacking both the motive and the means to seek new worlds, by sea, beyond. Time, however, will furnish both the motive and the means: we shall find the one, as we proceed, in the Spice Islands of the East, the other in the Mariner's Compass. The next division of our subject will narrate how the contests between the Crescent and the Cross over the tomb of Christ brought Europe and Asia into contact and acquaintanceship; and how the commerce and intercourse which were the immediate consequences led to that general and absorbing interest in the sea and ships which eventually produced Columbus and Magellan. The influence of nutmeg and cinnamon upon the spread of the gospel and the development of science is a theme which we shall show to be not unworthy of earnest and philosophical inquiry.

SUPPOSED FORM OF THE SHIPS OF NEARCHUS.

VENETIAN GALLEY OF THE TENTH CENTURY.

Section II.

FROM THE COMMENCEMENT OF THE CHRISTIAN ERA TO THE APPLICATION OF THE MAGNETIC NEEDLE TO EUROPEAN NAVIGATION, A.D. 1300.

CHAPTER VIII.

NAVIGATION DURING THE ROMAN EMPIRE—THE RISE OF VENICE AND GENOA—THE CRUSADES—THEIR EFFECT UPON COMMERCE—WEDDING OF THE ADRIATIC—CREATION OF THE FRENCH NAVY—INTRODUCTION OF EASTERN ART INTO EUROPE—MAPS OF THE MIDDLE AGES—REMOTE EFFECT OF THE CRUSADES UPON GEOGRAPHICAL SCIENCE.

We have taken the birth of Christ as a point of departure in the history of navigation, merely because of the prominence of that event in the annals of the world, not on account of any connection that it has with the chronicles of the sea. So far from that, the first five centuries of the Christian era are an absolute blank in all matters which pertain to our subject. The Roman Empire rose and fell; and its rise and fall concerned the Mediterranean only. Not even Julius Cæsar, the greatest man in Roman history, has a place in maritime records; unless, when crossing the Adriatic in a fishing-boat during a storm, his memorable words of encouragement to the fisherman, "Fear nothing! you carry Cæsar and his fortunes!" are sufficient to connect him with the sea. Neither Pompey, nor Sylla, nor Augustus, nor Nero, nor Titus, nor Constantine, nor Theodosius, nor Attila, can claim part or lot in the dominion of man over the ocean. And so we glide rapidly over five centuries.

Upon the invasion of Italy by the barbarians, A.D. 476, the Veneti, a tribe dwelling upon the northeastern shores of the Adriatic, escaped from their ravages by fleeing to the marshes and sandy inlets formed by the deposits of the rivers which there fall into the gulf. Here they were secure; for the water around them was too deep to allow of an attack from the land, and too shallow to admit the approach of ships from the sea. Their only resource was the water and the employments it afforded. At first they caught fish; then they made salt, and finally engaged in maritime traffic. Early in the seventh century their traders were known at Constantinople, in the Levant, and at Alexandria. Their city soon covered ninety islands, connected together by bridges. They established mercantile factories at Rome, and extended their authority into Istria and Dalmatia. In the eighth century they chased the pirates, and in the ninth they fought the Saracens. At this period Genoa, too, rose into notice, and the Genoese and the Venetians at once became commercial rivals and the monopolists of the Mediterranean.

And now Peter the Hermit, barefooted and penniless, inveighing against the atrocities of the Turks towards Christians at Jerusalem, exhorted the warriors of the Cross to take up arms against the infidels. He inspired all Europe with an enthusiasm like his own, and enlisted a million followers in the cause. The passion of the age was for war, peril, and adventure; and fighting for the Sepulchre was a more agreeable method of doing penance than wearing sackcloth or mortifying the flesh. The First Crusade, a motley array of knights, spendthrifts, barons, beggars, women, and children, set out upon their wild career. Then came the Second, the Third, and the

Fourth. Crusading was the amusement and occupation of two centuries. Two millions of Europeans perished in the cause before it was abandoned. A few words concerning its effect upon the civilization of Europe are necessary here, in direct pursuance of our subject.

During their stay in Palestine the Crusaders learned, and in a measure acquired, the habits of Eastern life. They brought back with them a taste for the peculiar products of that region, —jewels, silks, cutlery, perfumes, spices. A brisk commerce through the length and breadth of the Mediterranean was the speedy consequence. Genoa, Pisa, Florence, Venice, covered the waters of their inland sea with sails, trafficking from the ports of Italy to those of Syria and Egypt. In every maritime city conquered by the Crusaders, trading-stations and bazaars were established. Marseilles obtained from the kings of Jerusalem privileges and monopolies of trade upon their territory. Venice surpassed all her rivals in the splendor and extent of her commerce, and it was for this that the Pope, Alexander III., sent the Doge the famous nuptial ring with which, in assertion of his naval supremacy, "to wed the Adriatic." The ceremony was performed from the deck of the Bucentaur, or state-galley, with every possible accompaniment of pomp and parade. The vessel was crowned with flowers like a bride, and amid the harmonies of music and the acclamations of the spectators the ring was dropped into the sea. The Republic and the Adriatic, long betrothed, were now indissolubly wedded. This ceremony was repeated from year to year.

The Normans, the Danes, the Dutch, imitated the example of the Italians, or, as they were then called, the Lombards, but were rather occupied in conveying provisions to the armies than in trading for their own account.

It was during the Crusades that the French navy was created. Philip Augustus, who, on his way to Syria, and thence home again, could not have remained insensible to the advantages of

THE DOGE OF VENICE WEDDING THE ADRIATIC.

possessing a strong force upon the ocean, formed, upon his return, the nucleus of a national fleet, for the purpose of defending his coasts either against pirates or foreign invasion.

While the necessity of transporting articles from the East to supply the demand thus created in the West gave a stimulus to commerce and navigation, manufactures were encouraged and developed by the operation of the same cause. The Italians learned from the Greeks the art of weaving silk, which soon resulted in the weaving of cloth of gold and silver. They learned to mould glass in a multitude of new and curious forms. From the manufactories of Syria, where stuffs were made of camels' hair, improvements were introduced into the manufactures of Europe, where they were woven of no other material than lambs' wool. Palestine also suggested to crusaders returning home the advantages of windmills for grinding flour. Arabia furnished the art of tempering arms and polishing steel, of chasing gold and silver, of mounting stones in rich and massive settings. Constantinople furnished the Christians with many splendid specimens of ancient art,—groups, statues, and the Corinthian horses, and thus awakened European taste.

Nearly all the Gothic monuments of Europe which still excite the admiration of the tourist owe their existence to this communication with the Greeks by means of the Crusades, and to the wonder which seized the Frank and Lombard at the sight of the churches and palaces of Byzantium. The Europeans carried back with them the architecture of the Saracens. Saint Mark's at Venice was built from the plans, and under the direction, of an unbeliever. The Cathedral and Spire of Strasburg, with their gigantic and yet delicate proportions, the Minster of Amiens, the Sainte Chapelle of Paris, were constructed in close imitation of the chef-d'œuvres of Eastern art. Painting upon glass was also brought from Constantinople, and the early painters of Christendom were speedily employed in tracing in colors, upon the windows of abbeys and cathedrals, the exploits of the Crusaders and the triumphs of the Cross.

From the Arabs and the Greeks, too, the Europeans received their first lessons in the natural and exact sciences. Imperfect and incomplete as were the astronomy, the botany, the mathematics, and the geography of the Arabians, they were far in advance of the same professions as understood and practised in Europe. The languages were improved and enriched by the association and exchange of ideas into which English, Germans, Italians, and French were forced. The confusion of tongues, which was as complete as at Babel, was somewhat corrected by the harmony of interest and oneness of purpose which animated all, of whatever name and lineage, who gathered around the Sepulchre.

It is obvious, therefore, that the effect of the Crusades, so far as it is the object of a work like the present to trace and delineate it, was to give the people of Europe a new motive for maintaining an intercourse with the people of Asia. They had seen their superior civilization, and sought to introduce it among themselves. They had learned to appreciate their skill in the arts, and resolved to acclimate those arts at home. They had accustomed themselves to many articles of luxury, which had become articles of necessity, and which it was now essential, therefore, to transport from the Levant, from the Red Sea, and the Persian Gulf, to the Bay of Venice and the Gulf of Genoa. There was a demand, in short, in the West, for the products, the manufactures, the arts, of the East. Here was the origin of the immense Eastern commerce which now fell into the hands of the Genoese and Venetians, and which, resulting from the Crusades, compelled us to the digression we have made. It is not our purpose, however, to refer more at length to this commerce, as it was carried on upon seas which had been navigated for twenty centuries; and we must hasten forward to the period when new paths were laid out over the immensity of the waters.

A map, published just anterior to the First Crusade, fully displays the ignorance which then prevailed in geographical science. The sea, as in the age of Homer, is made to surround the world as a river, the land being divided into three parts, Europe, Asia, and Africa. Africa and Asia are joined together in the South, and the Indian Ocean is an inland sea. Asia is as large as the other two continents combined. On the east there is a small spot indicated as the position of the Garden of Eden by the words *Hic est Paradisus.* Europe and Africa are separated from Asia by a long canal, which may be either the Nile or the Hellespont. Africa is still considered the land of mystery and fable: its northern part only is considered inhabitable, the south being even unapproachable, on account of the torrents of flame poured on it by the sun. The Frozen Ocean, the Baltic, the White Sea, and the Caspian, are all united. The Northern regions are represented as forming one single island. Scandinavia is made the birthplace and residence of the Amazons, the famous women-warriors to whom antiquity had given a home in the Caucasus.

We shall, in due order, proceed to show that the indirect and remote effect of the Crusades, and of the intercourse produced by them between two totally separated regions, was to induce the *Discovery of America*, the *Doubling of the Cape of Good Hope*, and the *Passage of the Straits* at the southern extremity of Patagonia,—results due to COLUMBUS, VASCO DA GAMA, and MAGELLAN, every one of whom were seeking, in the voyages which have rendered them immortal, another passage to the Indies than that held by the Italians—so far as they could prosecute it in vessels upon the Mediterranean. But, before we can proceed from the coasting enterprises of the Lombards upon the land-locked waters of their inland sea, to the daring ventures of the Portuguese and Spaniards upon the raging billows of the Tropical and South Atlantic, we must turn for a moment to the North of Europe, and inquire into the maritime achievements of the Anglo-Saxons and the Northmen during the Dark and Middle Ages.

DANISH VESSEL OF THE TENTH CENTURY: FROM AN INSCRIPTION.

CHAPTER IX.

THE SCANDINAVIAN SAILORS—THEIR PIRACIES AND COMMERCE—THE ANGLO-SAXONS—ALFRED THE GREAT A SHIP-BUILDER—THE VOYAGE OF BEOWULF—DISCOVERY OF ICELAND BY THE DANES—DISCOVERY OF GREENLAND—THE VOYAGE OF BJARNI AND LEIF TO THE AMERICAN CONTINENT—THEIR DISCOVERY OF NEWFOUNDLAND, NOVA SCOTIA, NANTUCKET, AND MASSACHUSETTS—ADVENTURES OF THORWALD AND THORFINN—COMPARISON OF THE DISCOVERIES OF THE NORTHMEN WITH THOSE OF COLUMBUS.

THE nations inhabiting the borders of the Baltic and the coasts of Norway, as well as those dwelling on the shores of the German Ocean, were situated quite as favorably for maritime enterprise as those upon the banks of the Mediterranean. Though their earliest expeditions by sea were not stimulated by the same cause,—the desire for commercial intercourse,—they arose from causes equally active. While the Mediterranean countries possessed a fruitful soil and a balmy climate, those of the North, under a sky comparatively ungenial, afforded their inhabitants but a few of the articles which they needed: they were led, therefore, to increase their power by sea, in order to establish themselves in more favored climes, or at least to obtain from them by plunder what their own country could not furnish. Thus they neglected the arts of agriculture, and became inured to a life of piracy upon the sea. They spent their lives in planning and executing maritime expeditions. Fathers gave fleets to their sons, and bade them seek their fortune on the ocean-highway. The ships, at first small,—being mere barks propelled by twelve oars,—came at last to be capable of carrying one hundred or one hundred and twenty men. They were supplied with stones, arrows, ropes with which to overset small vessels, and grappling-irons with which to come to close quarters.

It would be remote from our purpose to notice these piratical excursions, were it not that they sometimes resulted in discovery or commerce. Many of the marauders settled permanently in England in the seventh century, and established there the Anglo-Saxon dominion. Alfred, their most celebrated king, obliged to defend his territory from the Danes, turned his attention zealously to every thing connected with ships, commerce, discovery, and geography, and became the first founder of that naval power which was at a later period to be the world's dread and admiration. The idea of ship-building once conceived, it was prosecuted with astonishing vigor. Alfred not only multitiplied their number, but introduced material improvements. Towards the latter part of his reign, his fleet numbered one hundred sail: it was divided into small squadrons and stationed at various places along the coast.

The oldest epic in any modern language, the Anglo-Saxon poem of "Beowulf," the Sea-Goth, written in forty-three cantos, and containing some six thousand lines, is occupied mainly in narrating the marvellous exploits of its hero, his combats with a pestilential fire-drake, and his slaying of "a grim giant named Grendel, a descendant of Cain." It incidentally describes a voyage made by Beowulf previous to the ninth century, and from this we may gather a few details, at best barren and unsatisfactory, of the equipments of a vessel in those days. In the extract which we give, the word "sea-nose" will readily be understood as meaning headland, or promontory:

"When the king had awaited
The time he should stay,
Came many to fare
On the billows so free.
His ship they bore out
To the brim of the ocean,
And his comrades sat down
At their oars as he bade.
A word could control
His good fellows, the Shylds.
On the deck of the ship
He stood, by the mast.
Ne'er did I hear
Of a vessel appointed
Better for battle,
With weapons of war,
And waistcoats of wool,
And axes and swords.
* * * *
The ship was on the waves,
Boat under the cliffs.
The barons ready
To the prow mounted.
The chieftains bore
On the naked breast
Bright ornaments,
War-gear, Goth-like.
The men shoved off,
Men on their willing way,
The bounden wood.
Then went over the sea-waves,
Hurried by the wind,
The ship with foamy neck,
Most like a sea-fowl,
Till about one hour
Of the second day
The curved prow
Had passed onward.
So that the sailors
The land saw,

The shore-cliffs shining,
Mountains steep,
And broad sea-noses.
Then was the sea-sailing
Of the Earl at an end.
God thanked he
That to him the sea-journey
Easy had been."

In the year 863, a Dane of Swedish origin, named Gardar, adventurously pushing off into the Northern Ocean, though upon an object which history has not recorded, discovered the island-rock whose appropriate name is Iceland. Eleven years later, a navigator named Ingolf colonized the country, the colonists, many of whom belonged to the most esteemed families in the North, establishing a flourishing republic. The situation of these people, isolated in the midst of an Arctic ocean, and their relation to the mother-country, compelled them to exert and develop their hereditary maritime proclivities. In 877, a sailor named Gunnbjörn saw a mountainous coast far to the west, supposed to be now concealed or rendered inaccessible by the descent of Arctic ice. Erik the Red, who had been banished from Norway for murder and had settled in Iceland, was in his turn outlawed thence in 983: he sailed to the west and discovered a land which he called Greenland, because, as he said, "people will be attracted hither if the land has a good name." He returned to Iceland, and, in the year 985, a large number of ships—according to some authorities, thirty-five—followed him to the new settlement and established themselves on its south-western shore.

In 986, Bjarni Herjulfson-Bjarni the son of Herjulf, in a voyage from Iceland to Greenland, was driven a long distance from the accustomed track. He at last saw land to the west, and took counsel with his men as to what land it could be. Bjarni declared it his opinion that it was not Greenland. They sailed close in shore, and noticed that there were no mountains, but that the land was undulating and well wooded. They left the land on their larboard side, and sailed away for two days, when they saw land again. They asked Bjarni if he thought this was Greenland; and he replied that "he thought it as little to be Greenland as the other, as he saw no high ice-hills." The sailors wished to wood and water there, but Bjarni would not consent. They sailed for three days to the north, and saw a bold shore with high mountains and ice-hills. Bjarni would not land, saying, "To me this land appears little inviting." Sailing for four days more to the northeast, they came to a country which Bjarni confidently pronounced to be Greenland, where he landed and afterwards settled. Various data furnished by this narrative, in the original Icelandic records, have enabled geographers to determine the various coasts thus dimly seen by Bjarni, but upon which he did not land. They are supposed to have been those of Long Island, Rhode Island, Massachusetts, Nova Scotia, and Newfoundland.

In the year 994, Leif Erikson—Leif the son of Erik the Outlaw—bought Bjarni's ship, and engaged thirty-five men to navigate it, as he intended to sail upon a voyage of discovery. He asked his father Erik to be the captain; but Erik declined, being, as he said, well stricken in years. They sailed away into the sea, and discovered first the land which Bjarni had discovered last. They went ashore, saw no grass, but plenty of icebergs, and an abundance of flat stones. From the latter circumstance they named the place *Helluland*, *hellu* signifying a flat stone. There can be no doubt that the spot thus named is the modern Newfoundland. They went on board again, and proceeded on their way. They went ashore a second time, where the land was flat and covered with wood and white sand. "This," said Leif, "shall be named after its qualities, and called Markland," (woodland.) This is undoubtedly Nova Scotia. They sailed again to the south for two days and came to an island which lay to the eastward of the mainland. They observed dew upon the grass, and this dew, upon being touched with the finger and raised to the mouth, tasted exceedingly sweet. This appears to have been Nantucket, where honey-dew is known to abound.

THE NORTHMEN IN AMERICA.

They proceeded on through a tract of shoal water, which corresponds with the sound between Nantucket and Cape Cod, and appear to have run across the mouth of Buzzard's Bay, and to have ascended the Pocasset River as far as Mount Hope Bay, which they took for a lake. Here they cast anchor, and, "bringing their skin cots from the ship, proceeded to make booths." They remained during the winter, finding plenty of salmon in the river and lake. "The nature of the country was, as they thought, so good, that cattle would not require house-feeding in winter, for there came no frost, and little did the grass wither there." Their statement that on the shortest day the sun was above the horizon from half-past seven till half-past four enables geographers to fix the latitude of the place where they were at 41° 43′ 10″, which is very nearly that of Mount Hope Bay.

One evening a man of the party was missing,—a German named Tyrker, whom Leif regarded as his foster-father. He determined to seek for him, and for this purpose chose twelve reliable men. Tyrker soon returned and said that he had been a long distance into the interior, and had found vines and grapes. "But is this true, my fosterer?" said Leif. "Surely is it true," he returned; "for I was bred up in a land where there is no want of either vines or grapes." The next morning Leif said to his sailors, "We will now set about two things, in that the one day we gather grapes, and the other cut vines and fell trees, so from thence will be a loading for my ship." The record states that the long-boat was filled with grapes. Leif gave the country the name of Vinland, from its vines.

To the reader of the present day it may seem that the wild vines of Massachusetts and Rhode Island can hardly have been so prominent a feature of the native products as to have given a name to the whole region. But it is certain that six centuries later the Puritans found wild maize and grapes growing there in profusion, while the neighboring island of Martha's Vineyard received its name from the English for a precisely similar reason.

Upon the return of Leif to Greenland, his brother Thorwald thought that "these new lands had been much too little explored." Leif gave him his ship, and he put out to sea, with thirty men, in the year 1002. Nothing is known of their voyage till they came to Leif's booths in Vinland. They laid up their ship, caught fish for their support, and spent a pleasant winter. They passed two years in exploring the interior, and then returned by the north, where Thorwald was killed in a battle with the Esquimaux.

But a more successful discoverer than any of these was Thorfinn Karlsnefne,—that is, Thorfinn the Predestined Hero.

He was a wealthy merchant of Iceland, the heir of Danish, Swedish, and Norwegian princes. He visited Greenland in 1006, where he married Gudrida, the widow of an Icelandic adventurer, and in 1007 sailed, in three ships and with one hundred and sixty men, upon a voyage to Vinland. His wife went with him, and, in the autumn of the same year, bore him a son named Snorri, who was, of course, the first of European blood born in America. From him the celebrated Swedish sculptor Thorwaldsen was lineally descended. Thorfinn remained here three years, and had many communications with the aborigines. A singular result of this relation may perhaps be traced in the names successively given to one spot. The Northmen called one of their settlements Hóp, and the Puritans, six centuries later, found that the Indians called it Haup. It would appear that they had continued, in their own tongue, the appellation bestowed upon the place in the Norse language. The Puritans anglicized it, and called it Mount Hope.

We have no accounts of any further voyages made by the Northmen to America. The records were preserved in the literature of the island, but the memory of them gradually faded away from the popular mind.

Several writers claim for these early navigators a degree of merit beyond that which they are willing to accord to Columbus. They reply to the argument that Bjarni's discovery of the American coast was merely accidental, as he had started in search of Greenland, that Columbus' discovery of America was accidental also, as he started in search of Asia, and as he believed the land to be Asia to the day of his death. "Besides," they say, "how different were the circumstances under which the two voyages were made! The Northmen, without compass or quadrant, without any of the advantages of science, geographical knowledge, personal experience, or previous discoveries, without the support of either kings or governments,—which Columbus, however discouraged at the outset, eventually obtained,

—but guided by the stars, and upheld by their own private resources and a spirit of adventure which no dangers could repress, crossed the broad Northern ocean and explored these distant lands."

This is all true; and doubtless our wonder at the success with which these early voyages were prosecuted would be augmented tenfold, could we obtain authentic information upon the character and capacity of the ships in which they were made. Nothing reliable exists upon this subject, except a few rude inscriptions; and from these, as reproduced in the engravings we have given, it would actually appear that the vessels used had no decks, and that they were partly propelled by oars. However navigation may have improved since the days of the Northmen, it is certain that no sailor would now attempt an Arctic voyage in an open boat; and when we read of the perils and sufferings of our modern Polar adventurers, it is impossible not to be amazed at the success with which the Danes and Norwegians, with their slender appliances, endured and outlived them.

CHAPTER X.

THE TRAVELS OF MARCO POLO—THE FIRST MENTION OF JAPAN IN HISTORY—KUBLAI KHAN—MARCO POLO'S VOYAGE FROM AMOY TO ORMUZ—MALACCA—SUMATRA—PYGMIES—SINGULAR STORIES OF DIAMONDS—THE ROC—POLO NOT RECOGNISED UPON HIS RETURN—HIS IMPRISONMENT—THE PUBLICATION OF HIS NARRATIVE—THE INTEREST AWAKENED IN CHINA, JAPAN, AND THE ISLANDS OF SPICES.

THE call to arms against the Moslems fixed, as we have said, the attention of Europe upon the East. The travels of Carpini, Rubruquis, and Ascelin, in Tartary and in China, revealed the existence of numerous tribes in localities believed to be occupied by the ocean. Hordes of savages, we are told, and whole nations of powerful and warlike people, emerged from the imaginary waters of Eoüs, the fabulous sea of antiquity and bed of Aurora. Marco Polo, whose celebrated journey was performed during the twenty years closing the thirteenth century, made known the centre and eastern extremity of Asia, Japan, a portion of the islands of the Indian Archipelago, a part of the continent of Africa, and, by hearsay, the large island of Madagascar. We subjoin a brief account of that portion of his travels which was prosecuted by sea.

He became a great favorite with Kublai Khan, whose winter capital was Khanbalik or Pekin, and served him for many years as one of his confidential officers. He was the first European who heard of the island of Japan, of which he speaks thus:—"Zipangu, or Cipango, is an island in the Eastern Ocean, situated about fifteen hundred miles from the mainland. It is quite large. The inhabitants have fair complexions, are civilized in their manners, though their religion is idolatry. They have gold in the greatest abundance, but its exportation is forbidden. The entire roof of the sovereign's palace is stated to be covered with a plating of gold, as we cover churches and other buildings with lead. So famous is the wealth of this island that Kublai Khan was fired with the desire of annexing it to his dominions. He sent out a numerous fleet and a powerful army; but a violent storm dispersed and wrecked the ships, and thirty thousand men were thrown upon a desert island a few miles from Cipango. They expected nothing but death or captivity, as they could obtain no means of subsistence. Being attacked from Cipango, they got in the rear of the enemy, took possession of their fleet, and put off for the main island. They kept the colors flying from the masts, and entered the chief city unsuspected. All the inhabitants were gone except the women. They took possession, but were closely besieged for six months, until, despairing of relief, they surrendered, on condition of their lives being spared. This took place in the year 1284." Such was the first intelligence of the island of Japan which ever reached the ears of Europeans.

After a stay of seventeen years in China, Marco and his companions resolved to make an attempt to return to their native land. Kublai Khan, however, was unwilling to part with them; and they owed their final release to a circumstance wholly unexpected. An embassy from Persia had visited Pekin, and had selected one of Kublai's grand-daughters for the wife of their prince. They set out with her on their journey to Persia, but, after meeting with incredible obstacles, were obliged to return to the Chinese capital. Marco had, at this time, just returned from a voyage among the islands of the Indian Sea, and had laid before the khan his observations upon the feasibility of navigation in those waters. The ambassadors sought an interview with Marco Polo, and found that they had all a common interest,—

that of getting away as speedily as possible. The khan was forced to facilitate the departure of the envoys, though it deprived him of his friends the Venetians. Preparations were made upon a grand scale for the expedition. Fourteen four-masted ships, a part of them with crews of two hundred and fifty men, were equipped and victualled for two years. The khan bade the Polo party an affectionate adieu, making them his ambassadors to the principal courts of Europe, and extorting from them a promise to return to his service after a visit to their own country.

Thus honorably dismissed, they set sail from the port of Amoy, in 1291. They coasted along the shores of Cochin China, and came in sight of the islands of Borneo and Java, though they did not land there. At the island of Bintan, near the Straits of Malacca, they obtained some knowledge of the kingdom of the Malays at the southern extremity of the peninsula. They landed upon Sumatra, and visited many parts of the island. Marco thus speaks of one branch of the trade of the inhabitants:—"It should be known that what is reported respecting the mummies of pygmies sent to Europe from India is only an idle tale, these pretended human dwarfs being manufactured in this island in the following manner. The country produces a large species of monkey having a countenance resembling that of a man. The Sumatrans catch them, shave off their hair, dry and preserve their bodies with camphor and other drugs, and prepare them generally so as to give them the appearance of little men. They then pack them in wooden boxes and sell them to traders, by whom they are vended for pygmies in all parts of the world. But there are no such things as pygmies in India or anywhere else. It is mere monkey-trade."

From Sumatra, Marco and his companions sailed into the Bay of Bengal, touched at the Andaman and Nicobar Islands, arrived at Ceylon, and, doubling the southern point of Hindostan, continued to the northward along its western coast. The pearl-fishery here attracted their attention; and Marco, in his description of the diamonds of a kingdom named Murphili, narrates, as a fact, a story which was afterwards incorporated in the Adventures of Sinbad the Sailor,—that of pieces of meat being thrown by the jewel-hunters into inaccessible valleys, whence they were brought back again by eagles and storks with quantities of diamonds clinging to them. But the story occurs in the writings of one of the Christian Fathers of the fourth century, and Marco Polo only gives it as a legend which he heard. He also alludes to the bird called the roc, which was so large that it lifted elephants into the air; its feathers measured ninety spans. The locality frequented by these monstrous ornithological specimens was the island of Madagascar.

The voyage appears to have ended at Ormuz, at the mouth of the Persian Gulf, after a navigation of a year and a half. Six hundred men of the various crews had died upon the way. There is no mention made in history of the return of the fleet to China, though Kublai Khan is known to have died three years after the departure of the Venetians. After various adventures, Marco Polo and his companions arrived in Venice, in 1295. They had been absent twenty-one years, and their nearest relatives did not know them. When they attempted to converse in Italian, their use of foreign idioms and barbarous forms of expression rendered their language hardly intelligible. Possession had been taken of their houses by some of their kindred, and they found it difficult to expel them. Their statements were disbelieved, till, by displaying their immense wealth and their priceless collections of jewels and precious stones, they forced their countrymen to give credit to adventures which must clearly have been extraordinary, to have resulted in such acquisitions of treasure. Marco's riches gave him the name of Milione; and he is designated, in the records of the Venetian Republic, and upon the title-page of his work,—still extant,—as Messer Marco Milione.

He was induced to write an account of his adventures in the

following manner. A war between the Venetians and the Genoese resulted in the capture of the galley of which he was commander. He was imprisoned during four years at Genoa. His surprising history becoming known, he was visited by all the principal inhabitants, who were anxious to listen to his narrative. The frequent necessity of repeating the same story became intolerably irksome to him, and he resolved to commit it to writing. He thus gave the first impulse to the promotion of geographical science. He procured from Venice the original notes he had made in the course of his travels, and, with their assistance and that of a Genoese amanuensis, the narrative was composed in his cell. It is a work of great research and deep interest. Formerly read for its marvels, it is now perused as the earliest authentic account of a region which still remains a *terra incognita*, and whose inhabitants repel curiosity and decline mingling with other nations upon the usual reciprocal terms of fellowship and good-will. Marco Polo is now justly considered the founder of the modern geography of Asia. It was long before any new discoveries were added to those of the illustrious Venetian, but his original statements were confirmed in many quarters:—by Oderic, who visited India and China in 1320; by Schiltberger, of Munich, who accompanied Tamerlane in his expeditions through Central Asia; by Pegoletti, an Italian merchant who went to Pekin, through the heart of Asia, in 1335; and by Clavijo, in 1403, who was sent by Spain as ambassador to Samarcand.

Thus, a European had been to the regions of spices and had returned. From this time forward the world was to know no rest till the route by sea had been discovered.

ANCIENT CHINESE COMPASS.

CHAPTER XI.

THE FIRST MENTION OF THE LOADSTONE IN HISTORY—ITS EARLY NAMES—THE FIRST MENTION OF ITS DIRECTIVE POWER—A POEM UPON THE COMPASS SIX HUNDRED YEARS OLD—FRIAR BACON'S MAGNET—THE LOADSTONE IN ARABIA—AN EYE-WITNESS OF ITS EFFICIENCY IN THE SYRIAN WATERS IN THE YEAR 1240—THE MAGNET IN CHINA—EARLY MENTION OF IT IN CHINESE WORKS—THE VARIATION NOTICED IN THE TWELFTH CENTURY—OTHER DISCOVERIES MADE BY THE CHINESE—MODERN ERRORS—FLAVIO GIOIA—THE ARMS OF AMALFI—ALL RECORDS LOST OF THE FIRST VOYAGE MADE WITH THE COMPASS BY A EUROPEAN SHIP.

WE have arrived at a momentous epoch in the history of the sea. It was at this period that the mariner's compass was—we do not say invented—but introduced into European navigation. That this admirable instrument, which, in half a century, changed the face of the earth, by leading to the discovery of America and thus proving the sphericity of the world, should remain unclaimed by its author, and that we are unable to point to him who thus blessed and benefited his race, must always be a subject of regret. So far from being able to name the individual to whom the invention is due, it has long been deemed impossible to fix even upon the nation who first used the needle at sea. We hope, however, by availing ourselves of recent researches made in France, to arrive at a conclusion not only satisfactory, but inevitable. In tracing the history of the compass, we must naturally begin with the magnet.

The ancients were fully acquainted with the loadstone, and with its power of attracting iron, though they were totally ignorant of its polarity. That they were so, is evident from the fact that the classic authors and ancient works upon navigation and kindred subjects do not furnish one word upon the subject. Claudian has left, in one of his idyls, a long description of the stone, and of its peculiar, indeed, magical, affinity for iron. Had he entertained the most distant idea that this stone could communicate to a steel needle the power of indicating the north, it is not to be supposed for an instant that he would have omitted mentioning it. The earliest name of the loadstone was Hercules' Stone, which was soon changed to *magnes*, from the fact that it was found in abundance in a region called Magnesia, in Lydia. Hence our word magnet. It was not till the fourth century of our era that the quality of repelling as well as of attracting iron seems to have been discovered. Marcellus, the physician of Theodosius the Great, is the first author who mentions this new quality.

The Romans, who acquired a knowledge of the magnet from the Greeks, preserved the name, though several of their authors, and Pliny among them, mention a tradition, that the magnet was so called from a shepherd named Magnes, who was the first to discover a mine of loadstone, by the nails in his shoes clinging to the metal.

The first mention in European history of the polarity of the magnetized needle, and of its importance to mariners, occurs in a satirical French poem written in 1190 by one Guyot de Provins. His object was to level, by implication, an invective against the Court of Rome; and he did it in the following neat manner. The translator has endeavored to preserve the quaint style of the original:

"As for our Father the Pope,
I would he were like the star

Which moves not. Very well see it
The sailors who are on the watch.
By this star they go and come,
And hold their course and their way.
They call it the Polar Star.
It is fixed, very unchangeable:
All the others move,
And alter their places and turn,
But this star moves not.
They make a contrivance which cannot lie,
By the virtue of the magnet.
An ugly and brownish stone,
To which iron spontaneously joins itself,
They have: and they observe the right point,
After they have caused a needle to touch it,
And placed it in a rush:
They put it in the water, without any thing more,
And the rush keeps it on the surface;
Then it turns its point direct
Towards the star with such certainty,
That no man will ever have any doubt of it;
Nor will it ever for any thing go false.
When the sea is dark and hazy,
That they can neither see star nor moon,
Then they place a light by the needle,
And so they have no fear of going wrong:
Towards the star goes the point,
Whereby the mariners have the skill
To keep the right way.
It is an art which cannot fail."

It may be very properly inferred, from the fact that the poet does not merely allude to the compass, but describes it and the polar star at some length, that it was not generally known, and, in fact, had been lately introduced into the Mediterranean. Whence it had been introduced there, we shall learn as we proceed.

The second historical mention of the compass occurs in a description of Palestine by Cardinal Jacques de Vitry, in the year 1218, in which is the following passage:—"The loadstone is found in India, to which, from some hidden cause, iron spontaneously attaches itself. The moment an iron needle is touched by this stone, it at once points towards the North Star, which, though the other stars revolve, is fixed as if it were the axis of the firmament: from whence it has become necessary to those who navigate the seas."

Brunetto Latini, a grammarian of Florence, and preceptor of Dante, settled in Paris about the year 1260, and composed a work entitled the "Treasure," in which he distinctly describes the process and the consequence of magnetizing a needle. He also went to England, and, in a letter of which fragments have been published, writes thus:—"Friar Bacon showed me a magnet, an ugly and black stone, to which iron doth willingly cling: you rub a needle upon it, the which needle, being placed upon a point, remains suspended and turns against the Star, even though the night be stormy and neither star nor moon be seen; and thus the mariner is guided on his way."

The Italian Jesuit Riccioli, in his work upon Geography and Hydrography, states, that before 1270, the French mariners used "a magnetized needle, which they kept floating in a small vessel of water, supported on two tubes, so as not to sink."

All these authors agree in fixing the period at which the use of the needle was popularized in Europe, at the latter part of the twelfth and the commencement of the thirteenth century. Not one of them mentions the inventor by name, or even indicates his nation. This circumstance leads to the conviction that it was unknown to them, and that, consequently, the inventor was not a European. The theory that the Europeans obtained it from the Arabians, and the Arabians from the Chinese, is supported by the following facts:

A manuscript work, written by an Arabian named Bailak, a native of Kibdjak, and entitled "The Merchant's Guide in the Purchase of Stones," thus speaks of the loadstone in the year 1242:—"Among the properties of the magnet, it is to be noticed that the captains who sail in the Syrian waters, when the night is dark, take a vessel of water, upon which they place a needle buried in the pith of a reed, and which thus floats upon the water. Then they take a loadstone as big as the palm of the hand, or even smaller. They hold it near the surface of the water, giving it a rotary motion until the needle turns upon the water: they then withdraw the stone suddenly, when the needle, with its two ends, points to the north and south. I saw this with my own eyes, on my voyage from Tripoli, in Syria, to Alexandria, in the year 640. [640 of the Hegira, 1240 A.D.]

"I heard it said that the captains in the Indian seas substitute for the needle and reed a hollow iron fish, magnetized, so that, when placed in the water, it points to the north with its head and to the south with its tail. The reason that the fish swims, not sinks, is that metallic bodies, even the heaviest, float when hollow, and when they displace a quantity of water greater than their own weight."

It may fairly be inferred, from this passage, that, at the time spoken of, (1240,) the practice was already of long standing in this quarter, and that the needle and its polarity had been long known and employed at sea. That is, the Arabs had become familiar with the loadstone in 1240, while Friar Bacon regarded it, in England, as a huge curiosity in 1260,—twenty years afterwards. The priority of the invention would seem to be thus incontestably proven for the Arabs. But we shall see speedily that it derived its origin from a region situated still farther to the east, and many centuries earlier.

A famous Chinese dictionary, terminated in the year 121 of our era, thus defines the word magnet:—"The name of a stone which gives direction to a needle." This is quoted in numerous modern dictionaries. One published during the Tsin dynasty—that is, between 265 and 419—states that ships guided their course *to the south* by means of the magnet. The Chinese word for magnet—*Tchi nan*—signifies, Indicator of the South. It was natural for the Chinese, when they first saw a needle point both north and south, to take the Antarctic pole for the principal point of attraction, for with them the south had always been the first of the cardinal points,—the emperor's throne and all the Government edifices invariably being built to face the south. A Chinese work of authority, composed about the year 1000, contains this passage:—"Fortune-tellers rub the point of a needle with a loadstone to give it the power of indicating the south."

A medical natural history, published in China in 1112, speaks even of the variation of the needle,—a phenomenon first noticed in Europe by Christopher Columbus in 1492:—"When," it says, "a point of iron is touched by a loadstone, it receives the power of indicating the south: still, it declines towards the east, and does not point exactly to the south." This observation, made at the beginning of the twelfth century, was confirmed by magnetic experiments made at Pekin, in 1780, by a Frenchman; only the latter, finding the variation to be from the north, set it down as from 2° to 2° 30′ to the west, while the Chinese, persisting in calling it a variation from the south, set it down as being from 2° to 2° 30′ to the east.

Thus, the Chinese, who were acquainted with the polarity of a magnetized needle as early as the year 121, and who noticed the variation in 1112, may be safely supposed to have employed it at sea in the long voyages which they made in the seventh and eighth centuries, the route of which has come down to us. Their vessels sailed from Canton, through the Straits of Malacca, to the Malabar coast, to the mouths of the Indus and the Euphrates. It is difficult to believe that, aware of the use to which the needle might be applied, they did not so apply it.

While thus claiming for the Chinese the first knowledge and application of the polarity of the needle, we may say, incidentally, that it is now certain that they made numerous other discoveries of importance long before the Europeans. They knew the attractive power of amber in the first century of our era, and a Chinese author said, in 324, "The magnet attracts iron, and amber attracts mustard-seed." They ascribed the tides to the influence of the moon in the ninth century. Printing was invented in the province of Chin about the year 920, and gunpowder would seem to have been made there long before Berthold Schwartz mixed it in 1330. Still, it is not necessary to resort to the argument of analogy to support the claims of the Chinese to this admirable invention: the direct evidence, as we have rehearsed it, is amply sufficient.

FRAGMENT OF AN ANCIENT CHINESE VESSEL.

A century ago, Flavio Gioia, a captain or pilot of Amalfi, in the kingdom of Naples, was recognised throughout Europe as the true inventor of the compass. He lived in the beginning of the fourteenth century, and biographers have even fixed the date of the memorable invention at the year 1303. The principal foundation for this assertion was the following line from a poem by Antonio of Bologna, who lived but a short time after Gioia:—

"Prima dedit nautis usam magnetis Amalphis."
Amalfi first gave to sailors the use of the magnet.

The tradition was subsequently confirmed by the statement made by authors of repute, that the city of Amalfi, in order to commemorate an invention of so much importance, assumed a compass for its coat of arms. This was believed till the year 1810, when the coat of arms of Amalfi was found in the library at Naples. It did not answer at all to the description given of it: instead of the eight wings which were said to represent the four cardinal points and their divisions, it had but two, in which no resemblance to a compass could be traced. Later investigations have, as we have said, completely demolished all the arguments by which the compass was maintained to be of European origin and of modern date. The curious reader will find the extracts from Chinese works which substantiate the Chinese claim, in a volume upon the subject published in 1834, at Paris, by M. J. Klaproth, and composed at the request of Baron Humboldt.

In the sketch which we are now about to give of the Portuguese voyages to the African coast, it will be remarked that the compass was already introduced and acclimated. No mention whatever is extant of the first venture made upon the Atlantic under the auspices of this mysterious but unerring guide. Science and history must forever regret that the first European navigator who employed it did not leave a record of the experiment. What would be more interesting to-day than the log of the earliest voyage thus accomplished in European waters? The modern reader would surely give his sympathy, unreservedly, to a narrative in which the navigator should describe his wonder, his terror, his joy, when, throughout the voyage, he saw the tremulous index point invariably north; when, upon the dispersion of the clouds which had concealed the Star from view, it was found precisely where the needle indicated; when, upon its being diverted from the line of direction by some curious and perhaps incredulous experimenter, it slowly but surely returned, remaining fixed and constant through storm and calm, at midnight and at noon. What would be more interesting than the speculations of such a captain upon the cause of the marvellous dispensation? And what more amusing than the commentaries of the forecastle, and the learned explanations of the veteran salts to the raw recruits? But all this absorbing lore has hopelessly disappeared, and the mariner's compass will forever remain mysterious in its principle, mysterious in its origin, mysterious in its history. We shall have occasion to return to the subject from another point of view, when, in describing the Arctic voyages of the present century, we shall find James Clarke Ross standing upon the North Magnetic Pole.

TENERIFFE.

Section III.

FROM THE APPLICATION OF THE MAGNETIC NEEDLE TO EUROPEAN NAVIGATION TO THE FIRST VOYAGE ROUND THE WORLD UNDER MAGELLAN—1300—1519.

CHAPTER XII.

THE PORTUGUESE ON THE COAST OF AFRICA—THE SPANIARDS AND THE CANARY ISLES—DON HENRY OF PORTUGAL—THE TERRIBLE CAPE, NOW CAPE BOJADOR—THE SACRED PROMONTORY—DISCOVERY OF THE MADEIRAS—A DREADFUL PHENOMENON—A PROLIFIC RABBIT AND A WONDERFUL CONFLAGRATION—HOSTILITY OF THE PORTUGUESE TO FURTHER MARITIME ADVENTURE—THE BAY OF HORSES—THE FIRST GOLD DUST SEEN IN EUROPE—DISCOVERY OF CAPE VERD AND THE AZORES—THE EUROPEANS APPROACH THE EQUATOR—JOURNEY OF CADA-MOSTO—DEATH OF DON HENRY—PROGRESS OF NAVIGATION UNDER THE AUSPICES OF THIS PRINCE.

We are now to consider at some length a series of voyages, tedious and fruitless at first, successful in the end, undertaken by the Portuguese, in their age of maritime heroism, to discover a passage by sea to the famous commercial region of the Indies, some general knowledge of which had been preserved since the Persian, Macedonian, and Roman Empires. The achievements which we are about to narrate were so surprising, so significant, and so complete, that, as has been aptly remarked, they can never happen again in history, unless, indeed, Providence were to create new and accessible worlds for discovery and conquest, or to replunge mankind for ages into ignorance and superstition. But, before proceeding with the discoveries of the Portuguese, we must mention a previous discovery made by accident in the same region by the French and Spanish.

About the year 1330, a French ship was driven among a number of islands which lay off the coast of the Desert of Sahara. These had been known to the ancients as the Fortunate Islands, and Juba of Mauritania, who is quoted by Pliny, calls two of them by name,—Trivaria, or Snow Island, and Canaria, or Island of Dogs. They had been lost to the knowledge of the Europeans for a thousand years, and it was a storm which revealed their existence, as we have said, to a vessel forced by stress of weather to escape from the coast into the open sea. The Spaniards profited by the vicinity of the group to make discoveries and settlements among them. Trivaria became Teneriffe, and Canaria the Grand Canary. It was here that superstition now placed the limits of navigation, and expressed the idea upon maps, by representing a giant armed with a formidable club, and dwelling in a tower, as threatening ships with destruction if they ventured farther out to sea. It is in this immediate neighborhood that we are now about to follow the daring and patient enterprises of the Portuguese.

Don Henry, the fifth son of John I. of Portugal, was placed by his father, in 1415, in command of the city of Ceuta, in Africa, which he had just conquered from the Moors. During his stay here, the young prince acquired much information relative to the seas and coasts of Western Africa, and this first suggested in his mind a plan for maritime discovery, which afterwards became his favorite and almost exclusive pursuit. He sent a vessel upon the first voyage of exploration undertaken by any nation in modern times. The commander was instructed to follow the western coast of Africa, and, if possible, to pass the cape called by the Portuguese Cape Non, Nun, or Noun. This had hitherto been considered the utmost southern limit of navigation by the Europeans, and had obtained its name from the negative term in the Portuguese language—implying that there was *nothing* beyond. A current proverb expressed the idea thus:

Whoe'er would pass the Cape of Non
Shall turn again, or else begone.

The fate of this vessel has not been recorded; but Don Henry continued for many years to send other vessels upon the same errand. Several of them proceeded one hundred and eighty miles beyond Cape Non, to another and more formidable promontory, to which they gave the name of Bojador—from *bojar*, to double—on account of the circuit which must be made to get

CAPE BOJADOR.

around it, as it stretches more than one hundred miles into the ocean. The tides and shoals here formed a current twenty miles wide; and the spectacle of this swollen and beating surge, which precluded all possibility of creeping along close to the coast, filled these timid navigators with terror and amazement. They dared not venture out of sight of land, and, seized with a sudden remembrance of the fabulous horrors of the torrid zone, they regarded the interposition of this terrific cape as a providential warning, and sailed hastily back to Portugal. There, with that fancy for embellishment peculiar to sailors of all ages, they narrated stories, or, as would be said in the present day, yarns, calculated forever to dissuade from further ventures in the latitudes of Capes Non and Bojador.

Don Henry, who had returned from Ceuta, resolved, in spite of these obstacles, to employ a portion of his revenue as Grand Master of the Order of Christ, in further maritime experiments. He fixed his residence upon the Sacrum Promontorium of the Romans, of which we have given a representation in the chapter describing the voyage of Pytheas. Here he indulged that passion for navigation and mathematics which he had hitherto been compelled to neglect. In 1418, two naval officers of his household volunteered their lives in an attempt to surmount the perils of Bojador. Juan Gonzalez Vasco and Tristan Vax Texeira embarked in a vessel called a *barcha* and resembling a brig with topsails, and steered for the tremendous cape.

Before reaching it, however, a violent storm drove them out to sea, and the crew, on losing sight of their accustomed landmarks, gave themselves up to despair. But, upon the abatement of the tempest, they found themselves in sight of an island four hundred miles to the west of the coast. Thus was discovered Porto Santo, the smallest of the group of the Madeiras, and thus was the feasibility and advantage of abandoning coasting voyages and venturing boldly out to sea made manifest. The adventurers returned to Portugal, and gave glowing accounts of the fertility of the soil, of the mildness of the climate, and the character of the inhabitants. Vessels were fitted out to colonize and cultivate the island; but a singular and most untoward event rendered it useless as a place of refreshment for navigators. A single rabbit littered during the voyage, and was let loose upon the island with her progeny: these multiplied so rapidly that in two years they eat every green thing which its soil produced. Porto Santo was therefore, for a time, abandoned.

During their residence there, however, Gonzalez and Vax noticed with wonder a strange and perpetual appearance in the horizon to the southwest. A thick, impenetrable cloud hovered over the waves, and thence extended to the skies. Some believed it to be a dreadful abyss, and others a fabulous island, while superstition traced amid the gloom Dante's inscription on the portal of the Inferno:

Abandon hope, all ye who enter here!

Gonzalez and Vax bore this state of suspense with the impatience of seamen, while from dawn to sunset the meteor, or the portent, preserved its uniform sullen aspect. At last they started in pursuit. It was urged, by a Spaniard named Juan de Morales, that the shadows hanging in the air could be accounted for by supposing that the soil of an island in the vicinity, being shaded from the sun by thick and lofty trees, exhaled dense and opaque vapors, which spread throughout the sky. As the ship advanced, the towering spectre was observed to thicken and to expand until it became horrible to view. The roaring of the sea increased, and the crew called on Gonzalez to flee from the fearful scene. But soon the weather became calm, and deeper shadows were observed through the portentous gloom. Faint images of rocks seemed to the excited crew the menacing figures of giants. The atmosphere was now transparent; the hoarse echo of the waves abated; the clouds dispersed, and the woodlands were unveiled. The seamen rested on their oars, while Gonzalez admired the wild luxuriance of nature in a spot which superstition had so long dreaded to approach. A rivulet, issuing from a glen, whose paler verdure formed a striking contrast with the deep green of venerable cedars, seemed to pour a stream of milk into a spacious basin. They searched in vain for traces of either inhabitants or cattle. The abundance of building-wood which the island furnished suggested the name of Madeira; and a tract covered with fennel (funcha) marked the site of the future town of Funchal.

A modern poet thus describes in verse the scene which we have narrated in prose:

> "Bojador's rocks
> Arise at distance, frowning o'er the surf,
> That boils for many a league without. Its course
> The ship holds on, till, lo! the beauteous isle
> That shielded late the sufferers from the storm
> Springs o'er the wave again. Then they refresh
> Their wasted strength, and lift their vows to Heaven.
> But Heaven denies their further search; for ah!
> What fearful apparition, pall'd in clouds,
> Forever sits upon the western wave,
> Like night, and, in its strange portentous gloom
> Wrapping the lonely waters, seems the bounds
> Of nature? Still it sits, day after day,
> The same mysterious vision. Holy saints!
> Is it the dread abyss where all things cease?
> The favoring gales invite: the bowsprit bears
> Right onward to the fearful shade: more black
> The cloudy spectre towers: already fear
> Shrinks at the view, aghast and breathless. Hark!
> 'Twas more than the deep murmur of the surge
> That struck the ear; whilst through the lurid gloom
> Gigantic phantoms seem to lift in air
> Their misty arms. Yet, yet—bear boldly on:
> The mist dissolves: seen through the parting haze,
> Romantic rocks, like the depicted clouds,
> Shine out: beneath, a blooming wilderness
> Of varied wood is spread, that scents the air;
> Where fruits of golden rind, thick interspersed
> And pendent, through the mantling umbrage gleam
> Inviting."

Gonzalez and Vax returned at once to Lisbon, where a public day of audience was appointed by the king to give every celebrity to this successful voyage. Madeira was at once colonized and cultivated; and it is said that Gonzalez, in order to clear a space for his intended city of Funchal, set the shrubs and bushes on fire, and that the flames, being communicated to the forests, burned for seven years. The sugar-cane was planted, and its cultivation yielded immense sums until sugar-plantations were established in Brazil and thus interfered with the monopoly. The attention of the islanders was then transferred to the grape, and from that time to this Madeira has supplied the world with a favorite—nay, almost indispensable—brand of wine.

Don Henry had now, it would appear, surmounted the principal obstacles opposed by ignorance or prejudice to the object of his laudable ambition. But there were many interests threatened by a continuance of discovery by sea. The military beheld with jealous dislike the distinction obtained by, and now willingly accorded to, a profession they held inferior to their own. The nobility dreaded the opening of a source of wealth which would raise the mercantile character, and in an equal degree lower the assumptions and pretensions of artificial social rank. Political economists suggested that there were barren spots in Portugal as capable of cultivation as any desert islands in the sea or any sandy coasts within the tropics. It was urged, too, that any Portuguese who should pass Cape Bojador would inevitably be changed into a negro, and would forever retain this brand of his temerity.

While Henry was resisting the arguments of his detractors, his father died, and was succeeded upon the throne by his son Edward. The latter gave every encouragement to the maritime projects of his brother, and, in 1433, one Gilianez, having incurred the displeasure of Henry, determined to regain his favor by doubling Cape Bojador. Though we are without details of the voyage, we know at least that it was successful, and that the historians of the time represent the feat as more remarkable than any of the labors of Hercules. Gilianez reported that the sea beyond Bojador was quite as navigable as the Mediterranean, and that the climate and soil of the coast were agreeable and fertile. He was sent the next year, with Henry's cup-bearer,

Baldoza, over the same route, and they advanced ninety miles beyond the cape with the conscious pride of being the first Europeans who had ventured so far towards the fatal vicinity of the equator. Though they saw no inhabitants, they noticed the tracks of caravans.

They were ordered, in 1435, to resume their discoveries, and to prolong their voyage till they should meet with inhabitants. In latitude 24° north, one hundred and thirty miles beyond Bojador, two horses were landed, and two Portuguese youths, sixteen years of age, were directed to mount them and advance into the interior. They returned the next morning, saying that they had seen and attacked a band of nineteen natives. A strong force was despatched to the cave in which they were said to have taken shelter: their weapons only were found. This spot was called *Angra dos Cavallos*, or Bay of Horses. The two vessels continued on forty miles farther, to a place where they killed a large number of seals and took their skins on board. Their provisions were now nearly exhausted, and the expedition, having penetrated nearly two hundred miles beyond the cape, returned to Lisbon.

The Portuguese war with Tangiers now absorbed the entire naval and maritime resources of the country, and the plague of Lisbon stayed for a time the patriotic enterprises of Don Henry. In 1440–42, expeditions sent in the same direction resulted in the capture and transfer of several Moors to Portugal, and in the payment to their captors, as ransom, of the first GOLD DUST ever beheld by Europeans. A river, or arm of the sea, near the spot where this gold was paid, received, from that circumstance, the name of *Rio del Ouro*. This gold dust at once operated as a sovereign panacea upon the obstinacy and irritation of the public mind. It has been well remarked that "this is the primary date to which we may refer that turn for adventure which sprang up in Europe, and which pervaded all the ardent spirits in every country for the two succeeding centuries, and which never ceased till it had united the four quarters of the globe in commercial intercourse. Henry had stood alone for almost forty years; and, had he fallen before those few ounces of gold reached his country, the spirit of discovery might have perished with him, and his designs have been condemned as the dreams of a visionary." The sight of the precious metal placed the discoveries and enterprises of Don Henry beyond the reach of detraction or prejudice. Numerous expeditions were successively fitted out:—that of Nuno Tristan, in 1443, who discovered the Arguin Islands, thirty miles to the southeast of Cape Blanco; that of Juan Diaz and others in 1444; that of Gonzalez da Cintra in 1445, who, with seven others, was killed fifty miles south of the Rio del Ouro,—this being the first loss of life on the part of the Portuguese since they had undertaken their explorations. In 1446, a gentleman of Lisbon, by the name of Fernandez, determined to proceed farther to the southward than any other navigator, and accordingly fitted out a vessel under the patronage of the prince. Passing the Senegal River, he stood boldly on till he reached the most western promontory of Africa, to which, from the number of green palms which he found there, he gave the name of Cape Verd. Being

CAPE VERD.

alarmed by the breakers with which this shore is lined, he returned to Portugal with the gratifying news of his discovery. In 1447, Nuno Tristan sailed one hundred and eighty miles beyond Cape Verd, and reached the mouth of a river, which he called the Rio

Grande, now the Gambia. He was attacked by the natives with volleys of poisoned arrows, of the effects of which all his crew and officers died but four; and the ship was at last brought home by these four survivors, after wandering two months upon the Atlantic. The next expedition, under Alvaro Fernando, carried out an antidote against the poisoned shafts of the enemy, which successfully combated the venom, as all who were wounded recovered.

The Açores, or Azores, were now discovered, about nine hundred miles to the west of Portugal; but some doubts exist both as to the discoverer and the date. They doubtless received their name from the number of hawks which were seen there, Açor signifying hawk in Portuguese. Santa Maria and San Miguel were named from the saints upon whose days they were first seen. Terceira obtained its name from the circumstance that it was the third that was discovered. Fayal was so called from the beech-trees it produced; Graciosa, from its agreeable climate and fertile soil; Flores, from its flowers; and Corvo, from its crows. The various clusters of islands which thus arose in the Atlantic, from the Azores to Cape Verd, now formed a succession of maritime colonies and nurseries for seamen, and thus enabled navigators to avoid the coast, where the outrages they endured from Moors and negroes threatened to exhaust their patience. The ships of Don Henry had now penetrated within ten degrees of the equator, and the outcry against venturing into a region where the very air was fatal broke out afresh. In this point of view, therefore, the settlement of the Azores was a matter of no little importance. In 1449, King Alphonso gave his uncle, Don Henry, permission to colonize these islands. In 1457, Henry obtained for them several important privileges, the principal of which was the exemption of their inhabitants from any duties upon their commerce in Portuguese and Spanish ports.

In the years 1455–56–57, a Venetian, by the name of Cada-Mosto, undertook, under the patronage of Don Henry, two voyages of discovery along the African coast. The narrative of his adventures, being in the first person, is the oldest nautical journal extant, with the single exception of one of Alfred the Great, still in existence. But, as it is principally occupied with descriptions of the manners and customs of the Africans, and as he did not proceed beyond the Rio Grande, thus adding little or nothing to maritime discovery, an account of his voyage would be out of place here. Don Henry died shortly after the return of Cada-Mosto from his second voyage, and for a season this calamity palsied the naval enterprise of his countrymen. They had been accustomed to derive from him, not only the encouragement necessary for the prosecution of such attempts, but even sailing directions and instructions upon all matters of detail. It can easily be conceived that the demise of this illustrious prince should temporarily dishearten navigators and paralyze discovery. Under his auspices the Portuguese had pushed their discoveries from Cape Non to Sierra Leone,—from the twenty-ninth to the eighth degree of north latitude. He died at Sagres—the city, half ship-yard, half arsenal, which he had founded upon the Sacrum Promontorium.

CHAPTER XIII.

THE PORTUGUESE CROSS THE EQUATOR FROM GUINEA TO CONGO—JOHN II. CONCEIVES THE IDEA OF A ROUTE BY SEA TO THE INDIES—HIS ARTIFICES TO PREVENT THE INTERFERENCE OF OTHER NATIONS—THE OVERLAND JOURNEY OF COVILLAM TO INDIA—THE VOYAGE OF BARTHOLOMEW DIAZ—THE DOUBLING OF THE TREMENDOUS CAPE—ITS BAPTISM BY THE KING—INJURIOUS EFFECTS OF SUCCESS UPON PORTUGUESE AMBITION.

During the remainder of the reign of Alphonso V.—which terminated in 1481—the Portuguese advanced over the coast and Gulf of Guinea and the adjacent islands to the northern boundary of the great kingdom of Congo, and had therefore arrived within six hundred and fifty marine leagues of the cape which forms the southern point of the African continent. They had crossed the equator, and not a man had turned black. They had entered into a brisk gold-trade with the savages of Guinea. John II., the son and successor of Alphonso, determined to fortify a point called Mina, from its abundant mines, and sent out twelve vessels with building materials and six hundred men. The negroes at first resisted, but finally yielded their consent. The fort was constructed and named St. Jorge da Mina; the quarry from which the first stone was taken being the favorite god of the tribe that inhabited the coast.

John II. now added to his other titles that of Lord of Guinea. In the hope of opening a passage by sea to the rich spice-countries of India, he asked the support and countenance of the different states of Christendom. But the established mercantile interest of these countries was naturally hostile to a project which aimed at changing the route of Eastern commerce. John next applied to the Pope for an increase of power, and obtained from his holiness a grant of all the lands which his navigators should discover in sailing *from west to east.* The grand idea of sailing from east to west—one which implied a knowledge of the sphericity of the globe—had not yet, to outward appearance, penetrated the brain of either pope or layman. One Christopher Columbus, however, was already brooding over it in secret and in silence.

It had hitherto been customary for Portuguese navigators to erect wooden crosses upon all lands discovered by them. John II. now commanded them to employ stone pillars six feet high, and to inscribe upon them, in the Latin and Portuguese languages, the date, the name of the reigning monarch, and that of the discoverer. Diego Cam was the first to comply with this command; he set up a column at the mouth of the river Congo, at which he arrived in 1484. An ambassador was sent by the chief of the territory to Portugal, where he embraced Christianity and was baptized by the name of John. The anxiety of the king now increased in reference to interference by other nations: he therefore sent to King Edward, of England, an earnest request that he would prevent the intended voyage to Guinea of two of his subjects, John Tintam and William Fabian, with which request Edward saw fit to comply. The Portuguese monarch now carefully concealed the progress of his navigators upon the African coast, and on all occasions magnified the perils of a Congo voyage. He declared that every quarter of the moon produced a tempest; that the shores were girt with inhospitable rocks; that the inhabitants were cannibals, and that the only vessels which could live in the waters of the torrid zone were caravels of Portuguese build. Suspecting that three sailors who had left Portugal for Spain intended to sell the secret to the foreign king, he ordered them to be pursued and taken. Two were killed, and the third was broken upon the wheel. "Let every man abide in his element:" said John; "I am not partial to travelling seamen."

We now approach an era of great achievements. John determined, in 1486, to assist the attempts made on sea by journeys over land. Accordingly a squadron was fitted out under Bartholomew Diaz, one of the officers of the royal household, while Pedro de Covillam and Alphonso de Payra, both well versed in Arabic, received the following order respecting a land journey:— "To discover the country of Prester John, the King of Abyssinia, to trace the Venetian commerce in drugs and spices to its source, and to ascertain whether it were possible for ships to sail round the extremity of Africa to India." They went by way of Naples, the Island of Rhodes, Alexandria, and Cairo, to Aden in Arabia. Here they separated, Covillam proceeding to Cananor and Goa, upon the Malabar coast of Hindostan, and being the first Portuguese that ever saw India. He went from there to Sofala, on the eastern coast of Africa, and saw the Island of the Moon, now Madagascar. He penetrated to the court of Prester John, the King of Abyssinia, and became so necessary to the happiness of that potentate, that he was compelled to live and die in his dominions. An embassy sent by Prester John to Lisbon made the Portuguese acquainted with Covillam's adventures. Long ere this, however, Bartholomew Diaz had sailed upon the voyage which has immortalized his name. He received the command of a fleet, consisting of two ships of fifty tons each, and of a tender to carry provisions, and set sail towards the end of August, 1486, steering directly to the south. It is much to be regretted that so few details exist in reference to this memorable expedition. We know little more than the fact that the first stone pillar which Diaz erected was placed four hundred miles beyond that of any preceding navigator. Striking out boldly here into the open sea, he resolved to make a wide circuit before returning landward. He did so; and the first land he saw, on again touching the continent, lay one hundred miles to the eastward of the great southern cape, which he had passed without seeing it. Ignorant of this, he still kept on, amazed that the land should now trend to the east and finally to the north. Alarmed, and nearly destitute of provisions, mortified at the failure of his enterprise, Diaz unwillingly put back. What was his joy and surprise when the tremendous and long-sought promontory—the object of the hopes and desires of the Portuguese for seventy-five years, and which, either from the distance or the haze, had before been concealed—now burst upon his view!

Diaz returned to Portugal in December, 1487, and, in his narrative to the king, stated that he had given to the formidable promontory he had doubled the name of "Cape of Tempests." But the king, animated by the conviction that Portugal would now reap the abundant harvest prepared by this cheering event, thought he could suggest a more appropriate appellation. The Portuguese poet, Camoens, thus alludes to this circumstance:

"At Lisboa's court they told their dread escape,
And from her raging tempests named the Cape.
'Thou southmost point,' the joyful king exclaimed,
'Cape of Good Hope be thou forever named!'"

Successful and triumphant as was this voyage of Diaz, it eventually tended to injure the interests of Portugal, inasmuch as it withdrew the regards of King John from other and important plans of discovery, and rendered him inattentive to the efforts of rival powers upon the ocean. It caused him, amid the intoxication of the moment, to refuse the services and reject the science of one who now offered to conduct the vessels of Portugal to the Indies by an untried route. It caused him, as we shall soon have occasion to narrate, to turn a deaf ear to the proposals of Columbus, who had humbly brought to Lisbon the mighty scheme with which he had been contemptuously repulsed from Genoa. We have arrived at the Great Era in Navigation,—the age of Columbus, da Gama, and Magellan.

CHRISTOPHER COLUMBUS.

CHAPTER XIV.

BIRTH OF CHRISTOPHER COLUMBUS—HIS EARLY LIFE AND EDUCATION—HIS FIRST VOYAGE—HIS MARRIAGE—HIS MARITIME CONTEMPLATIONS—HE MAKES PROPOSALS TO THE SENATE OF GENOA, THE COURT OF VENICE, AND THE KING OF PORTUGAL—THE DUPLICITY OF THE LATTER—COLUMBUS VISITS SPAIN—JUAN DE MARCHENA—COLUMBUS REPAIRS TO CORDOVA—HIS SECOND MARRIAGE—HIS LETTER TO THE KING—THE JUNTO OF SALAMANCA—COLUMBUS RESOLVES TO SHAKE THE DUST OF SPAIN FROM HIS FEET—MARCHENA'S LETTER TO ISABELLA—THE QUEEN GIVES AUDIENCE TO COLUMBUS—THE CONDITIONS STIPULATED BY THE LATTER—ISABELLA ACCEPTS THE ENTERPRISE, WHILE FERDINAND REMAINS ALOOF.

CRISTOFERO COLOMBO (in Spanish Colon, in French Colomb, in Latin and English Columbus) was born in Genoa, in the year 1435.* His father was a wool-comber, and Christopher followed, for a time, the same occupation. He was sent, however, at the age of ten years, to the University of Pavia, where he seems to have studied, though with little advantage, natural philosophy and astronomy, or, as it was then called, astrology. Returning to his father's bench, he worked at wool-combing, with his brother Bartholomew, till he was fourteen years of age. By this time the natural influence of the situation, the atmosphere, and the traditions of Genoa had awakened in him the tastes and the ambition of a sailor. The sea had long been the home and the life of the Genoese: it was the theatre of their glory, and their avenue to wealth. Christopher's great-uncle, Colombo, commanded a fleet intrusted to him by the king, and with which he carried on a predatory warfare against the Venetians and Neapolitans. His nephew joined his ship, and thus became acquainted with the whole extent of the Mediterranean, which was at that period ploughed by the pirates of the Archipelago and the corsairs of the Barbary States. As the vessel went armed to the teeth, the young sailor not only learned the art of navigation, but acquired those habits of discipline and subordination, of self-command and presence of mind, which afterwards served him in so good stead. This manner of life lasted for many years, till Columbus, at the age of thirty, was wrecked off the coast of Portugal, and reached, with some difficulty, the city of Lisbon. Here he found his brother Bartholomew settled, and occupying himself in drawing plans, charts, and maps for the use of navigators. Christopher joined him, and gained a sufficient livelihood by copying manuscripts and black-letter books, and aiding his brother in his avocations. He soon married an Italian lady named Felippa di Perestrello, whose

* A late French biography of Columbus, a work of profound research and erudition, by M. Roselly de Lorgues, proves beyond a cavil the accuracy of this assertion. The work in question was published under the auspices of the Pope.

father, now dead, had been Governor of the island of Porto Santo, one of the Madeiras. This union between the humble son of a wool-comber and the daughter of an Italian gentleman is deemed, by several of the biographers of Columbus, a strong proof of the nobility of his ancestry. After his marriage, he left for Porto Santo,—the sterile dowry of his wife,—where his first son, Diego, was born.

We have already seen that the period was one of the greatest excitement and expectancy in regard to maritime discovery. Columbus had long reflected upon the existence of land in the west, upon the sphericity of the earth, and upon the possibility of crossing the Atlantic. He had already conceived the idea of reaching Asia by following the setting sun across the immensity of the waters. His mind, too, was kindled to religious enthusiasm by the allusions in the Bible to the universal diffusion of the gospel, and, in his dreams of nautical discovery, the belief that he was destined to be an apostle, sent to extend the dominion of the cross, predominated over more worldly aspirations. For years, while struggling with disappointment and harassed by poverty, he pursued this idea with the pertinacity of a monomaniac. When forty years old, and residing at Lisbon, he proposed to the Senate of Genoa to leave the Mediterranean by the Straits of Gibraltar and to proceed to the west, in the sea known as the Ocean, as far as the "lands where spices bloom," and thus circumnavigate the earth. The Genoese, whose maritime knowledge was confined to the Mediterranean, and who had no fancy for adventures upon the ocean, declined listening to the proposition, pretexting the penury of the treasury. It would also seem that overtures made by Columbus to the Council of Venice were similarly rejected. For a time, therefore, he abandoned all efforts to further his desires. In 1477, he made a voyage to Iceland, in order to discover whether it was inhabited, and even sailed one hundred leagues beyond it,—where, to his astonishment, he found the sea not frozen.

Upon the accession of John II. to the throne of Portugal,—a sovereign whom we have already shown to be deeply interested in the progress of the art of navigation,—Columbus made known to him his opinions and his plans, assigning the extension of the gospel as the avowed and final object of the expedition. The subject was referred to a maritime junto and to a high council, by both of whom it was rejected as visionary and absurd. The king was induced, however, by one of his councillors, to equip a caravel and send it on a voyage of discovery upon the route traced out by Columbus, and thus obtain for himself the glory of the expedition, if successful. Columbus was invited to hand in to the Government his maps and charts, together with his written views upon the whole subject. This he did, supposing, in his simplicity, that another examination was to be made of the practicability of the venture. The king despatched a caravel, under the command of one of the ablest pilots of his marine, to follow the track indicated. The vessel left, but soon returned, her crew having been appalled at sight of the boundless horizon, and her captain having lost his courage in a storm. Columbus, indignant at this duplicity, secretly left Lisbon and returned home to Genoa. At this period he had the misfortune to lose his wife Felippa, who had shared his confidence in the existence of unknown lands, and whose encouragement had sustained him in his disappointments. This was in the year 1484. He renewed his proposal to the Senate of Genoa, which was again rejected. He now cast his eyes upon the other European powers, among whom the two sovereigns of Spain, Ferdinand of Aragon and Isabella of Castile, seemed to deserve the preference.

Not far from Palos, upon the Spanish coast, and in sight of the ocean, stood, upon a promontory half hidden by pine-trees, a monastery—known as La Rabida—dedicated to the Virgin, and inhabited by Franciscan friars. The Superior, Juan Perez de Marchena, offered an example of fervent piety and of theological erudition, at the same time that he was a skilful mathematician and an ardent practitioner of the exact sciences. He was at once an astronomer, a devotee, and a poet. During the hours of slumber, he often ascended to the summit of the abbey, and, looking out upon the ocean,—known as the Sea of Darkness,—would ask himself if beyond this expanse of waters there was no land yet unclaimed by Christianity. He rejected as fabulous the current idea that a vessel might sail three years to the west without reaching a hospitable shore. The ocean, formidable to others and intelligible to few, was to him the abode of secrets which man was invited to unfold.

One day a traveller rang at the gate and asked for refreshment for himself and his son. Being interrogated as to the object of his journey, he replied that he was on his way to the court of Spain to communicate an important matter to the king and queen. The traveller was Christopher Columbus. How he came to pass by this obscure monastery—which lay altogether off his route—has never been explained. A providential guidance had brought him into the presence of the man the best calculated to comprehend his purpose, in a country where he was totally without friends and with whose language he was completely unacquainted. A common sympathy drew them together; and Columbus, accepting for a period the hospitality of Marchena, made him the confidant of his views. Thus, while the colleges and universities of Christendom still held the childish theory that the earth was flat, and that the sea was the path to utter and outer darkness, Columbus and Marchena, filled with a spontaneous and implicit faith, intuitively believed in the sphericity of the globe and the existence of a nameless continent beyond the ocean. In theory they had solved the great question whether the ship which should depart by the west would come back by the east.

Marchena gave Columbus a letter of recommendation to the queen's confessor, and, during his absence, promised to educate and maintain his son Diego. Thus tranquillized in his affections, and aided in his schemes, Columbus departed for Cordova. Here he was destined to undergo another disappointment; for the queen's confessor, his expected patron, treated him as a dreaming speculator and needy adventurer. He soon became again isolated and forgotten. In the midst of his indigence, however, a noble lady, Beatrix Enriquez, young and beautiful, though not rich, noticed his manners and his language, so evidently above his condition, and detained him at Cordova long after his hopes were extinguished. He married her: she bore him a son, Fernando, who afterwards became his father's biographer and historian.

Columbus now wrote to the king a brief and concise letter, setting forth his desires. It was never answered. After a multitude of similar deceptions and disappointments, Geraldini, the ambassador of the Pope, presented him to Mendoza, the Grand Cardinal, through whose influence Columbus obtained an audience of Ferdinand, who appointed a junto of wise men to examine and report upon his scheme. This junto, made up of theologians and not of navigators and geographers, and which sat at Salamanca, opposed Columbus on biblical grounds, declared the theory a dangerous if not heretical innovation, and finally reported unfavorably. This decision was quite in harmony with public opinion in Salamanca, where Columbus was spoken of as "a foreigner who asserted that the world was round like an orange, and that there were places where the people walked on their heads." Seven years were thus wasted in solicitation, suspense, and disappointment. From time to time Columbus had reason to hope that his proposals would be reconsidered; but in 1490 the siege of Baza, the last stronghold of the Moors, and in 1491 the marriage of Isabella, the daughter of Ferdinand and Isabella, with Don Alonzo of Portugal, absorbed the attention of their majesties to the exclusion of all scientific pre-occupations. Finally, when the matter was reopened, and the junto was reassembled, its president, Fernando de Talavera, was instructed to say that the exhaustion of the treasury necessitated the postponement of the whole subject until the close of the war with Grenada. At last, Columbus, reflecting upon the delays, refusals, affronts, and suspicions of which he had been the object, the time he had wasted, and the antechambers in which he had waited the condescension of the great, resolved to shake the dust of Spain from his feet, and returned to the abbey of his friend Marchena. He arrived there bearing upon his person the impress of poverty, fatigue, and exhausted patience. Marchena was profoundly annoyed by the reflection that the glory of the future discoveries of Columbus would be thus taken from Spain and conferred upon some rival power. Fearing, however, that he had too readily lent his ear to theories which had been twice rejected as puerile by a competent junto, he sent for an eminent mathematician of Palos, Garcia Hernandez, a physician by profession. They then conferred together upon the subject and pronounced the execution of the project feasible. The assertion that the famous sailor Martin Alonzo Pinzon was a party to the conference would appear to be an error. Pinzon was at this period at Rome, and did not see Columbus for a year or more afterwards.

Marchena at once wrote an eloquent letter to Queen Isabella, and intrusted it to a pilot whose relations with the court rendered him a safe and reliable messenger. He gave the missive into the hands of the queen, and returned to the monastery the bearer of an invitation to Marchena to repair at once to Santa Fe, where the court then was, engaged in investing Grenada. Columbus borrowed a mule for the friar, who left secretly at midnight and arrived safely at Santa Fe. That Isabella should, at such a moment, when engaged in war and harassed by financial embarrassments, listen to a proposition which had been twice condemned by a learned body of men, is a circumstance which entitles her in the highest degree to a share in the glory which her protégé Columbus was, through her, destined to obtain. She received Marchena graciously, and instructed him to summon

Columbus, to whom she sent twenty thousand maravedis—seventy dollars, nearly—with which to purchase a horse and a proper dress in which to appear before her.

Columbus arrived at Santa Fe just before the surrender of Grenada and the termination of the struggle between the Crescent and the Cross. He was present at the delivery of the keys of the city and the abandonment of the Alhambra to Isabella by the Moorish king, Boabdil el Chico. After the official rejoicings, the queen gave audience to Columbus. As she already believed in the practicability of the scheme, the only subjects to be discussed were the means of execution, and the recompense to be awarded to Columbus in case of success. A committee was appointed to consider this latter point. Columbus fixed his conditions as follows:

He should receive the title of Grand Admiral of the Ocean:

He should be Viceroy and Governor-General of all islands and mainlands he might discover:

He should levy a tax for his own benefit upon all productions—whether spices, fruits, perfumes, gold, silver, pearls, or diamonds—discovered in, or exported from, the lands under his authority:

And his titles should be transmissible in his family, forever, by the laws of primogeniture.

These conditions, being such as would place the threadbare solicitor above the noblest house in Spain, were treated with derision by the committee, and Columbus was regarded as an insolent braggart. He would not abate one tittle of his claims, though, after eighteen years of fruitless effort, he now saw all his hopes at the point of being again dashed to earth. He mounted his mule, and departed for Cordova before quitting Spain forever.

Two friends of the queen now represented the departure of Columbus as an immense and irreparable loss, and, by their supplications and protestations, induced her once more to consider the vast importance of the plans he proposed. Moved by their persuasions, she declared that she accepted the enterprise, not jointly, as the wife of the King of Spain, but independently, as Queen of Castile. As the treasury was depleted by the drains of war, she offered to defray the expenses with her own jewels. A messenger was despatched for Columbus, who was overtaken a few miles from Grenada. He at first hesitated to return; but, after reflecting upon the heroic determination of Isabella, who thus took the initiative in a perilous undertaking, against the report of the junto, the advice of her councillors, and in spite of the indifference of the king, he obeyed with alacrity, and returned to Santa Fe.

He was received with distinction by the court and with affectionate consideration by the queen. Ferdinand remained a stranger to the expedition. He applied his signature to the stipulations, but caused it to be distinctly set down that the whole affair was undertaken by the Queen of Castile, at her own risk and peril,—thus excluding himself forever from lot or parcel in this transcendent enterprise.

THE FLEET OF COLUMBUS.

CHAPTER XV.

THE PORT OF PALOS—THE SUPERSTITION OF ITS MARINERS—THE HAND OF SATAN—A BIRD WHICH LIFTED VESSELS TO THE CLOUDS—THE PINTA AND THE NINA—THE SANTA MARIA—CAPACITY OF A SPANISH CARAVEL—THE THREE PINZONS—THE DEPARTURE—COLUMBUS' JOURNAL—THE HELM OF THE PINTA UNSHIPPED—THE VARIATION OF THE NEEDLE—THE APPEARANCE OF THE TROPICAL ATLANTIC—FLOATING VEGETATION—THE SARGASSO SEA—ALARM, AND THREATENED MUTINY, OF THE SAILORS—PERPLEXITIES OF COLUMBUS—LAND! LAND! A FALSE ALARM—INDICATIONS OF THE VICINITY OF LAND—MURMURS OF THE CREWS—OPEN REVOLT QUELLED BY COLUMBUS—FLOATING REEDS AND TUFTS OF GRASS—LAND AT LAST—THE VESSELS ANCHOR OVER-NIGHT.

Columbus received his letters-patent, granting him all the privileges and titles he had demanded, on the 30th of April, 1492. His son Diego was made page to the prince-royal,—a favor only accorded to children of noble families. The harbor of Palos was chosen as the port of departure; and its inhabitants, whose annual taxes consisted in furnishing two caravels, armed and manned, to the Government, were instructed to place them, within ten days, at the orders of Columbus. Persons awaiting trial or condemnation were to have the privilege of escaping verdict and punishment by embarking upon this terrible and perhaps fatal voyage.

The mariners of Palos received these tidings with dismay. Nothing was certainly in those days more calculated to strike with terror the cautious coaster than a voyage upon the boundless, endless Mare Tenebrosum, which, in the imagination not only of the ignorant, but even of the educated, was the home of chaos, if not the seat of Erebus. Upon the maps of the world designed at this period, the words Mare Tenebrosum were surrounded with figures of imps and devils, compared to which the Cyclops, griffins, and centaurs of mythology were modest and benign creations. The Arabians, who were forbidden by the Koran to depict the forms of animals, gave, as they thought, a fitting character to the sea, by representing the hand of Satan upon their charts, ready to clutch and drag beneath the waves all who should be so rash as to brave the displeasure of Bahr-al-Talmet. Besides Satan, besides the Leviathan and Behemoth, and other similar submarine terrors, the adventurer upon the open sea would find adversaries in the air; and, if he escaped the blast and the thunderbolt, it would be to fall a victim to the roc, that gigantic bird which lifted ships into the air and crunched them in the clouds. This roc, from terrifying the companions of Columbus, has descended to amuse children in the nautical romance of Sinbad the Sailor.

Time passed, and the authorities of Palos had yet furnished nothing towards the voyage. Owners of vessels hid them in distant creeks, and the port became gradually a desert. The court ordered stringent measures, and at last a caravel named the Pinta was seized and laid up for repairs. All the carpenters turned sick, and neither rope, wood, nor tar were to be found. In vain did Marchena, the zealous Franciscan of Palos, who was beloved by all its inhabitants, undertake a crusade among the seafaring population in favor of the project: the whole Andalusian coast considered it chimerical and a temptation of Providence.

Martin Alonzo Pinzon, one of three brothers, all seamen, and who had at this period lately returned from Rome, where the Pope's librarian had shown him a map bearing the representation of land in the Atlantic to the west, was introduced by Marchena to Columbus. The report soon became current that the brothers, whose credit and influence at Palos were very great, intended to risk the adventure on board of the caravel Nina, belonging to the younger of the three. The mariners took courage, and the city of Palos contributed its second caravel, the Gallega, making three in all. This Gallega, though old and heavy and unfit for the service, was stout and solid, and Columbus chose her for his flag-ship, rebaptizing her, however, the Santa Maria. Towards the end of July, the vessels were nearly ready for sea, and Columbus retired for a period to the monastery, where he passed his days in prayer and his nights in contemplation. On one occasion he left the convent and appeared among the workmen: he surprised the sailors, condemned by the city to accompany him to the west, engaged in putting the rudder of the Pinta together in such a manner that the first storm would unship it. Marchena redoubled his exhortations, and at last the expedition was ready.

Popular belief has, in modern times, represented these vessels as much smaller than they probably really were. The term *caravel*, of doubtful etymology, affords no indication of their tonnage or capacity. Caravels were used, however, to transport troops, provisions, and artillery, and even to fight upon the high seas. They were sent by Portugal to the coast of Africa. John II. had, as we have narrated, sent a vessel to the west in order to anticipate Columbus; and this vessel was a caravel. The smallest of the three—the Nina—subsequently, when at sea, took on board fifty-six men, in addition to her own crew, a number of cannon, and a portion of the rigging of the Santa Maria, without lowering her water-line; and Columbus once threatened a Portuguese officer to take one hundred of his men on board the Nina and carry them to Castile. Neither she, nor the other two caravels, were the "light barks" or "shallops" which historians have delighted to represent them. The importance of the subject requires that we describe the three vessels with all the minuteness which the late researches of which we have spoken will authorize.

The Santa Maria measured about ninety feet at the keel. She had four masts, two of them square-rigged, and two furnished with the lateen-sails of the Mediterranean. She had a deck extending from stem to stern, and a double deck at the poop, twenty-six feet long,—one-third, nearly, of her entire length. The double deck was pierced for cannon, the forward-deck being armed with smaller pieces, used for throwing stones and grape. From the journal of Columbus we know that he employed, in the manœuvres, quite a complicated system of ropes and pulleys. Eight anchors hung over her sides. She represented in her general characteristics a modern vessel of twenty guns. She was manned by sixty-six men, not one of whom was from Palos,—one of them being an Englishman, and one an Irishman,—and was commanded by Columbus.

The Pinta and the Nina were decked only forward and aft, the space in the middle being entirely uncovered. Their armament was equal to that of sloops of sixteen and ten guns respectively. Alonzo Pinzon commanded the Pinta, whose total crew, including the officers, numbered thirty men. The youngest of the three Pinzons, Vincent Yanez, commanded the Nina, with twenty-three men. The provisions of the fleet consisted of smoked beef, salt pork, rice, dried peas and other vegetables, herrings, wine, oil, vinegar, &c., sufficient for a year.

As the day approached and the danger grew more imminent, the apprehension increased, and the sailors expressed a desire to reconcile themselves with Heaven and obtain absolution for their sins. They went in procession to the monastery of La Rabida, with Columbus at their head, and received the Eucharist from the hands of the Franciscan Marchena. Columbus, while waiting for the land-breeze, retired for a last time to the convent, to meditate upon the duties before him and to peruse his favorite book, the Gospel of St. John. At three o'clock in the morning of the 3d of August he was awakened by the murmuring of the long wished for wind in the tops of the pine-trees which bordered his cell. The coming day was Friday, a day inauspicious to sailors, but to him a day of good omen. He arose, summoned Marchena, from whom he received the communion, and then descended, on foot, the steep declivity which leads to Palos.

The Santa Maria at once sent her boat to receive the admiral, and at the sound of the preparations and the orders of the pilots, the inhabitants awoke and opened wide their windows. Mothers, wives and sisters, fathers and brothers, ran in confusion to the shore, to bid a last farewell to those whom they might perhaps never see again. The royal standard, representing the Crucifixion, was hoisted at the main; and Columbus, standing upon the quarter-deck, gave the order to spread the sails in the name of Jesus Christ. Thus commenced the most memorable venture upon the ocean that man had then made or has made since,—the record of whose shortest day is more stored with incident than was the whole voyage of Jason, from the Whirling Rocks to the Golden Fleece.

Columbus commenced his journal at once, and it is from the passages of this narrative which are still extant, that we shall derive an account of the voyage. He begins by declaring the object of the expedition to be to extend the blessings of the gospel to nations supposed to be without it. He adds, that he shall write at night the events of the day, and each morning the occurrences of the night. He will mark the lands he shall dis-discover upon the chart, and will banish sleep from his eyelids in order to watch the progress of his vessel.

All went well till Monday, when the helm of the Pinta fell to pieces,—this accident having been a second time prepared by her refractory owners. The fleet made the best of their way to the Canaries, where the Pinta was repaired. They sailed again on the 6th of September, narrowly escaping attack from three Portuguese caravels that King John had sent against Columbus, indignant that he should have transferred to another power the proposal he had once made to himself.

Thus far the route had lain over the beaten track between the continent and the Canaries, along the coast of Africa. As they now launched into the open sea, and as the Peak of Teneriffe sank under the horizon behind them, the heart of Columbus beat high with joy, while the courage of his officers and men died away within them. The Admiral kept two logs, one for himself and one for the crew, the latter scoring a distance less than that which they had really made, and thus keeping them in ignorance of their actual distance from home. His course was to the southwest. The sky, the stars, the horizon, the water, changed visibly as they advanced. Familiar constellations disappeared, others took their place. On the 13th of September, Columbus observed a strange and fearful phenomenon. The needle, which till then had been infallible, swerved from the Polar star, and tremblingly diverged to the northwest. The next day this variation was still more marked. Columbus took every precaution to conceal a discovery so discouraging from the fleet, and one which alarmed even him. The water now became more limpid, the climate more bland, and the sky more transparent. There was a delicate haze in the air, and a fragrance peculiar to the sea in the fresh breeze. Aquatic plants, apparently newly detached from the rocks or the bed of the ocean, floated upon the waves. For the first time in the history of the world, the tranquil beauties and the solemn splendors of the tropical Atlantic were passing before the gaze of human beings. According to the journal of Columbus, "nothing was wanting in the scene except the song of the nightingale to remind him of Andalusia in April."

The proximity of land seemed often to be indicated by the odor with which the winds were laden, by the abundance of marine plants, and the presence of birds. Columbus would not alter his course, as he did not wish to abate the confidence of his men in his own belief that land was to be found by steering west. The floating vegetation now became so abundant that it retarded the passage of the vessels. The sailors became seriously alarmed. They thought themselves arrived at the limit of the world, where an element, too unstable to tread upon, too dense to sail through, admonished the rash stranger to take warning and return. They feared that the caravels would be involved beyond extrication, and that the monsters lying in wait beneath the floating herbage would make an easy meal of their defenceless crews. The trade-winds, then unknown, were another cause of anxiety; for, if they always blew to the westward, as they appeared to do, how could the ships ever return eastward to Europe? In the midst of the apprehensions excited by these causes, which nearly drove the terrified men to mutiny, a contrary wind sprang up, and the revolt was thus providentially quelled. Columbus wrote in his journal, "this opposing wind came very opportunely, for my crew was in great agitation, imagining that no wind ever blew in these regions by which they could return to Spain."

But the terrors of the ignorant men soon broke out afresh. Seaweed and tropical marine plants reappeared in heavy masses, and seemed to shut in the ships among their stagnant growth. The breeze no longer formed billows upon the surface of the waters. The sailors declared that they were in those dismal quarters of the world where the winds lose their impulse and the waters their equilibrium, and that soon fierce aquatic monsters would seize hold of the keels of the ships and keep them prisoners amid the weeds. In the midst of the perplexities to which Columbus was thus exposed, the sea became suddenly agitated, though the wind did not increase. This revival of motion in the element they thought relapsed into sullen inactivity, again cheered the crew into a temporary tranquillity.*

* This tract, so thickly matted with Gulf-weed, and covering an area equal in extent to the Mississippi Valley, has since been called by the Portuguese the Sargasso Sea. It still exists in the same spot, and if we now hear very little of it, it is because navigators have learned to avoid it. Lieut. Maury ac-

At sunset on the 25th, Alonzo Pinzon, rushing excitedly upon the quarter-deck of the Pinta, shouted, "Land! land! My lord, I was the first to see it!" The sailors of the Nina clambered joyfully into the tops, and Columbus fell upon his knees in thanksgiving. But the morn dissipated the illusion, and the ocean stretched forth its illimitable expanse as before. On the 1st of October, one of the lieutenants declared with anguish that they were seventeen hundred miles from the Canaries, intelligence which terribly alarmed the crew, though they had really made a much greater distance, being actually twenty-one hundred miles from Teneriffe, according to Columbus' private reckoning.

The indications of the vicinity of land had been so often deceitful, that the crew no longer put faith in them, and fell from discouragement into taciturnity, and from taciturnity into insubordination. The discontent was general, and no efforts were made to conceal it. In their mutinous conversations, they spoke contemptuously of Columbus as "the Genoese," as a charlatan and a rogue. Was it just, they said, that one hundred and twenty men should perish by the caprice and obstinacy of one single man, and that man a foreigner and an impostor? If he persisted in proceeding "towards his everlasting west, which went on and on, and never came to an end," he ought to be thrown into the sea and left there. On their return they could easily say that he had fallen into the waves while gazing at the stars. A revolt was agreed upon between the crews of the three ships,

---

counts for its existence in the following manner:—"Patches of this weed are always to be seen floating along the Gulf Stream. Now, if bits of cork, or chaff, or any floating substance, be put in a basin, and a circular motion be given to the water, all the light substances will be found crowding together near the centre of the pool, where there is the least motion. Just such a basin is the Atlantic Ocean to the Gulf Stream, and the Sargasso Sea is the centre of the whirl. Columbus found this weedy sea in his voyage of discovery, and there it has remained to this day."

who were on several occasions brought into communication by the sending of boats from the one to the other. The captains of the Pinta and the Nina were aware of what was transpiring, but for the time being maintained a cautious neutrality. The sea continued calm as the Guadalquivir at Seville, the air was laden with tropical fragrance, and in twenty-four hours the fleet, apparently at rest, glided imperceptibly over one hundred and eighty miles. This motionless rapidity, as it were, thoroughly terrified the crew, and, breaking out into open mutiny, they refused, on the 10th of October, to go any farther westward. The Nina and the Pinta rejoined the Santa Maria; the brothers Pinzon, followed by their men, leaped upon her deck, and commanded Columbus to put his ship about and return to Palos.

At this most vital point of the narrative, our authorities are contradictory, while the journal of Columbus himself is silent. According to Oviedo,—a writer who obtained his information from an enemy of Columbus,—the latter yielded to his men so far as to propose a compromise, and to consent to return unless land was discovered in three days' sail. To say the least, such a submission to the menaces and behests of his infuriated subalterns was not an act compatible with the character of Columbus, with his well known self-reliance, and his openly expressed and constantly reiterated confidence in the Divine protection. The Catholic biography, which we have quoted, attributes the pacification of the revolt directly to the Divine interference, asserting that no human philosophy can explain this sudden and complete suspension of the prevailing exasperation and animosity. It is certain, at any rate, that the demonstration, which began at night-fall, had ceased long before the morning's dawn.

And now pigeons flew in abundance about the ships, and green canes and reeds floated languidly by. A bush, its branches red with berries, was recovered from the water by the Nina. A tuft of grass and a piece of wood, which appeared to have been cut by some iron instrument, were picked up by the Pinta. Such indications were sufficient to sustain the most dejected. Still the sun sank to rest in a horizon whose pure line was unbroken by land and unsullied by terrestrial vapor. The caravels were called together, and, after the usual prayer to the Virgin, Columbus announced to them that their trials were at an end, and that the morrow's light would bring with it the realization of all their hopes. The pilots were instructed to take in sail after midnight, and a velvet pourpoint was promised to him who should first see land. The crews which, two days before, considered Columbus as a trickster and a cheat, now received his word as they would a gospel from on high. The expectation and impatience which pervaded the three ships were indescribable. No eye was closed that night. The Pinta, being the most rapid sailer, was a long way in advance of the others. The Nina and the Santa Maria followed slowly, for sail had now been shortened, in her track. Suddenly a flash and a heavy report from the Pinta announced the joyful tidings. A Spaniard of Palos, named Juan Rodriguez Bermejo, had seen the land and won the velvet pourpoint. Columbus fell upon his knees, and, raising his hands to heaven, sang the Te Deum Laudamus. The sails were then furled and the fleet lay to. Arms and holiday dresses were prepared, for they knew not what the day would bring forth, whether the land would offer hospitality or challenge to combat. The great mystery of the ocean was to be revealed on the morrow: in the meantime, the night and the darkness had in their keeping the mighty secret—whether the land was a savage desert or a spicy and blooming garden.

THE NINA HOMEWARD BOUND.

COLUMBUS TAKING POSSESSION OF GUANAHANI.

CHAPTER XVI.

DISCOVERY OF GUANAHANI—CEREMONIES OF TAKING POSSESSION—EXPLORATION OF THE NEIGHBORING ISLANDS—SEARCH FOR GOLD—CUBA SUPPOSED BY COLUMBUS TO BE JAPAN—THE CANNIBALS—HAITI—RETURN HOMEWARDS—A STORM—AN APPEAL TO THE VIRGIN—ARRIVAL AT THE AZORES—CONDUCT OF THE PORTUGUESE—COLUMBUS AT LISBON—AT PALOS—AT BARCELONA—COLUMBUS' SECOND VOYAGE—DISCOVERY OF GUADELOUPE, ANTIGOA, SANTA CRUZ, JAMAICA—ILLNESS OF COLUMBUS—TERRIBLE BATTLE BETWEEN THE SPANIARDS AND THE SAVAGES—COLUMBUS RETURNS TO SPAIN—HIS RECEPTION BY THE QUEEN—HIS THIRD VOYAGE—THE REGION OF CALMS—DISCOVERY OF TRINIDAD AND OF THE MAIN LAND—ASSUMPÇION AND MARGARITA—COLUMBUS IN CHAINS.

ON Friday, the 12th of October, 1492, the kindling dawn revealed to the wondering eyes of our adventurers the bright colors and early-morning beauties of an island clothed in verdure, and teeming with the fruits and vegetation of mid-autumn in the tropics. Its surface undulated gently, massive forests skirted the spots cleared for cultivation, and the sparkling water of a fresh lake glittered amid the luxuriant foliage which encircled it. An anchorage was easily found, and Columbus, dressed in official costume, and bearing the royal standard in his hand, landed upon the silent and deserted shore. He planted the standard, and, prostrating himself before it, kissed the earth he had discovered; he then uttered the since famous prayer, the opening lines of which were, by order of the Spanish sovereigns, repeated by subsequent discoverers upon all similar occasions. He drew his sword, and, naming the land San Salvador, in memory of the Saviour, took possession of it for the Crown of Castile. The crews recognised Columbus as Admiral of the Ocean and Viceroy of the Indies. The most mutinous and outrageous thronged closely about him, and crouched at the feet of one who, in their eyes, had already wealth and honors in his gift.

The island at which Columbus had landed was called by the natives Guanahani, and is now one of the archipelago of the Bahamas. The inhabitants had retreated to the woods at the arrival of the strangers; but, being gradually reassured, suffered their confidence to be won, and received from them fragments of glass and earthen-ware as presents possessing a supernatural virtue. Columbus took seven of them on board, being anxious to convey them to Spain and offer them to the king, promising however to return them. Then he weighed anchor and explored the wonderful region in which these lovely islands lie. New lands were constantly, as it were, rising from the waves; the eye could hardly number them, but the seven natives called over a hundred of them by name. He landed successively at Concepçion, la Fernandine, and Isabella; at all of which he was enchanted by the magnificence of the vegetation, the superb plumage of the birds, and the delicious fragrance with which the forests and the air were filled. He sought everywhere for traces of gold in the soil, for he hoped thus to interest Spain in a continuance of his explorations. Such was his desire to obtain a sight of the precious metal, that he passed rapidly from island to island, indifferent to every other subject. At last, the natives spoke of a large and marvellous land, called Cuba, where there were spices, gold, ships, and merchants. Supposing this to be the wonderful Cipango, described by Marco Polo, he set sail at once. It was now the 24th of October.

On the 28th, at dawn, Columbus discovered an island, which, in its extent and in its general characteristics, reminded him strongly of Sicily, in the Mediterranean. As he approached, his senses underwent a species of confusion from the miraculous fertility and luxuriance of the vegetation. In his journal, he does not attempt to describe his emotions, but, preserving the silence of stupefaction, says simply that "he never saw any thing so magnificent." He no longer doubted that this beautiful spot was the real Cipango. He landed, gave to the island the name of Juana, and commenced a search for gold, which resulted in a complete disappointment. On leaving Cuba, he gave it a name which he thought more appropriate than Juana, styling its eastern extremity Alpha and Omega, being, as he thought, the region where the East Indies finished and where the West Indies began. This error of Columbus was the cause of the North American savages being called Indians—an error which has been perpetuated in spite of the progress of geographical discovery, and which will doubtless endure forever.

On the 6th of December, he discovered an island, named Haiti by the natives, and which he called Hispaniola, as it reminded him of the fairest tracts of Spain. He found that the inhabitants had the reputation with their neighbors of devouring human flesh; they were called *Caniba* people, an epithet which, after the necessary modifications, has passed into all European languages. The Caribs were the nation meant. At this point, the captain of the Pinta deserted the fleet, in order to make discoveries on his own account. Soon after, the Santa Maria was wrecked upon the coast of Haiti, and Columbus, thinking that this accident was intended as an indication of the Divine will that he should establish a colony there, built a fort of live timber, in which he placed forty-two men. He weighed anchor in the Nina, on the 11th of January, 1493, and shortly after fell in with the Pinta. He pretended to believe and accept the falsehoods and contradictions which Pinzon alleged as the reasons for his abandonment of the fleet. The two vessels now turned their heads east, Columbus hoping to discover a cannibal island on his way, as he wished to carry a professor of the disgusting practice to Spain.

No event of moment happened until the 12th of February, a month afterwards, when a terrible storm burst over the hitherto tranquil waters. Its violence increased to such a degree that nothing remained but a desperate appeal to "Mary, the Mother of God." A quantity of dried peas, equal in number to the number of men on board the Nina, were placed in a sailor's woollen cap, one of them being marked with a cross. He who should draw this pea, was to go on a pilgrimage to the church of Saint Mary at Guadeloupe, bearing a candle weighing five pounds, in case the ship were saved. Columbus was the first to draw, and he drew the marked pea. Other vows of this sort were made, and, finally, one to go in procession, and with bare feet, to the nearest cathedral of whatever land they should first reach. The admiral, fearing that his discovery would perish with him, withdrew to his cabin, during the fiercest period of the tumult, and wrote upon parchment two separate and concise narratives of his discoveries. He enclosed them both in wax, and, placing one in an empty barrel, threw it into the sea. The other, similarly enclosed, he attached to the poop of the Nina, intending to cut it loose at the moment of going down. Happily, the storm subsided; and, on the 17th, the shattered vessels arrived at the southernmost island of the Azores, belonging to the King of Portugal. Here half the crew went in procession to the chapel, to discharge their vow; and, while Columbus was waiting to go with the other half, the Portuguese made a sally, surrounded the first portion, and made them prisoners. After a useless protest, Columbus departed with the men that remained, having with him, in the Nina, but three able-bodied seamen. Another storm now threw him upon the coast of Portugal, at the mouth of the Tagus. Here he narrowly escaped shipwreck

RECEPTION OF COLUMBUS BY FERDINAND AND ISABELLA.

a second time, but, with the assistance of the wonder-stricken inhabitants, reached in safety the roads of Rostello. The king, though jealous of the maritime renown he was acquiring for Spain, received him with distinction and dismissed him with presents. Columbus arrived, in the Nina, at Palos on Friday, the 15th of March, seven months and twelve days after his departure. Alonzo Pinzon had already arrived in the Pinta, and, believing Columbus to have perished in the storm, had written to the court, narrating the discoveries made by the fleet, and claiming for himself the merit and the recompense.

It is not our province to relate the history of the career of Columbus upon land, nor have we space so to do. We can only briefly allude to his discharge, by pilgrimages to holy shrines, of the vows, which, three times out of four, had, by lot, devolved upon him: to the week he spent with Marchena, and in the silence of the cloister, at la Rabida; to the princely honors he received in his progress to Barcelona, whither the court had gone; to his reception by the king and queen, in which Ferdinand and Isabella rose as he approached, raised him as he kneeled to kiss their hands, and ordered him to be seated in their presence.

The Spanish sovereigns soon fitted out a new expedition; and, on the 25th of September, 1493, Columbus left the port of Cadiz with seventeen vessels, five hundred sailors, soldiers, citizens and servants, and one thousand colonists, three hundred of whom had smuggled themselves on board. He sailed directly for the Carib or Cannibal Islands, and on the 3d of November arrived in their midst. He named one of them Maria-Galanta, from his flag-ship; another, Guadeloupe, from one of the shrines of Spain where he had discharged a vow. He here found numerous and disgusting evidences of the truth of the story that these people lived on human flesh. The island which he named Montserrat, in honor of the famous sanctuary of that name, had been depopulated by the Caribs. He gave to the next land the name of Santa Maria l' Antigoa; it is now known as Antigoa, simply. Another he called Santa Cruz, in honor of the cross. Returning to Hispaniola, he found the fort destroyed and the garrison massacred. Having founded the city of Isabella upon another part of the island, he sent back twelve of his ships to Spain, and with three of the remaining five, one of which was the famous Nina, started upon a voyage of discovery in the surrounding waters. He touched at Alpha and Omega, and inquired of the savages where he could find gold. They pointed to the south. Two days afterwards, Columbus descried lofty mountains, with blue summits, upon an island to which he gave the name of Jamaica, in honor of St. James. Then returning to Cuba, and following the southern coast a distance sufficient to convince the three crews that it was a continent and not an island, he took possession of it as such. He then wished to revisit the Caribbean Islands and destroy the boats of the inhabitants, that they might no longer prey upon their neighbors, but the direction of the winds would not permit him to sail to the west. Returning to Isabella, he met his brother Bartholomew, who had just arrived from Spain, bearing a letter from the queen. He also found, to his extreme regret, that the officers he had left in charge of the colony had transcended their authority and had abandoned their duties. Margarit, the commander, and Boil, the vicar, had departed in the ship that had brought Bartholomew. Overcome by the toils and privations he had undergone, and sick at heart at the sight of the disasters under which the colony was laboring, he fell into a deep lethargy, and for a long time it was doubtful whether he would ever awake again.

He did awake, however, but only to a poignant consciousness of the miseries the Spanish invasion had brought upon the island. The Spaniards and Indians had become, through the treachery of the former, hostile during his absence, and battles, surprises, and murders were of daily occurrence. Seeing the necessity of a vigorous effort in order to maintain his authority over the natives, he led his two hundred and twenty men against a furious throng of naked, painted savages, whose numbers were declared by the Spaniards to be no less than one hundred thousand. The Indians were defeated with great slaughter, and were subjected to the payment of tribute and to the indignity of taxation. At this period, an officer, named Juan Aguado, sent out by Ferdinand and Isabella upon the malicious representations of Margarit and Father Boil, to inquire into the state of the colony and the conduct of Columbus, arrived in the island. Columbus determined to return himself to Spain, to present in person a justification of his course. A violent storm having destroyed all the vessels except the Nina, Columbus took the command of her, Aguado building a caravel for himself from the wrecks of the others. They both left Isabella on the 10th of March, 1496, taking with them the sick and disappointed, to the number of two hundred and twenty-five, and thirty-two Indians, whom they forced to accompany them. They touched at Guadeloupe for wood and water, and, after repulsing an attack of Caribs, contrived to gain their confidence, and to obtain the articles of which they stood in need. They left again on the 20th of April. After a long and painful voyage, in the course of which it was proposed to throw the Indians overboard in order to lessen the consumption of food, they arrived, without material damage, at the port of Cadiz. Columbus wrote to the king and queen, and during the month that elapsed before their answer was received, allowed his beard to grow, and, disgusted with the world, assumed the garments and the badges of a Franciscan friar. He was soon summoned to Burgos, then the residence of the court, where Isabella, forgetting the calumnies of which he had been the object and the accusations his enemies had heaped upon him, loaded him with favors and kindness.

Numerous circumstances prevented Columbus from requesting the immediate equipment of another expedition. It was not till the 30th of May, 1498, that he sailed again for his discoveries in the West. He left San Lucar with six caravels, three laden with supplies and reinforcements for the colony at Isabella, and three intended to accompany himself upon a search for the mainland, which he believed to exist west of Hispaniola, Cuba, and Jamaica. On the 15th of July, in the latitude of Sierra Leone, they came into the region of calms, where the water seemed like molten silver beneath a tropical sun. Not a breath of air stirred, not a cloud intercepted the fiery rays which fell vertically upon them from the skies. The provisions decayed in the hold, the pitch and tar boiled upon the ropes. The barrels of wine and water opened in wide seams, and scattered their precious contents to waste. The grains of wheat were wrinkled and shrivelled as if roasting before the fire. For eight days this incandescence lasted, till an east wind sprang up and wafted them to a more temperate spot in the torrid zone.

On the 31st of July land was discovered in the west,—three mountain peaks seeming to ascend from one and the same base. Columbus had made a vow to give the name of the Trinity to the first land he should discover, and this singular triune form of the land now before them was noticed as a wonderful coincidence by all on board. It was named, therefore, Trinidad; it lies off the northern coast of Venezuela, in the Continent of South America. The innumerable islands, formed by the forty mouths of the Orinoco, were next discovered, and shortly afterwards the continent to the north, which Columbus judged to be the mainland from the volume of water brought to the sea by the Orinoco. Columbus was not the first to set foot upon the New World he had discovered: being confined to his cabin by an attack of ophthalmia, he sent Pedro de Terreros to take possession in his stead. This discovery of the Southern portion of the Western Continent was, however, as we shall soon have occasion to show, subsequent to that of the Northern portion by John Cabot, who visited Labrador in 1497.

The fleet was unable to remain in these seductive regions, owing to the scarcity of provisions and the increasing blindness of the admiral. He would have been glad to stay in a spot which, in his letter to his sovereigns, he describes as the Terrestrial Paradise, the Orinoco being one of the four streams flowing from it, as described in the Bible. The fact that this river throws from its forty issues fresh water enough to overcome the saltness of the sea to a great distance from the shore, was one of the circumstances which gave to this portion of the world the somewhat marvellous and fantastic character with which the imagination of Columbus invested it. He sailed at once from the continent to Hispaniola, discovering and naming the islands of Assumpçion and la Margarita. At Hispaniola he again found famine, distress, rebellion, and panic on every side. Malversation and mutiny had brought the colony to the very verge of ruin.

We have not space to detail the manœuvres and machinations by which the mind of Ferdinand was prejudiced towards Columbus, and, in consequence of which, Francesco Bobadilla was sent by him in July, 1500, to investigate the charges brought against the admiral. Arrogant in his newly acquired honors, Bobadilla took the part of the malcontents, and, placing Columbus in chains, sent him back to Spain. He arrived at Cadiz on the 20th of November, after the most rapid passage yet made across the ocean. The general burst of indignation at the shocking spectacle of Columbus in fetters, compelled Ferdinand to disclaim all knowledge of the transaction. Isabella accorded him a private audience, in which she shed tears at the sufferings and indignities he had undergone. The king kept him waiting nine months, wasting his time in fruitless applications for redress, and finally appointed Nicholas Ovando Governor of Hispaniola in his place.

COLUMBUS IN CHAINS AT CADIZ.

CHAPTER XVII.

THE FAILING HEALTH OF COLUMBUS—HIS FOURTH VOYAGE—MARTINIQUE, PORTO RICCO, NICARAGUA, COSTA RICCA, PANAMA—HIS SEARCH FOR A CHANNEL ACROSS THE ISTHMUS—HE PREDICTS AN ECLIPSE OF THE MOON AT JAMAICA—HIS RETURN—THE DEATH OF ISABELLA—COLUMBUS PENNILESS AT VALLADOLID—HIS DEATH—HIS FOUR BURIALS—THE INJUSTICE OF THE WORLD TOWARDS COLUMBUS—CHRISTOPHER PIGEON—AMERIGO VESPUCCI—THE NEW WORLD NAMED AMERICA—ERRORS OF MODERN HISTORIANS—THE DISTRICT OF COLUMBIA—JOHN CABOT IN LABRADOR—SEBASTIAN CABOT IN HUDSON'S BAY—VINCENT YANEZ PINZON AT THE MOUTHS OF THE AMAZON.

COLUMBUS was now advanced in years, and his sufferings and labors had dimmed his eyesight and bowed his frame; but his mind was yet active, and his enthusiasm in the cause of discovery irrepressible. He had convinced himself, and now sought to convince the queen, that to the westward of the regions he had visited the land converged, leaving a narrow passage through which he hoped to pass, and proceed to the Indies beyond. This convergence of the land did in reality exist, but the strait of water he expected to find was, and is, a strait of land—the Isthmus of Panama. However, the queen approved of the plan, and gave him four ships, equipped and victualled for two years. Columbus had conceived the immense idea of passing through the strait, and returning by Asia and the Cape of Good Hope, thus circumnavigating the globe and proving its spherical form. He departed from Cadiz on the 8th of May, 1502.

He touched at, and named, Martinique early in June, and afterwards at St. Jean, now Porto Ricco. Ovando refused his request to land at Isabella to repair his vessel and exchange one of them for a faster sailer. Escaping a terrible storm, which wrecked and utterly destroyed the splendid fleet in which the rapacious pillagers of the island had embarked their ill-gotten wealth, he was driven by the winds to Jamaica, and thence by the currents to Cuba. Here a strong north wind enabled him to sail south southwest, towards the latitude where he expected to find the strait. He touched the mainland of North America at Truxillo, in Honduras, and coasted thence southward along the Mosquito shore, Nicaragua, Costa Ricca, and Panama. Here he explored every sinuosity and indentation of the shore, seeking at the very spot where civilization and commerce now require a canal, a passage which he considered as demanded by Nature and accorded by Providence. He followed the isthmus as far as the Gulf of Darien, and then, driven by a furious tropical tempest, returned as far as Veragua, in search of rich gold mines of which he had heard. The storm lasted for eight days, concluding with a terrible display of water-spouts, which Columbus is said to have regarded as a work of the devil, and to have dispelled by bringing forth the Bible and exorcising the demon.

One of the water-spouts passed between the ships without injuring them, and spun away, muttering and terrible, to spend its fury elsewhere.

On reaching Veragua, Columbus sent his brother up a river, which he called Bethlehem, or by contraction Belem, to seek for gold. His researches seeming to indicate the presence of the precious metal, Columbus determined to establish a colony upon the river, an attempt which was defeated by the hostility of the natives. Their fierce resistance and the crazy state of his vessels forced Columbus, in April, 1503, to make the best of his way to Hispaniola with two crowded vessels, which, being totally unseaworthy, he was obliged to run ashore at Jamaica. There Columbus awed the natives and subdued them to obedience and submission, by predicting an eclipse of the moon.

Thus left without a single vessel, he had no resource but to send to Hispaniola for assistance. After a period of fifteen months, lost in quelling mutinies and in opposing the cruelties and exactions of the new masters of the island, he obtained a caravel, and again sailed for Spain on the 12th of September, 1504. During the passage, he was compelled, by a severe attack of rheumatism, to remain confined to his cabin. His tempest-tossed and shattered bark at last cast anchor in the harbor of San Lucar. He proceeded to Seville, where he heard, with dismay, of the illness, and then of the death, of his patroness Isabella. Sickness now detained him at Seville till the spring of 1505, when he arrived, exhausted and paralytic, before the king. Here he underwent another courtly denial of redress. He was now without shelter and without hope. He was compelled to borrow money with which to pay for a shabby room at a miserable inn. He lingered for a year in poverty and neglect, and died at last in Valladolid, on the 20th of May, 1506. The revolting ingratitude of Ferdinand of Spain thus caused the death, in rags, in destitution, and in infirmity, of the greatest man that has ever served the cause of progress or labored in the paths of science. Had we written the life of Columbus, and not thus briefly sketched the history of his voyages, we should have found it easy to assert and maintain his claim to this commanding position.

The agitation of the life of Columbus followed his remains to the grave,—for he was buried four successive times, and his dead body made the passage of the Atlantic. It was first deposited in the vaults of the Franciscan Convent of Valladolid, where it remained seven years. In 1513, Ferdinand, now old and perhaps repentant, caused the coffin to be brought from Valladolid to Seville, where a solemn service was said over it in the grand cathedral. It was then placed in the chapel belonging to the Chartreux. In 1536, the coffin was transported to the city of St. Domingo, in the island of Hispaniola. Here it remained for two hundred and sixty years. In 1795, Spain ceded the island to France, stipulating that the ashes of Columbus should be transferred to Spanish soil. In December of the same year, the vault was opened, and the fragments which were found—those of a leaden coffin, mingled with bones and dust returned to dust—were carefully collected. They were carried on board the brigantine Discovery, which transported them to the frigate San Lorenzo, by which they were taken to Havana, where, in the presence of the Governor-General of Cuba and in the midst of imposing ceremonies, they were consigned to their fourth and final resting-place.

It will not be altogether out of place to group together here the numerous and remarkable instances of the world's injustice and ingratitude towards Columbus. We have said that he died in penury at Valladolid. A publication, issued periodically in that city from 1333 to 1539, chronicling every event of local interest—births, marriages, deaths, fires, executions, appointments, church ceremonies—did not mention, or in any way allude to, the death of Columbus. Pierre Martyr, a poet of Lombardy, once his intimate friend, and who had said, at the time of his first voyage, that by singing of his discoveries he would descend to immortality with him, seemed to think, later in life, that he should peril his chances of immortality were he to sing of his death, for his muse held her peace. In 1507, a collection of voyages was published by Fracanzo de Montalbodo, in which no mention was made of Columbus' fourth voyage, and in which Columbus himself was alluded to as still alive. In 1508, a Latin translation of this work was published, in the preface to which Columbus was mentioned as still living in honor at the court of Spain. Another famous work of the time attributes the discovery of the New World, not to the calculations and science of a man, but to the accidental wanderings of a tempest-driven caravel. Not ten years after the death of Columbus, the chaplain of one of the kings of Italy, in a work upon "Memorable Events in Spain," stated that a New World had been discovered in the West by one PETER COLUMBUS. And, in the same taste and spirit, a German doctor, in the first German book which spoke of the New World, did not once mention the name of Columbus, but, translating the proper name as if it were a common noun, calls him Christoffel Dawber, which, being translated back again, signifies CHRISTOPHER PIGEON.

We shall now speak of that signal instance of public ingratitude and national forgetfulness which is universally regretted, yet will never be repaired,—the giving to the New World the name of America and not that of Columbia,—a substitution due to an obscure and ignorant French publisher of St. Dié, in Lorraine.

Amerigo Vespucci, born at Florence fifteen years after Columbus, and the third son of a notary, appears to have been led by mercantile tastes to Spain in 1486, where he became a factor in a wealthy house at Seville. He abandoned the counter, however, for navigation and mathematics, and took to the sea for a livelihood. He was at first a practical astronomer, and finally a pilot-major. He went four times on expeditions to the New World, in 1499, 1500, 1501, 1502. During the first, he coasted along the land at the mouths of the Orinoco, which had been discovered by Columbus the preceding year. Even had he been the first to discover the mainland,—which he was not,—there would have been no merit in it, for he was merely a subordinate officer on board a ship following in the track of Columbus, seven years after the latter had traced it upon the ocean and the charts of the marine. He published an account of his voyage. But it does not appear that he ever claimed honor as the first discoverer, and the friendly relations he maintained with the family of Columbus after the death of the latter show that they did not consider him as attempting to obtain a distinction which did not belong to him. The error flowed from another and more distant source.

Columbus had died in 1506, and had been forgotten. In 1507, a Frenchman of St. Dié republished Vespucci's narrative, substituting the date of 1497 for that of 1499,—thus making it appear that Vespucci had preceded, instead of followed, Columbus in his discovery of the mainland. He did not once mention Columbus, and attributed the whole merit of the western voyages to Vespucci. He added that he did not see why from the name of Amerigo an appellation could not be derived for the continent he had discovered, and proposed that of America, as having a feminine termination like that of Europa, Asia, and Africa, and as possessing a musical sound likely to catch the public ear. This work was dedicated to the Emperor Maximilian, and passed rapidly through editions in various languages.

Thus far no specific name had been given to the continent. Its situation was sometimes indicated upon maps by a cross, and sometimes by the words TERRA SANCTÆ CRUCIS, SIVE MUNDUS NOVUS, often printed in red capitals. In 1522, for the first time, the name of America, under its French form of *Amérique*, was printed upon a map at Lyons. Germany followed, and the presses of Basle and Zurich aided the usurpation. Florence was but too eager to accept a name which flattered her vanity; and, as Genoa did not protest in the name of Columbus, Italy yielded to the current, and did a large share in the labor of injustice. In 1570, the name of America was for the first time engraved upon a metal globe, and from this time forward the spoliation may be regarded as accomplished. Columbus had been twice buried and twice forgotten; and now his very name was lost,—the continent he had found having been baptized in honor of another, and his race in the male line being extinct,—for Diego and Fernando had died without heirs.

In modern times, in our own day even, it has been a common practice to depreciate the services of Columbus, and eminent writers have thought it no disgrace to profess and testify ignorance of his history and life. Raynal, a French philosopher of distinction, declared, about the year 1760, that the passage of the Cape of Good Hope by Vasco da Gama was a greater achievement than the crossing of the Atlantic by Columbus. He offered a prize for disquisitions upon the question, "Has the discovery of America been useful or prejudicial to the human race?" Buffon seems, too, to have considered the discoveries of the Portuguese in the East as more important than those of Columbus in the West. Robertson, in his History of America, says that even without Columbus some happy accident would have discovered the New World a few years later. Fontenelle, and many others, attribute the first notice of the variation of the compass to Cabot in 1497, though Columbus distinctly mentions noticing it in his journal on the 13th of September, 1492. A late Spanish historian writes:—"Columbus made nothing but discoveries in these regions; conquest was reserved for Cortez and Pizarro." Lamartine makes an error of fifteen years in stating the period of the return of Columbus to Spain. Dumas asserts that Columbus passed "a portion of his life in prison,"—an expression he would not probably have used, knowingly, to designate a period of three months. Granier de Cassagnac places the last voyage of Columbus in 1493, instead of 1502. St. Hilaire makes the celebrated Las Casas cross the sea with Columbus nine years too soon. These mis-statements, though not resulting in distortion or misrepresentation of character, are the effects of that indifference which for centuries history has manifested towards the life, services, and death of Columbus.

Columbia is the poetic and symbolical name of America, occurring in the National Anthem and in numerous effusions of patriotic verse. An effort to avenge the memory of the discoverer was made by giving his name, officially, to a tract borrowed from Virginia and Maryland, and measuring one hundred miles square,—the seat of the American Government. So far from this tardy acknowledgment being a reparation, however, it is probable that the spirit of the departed benefactor, if summoned to speak, would declare it the last, and by no means the least, of the long line of insults that an ungrateful posterity had heaped upon his memory.

It will be proper to add to this view of the voyages of Columbus a brief account of those effected immediately afterwards by John and Sebastian Cabot, and by Vincent Yanez Pinzon.

In the year 1496, Henry VII. of England, stimulated by the success of Columbus, granted a patent to one Giovanni Gabotto, a Venetian dwelling in Bristol, to go in search of unknown lands. Little is known of this person, whose name has been Anglicized into John Cabot, except that he was a wealthy and intelligent merchant and fond of maritime discovery. He had three sons, one of whom, named Sebastian, was nineteen years old at the time of the voyage, upon which, with his brothers, he accompanied his father. They sailed in a ship named the Matthew, and on the 24th of June, 1497, discovered the mainland of America, eighteen months before Columbus set foot upon it at the mouths of the Orinoco. For a long time it was supposed that Cabot had landed upon Newfoundland, but it is now considered settled that Labrador was the portion of the continent first discovered by a European. No account of the further prosecution of the voyage has reached us, and the only official record of Cabot's return is an entry in the privy-purse expenses of Henry, 10th August, 1497:—"To hym that found the New Isle, 10*l*." Thus, fifty days had not elapsed between the discovery and its recompense in England,—a fact which shows that Cabot returned home at once. He is supposed to have died about the year 1499.

Sebastian Cabot, the second son, who is regarded as by far the most scientific navigator of this family of seamen, appears to have lived in complete obscurity during the following twelve years. Disgusted, however, by the want of consideration of the English authorities towards him, he accepted an invitation from King Ferdinand to visit Spain in 1512. Here, for several years, he was employed in revising maps and charts, and, with the title of Captain and a liberal salary, held the honorable position of Member of the Council of the Indies. The death of Ferdinand and the intrigues of the enemies of Columbus induced him to return to England in 1517. He was employed by Henry VIII., in connection with one Sir Thomas Perte, to make an attempt at a Northwest passage. On this voyage he is said to have gained Hudson's Bay, and to have given English names to sundry places there. So few details of the expedition have been preserved, that the latitude reached (67½ degrees) is referred by different authorities both to the north and the south. The malice or cowardice of Sir Thomas Perte compelled Cabot to return without accomplishing any thing worthy of being recorded. It was often said afterwards, that if the New World could not be called Columbia, it would be better to name it Cabotiana than America.

Vincent Yanez Pinzon, the youngest of the three brothers who had accompanied Columbus upon his first voyage, determined, upon hearing, in 1499, that the continent was discovered, on trying his fortunes at the head of an expedition, instead of in a subordinate position. He found no difficulty in equipping four caravels, and in inducing several of those who had seen the coast of Paria to embark with him as pilots. He sailed from Palos in December, 1499, and proceeded directly to the southwest. During a storm which obscured the heavens he crossed the equator, and on the disappearance of the clouds no longer recognised the constellations, changed as they were from those of the Northern to those of the Southern hemisphere. Pinzon was thus the first European who crossed the line in the Atlantic. The sailors, unacquainted with the Southern sky, and dismayed at the absence of the polar star, were for a time filled with superstitious terrors. Pinzon, however, persisted, and, on the 20th of January, 1500, discovered land in eight degrees of south latitude. He took possession for the Crown of Spain, and named it Santa Maria de la Consolaçion. We shall soon have occasion to mention why this name was superseded by that of Brazil.

Pinzon explored with amazement the huge mouths of the Amazon, whose immense torrents, as they emptied into the sea, freshened its waters for many leagues from the land. Sailing to the north, he followed the coast for four hundred leagues, and then returned to Palos, carrying with him three thousand pounds' weight of dye-woods and the first opossum ever seen in Europe.

And now, having closed the fifteenth century with the achievements of the Spanish in the West, we open the sixteenth with those of the Portuguese in the East.

VASCO DA GAMA.

CHAPTER XVIII.

PORTUGUESE NAVIGATION UNDER EMMANUEL—POPULAR PREJUDICES—THE LUSIAD OF CAMOENS—VASCO DA GAMA—MAPS OF AFRICA OF THE PERIOD—PREPARATIONS FOR AN INDIAN VOYAGE—RELIGIOUS CEREMONIES—THE DEPARTURE—RENDEZVOUS AT THE CAPE VERDS—LANDING UPON THE COAST—THE NATIVES—AN INVITATION TO DINNER, AND ITS CONSEQUENCES—A STORM—MUTINY—THE SPECTRE OF THE CAPE.

In the year 1495, John II. of Portugal was succeeded by his cousin, Emmanuel, into whose mind he had a short time before his death instilled a portion of his own zeal for maritime discovery and commercial supremacy. He had especially dwelt upon the necessity of continuing the progress of African research beyond the point which Bartholomew Diaz had lately reached, into the regions where lay the East Indies with their wealth and marvellous productions, and thus substituting for the tedious land-route a more expeditious track by sea. Upon his accession, Emmanuel found that a strong opposition existed to the extension of Portuguese commerce and discovery. Arguments were urged against it in his own councils, and had a marked effect upon the public mind by heightening the danger of the intended voyage.

In our narrative of the first East Indian expedition, we shall often have occasion to quote from a poem written in commemoration of it,—the Lusiad of Camoens, a semi-religious epic and the masterpiece of Portuguese literature,—Lusiade being the poetic and symbolical name of Portugal. Camoens describes at the outset the hostility of the nation to further maritime adventure, and places in the mouth of a reverend adviser of the king the following forcible appeal:

> "Oh, frantic thirst of Honor and of Fame,
> The crowd's blind tribute, a fallacious name;
> What stings, what plagues, what secret scourges cursed,
> Torment those bosoms where thy pride is nursed!
> What dangers threaten and what deaths destroy
> The hapless youth whom thy vain gleams decoy!
> Thou dazzling meteor, vain as fleeting air,
> What new dread horror dost thou now prepare?
> Oh, madness of Ambition! thus to dare
> Dangers so fruitless, so remote a war!
> That Fame's vain flattery may thy name adorn,
> And thy proud titles on her flag be borne:
> Thee, Lord of Persia, thee of India lord,
> O'er Ethiopia vast, and Araby adored!"

Never was any expedition, whether by land or water, so unpopular as this of King Emmanuel. The murmurs of the cabinet were re-echoed by the populace, who were wrought upon to such an extent that they believed the natural consequence of an invasion of the Indian seas would be the arrival in the Tagus of the wroth and avenging Sultan of Egypt. But Emmanuel, who, we are told, "regarded Diffidence as the mark of a low and grovelling mind, and Hope the quality of a noble and aspiring soul," discerned prospects of national advantage in the scheme, and determined to pursue it to a prosperous issue.

King John, before his death, and shortly after the return of Diaz, had ordered timber to be purchased for the construction of ships fit to cope with the storms of the redoubtable Cape. Emmanuel now sought a capable commander, and, after much deliberation, fixed upon a gentleman of his own household, Vasco da Gama by name, a native of the seaport of Sines, and already favorably known for enterprise and naval skill. We are told that "he was formed for the service to which he was called,—violent indeed in his temper, terrible in anger, and sudden in the execution of justice, but at the same time intrepid, persevering, patient in difficulties, fertile in expedients, and superior to all discouragement. He devoted himself to death if he should not succeed, and this from a sense of religion and loyalty." When the king acquainted him with the mission intrusted to his charge, Vasco replied that he had long aspired to the honor of conducting such an undertaking. Camoens makes da Gama thus describe his acceptance of the honor:

"'Let skies on fire,
Let frozen seas, let horrid war, conspire:
I dare them all,' I cried, 'and but repine
That one poor life is all I can resign.'"

The most distinguished members of the Portuguese nobility were present at this interview. The king gave da Gama, with his own hands, the flag he was to bear,—a white cross enclosed within a red one,—the Cross of the military Order of Christ. Upon this he took the oath of allegiance. Emmanuel then delivered him the journal of Covillam, with such charts as were then in existence, and letters to all the Indian potentates who had become known to the Portuguese. Among these was of course one addressed to the renowned Prester John.

A map of Africa had been lately designed, in accordance with the discoveries made by land, as we have mentioned, by Covillam. The accompanying specimen is a fac-simile of one which belonged to Juan de la Cosa—the pilot of Columbus.

Upon it the principal cities are indicated by a roughly sketched house or church; the government is denoted by a picture of a king, closely resembling the royal gentry in a pack of cards; while flags, planted at intervals, indicate boundary lines and frontier posts. The winds are represented by fabulous divinities sitting round the world upon leathern bottles, whose sides they are pressing to force out the air. The celebrated statue of the Canaries is often seen flourishing his club at the top of his tower.

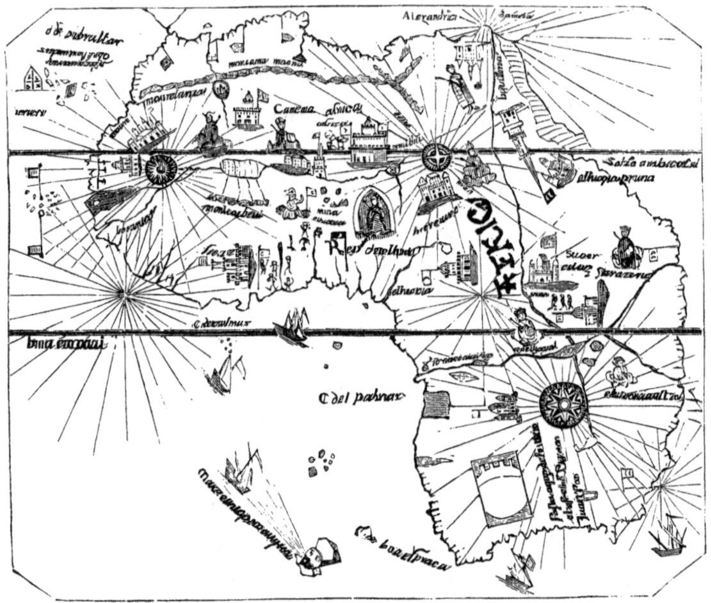

MAP OF AFRICA DRAWN IN THE YEAR 1497.

Abyssinia figures with its Prester John, his head being adorned with a brilliant mitre. Other kingdoms are marked out by portraits of their kings in richly embroidered costumes. The inhabitants of Africa, in maps of the world, are represented as giraffes, black men, and elephants. Portuguese camps are denoted by colored tents, while groups of light cavalry, splendidly caparisoned, dotting the territory at numerous points, indicate that the Portuguese army is making the tour of that mysterious continent. These quaint specimens of chartographical art are, in short, the faithful expression of the geographical science of the age.

The fleet equipped for da Gama's voyage consisted of three ships and a caravel,—the San Gabriel, of one hundred and twenty tons, commanded by da Gama, and piloted by Pero Dalemquer, who had been pilot to Bartholomew Diaz; the San Rafael, of one hundred tons, commanded by Paulo da Gama, the admiral's brother; a store-ship of two hundred tons; and the caravel, of fifty tons, commanded by Nicolao Coelho. Besides these, Diaz, who had already been over the route, was ordered to accompany da Gama as far as the Mina. The crews numbered in all one hundred and sixty men, among whom were ten malefactors condemned to death, and who had consequently nothing to hope for in Portugal. Their duty in the fleet was to go ashore upon savage coasts and attempt to open intercourse with the natives. In case of rendering essential service and escaping with their lives, their sentence was to be remitted on their return home.

A small chapel stood upon the seaside about four miles from Lisbon. Hither da Gama and his crew repaired upon the day preceding that fixed for their departure. They spent the night in prayer and rites of devotion, invoking the blessing and protection of Heaven. On the morrow, the adventurers marched to their ships in the midst of the whole population of Lisbon, who now thronged the shore of Belem. A long procession of priests sang anthems and offered sacrifice. The vast multitude, catching the fire of devotion and animated with the fervor of religious zeal, joined aloud in the prayers for their safety. The parents and relatives of the travellers shed tears, and da Gama himself wept on bidding farewell to the friends who gathered round him.

Camoens thus describes the emotions of the adventurers as they gazed at the receding shore:

"As from our dear-loved native shore we fly,
Our votive shouts, redoubled, rend the sky:

'Success! Success!' far echoes o'er the tide,
While our broad hulks the foaming waves divide.
When slowly gliding from our wistful eyes,
The Lusian mountains mingle with the skies;
Tago's loved stream and Cintra's mountains cold,
Dim fading now, we now no more behold;
And still with yearning hearts our eyes explore,
Till one dim speck of land appears no more."

The admiral had fixed upon the Cape Verd Islands as the first place of rendezvous in case of separation by storm. They all arrived safely in eight days at the Canaries, but were here driven widely apart by a tempest at night. The three captains subsequently joined each other, but could not find the admiral. They therefore made for the appointed rendezvous, where, to their great satisfaction, they found da Gama already arrived; "and, saluting him with many shots of ordnance, and with sound of trumpets, they spake unto him, each of them heartily rejoicing and thanking God for their safe meeting and good fortune in this their first brunt of danger and of peril." Diaz here took leave of them and returned to Portugal. Then, on the 3d of August, they set sail finally for the Cape of Good Hope.

They continued without seeing land during the months of August, September, and October, greatly distressed by foul weather, or, in the quaint language of those days, "by torments of wind and rain." At last, on the 7th of November, they touched the African coast, and anchored in a capacious bay, which they called the Bay of St. Helena, and which is not far to the north of the Cape. Here they perceived the natives "to bee lyttle men, ill favored in the face, and of color blacke; and when they did speake, it was in such manner as though they did alwayes sigh." Camoens rhapsodizes at length over this approach to the land; and it must be remembered that, having followed in da Gama's track as early as the year 1553, his descriptions of scenery are those of an eye-witness:

"Loud through the fleet the echoing shouts prevail:
We drop the anchor and restrain the sail;

And now, descending in a spacious bay,
Wide o'er the coast the venturous soldiers stray,
To spy the wonders of the savage shore
Where strangers' foot had never trod before.
I and my pilots, on the yellow sand,
Explore beneath what sky the shores expand.
Here we perceived our venturous keels had pass'd,
Unharmed, the Southern tropic's howling blast,
And now approached dread Neptune's secret reign:
Where the stern power, as o'er the Austral main
He rides, wide scatters from the Polar Star
Hail, ice, and snow, and all the wintry war."

Trade was now commenced between da Gama and the natives, and, by means of signs and gestures, cloth, beads, bells, and glass were bartered for articles of food and other necessaries. But this friendly intercourse was soon interrupted by an act of imprudent folly on the part of a young man of the squadron. Being invited to dine by a party of the natives, he entered one of their huts to partake of the repast. Being disgusted at the viands, which consisted of a sea-calf dressed after the manner of the Hottentots, he fled in dismay. He was followed by his perplexed entertainers, who were anxious to learn how they had offended him. Taking their officious hospitality for impertinent aggression, he shouted for help; and it was not long before mutual apprehension brought on open hostilities. Da Gama and his officers were attacked, while taking the altitude of the sun with an astrolabe, by a party of concealed negroes armed with spears pointed with horn. The admiral was wounded in the foot, and with some difficulty effected a retreat to the ships. He left the Bay of St. Helena on the 16th of November.

He now met with a sudden and violent change of weather, and the Portuguese historians have left animated descriptions of the storm which ensued. During any momentary pause in the elemental warfare, the sailors, worn out with fatigue and yielding to despair, surrounded da Gama, begging that he would not devote himself and them to a fate so dreadful. They declared that the gale could no longer be weathered, and that every one must be buried in the waves if they continued to proceed. The admiral's firmness remained unshaken, and a conspiracy was soon formed against him. He was informed in time of this desperate plot by his brother Paulo. He put the ringleaders and pilots in irons, and, assisted by his brother and those who remained faithful to their duty, stood night and day to the helm. At length, on Wednesday, the 20th of November, the whole squadron doubled the tremendous promontory. The mutineers were pardoned and released from their manacles.

The legend of the Spectre of the Cape is given by Camoens in full; and it is so characteristic of the age, and, as an episode, is itself so interesting, that we cannot refrain from quoting it entire. Da Gama is supposed to be relating his experience in the first person:

"I spoke, when, rising through the darken'd air,
Appall'd, we saw a hideous phantom glare.
High and enormous o'er the flood he tower'd,
And thwart our way with sullen aspect lower'd:
An earthly paleness o'er his cheeks was spread,
Erect uprose his hairs of wither'd red;
Writhing to speak, his sable lips disclose,
Sharp and disjoin'd, his gnashing teeths' blue rows;
His haggard beard flow'd quivering in the wind;
Revenge and horror in his mien combined;
His clouded front, by withering lightnings sear'd,
The inward anguish of his soul declared.
Cold, gliding horrors fill'd each hero's breast;
Our bristling hair and tottering knees confess'd
Wild dread. The while, with visage ghastly wan,
His black lips trembling, thus the fiend began:
'Ye sons of Lusus, who, with eyes profane,
Have view'd the secrets of my awful reign,
Have pass'd the bounds which jealous nature drew
To veil her secret shrine from mortal view;
Hear from my lips what direful woes attend,
And, bursting soon, shall o'er your race descend:
With every bounding keel that dares my rage,
Eternal war my rocks and storms shall wage.
The next proud fleet that through my drear domain
With daring hand shall hoist the streaming vane,
That gallant navy, by my whirlwinds toss'd,
And raging seas, shall perish on my coast.

Then he who first my secret reign descried,
A naked corpse, wide floating o'er the tide,
Shall drive. Unless my heart's full raptures fail,
O Lusus, oft shalt thou thy children wail!
Each year thy shipwreck'd sons shalt thou deplore,
Each year thy sheeted masts shall strew my shore!'"

The frontispiece to this volume—a copy from an antique original—represents da Gama's ship and the Spectre of the Cape. The table-land of the promontory is seen through the drift of the tempest, towards the east. The ship is broached to, her sails close-furled, with the exception of the foresail, which has broken loose and is flapping wildly in the hurricane. Both the engraving and the description we have quoted from Camoens are strikingly illustrative of those visionary horrors which pervaded the minds of the navigators of the period, and are also characteristic of that peculiar cloud whose sudden envelopment of the Cape is the sure forerunner of a storm. The artist seems to have chosen the moment when the spectre, having uttered his dreadful prophecy, is vanishing into air.

THE MAN OVERBOARD, AND THE ALBATROSS.

CHAPTER XIX.

DA GAMA AND THE NEGROES—THE HOTTENTOTS AND CAFFRES—ADVENTURE WITH AN ALBATROSS—THE RIVER OF GOOD PROMISE—MOZAMBIQUE—TREACHERY OF THE NATIVES—MOMBASSA—MELINDA, AND ITS AMIABLE KING—FESTIVITIES—THE MALABAR COAST—CALICUT—THE ROUTE TO THE INDIES DISCOVERED.

DA GAMA landed some two hundred miles beyond the Cape, and, discharging the victualling-ship of her stores, ordered her to be burned, as the king had directed. He then entered into commercial relations with the natives, and exchanged red night-caps for ivory bracelets. "Then came two hundred blacke men, some lyttle, some great, bringing with them twelve oxen and four sheep, and as our men went upon shore they began to play upon four flutes, according with four sundry voices, the music whereof sounded very well. Which the generall hearing, commanded the trumpets to sound, and so they danced with our men. In this pastime and feasting, and in buying their oxen and sheep, the day passed over." Da Gama had reason before long to suspect treachery, however, and withdrew his men and re-embarked. It was in this place that a man falling overboard, and swimming for a long time before the accident was observed, was followed by an albatross, who hovered in the air just above him, waiting the propitious moment when he could make a quiet meal upon him. The man was subsequently rescued, and the albatross disappointed.

Da Gama now passed the rock de la Cruz, where Diaz had erected his last pillar, and by the aid of a brisk wind escaped the dangers of the currents and shoals. Losing sight of land, he recovered it again on Christmas-day, and in consequence named the spot Tierra da Natal,—a name which it still preserves. From this point his course was nearly north, along the eastern coast of the continent. Farther on he landed two of his malefactors, with instructions to inform themselves of the character and customs of the inhabitants, promising to call for them on his return. On the 11th of January, 1498, he anchored off a portion of the coast occupied by people who seemed peaceably and honestly disposed. They were, in fact, Caffres,—the fleet having passed the territory of the Hottentots. One of the sailors, Martin Alonzo, understood their language,—a circumstance very remarkable, yet perfectly authenticated. As he had not been lower than the Mina, on the western coast, and of course never upon the eastern at all, the inference seems inevitable that some of the negro tribes of Africa extend much beyond the limits usually assigned them in modern geography. After two days spent in the exchange of civilities of the most courteous nature, the ships proceeded on their way,—da Gama naming the country *Tierra da Boa Gete,*—Land of Good People.

He next found, at the mouth of a large river, a tribe of

negroes who seemed to have made greater progress in civilization than their neighbors. They had barks with sails made of palm-leaves,—the only indication of any knowledge of navigation the Portuguese had yet met with upon the African coast. No one—not even Martin Alonzo—understood their language: as far as could be gathered from their pantomime, they had come from a distance where they had seen vessels as large as the San Gabriel, whence da Gama conjectured that the Indies were not far off. He gave to the river the name of *Rio dos bos Sinaes*, or River of Good Promise. The crew suffered greatly here from the effects of scurvy,—many of them dying of the disease and others succumbing under the consequences of amputation. The ships were careened and repaired: thirty-two days were spent in this labor. These incidents are thus graphically described in the Lusiad:

"Far from the land, wide o'er the ocean driven,
Our helms resigning to the care of Heaven,
By hope and fear's keen passions toss'd, we roam;
When our glad eyes behold the surges foam
Against the beacons of a shelter'd bay,
Where sloops and barges cut the watery way.
The river's opening breast some upward plied,
And some came gliding down the sweepy tide.
Quick throbs of transport heaved in every heart,
To view this knowledge of the seaman's art;
For here we hoped our ardent wish to gain,
To hear of India's strand,—nor hoped in vain:
Though Ethiopia's sable hue they bore,
No look of wild surprise the natives wore;
Wide o'er their heads the cotton turban swell'd,
And cloth of blue the decent loins conceal'd.
Their speech, though rude and dissonant of sound,
Their speech a mixture of Arabian own'd.
Alonzo, skill'd in all the copious store
Of fair Arabia's speech and flowery lore,
In joyful converse heard the pleasing tale,
'That o'er these seas full oft the frequent sail,
And lordly vessels, tall as ours, appear'd,
Which to the regions of the morning steer'd:
Whose cheerful crews, resembling ours, display
The kindred face and color of the day.'

Elate with joy, we raise the glad acclaim,
And River of Good Signs the port we name.

"Our keels, that now had steer'd through many a clime,
By shell-fish roughen'd, and incased with slime,
Joyful we clean; while bleating from the field
The fleecy dams the smiling natives yield.
Alas! how vain the bloom of human joy!
How soon the blasts of woe that bloom destroy!
A dread disease its rankling horrors shed,
And death's dire ravage through mine army spread.
Never mine eyes such dreary sight beheld!
Ghastly the mouth and gums enormous swell'd;
And instant, putrid like a dead man's wound,
Poison'd with fetid steam the air around.
Long, long endear'd by fellowship in woe,
O'er the cold dust we give the tears to flow;
And in their hapless lot forebode our own,—
A foreign burial, and a grave unknown."

The fleet joyfully left the River of Good Promise on the 24th of February, and not long after discovered two groups of islands. Near the coast of one of these they were followed by eight canoes, manned by persons of fine stature, less black than the Hottentots, and dressed in cotton cloth of various colors. Upon their heads they wore turbans wrought with silk and gold thread. They were armed with swords and daggers like the Moors, and carried musical instruments which they called sagbuts. They came on board as if they had known the strangers before, and spoke in the Arabic tongue, repelling with disdain the supposition that they were Moors. They said that their island was called Mozambique; that they traded with the Moors of the Indies in spices, pearls, rubies, silver, and linen, and offered to take the ships into their harbor. The bar permitting their passage, they anchored at two crossbow-shots from the town. This was built of wood and thatch,—the mosques alone being constructed of stone. It was occupied principally by Moors, the rest of the island being inhabited by the natives, who were the same as those of the mainland opposite. The Moors traded with the Indies and with the African Sofala in ships without decks and built without the use of nails,—the planks being bound together by cocoa fibres, and the sails being made of palm-leaves. They had compasses and charts.

The Moorish governor of Mozambique and the other Moors supposed the Portuguese to be Turks, on account of the whiteness of their skin. They sent them provisions, in return for which da Gama sent the shah a quantity of red caps, coral, copper vessels, and bells. The shah set no value upon these articles, and inquired disdainfully why the captain had not sent him scarlet cloth. He afterwards went on board the flag-ship, where he was received with hospitality, though not without secret preparations against treachery. The Portuguese learned from him that he governed the island as the deputy of the King of Quiloa; that Prester John lived and ruled a long distance towards the interior of the mainland; that Calicut, whither da Gama was bound, was two thousand miles to the northeast, but that he could not proceed thither without the guidance of pilots familiar with the navigation. He promised to furnish him with two. Discovering subsequently, however, that the strangers were Christians, the shah contrived a plot for their destruction. The vessels escaped, but with only one pilot, whose treachery throughout the voyage was a source of constant annoyance and peril. On departing, da Gama gave the traitors a broadside, which did considerable damage to their village of thatch.

On the 1st of April, da Gama gave to an island which he discovered the name of Açoutado, in commemoration of a sound flagellation which was there administered to the pilot for telling him it formed part of the continent,—upon which he confessed that his purpose in thus misrepresenting the case was to wreck and destroy the ships. On the 7th, they came to the large island of Mombassa, where they found rice, millet, poultry, and fat cattle, and sheep without tails. The orchards were filled with fig, orange, and lemon trees. This island received honey, ivory, and wax from a port upon the mainland. The houses were built of stone and mortar, and the city was defended by a small fort almost even with the water. "They have a king," says the chronicle, "and the inhabitants are Moores, whereof some bee white. They goe gallantly arrayed, especially the women, apparelled in gownes of silke and bedecked with jewells of golde and precious stones. The men were greatly comforted, as having confidence that in this place they might cure such as were then sick,—as in truth were almost all; in number but fewe, as the others were dead."

The King of Mombassa, however, was as great a rogue as the Shah of Mozambique, from whom he had heard, by overland communication, of what had happened in his island. During the night following a grand interchange of civilities and of protestations, da Gama was informed that a sea-monster was devouring the cable. It turned out that a number of Moors were endeavoring to cut it, that the ship might be driven ashore. Anxious to quit this inhospitable coast, the fleet profited by the first wind to continue their course to the north. They captured a zambuco, or pinnace, from which they took seventeen Moors and a considerable quantity of silver and gold. On the same day they arrived off the town of Melinda, situated three degrees only to the south of the equator. The city resembled the cities of Europe, the streets being wide, and the houses being of stone and several stories high. "The generall," we are told, "being come over against this citie, did rejoyce in his heart very much, that he now sawe a citie lyke unto those of Portingale, and rendered most heartie and humble thanks to God for their good and safe arrival." The chief of the captured zambuco offered to procure da Gama a pilot to take the fleet to Calicut, if he would permit him to go ashore. He was landed upon a beach opposite the city. The chief performed his promise, and induced the King of Melinda to treat the strangers with courtesy and respect. Camoens thus describes the festivities upon the alliance:

"With that ennobling worth whose fond employ
Befriends the brave, the monarch owns his joy;
Entreats the leader and his weary band
To taste the dews of sweet repose on land,
And all the riches of his cultured fields
Obedient to the nod of Gama yields.
'What from the blustering winds and lengthening tide
Your ships have suffer'd, here shall be supplied;
Arms and provisions I myself will send,
And, great of skill, a pilot shall attend.'
So spoke the king; and now, with purpled ray,
Beneath the shining wave the god of day
Retiring, left the evening shades to spread,
When to the fleet the joyful herald sped.
To find such friends each breast with rapture glows:
The feast is kindled, and the goblet flows;
The trembling comet's irritating rays
Bound to the skies, and trail a sparkling blaze;
The vaulting bombs awake their sleeping fire,
And, like the Cyclops' bolt, to heaven aspire;
The trump and fife's shrill clarion far around
The glorious music of the night resound.
Nor less their joy Melinda's sons display:
The sulphur bursts in many an ardent ray,
And to the heavens ascends in whizzing gyres,
Whilst Ocean flames with artificial fires."

During the interview which followed, the king remarked that he had never seen any men who pleased him so much as the Portuguese,—a compliment which da Gama acknowledged by setting at liberty the sixteen Moors of the captured pinnace. The king sent the promised pilot on his return; he proved to be as deeply skilled in the art of navigation as any of the pilots of Europe. He was acquainted with the astrolabe, compass, and quadrant. The fleet set sail from Melinda on the 24th of April. As they had now gone far enough towards the north, and as India lay nearly east, they bade farewell to the coast, of which they had hardly lost sight since leaving Lisbon, and struck into the open sea, or rather a wide gulf of the Indian Ocean, seven hundred and fifty leagues across. A few days after, having crossed the line, the crew were delighted to behold again the stars and constellations of the Northern hemisphere. The voyage was rapid and fortunate; for in twenty-three days they arrived off the Malabar coast, and, after a day or two of southing, discovered the lofty hills which overhang the city of Calicut. Da Gama amply rewarded the pilot, released the malefactors from their fetters, and summoned the crew to prayer. The anchor was then thrown, and a feast was spread in honor of the day. The route by sea had been discovered from the Tagus to the Ganges: da Gama had laid out the way from Belem to Golconda.

CALICUT IN THE SIXTEENTH CENTURY.

WRECK OF THE SAN RAFAEL.

CHAPTER XX.

THE MOORS IN HINDOSTAN—CONDITION OF THE COUNTRY UPON THE ARRIVAL OF DA GAMA—HOSTILITY OF THE MOORS—THEY PREJUDICE THE KING OF CALICUT AGAINST THE PORTUGUESE—CONSEQUENT HOSTILITIES—DA GAMA SETS OUT UPON HIS RETURN—WILD CINNAMON—A MOORISH PIRATE DISGUISED AS AN ITALIAN CHRISTIAN—A TEMPESTUOUS VOYAGE—WRECK OF THE SAN RAFAEL—HONORS AND TITLES BESTOWED UPON DA GAMA—AN EXPEDITION FITTED OUT UNDER ALVAREZ CABRAL—ACCIDENTAL DISCOVERY OF BRAZIL—COMETS AND WATER-SPOUTS—LOSS OF FOUR VESSELS—A BAZAAR ESTABLISHED AT CALICUT—ATTACK BY THE MOORS—CABRAL WITHDRAWS TO COCHIN—VISITS CANANOR AND TAKES IN A LOAD OF CINNAMON—IS RECEIVED WITH COLDNESS UPON HIS RETURN—VASCO DA GAMA RECALLED INTO THE SERVICE BY THE KING—HIS ACHIEVEMENTS AT SOFALA, CANANOR, AND CALICUT—HE HANGS FIFTY INDIANS AT THE YARD-ARM—PROTECTS COCHIN AND THREATENS CALICUT—WITHDRAWS TO PRIVATE LIFE.

SOME two hundred years before this time, the Malabar coast of Hindostan was united under one single native prince—named Perimal—whose capital was in the interior. It was at this period that the Arabians discovered India. Perimal embraced the Mohammedan religion, and resolved to make a pilgrimage to Mecca and to finish his days there. He intrusted the government to other hands, and embarked for Arabia from the spot where Calicut now stands. The Arabians were led by this circumstance to regard Calicut with peculiar veneration, and by degrees abandoned the former capital: it was thus that Calicut gradually became the great spice and silk market of the East.

In the time of Vasco da Gama, India Proper, or Hindostan, was divided into several independent kingdoms, such as Moultan, Delhi, Bengal, Orissa, Guzarate or Cambaia, Deccan, Canara, Bisnagar, and Malabar. The divisions of Farther India were Ava, Brama, Pegu, Siam, Cambodia, Cochin-China, and Tonkin. The Portuguese fleet had arrived upon the coast of Malabar, which is the edge of the southwestern promontory of Hindostan. It was here, and upon the western coast generally, that the Portuguese were now enabled to plant establishments and to form treaties of alliance and commerce.

The Moors of Arabia had already, as we have said, a foothold in the country, and were alarmed at seeing Europeans arrive by sea at the scene of a trade of which they had hitherto held the exclusive monopoly. They succeeded in throwing obstacles in the way of the Portuguese admiral, and in poisoning the ear of the Indian zamorin, or king, against him. They even laid a plot for the destruction of the fleet and all on board, that no one might return to Europe to tell of the new route to the Indies. The native monarch was induced by them to testify dissatisfaction with the presents da Gama had brought, and to ask for the golden statue of the Virgin that ornamented the admiral's ship, as a more suitable offering to one of his rank. Da Gama replied that it was not a golden Virgin, but a wooden one gilt; that it had nevertheless preserved him from the perils of the sea, and that he could not part with it. After many proofs of the hostility of the Moors and the treachery of the natives, da Gama obtained from the zamorin the following laconic epistle to his sovereign:—"Vasco da Gama, a gentleman of thy house, has visited my country. His arrival has given me pleasure. My land is full of cinnamon, cloves, pepper, and precious stones. What I desire to obtain in return from yours is gold, silver, coral, and scarlet." With this missive da Gama set sail upon his return early in September. The zamorin sent sixty armed barks to attack him, but a broadside or two and a favorable wind enabled him to make good his escape. Upon a neighboring island some of the crew discovered a large forest of wild cinnamon. Not far from here, da Gama discovered the Angedive, or Five Islands, and in the vicinity had a brush with Indian pirates. An elderly person, differing in appearance from the natives, came on board and represented himself as an Italian Christian. He had come from the Indians of the island of Goa, he said, to beg the admiral to go thither and trade. This well-behaved old gentleman proved to be a sort of Moorish buccaneer, and, upon being put to the torture, confessed that he was a spy, and that he had been sent to reconnoitre the fleet and count their numbers. Da Gama retained him as a trophy to present to King Emmanuel. He finally left the Indian coast on the 15th of October.

When they were fairly out at sea, the pirate-prisoner made a complete confession, and his evident sincerity quite won da Gama's heart. He gave him clothes and a supply of money. The Moor repented of his evil ways and of his pagan faith, and forthwith embraced Christianity. He was baptized by the name of Gaspardo da Gama.

The voyage back to Melinda, across the gulf, was disastrous in every sense. The weather was tempestuous and hot. The scurvy carried off thirty men in the first week, and consternation seized the officers and crew. After four months' navigation, when hardly sixteen men able to work were left on each vessel, they descried the African coast, thirteen leagues above Melinda. Descending to the latter city, they were received with joy by the king, who was anxiously awaiting their return. They took on board an ambassador sent by him to King Emmanuel. The San Rafael was lost upon this coast, and the fleet thus reduced to two vessels. Da Gama discovered the island of Zanzibar, and received offers of service from the sovereign. He doubled the Cape successfully on the 20th of March, and anchored soon after at the Cape Verds. Here, during the night, Nicolao Coelho, the captain of the caravel, slipped away, and made all haste to Portugal, in order to be the first to carry to Europe the intelligence of the grand discovery.

Da Gama now found that he could prosecute the voyage no further in his disabled vessel, the San Gabriel, and chartered a caravel in which to proceed to Lisbon. On the way his brother Paulo died, and was buried at the island of Terceira. Vasco arrived at Belem in September, 1499, two years and two months after his departure. The king, informed of his approach by the previous arrival of Coelho, sent a magnificent cortège to conduct him to court. He overwhelmed him with honors, wealth, and distinctions. He himself took the title of Lord of the Conquest of Ethiopia, Arabia, Persia, and the Indies. Coelho was ennobled, and a pension of one thousand ducats secured to him. Of the one hundred and sixty men who departed upon this voyage, only fifty-five had returned, and all these were munificently rewarded for their share in the brilliant achievements of their commander. The king ordered a series of public festivities, which were preceded by a solemn service of thanksgiving to Heaven for the glory vouchsafed to the Portuguese name and nation.

Emmanuel allowed not a week to pass before he directed the necessary preparations to be made for fitting out another and more powerful fleet, to follow in da Gama's track and attempt to colonize the Indies. He determined that da Gama should enjoy his dignities and renown in peace, however, and intrusted the command to one Pedro Alvarez Cabral, a gentleman of merit and distinction. The fleet numbered thirteen vessels, manned by twelve hundred men, among whom were eight Franciscans to convert the pagans, and some thirty condemned malefactors to undertake communications with the savages. Cabral carried a hat blessed by the Pope and deemed to possess miraculous virtues. Among the captains were Bartholomew Diaz and his brother Diego. The specific object of the expedition was to obtain permission from the Zamorin of Calicut to establish a trading station there, the Portuguese promising in return to furnish him the same articles which the Moors furnished him, and on more advantageous terms.

The squadron set sail on the 9th of March, 1500. It will appear almost incredible that, in order to avoid the calms known to prevail at that season off the coast of Guinea, they proceeded so far to the west that, late in April, they touched at the continent now known as South America; where, however, Yanez Pinzon had been before them. Cabral gave to it the name of Land of the Holy Cross; but this, as well as the name given by Pinzon, was subsequently changed to that of Brazil, from a species of dye-wood which grew in abundance there. The inhabitants were friendly, and exchanged parrots of brilliant plumage for bits of paper and cloth. Cabral put two of his criminals ashore and left them, with instructions to inquire into the history of the country and the customs of its inhabitants. He also sent one of his vessels back to Lisbon with intelligence of the discovery.

The fleet left Brazil on the 2d of May, steering to the south-east, in order to double the Cape. A terrible comet visible day and night, a storm which lasted three weeks, a water-spout reaching to the clouds,—this latter being a phenomenon which the Portuguese had never before seen,—now menaced and harrassed them in quick succession. Four vessels were lost, and among them that of Bartholomew Diaz, with all on board. The rest were severely injured; but Cabral was rejoiced to find that during the storm he had weathered the redoubtable promontory. Encountering some Moorish vessels laden with gold, he seized them, but not until the crews had thrown a portion of the precious metal into the sea. At Mozambique he took a pilot for the island of Quiloa, three hundred miles to the north, whose sovereign was enriched by his gold-trade with the African port of Sofala. Here he attempted to enter into a treaty of commerce; but the prejudices entertained against Christians prevented any concessions on the part of the Moors. At Melinda Cabral landed two criminals and the presents for the king sent out by Emmanuel. Obtaining pilots for the Indian coast, he departed on the 7th of August, and arrived at Calicut on the 13th of September.

From this point dates the first European establishment in the East Indies. Stimulated by considerations of interest, the zamorin, after many delays, granted the admiral an interview, in which the latter stated the ardent desire of his master, the King of Portugal, to furnish the zamorin's subjects with all articles of European production or manufacture, taking in exchange the spices and jewels of the East. A market or bazaar was at once opened, and the cargoes of the ships, being transferred to it, were rapidly converted into cinnamon, diamonds, and drugs.

The Moors now became seriously jealous of the activity, power, and success of their rivals. They resorted to every means to excite the hostility of the zamorin and his subjects against them. They attacked and destroyed the Portuguese market, plundering it of goods to the amount of four thousand ducats. The inconstant zamorin offering neither apology nor restitution, Cabral determined on vengeance. He boarded two large Moorish vessels, killed six hundred men, and salted down three elephants for food. He then bombarded the town: palaces, temples, and storehouses crumbled to dust beneath the thunders of the artillery. The zamorin fled, and Cabral withdrew with his victorious fleet to Cochin, a rich capital one hundred and fifty miles to the south of Calicut, where pepper was abundant and the king was poor. Trimumpara, the monarch, was informed of the summary vengeance wreaked by the fleet upon his brother of Calicut, and at once offered the strangers hospitality and protection. The admiral sent him a silver basin full of saffron and a silver vial filled with rose-water. Trade and barter rapidly loaded the ships with the fragrant commodities of the country. A fleet of twenty-five sail now appeared in the offing, and Trimumpara told Cabral that their object was to attack him, and that they were sent by the zamorin of Calicut. Cabral, having been separated from his most efficient ship, determined not to venture a combat, and made for the north, casting anchor before Cananor, a town a little above Calicut. Here he found a commodious roadstead, an independent prince, and a soil abounding in ginger, cardamom-seeds, tamarinds, and cinnamon. Of the latter article he took four hundred quintals. The king, judging, from the insignificance of this purchase, that he was short of money, offered him a further supply upon credit. Cabral expressed his sense of appreciation of this generosity, but declined the proposition. The fleet now sailed homewards: one of the vessels was lost upon the African coast, and, taking fire, was destroyed with its contents. The six ships remaining of the twelve which had left Brazil, arrived at Lisbon on the 31st of July, 1501. Cabral was received with coldness by the king, partly on account of the loss of ships and men he had met with, and partly on account of his failure at Calicut, to which place he,—the king,—relying on Cabral's success, had sent out, three months previous to his return, a fleet of four vessels under Juan de Nueva. This expedition was singularly happy in its results,—Nueva lading his vessels to great advantage at Cananor, and discovering the island of St. Helena upon his homeward voyage.

It was now evident to the Portuguese that without the employment of force it would be impossible to obtain a permanent foothold in the Indies. After listening to a deliberation as to whether it were not best to abandon the attempt altogether, Emmanuel ordered the equipment of a grand fleet of twenty

DA GAMA'S FLAGSHIP.

vessels, to be placed under the command of Vasco da Gama, who consented to resume active life. It was to be divided into three portions: the first, consisting of ten sail, under da Gama, was to undertake the subjugation of the refractory kings of Malabar; the second, of five sail, under Vincent Sodrez, was to guard the entrance of the Red Sea into the Indian Ocean, and thus prevent the Turks and Moors from trading with the ports of Africa and Hindostan; and the third, of five vessels, under Stefano da Gama, was to be detailed upon any service the admiral might direct. They sailed early in 1502, and formed a treaty of alliance and commerce with the king of Sofala, without difficulty. Da Gama obtained from the king of Quiloa an engagement to pay to the crown of Portugal an annual tribute in gold fresh from the mine. Upon the Indian coast near Cananor, he fell in with an Egyptian vessel of the largest size, laden with costly merchandise and crowded with Moors of high rank on their way to Mecca. He attacked, plundered, and burned her: three hundred men and women perished in the flames, in the sea, or by the sword. Twenty children were saved and conveyed to the ship of da Gama, who made a vow to educate them as Christians, in atonement for the apostasy of one Portuguese who had become a Mohammedan. After this sanguinary lesson, da Gama found no obstacles to the establishment of a trading station at Cananor, where his fleet landed a portion of their cargoes. He then sailed to Calicut, determined to inflict summary vengeance upon the faithless and treacherous zamorin.

Not far from the coast he seized a number of boats in which were fifty Indians. He sent word to the zamorin that, unless satisfaction were given for the late destruction of the Portuguese bazaar before noon, he would attack the city with fire and sword, and would begin with his fifty prisoners. The time having expired, the unfortunate captives were hung simultaneously at the yard-arms of the various vessels. The town was then reduced to ashes. A squadron was left to sweep the Moorish vessels from the seas, and da Gama proceeded down the coast to Cochin, the city of the friendly Trimumpara. Presents and compliments were here exchanged,—the offerings of the King of Portugal being a golden crown, vases of embossed silver, a rich tent, a piece of scarlet satin, and a bit of sandal-wood, while those of his majesty of Cochin were a Moorish turban of silver thread, two gold bracelets set with precious stones, two large pieces of Bengal calico, and a stone said to be a specific against poison, and taken from the head of an animal called bulgodolph,—a fabulous creature, declared by some to be a serpent and by others to be a quadruped.

An apology was now received from the zamorin, and da Gama returned to Calicut with only one vessel. Seeing him thus single-handed, the zamorin sent thirty-three armed canoes against him, and, without the prompt assistance of Sodrez' cruising squadron, da Gama would inevitably have perished. The zamorin now threatened Trimumpara with his vengeance if he continued to harbor the Portuguese and to trade with Christian infidels. Da Gama promised Trimumpara the assistance and alliance of the King of Portugal, and set sail with well-laden vessels. He met the zamorin's fleet of twenty-nine sail, and, having captured two, put the rest to flight with great slaughter. In the two that were taken he found an immense quantity of porcelain and Chinese stuffs, together with an enormous golden idol, with emeralds for eyes, a robe of beaten gold for a vestment, and rubies for buttons. Leaving Sodrez and his fleet to defend Cochin against Calicut and to exterminate the traders from Mecca, da Gama returned with thirteen vessels to Portugal. The king conferred upon him the titles of Admiral of the Indian Ocean and Count de Vidigueira. He again withdrew to privacy, and did not a second time emerge into public life till the year 1524, when the interests of the country under John III. again reclaimed his services in the East.

VESSELS EMPLOYED IN THE SPICE-TRADE: SIXTEENTH CENTURY.

CHAPTER XXI.

SPREAD OF THE PORTUGUESE EAST INDIAN EMPIRE—ALPHONZO D'ALBUQUERQUE—IMMENSE SACRIFICE OF LIFE—ANCIENT ROUTE OF THE SPICE-TRADE WITH EUROPE—COMMERCE BY CARAVANS—REVOLUTION PRODUCED BY OPENING THE NEW ROUTE—FRANCESCO ALMEIDA—DISCOVERY OF CEYLON—TRISTAN D'ACUNHA—THE PORTUGUESE MARS—HIS VIEWS OF EMPIRE—AN ARSENAL ESTABLISHED AT GOA—REDUCTION OF MALACCA—SIAM AND SUMATRA SEND EMBASSIES TO ALBUQUERQUE—THE ISLAND OF ORMUZ—DEATH OF ALBUQUERQUE—EXTENT OF THE PORTUGUESE DOMINION—ORMUZ BECOMES THE GREAT EMPORIUM OF THE EAST—FALL OF THE PORTUGUESE EMPIRE.

HAVING narrated, in the preceding chapters, the incidents which led to the circumnavigation of Africa, and having described the several voyages which introduced the Europeans into the East, by the new route of the Indian Ocean and the Cape of Tempests, we must briefly allude to the sequel,—the spread of European commerce among the islands and seaports of this highly favored region. Alphonzo and Francesco d'Albuquerque, with a fleet of nine vessels, and Edoardo Pacheco, with three vessels, carried terror and revenge to the Malabar coast: forts were built to protect the Portuguese commerce, kings were forced to pay tribute, fleets were swept from the seas; and, as a proverb of the time expressed it, pepper began to cost blood. Again the King of Portugal sent out a formidable squadron,—

thirteen ships of the line, the largest yet constructed, under Lopez Soarez. Sea-battles now took place, in which the proportions of the slain were one thousand infidels to seventy-five Portuguese,—in which a single European vessel contended successfully with myriads of the native barks. The sacrifice of life was truly awful; but gradually the whole eastern coast of Africa, and, opposite to it, the whole western coast of India, fell under Portuguese sway.

The entire commerce of this quarter of the world was of course revolutionized by these discoveries and conquests. Before this period the productions of the East had been carried to Europe in the following manner. The city of Malacca, in the peninsula of the same name, was the central market to which came the camphor of Borneo, the cloves of the Moluccas, the nutmegs of Banda, the pepper of Sumatra, the gums, drugs, and perfumes of China, Japan, and Siam. These products were taken by water, either in the clumsy boats of the natives or the more solid vessels of the Moors, to the ports of the Red Sea, were landed at Tor or at Suez, whence they were transported by caravans to Cairo, and thence by the Nile to Alexandria, where they were placed on board of vessels bound to all the ports of Europe. Those intended for Armenia, Trebizonde, Aleppo, Damascus, were taken by the Persian Gulf to Bassorah, and thence distributed by caravans. The Venetians and Genoese took their portion at Beyrout, in Syria. The East Indians preferred the manufactures of Europe to gold and silver, and consequently the trade was generally in the form of barter and exchange. In addition to the products of Farther India which we have mentioned must be added those of India Proper,—the fabrics of Bengal, the pearls of Orissa, the diamonds of Golconda, the cinnamon of Ceylon, the pepper of Malabar.

Thus, not only thousands of laborers, sailors, conductors of caravans, saw themselves suddenly deprived of their livelihood by this diversion of the traffic into the hands of the Portuguese, but rich cities lost their revenues and princes lost their tribute. While the Venetians resolved to appeal to arms, the Sultan of Egypt addressed a protestation to Rome. But the King of Portugal tranquillized the Pope by declaring his intention of extending the jurisdiction of the apostolic faith, and he prepared to resist violence by sending out, in 1507, Don Francesco Almeida, with twenty-two ships and fifteen hundred regular soldiers: he bestowed upon the new commander the title of Viceroy of the Indies. Almeida deposed the King of Quiloa, and crowned another of his own appointment; he built a fort in twenty days, garrisoned it with one hundred and fifty men, and left a brigantine and a caravel to scour and protect the coast. He bombarded Mombassa, killed fifteen hundred men and lost five. He erected forts and established trading stations at Onor, Cananor, Surat and Calicut, upon the Malabar coast. To the important point of Sofala, upon the African coast, Emmanuel sent a distinct expedition of six ships, under Pedro da Nayha and Juan da Quiros, who compelled the king to admit their nation to a share in the famous gold mines which constituted his kingdom and his wealth. In 1508, Lorenzo, the son of Almeida, while chasing the flying Moors with six men-of-war, discovered the island of Ceylon, to the south of Hindostan. Here he found the Moors and natives loading vessels with elephants and cinnamon.

Again King Emmanuel, drawing upon resources which seemed almost inexhaustible, sent out thirteen vessels, with thirteen hundred men, under Tristan d'Acunha. This fleet was driven to the coast of Brazil, and upon the way thence to the Cape of Good Hope the commander discovered the islands which now bear his name. He burned and pillaged the town of Oja, near Melinda; he reduced a neighboring shah to the payment of an annual tribute of six hundred golden ducats. His soldiers would not give the captured women of Brava time to remove their bracelets and ear-rings, but in their ruthless haste cut off their arms and ears.

It was now evident to the King of Portugal that his rule in the East could not be consolidated and extended by the same means which had obtained him his first foothold upon the coast,—chance, intrepidity, and unscrupulous violence. What was required was a carefully conceived system of government, and a man capable of administering it. Emmanuel's choice fell upon Alphonzo d'Albuquerque, whose services in the East had already been meritorious, and to whom, in 1509, he gave the title and power of viceroy. Albuquerque, whose courage obtained for him the name of the Portuguese Mars, ranks, by his talents, his severe virtues, and his disinterested zeal, among the greatest men whom the world has produced. He at once formed the plan of founding an empire which should extend from the Persian Gulf to the peninsula of Malacca; and, determining to abandon Calicut, which had thus far been looked upon as the best point for an arsenal, he selected the island of Goa, a little to the north, captured it, and made its admirable harbor a Portuguese roadstead and its town a Portuguese capital. He built bazaars and citadels along the coast from north to south, and then turned his eyes towards Malacca,—a magnificent country, ruled by a despot and inhabited by slaves. As we have said, its principal seaport was the central resort of the ships of China, Japan, Bengal, the Philippines and the Moluccas, Coromandel, Persia, Arabia, and Malabar.

The Portuguese had first visited Malacca two years previously, Emmanuel having sent one Siguiera to make a treaty with the king. He had been perfidiously treated, and Albuquerque now, in 1511, appeared before the city to call the monarch to account. A long and obstinate battle resulted in the defeat of the natives and the unconditional surrender of the peninsula. The Kings of Siam, Sumatra, and Pegu sent ambassadors to Albuquerque, asking the honor of his friendship. He built a citadel and returned to Cochin. But, as he left one spot to repair to another, revolt was sure to follow; and, as the Venetians now joined the Moors to repel the Portuguese, he saw that his dominion could not be complete till he controlled the navigation of the Red Sea and the Persian Gulf. The city of Aden, in Arabia, was the key to the Red Sea, commanding, as it did, the Straits of Babelmandel; and the island of Ormuz was the key to the Persian Gulf. He failed to take Aden, but he succeeded easily with Ormuz, whose king acknowledged himself the vassal of Emmanuel. Albuquerque then formed a gigantic plan in reference to the Red Sea. Unable to command it by the capture of Aden, he determined to ruin Suez, at the other extremity of the sea, by forming an alliance with the King of Ethiopia, and inducing that monarch to dig a new course for the Nile and make it empty into the Red Sea instead of into the Mediterranean, thus rendering Egypt uninhabitable and Suez desert. The invasion of Egypt by the Turks, however, prevented the accomplishment of this undertaking. Thus the people and kings of the East everywhere gave way before the grand plans and deeds of Albuquerque, whom they both feared for his energy and loved for his justice. When, in 1515, he died at Goa, disgraced by his king and worn out by a thankless service, the heathen monarchs wept over his grave, and for many years went in pilgrimage to his tomb, asking his protection against the cruelty or injustice of his successors.

The Portuguese, in little more than fifty years from the first expedition of Vasco da Gama, had established an empire in these seas of truly wonderful extent and power. They held exclusive possession of the Malabar and Coromandel coasts of India Proper, were masters of the Bay of Bengal, ruled the peninsula of Malacca, and held tributary the islands of Ceylon, Sumatra, Java, and the Moluccas. To the westward, towards Africa, their authority extended as far as the Persian boundary, and over all the islands of the Persian Gulf. In Arabia, even, they had tributaries and allies, and no Arabian prince dared confess himself their enemy. They exercised an influence in the Red Sea: and upon the eastern coast of Africa, they were the masters of Quiloa, Sofala, Mozambique, and Melinda.

As Albuquerque had foreseen, Ormuz—from its fortunate situation, as an emporium of trade, at the mouth of the Persian Gulf—became the most important of the Portuguese conquests. The island was by nature little more than a barren rock, and was entirely destitute of water. Its wealth and splendor, however, during the period of its commercial supremacy, gave the world an example of the power of trade which had never yet been witnessed. The trading season lasted from January to March and from August to November: during these months, the houses fronting on the streets were opened like shops, and decorated with piles of porcelain and Indian curiosities, and perfumed with fragrant dwarf shrubs set in gilded vases. Camels laden with skins of water stood at the corners of the streets. The richest wines of Persia and the most costly odors of Asia were offered in profusion to those who visited the city to trade. Thick awnings stretched from roof to roof across the promenades, excluding the rays of the sun. The luxury and magnificence of the place seemed to flow rather from the lavish extravagance of an idle prince than from the legitimate pomp of a stirring and active commercial population.

In 1580, Portugal was conquered and annexed to Spain, and the Portuguese Empire in the East at once declined, and the Dutch Empire sprang up upon its ruins. Ormuz was plundered by the Persians and English united in 1662: the very stones of which its edifices were built were carried away as ballast, and it speedily sank back into its primitive state—a barren and desolate rock. Hardly a vestige of the proud city now remains to vindicate history in its record that here once stood one of the most famous emporiums of commerce and most frequented resorts of man.

PONCE DE LEON AND THE FOUNTAIN OF YOUTH.

CHAPTER XXII.

PONCE DE LEON—THE FOUNTAIN OF YOUTH—DISCOVERY OF FLORIDA—THE MARTYRS AND THE TORTUGAS—THE BAHAMA CHANNEL—VASCO NUÑEZ DE BALBOA—HE GOES TO SEA IN A BARREL—MARRIES A LADY OF THE ISTHMUS—HIS SEARCH FOR GOLD—HEARS OF A MIGHTY OCEAN—UNDERTAKES TO REACH IT—PREPARATIONS FOR THE EXPEDITION—LEONCICO THE BLOODHOUND—BATTLE WITH A CACIQUE—ASCENT OF THE MOUNTAINS—BALBOA MOUNTS TO THE SUMMIT ALONE—THE FIRST SIGHT OF THE PACIFIC—CEREMONIES OF TAKING POSSESSION—BALBOA UP TO HIS KNEES IN THE OCEAN—EVERY ONE TASTES THE WATER—A VOYAGE UPON THE PACIFIC, AND A NARROW ESCAPE—IGNOMINIOUS FATE OF BALBOA—JUAN DIAZ DE SOLIS—DISCOVERS THE RIO DE LA PLATA—HIS HORRIBLE DEATH BY CANNIBALS.

WE now return, in due chronological progression, to the discoveries of the Spaniards in the West. We have not space to describe, or even to mention, all the successive expeditions made to various points of the great American Continent: we select, therefore, only the more important and interesting episodes among the Spanish maritime achievements. Three heroes will occupy our attention from 1510 to 1514,—Ponce de Leon, Juan Diaz de Solis, and Vasco Nuñez de Balboa.

Juan Ponce, surnamed de Leon from his native province, was one of the Spanish captains who emigrated to Hispaniola shortly after its discovery by Columbus. After an active and prosperous career, he found himself, in 1510, by the withdrawal of the king's favor, without place or occupation. He was, however, rich, and resolved to attempt to regain his credit by means of discoveries. He was avaricious, too, and would willingly have augmented his already large possessions. He had heard from the Indians of Cuba of the existence, to the north of Hispaniola, of an island named Bimini, where, they asserted, was a spring whose waters had the virtue of restoring youth to the aged and vigor to the decrepit. Ponce thought that if he could discover and seize this fountain it would be an inexhaustible source of revenue to him, as he could levy a tax upon all who derived benefit from its influence. He determined to set out in search of it, and fitted out two stout ships at his own expense. With these he left St. Genevieve, in Porto Rico, on the 1st of March, 1512, and steered boldly through the intricate group of the Lucayos. Wherever he stopped, he drank of all the running streams and standing pools, whether their waters were fresh or stagnant, that he might not miss the famous spring. He inquired of all the natives he met where he could find the wondrous Fountain of Youth.

At last he discovered a land till then unknown to Europeans. Early in April, and in Easter week, he touched what he supposed was an island, but what in reality was a portion of the continent. As the landscape was covered with flowers, he named the spot "Florida." He had several severe fights with the Indians, one of whom he made prisoner, that he might learn Spanish and give him information concerning the country. He now sailed to the south and doubled Cape Florida on the 8th of May, which, on account of the currents, he named Cabo de las Corrientes. On the 15th, he sailed along a line of small islands as far as two white ones, and called the whole group Los Martyros, or The Martyrs, from the high rocks at a distance which had the appearance of men undergoing crucifixion. The name was singularly applicable, for the large number of seamen who have since been wrecked upon these islands has made them in reality a place of martyrdom. He discovered another group to the southwest, which he called the Tortugas, as his men took one hundred and seventy tortoises upon one of them in a short time, and might have had more if they would. Ponce de Leon continued ranging about here till September, when he returned to Porto Rico, sending one of his ships to Bimini—the smallest of the Bahamas—to see if he could discover the spring. The vessel went and returned, the captain, Perez de Ortubia, reporting that the island was pleasantly diversified with hills, groves, and rivers, but that none of the latter possessed any unusual charm.

One great advantage which resulted from the voyage of Ponce de Leon was the discovery, by his second captain, Ortubia, of the passage now known as the Bahama Channel, by which ships bound from Havana to Spain pass out into the Atlantic Ocean. This new passage became the universal track even during Ponce de Leon's life. Upon his return to court, he was well rewarded for his discoveries both by land and sea, but his gathering years caused him often to regret that he had missed the Fountain of Youth.

We have now to relate the manner in which the Pacific Ocean, which had rolled for centuries in its accustomed bed, unknown to Europeans, was first seen by Continental eyes. The islands discovered by Columbus were still under the exclusive dominion of the Spaniards; Hispaniola was the central point of their operations of discovery and conquest. Settled here, upon a farm, was a man, still in the prime of life, named Vasco Nuñez de Balboa. He was a native of Xeres, in Spain, and had eagerly enlisted in the late voyages of adventure. He was known to be a mere soldier of fortune, and of loose, prodigal habits, and is described as an "egregius digladiator," or adroit swordsman. His farm had involved him in debt; and, to escape his embarrassments and elude his creditors, he caused himself, in 1511, to be nailed up in a cask, to be labelled "victuals for the voyage," and to be conveyed on board a ship starting upon an expedition to the mainland. When the vessel was out of sight of the shore, he emerged from the cask, and appeared before the surprised captain, Hernandez de Enciso. Being tall and muscular, evidently inured to hardships and of intrepid disposition, he found favor with the captain, especially when he told him that a venerable priest had asserted "that God reserved him for great things."

In the course of two years, Balboa had acquired authority over a tract of the Isthmus of Darien, and had married the young and beautiful daughter of the Cacique of Coyba. After a victory obtained over one of the neighboring monarchs, from whom four thousand ounces of gold and a quantity of golden utensils had been extorted, Balboa ordered one-fifth to be set apart for himself and the rest to be shared among his followers. While the Spaniards were dividing it by weight, a dispute arose respecting the fairness of the award, when the Indian who had given the gold spoke to the disputants as follows:

"Why should you quarrel for such a trifle? If gold is to you so precious that you abandon your homes for it and invade the peaceful lands of others, I will tell you of a region where you may gratify your wishes to the utmost. Beyond those lofty mountains lies a mighty sea, which from their summits may be easily discerned. It is navigated by people who have vessels almost as large as yours, and, like them, furnished with sails and oars. All the streams which flow from these mountains into the sea abound in gold: the kings who reign upon its borders eat and drink out of golden vessels. Gold, in fact, is as common there as iron among you Spaniards."

Fired by this discourse, Balboa inquired whether it would be difficult to penetrate to this sea and its golden shores. "The task," the prince replied, "is arduous and dangerous. Powerful caciques will oppose you with their warriors; fierce cannibals will attack you, and devour those whom they kill. To

BALBOA AND THE INDIAN.

accomplish your enterprise, you will require at least a thousand men, armed like those you have with you now." To prove his sincerity, the prince offered to accompany Balboa upon the expedition, at the head of his warriors. This was the first intimation received by a European of the splendid expanse of water which was so soon to receive the name of Pacific. It exerted an immediate and radical change upon the character and conduct of Balboa. The soldier of fortune became animated by an honorable and controlling ambition; the restless and reckless desperado saw before him a glorious path to immortality. He baptized the prince who had given him information so priceless, and proceeded to Darien to obtain the means of accomplishing his scheme.

For a long time he was baffled. A terrific tempest laid waste the fields and devastated the harvests. He sent to Hispaniola for men and provisions; but the emissary was wrecked upon the coast of Jamaica. He wrote to Don Diego Columbus, who governed at San Domingo, informing him of the existence of a new ocean, bordered with shores of gold, and asking for a thousand men with whom to prosecute its discovery. He forwarded the sum of fifteen thousand crowns in gold, to be transmitted to the king as his royal fifths. Many of his followers, too, sent sums intended for their creditors in Spain.

While waiting for a reply, Balboa learned indirectly that he had fallen into disfavor with the king. One brilliant achievement might restore him to consideration and forever fix him in the good graces of the monarch. He chose one hundred and ninety of the most vigorous and resolute of his men, and took with him a number of bloodhounds. His own peculiar body-guard was a dog named Leoncico,—one of the numerous progeny sired by the famous warrior-dog of Juan Ponce de Leon. Leoncico was covered with scars received in his innumerable fights with the natives. Balboa often lent him to others, and received for his services the same share of booty an able-bodied man would have claimed. Leoncico had earned for his master in this way several thousands of dollars.

On the 1st of September, 1513, Balboa embarked with his followers in a light brigantine and nine canoes, and ascended a stream which was navigable as far as Coyba. Here he received accessions of men, and, having sent back those who were ill or disabled, prepared to penetrate the wilderness on foot. In a battle with a cacique named Quaragua, he slew six hundred of the natives. Some were transfixed with lances, others hewn down with swords, and others torn to pieces by the bloodhounds. He advanced hardly seven miles a day, but at last reached a village lying at the foot of the mountain that commanded the long wished for prospect. Only sixty-seven men out of two hundred remained to make this last grand effort. Balboa ordered them to retire early to repose, that they might be ready at the cool hour of dawn. They set forth at daybreak on the morning of the 26th of September. In a short time they emerged from the forests, and arrived at the upper regions of the mountain, leaving the bald summit still to be ascended. Balboa ordered them to halt, that he might himself be alone to enjoy the scene and the first to discover the ocean. He reached the peak, and there the magnificent sight burst upon his view. The water was still at the distance of two days' journey; but there it lay, beyond the intervening space, grand, boundless, and serene. He fell upon his knees, and returned thanks

BALBOA DISCOVERING THE PACIFIC OCEAN.

to God. He summoned his followers to ascend, and thus addressed them:—"Behold, my friends," he said, "the glorious sight which we have so ardently longed for. Let us pray to God that he will aid and guide us to conquer the sea and land which we have discovered, and in which no Christian has ever entered to preach the holy doctrine of the Evangelists. By the favor of Christ you will thus become the richest Spaniards that have ever come to the Indies." The priest attached to the expedition chanted that impressive anthem, the Te Deum; and the Spaniards, in whom religious fervor and the thirst for pillage seemed to be mingled in equal proportions, joined in the chorus with heart and voice.

Balboa now called upon all present to witness that he took possession of the sea, its islands and surrounding lands, in the name of the sovereigns of Castile; and the notary of the expedition made a record to that effect, to which all present, to the number of sixty-seven men, signed their names. Balboa then caused a tall tree to be cut down and fashioned into the form of a cross: this he erected on the spot whence he had first beheld the ocean. A mound of stone was likewise piled up as a monument, and the names of Ferdinand and Juana were carved upon the neighboring trees.

A scouting party under Alonzo Martin, sent by Balboa to discover the best route to the sea, came after two days' journey to a beach, upon which were two canoes, stranded as it were, and apparently out of the reach of water. But the tide soon came rushing in, and floated them; upon which Alonzo Martin stepped into one of them, and was thus the first European who embarked upon the ocean which Balboa had discovered and which Magellan was to name. Balboa soon arrived upon the coast: the tide had ebbed, and the water was nearly two miles distant. But it soon returned, invading the place where the Spaniards were seated. Upon this Balboa arose, and, taking a banner representing the Virgin and Child and bearing the arms of Castile and Leon, marched knee-deep into the water, and, waving the flag, pronounced the following act of taking possession:

"Long live the high and mighty monarchs Don Ferdinand and Donna Juana, sovereigns of Castile, Leon, and Aragon, in whose name I take real and actual and corporeal possession of these seas, and lands, and coasts, and ports, and islands of the South, and all thereunto annexed; and of the kingdoms and provinces which do or may appertain to them in whatever manner or by whatever right or title, ancient or modern, in times past, present, or to come, without any contradiction; and if other

BALBOA TAKING POSSESSION OF THE PACIFIC OCEAN.

prince or captain, Christian or infidel, or if any law, condition, or sect whatsoever, shall pretend any right to these lands and seas, I am ready to maintain and defend them in the name of the Castilian sovereigns, whose is the empire and dominion over these Indies, islands, and terra firma, Northern and Southern, with all their seas, both at the Arctic and Antartic poles, on either side of the equinoctial line, whether within or without the tropics of Cancer and Capricorn, both now and in all time, as long as the world endure, and until the final day of judgment of all mankind."

As may be supposed, no one appeared to dispute these formidable pretensions, and no champion entered the lists in behalf of the original owners of the seas, islands, and surrounding lands in question; so that Balboa called upon his companions to bear witness that he had duly and uninterruptedly taken possession. The notary drew up the necessary legal document, which was signed by all present. Then they all tasted the water, which, from its saltness, they felt assured was the ocean. Balboa carved a cross on a tree whose roots were below high-water mark, and, lopping off a branch with his sword, bore it away as a trophy.

Balboa now wished to perform a voyage upon the bosom of the new-found ocean. In spite of the advice of friendly Indians, who represented the season as stormy, he embarked with sixty of his men in nine canoes. A tempest compelled them to seek refuge upon an island. In the night the tide completely submerged it, and rose to the girdles of the Spaniards. Their canoes were broken to pieces, and at low tide they managed with great difficulty to effect their escape to the mainland. After numerous forays against the caciques ruling the neighboring tribes, Balboa arrived at the Darien River, on the 19th of January, 1514, after having accomplished one of the most remarkable feats on record, and after an expedition which must ever be memorable among deeds of intrepidity and adventure.

The king created him Adelantado of the South Sea, and Governor of Panama and Coyba, but subject to Pedrarias, the Governor of Darien. The latter regarded him as his rival, and, by a successful series of treacherous arts, brought against him a well-contrived charge of treason to the king. He was reluctantly found guilty by the alcalde, and by Pedrarias condemned to be beheaded, as a traitor and usurper of the territories of the crown. The execution took place in the public square of a small town near Darien, and was witnessed by Pedrarias from between the reeds of the wall of a house some twelve paces from the scaffold. Balboa and four of his officers were beheaded in quick succession during the brief twilight of a tropical evening. Pedrarias confiscated Balboa's property, and ordered his head to be impaled upon a pole and exposed upon the public square till decomposition should ensue.

Thus perished, at the age of forty-two years,—the victim of the meanest envy and the most odious treachery,—a man who will be ever remembered as one of the most illustrious of the early discoverers. Events transformed him from a rash and turbulent adventurer into a discreet and patriotic captain; and, from the moment when he felt that he had drawn the attention of the world upon him, his conduct was that of a man born and predestined to greatness. He fell in the zenith of his glory, a worthy cotemporary of Columbus, da Gama, and Magellan.

Juan Diaz de Solis, who, with Yanez Pinzon, Amerigo Vespucci, and Juan de la Cosa, the pilot of Columbus, was a member of the Spanish council appointed to deliberate upon discoveries yet to be made, sailed to South America in 1514, and, doubling Capes St. Roque, St. Augustin, and Frio, entered the bay upon which now stands the city of Rio Janeiro, and was probably the first European to set foot upon the coast thus far to the south. He supposed the bay to be the mouth of a passage through to the South Sea so lately discovered by Balboa. He proceeded to the south, ascertaining the position of every headland and indentation with all the precision the instruments and science of the time would permit. At last he found a great opening of the sea towards the west: he took possession of the northern coast for the King of Spain, and named the gulf Fresh-Water Sea. Subsequently, finding that it was a river, and that silver-mines existed there, he named the stream Rio de la Plata. The Indians called it Paraguaza. He found the country fertile and attractive, and an abundance of the wood which had given to the whole region the name of Brazil. He went on shore with a small party, but soon fell into an ambuscade laid for them by

FATE OF DE SOLIS AND HIS COMPANIONS.

the natives. Solis and five of his companions were taken, killed, roasted, and devoured by the horrible cannibals who inhabited the country. The Spaniards who remained on board the ships witnessed the shocking catastrophe, which so appalled and horrified them that they fled in dismay and sailed hastily back to Spain.

FERDINAND MAGELLAN.

CHAPTER XXIII.

REMARKABLE FORESIGHT OF THE COURT OF ROME—A PAPAL BULL—FERDINAND MAGELLAN—HE OFFERS HIS SERVICES TO SPAIN—HIS PLANS—HIS FLEET—PIGAFETTA THE HISTORIAN—AN INAUSPICIOUS START—TENERIFFE AND ITS LEGENDS—ST. ELMO'S FIRE—THE CREW MAKE FAMOUS BARGAINS WITH THE CANNIBALS—HEAVY PRICE PAID FOR THE KING OF SPADES—PATAGONIAN GIANTS—PIGAFETTA'S EXAGGERATIONS—THE HEALING ART IN PATAGONIA—THE TRAGEDY OF PORT JULIAN—DISCOVERY OF A STRAIT—THE OPEN SEA—CAPE DESEADO—THE OCEAN NAMED PACIFIC—RAVAGES OF THE SCURVY—A PATAGONIAN PAUL—THE NEEDLE BECOMES LETHARGIC—DISCOVERY OF THE LADRONES—THE FIRST COCOANUT—A CATHOLIC CEREMONY UPON A PAGAN ISLAND.

THE Pope of Rome, whose authority was at this period supreme among the princes who were in communion with the Church, now thought proper to anticipate a possible collision between Spain and Portugal, the two monopolists of commerce and discovery. He declared by a bull, or papal decree, that all new countries which should be thereafter discovered to the east of the Azores were to belong to the crown of Portugal, while all that were discovered to the west should be the property of Spain. Thus, a potentate who claimed to be infallible issued a decree based upon the pontifical conviction that the world was flat, even after the very solid arguments to the contrary of Columbus and da Gama. His Holiness, in his wisdom, imagined that one nation might sail to the right, the other to the left, and go on forever: he did not foresee, what was now almost palpable to every eye but that of Roman infallibility, that the Spaniards and the Portuguese would at last meet at the antipodes. There, in time, they did meet, and the very pretty dispute which arose in consequence we shall narrate in the sequel. But a more immediate effect of the decree was this:—a Spaniard, if he felt himself neglected or maltreated by his own sovereign, would offer his services to the Portuguese king, confident of employment at his hands, as the latter would thus weaken Spain and profit by discoveries made by her subjects. A Portuguese, if similarly aggrieved, would in the same way desert to the Spanish king and accept service from the Spanish crown.

It so happened that one Fernâo Magalhaens, known in English as Ferdinand Magellan, a Portuguese by birth, and who had served with distinction in the East Indies under Albuquerque, addressed himself to the court of Lisbon for the recompense which was his due. His application was treated with disdain. He forthwith withdrew to Spain with a learned man who had been similarly neglected, one Ruy Falero, an astronomer, whom the Portuguese regarded as a conjurer and charlatan. Magellan made overtures for new discoveries to Cardinal Ximenes, then Prime Minister of Spain, and in reality its ruler during the absence of Charles V. The Portuguese ambassador sought by every means in his power to baffle his designs, and demanded of the court that he and Falero should be given up as deserters. He even offered Magellan a reward if he would desist from his purpose, or, at least, execute it in the service of Portugal. But the cardinal listened with favor to the plan presented by Magellan, which was briefly as follows:

Columbus, who started upon his voyage to the west in order to reach the East Indies by a western route, had failed in his object, discovering instead an intermediate continent. Magellan now proposed to seek the Portuguese Moluccas, or Spice Islands, by sailing, if possible, from the Atlantic Ocean into the South Sea, discovered by Balboa five years before. His idea was to attempt to find a passage through the mainland of South America by the Rio de la Plata, or some other channel opening upon its eastern coast. Should this succeed, Spain would possess the East Indies as well as the West, since, if the Moluccas were discovered by way of the west, even though situated to the east, they would fall expressly within the allotment made by the late papal bull. Magellan thought the world was round, in defiance of the pontifical declaration that it was flat.

In accordance with this proposal, the Spanish crown agreed to equip a fleet of five vessels and to give the command of it to Magellan. It was furthermore agreed that he should have a twentieth part of the clear profit of the expedition, and that the government of any islands he might discover should be vested in him and his heirs forever, with the title of Adelantado. The five vessels were accordingly fitted out at Seville, Magellan's flag-ship being named the Trinidada. They were manned by two hundred and thirty-seven men, thirty of whom were able-bodied Portuguese seamen, upon whom Magellan principally relied. The astronomer Falero declined accompanying him, having, in his astrological calculations, foreseen that the voyage would be fatal to him. A certain San Martino, of Seville, who went in his stead, was, as will be seen, assassinated in his place at the island of Zubu. An Italian gentleman, named Pigafetta, was permitted by the cardinal to form part of Magellan's suite. He afterwards became the historian of the voyage.

The fleet set sail from Seville on the 10th of August, 1519, its departure being announced by a discharge of artillery. Seville is nearly one hundred miles from the sea, by the river Guadalquivir, the seaport of which is San Lucar, whence they finally departed on the 20th of September. It would be difficult to imagine circumstances more inauspicious than those under which Magellan left the shores of Europe. The course he was to follow was unexplored: so rash was the attempt considered, that he dared not communicate to his men the real object of the expedition. The season was already advanced, and he would in all probability arrive in high southern latitudes at the coldest period of the year. To the perils naturally incident to such a voyage was to be added the unfortunate fact that the commanders of the other four ships were Spaniards, and consequently inimical to Magellan, who, though in the service of Spain, was of Portuguese birth.

In six days the squadron reached Teneriffe; of this island Pigafetta relates several curious legends current at that time. It never rained there, he says, and there was neither river nor spring in the island. The leaves of a tree, however, which was constantly surrounded by a thick mist, distilled excellent water, which was collected in a pit at its foot, whither the inhabitants and wild beasts repaired to quench their thirst. Early in October the fleet passed between Cape Verd and its islands, and coasted along the shores of Guinea and Sierra Leone. Here they met with contrary winds, sharks, and dead calms. One dark night, during a violent tempest, the St. Elmo fire blazed for two hours upon their topmast. This, which is now known to be an effect of electricity, which the ancient idolaters believed to be Castor and Pollux, which Catholics in Magellan's time regarded as a saint, and which English sailors call Davy Jones, was a great consolation to the Portuguese during the storm.

At the moment when it disappeared it diffused a light so resplendent that Pigafetta was almost blinded and gave himself up for lost; but, he adds, "the wind ceased momentaneously."

Passing the equinoctial line and losing sight of the polar star, Magellan steered south-southwest, and in the middle of December struck the coast of Brazil. His men made excellent bargains with the natives. For a small comb they obtained two geese; for a piece of glass, as much fish as would feed ten men; for a ribbon, a basket of potatoes,—a root then so little known that Pigafetta describes it as resembling a turnip in appearance and a roasted chestnut in taste. A pack of playing-cards was a fortune, for a sailor bought six fat chickens with the king of spades. The fleet remained thirteen days at anchor, and then pursued its way to the southward along the territory of the cannibals who had lately devoured de Solis. Stopping at an island in the mouth of a river sixty miles wide, they caught, in one hour, penguins sufficient for the whole five ships. Magellan anchored for the winter in a harbor found in south latitude 49° and called by him Port Julian. Two months elapsed before the country was discovered to be inhabited. At last a man of gigantic figure presented himself upon the shore, capering in the sands in a state of utter nudity, and violently casting dust upon his head. A sailor was sent ashore to make similar gestures, and the giant was thus easily led to the spot where Magellan had landed. The latter gave him cooked food to eat and presented him, incidentally, with a large steel mirror. The savage now saw his likeness for the first time, and started back in such fright that he knocked over four men. He and several of his companions, both men and women, subsequently went on board the ships, and constantly indicated by their gestures that they supposed the strangers to have descended from heaven. One of the savages became quite a favorite: he was taught to pronounce the name of Jesus and to repeat the Lord's prayer, and was even baptized by the name of John by the chaplain.

This profession of Christianity did the poor pagan no good, for he soon disappeared,—murdered, doubtless, by his people, in consequence of his attachment to the foreigners.

The whole description given by Pigafetta of these savages, whom Magellan called Patagonians,—from words indicating the resemblance of their feet, when shod with the skin of the lama, to the feet of a bear,—is now known to be much exaggerated. It is certain that they were by no means so gigantic as he represented them. He adds that they drank half a pail of water at a draught, fed upon raw meat, and swallowed mice alive; that when they were sick and needed bleeding they gave a good chop with some edged tool to the part affected; when they wished to vomit they thrust an arrow half a yard down their throat. The headache was cured by a gash in the forehead.

A fearful tragedy was enacted in Port Julian. The four Spanish captains conspired to murder Magellan. The plot was discovered and the ringleaders were brought to trial. Two were hung, another was stabbed to the heart, while a number of their accomplices were left among the Patagonians. Magellan quitted Port Julian in August, 1520, having planted a cross on a neighboring mountain and taken solemn possession of the country in the name of the King of Spain. On the 14th of September, he discovered a fresh-water river, which he named Santa Cruz, in honor of the anniversary of the exaltation of the cross. Here the crew, by Magellan's order, made confession and received the holy communion.

On the 21st of October, Magellan made the great discovery which has immortalized his name. He reached a strait communicating between the Atlantic Ocean and the South Sea: consulting the calendar for a name, he called it in honor of the day, the Strait of the Eleven Thousand Virgins. It is now Magellan's Strait. It was enclosed between lofty mountains covered with snow; the water was so deep that it afforded no anchorage. The crew were so fully persuaded that it possessed no western outlet, that, had it not been for Magellan's confidence and persistence, they would never have ventured to explore it. The strait was found to vary in breadth from one mile to ten, and to be four hundred and forty miles in length. During the first night spent in the strait, the Santo Antonio, piloted by one

CAPE VIRGIN—THE EAST ENTRANCE OF MAGELLAN'S STRAIT.

Emmanuel Gomez, who hated Magellan, found her way back into the Atlantic, and returned at once to Spain. The pilot's object was principally to be the first to tell the news of the discovery, and to carry to Europe a specimen of a Patagonian giant, one of whom he had on board of his vessel. On his way he stopped at Port Julian and took up two of the conspirators who had been abandoned there. The Patagonian was unable to bear the change of climate, and died of the heat on crossing the line.

One of Magellan's remaining four vessels was sent on in advance of the others to reconnoitre a cape which seemed to terminate the channel. The vessel returned, announcing that the strait indeed terminated at this cape and that beyond lay the open sea. "We wept for joy," says Pigafetta: "the cape was denominated Cabo Deseado,—Wished-for Cape,—for in good truth we had long wished to see it." The sight gave Magellan the most unbounded joy, for he was now able practically to demonstrate the truth of the theory he had advanced,—that it was possible to sail to the East Indies by way of the west. He now named the famous strait the Strait of the Patagonians, but a sense of justice induced the Europeans to change its name and to call it the Strait of Magellan. At every mile or two he found a safe harbor with excellent water, cedar-wood, sardines, and shell-fish, together with an abundance of sweet celery,—a specific against the scurvy.

On the 28th of November, the squadron, reduced to three ships by the loss of the Santiago, left the strait and launched into the Great South Sea, to which, from the steady and gentle winds that propelled them over waters almost unruffled, Magellan gave the name of Pacific,—a name which it has ever since retained. They sailed on and on during the space of three months and twenty days, seeing no land, with the exception of two sterile and deserted islands which they named the Unfortunate. During all this time they tasted no fresh provisions. Their biscuit was little better than dust and smelled intolerably, being impregnated with the effluvia of mice. The water was putrid and offensive. The crew were so far reduced that they were glad to eat leather, which they were obliged to soak for four or five days in the sea in order to render it sufficiently supple to be broiled, chewed, and digested. Others lived on sawdust, while mice were sought after with such avidity that they were sold for half a ducat apiece.

Scurvy now began to make its appearance, and nineteen of the sailors died of it. The gums of many were swollen over their teeth, so that, unable to masticate their leathern viands, they perished miserably of starvation. Those who remained alive became weak, low-spirited, and helpless. The Patagonian taken on board the Trinidada at Port Julian was attacked by the disease. Pigafetta, seeing that he could not recover, showed him the cross and reverently kissed it. The Patagonian besought him by gestures to forbear, as the demon would certainly enter his body and cause him to burst. When at death's door, however, he called for the cross, which he kissed: he then begged to be baptized, and was received into the bosom of the Church under the name of Paul.

The vessels kept on and on, seeing no fish but sharks, and finding no bottom along the shores of the stunted islands which they passed. The needle was so irregular in its motion that it required frequent passes of the loadstone to revive its energy. No prominent star appeared to serve as an Antarctic Polar guide. Two stars, however, were discovered, which, from the smallness of the circle they described in their diurnal course, seemed to be near the pole. "We traversed," says Pigafetta, "a space of from sixty to seventy leagues a day; and, if God and His Holy Mother had not granted us a fortunate voyage, we should all have perished of hunger in so vast a sea. I do not think any one for the future will venture upon a similar voyage." It was, indeed, nearly sixty years before Drake, the second circumnavigator, entered the Pacific Ocean.

Early in March, 1521, Magellan fell in with a cluster of islands, where he and his men went ashore to refresh themselves after the fatigues and privations of their voyage. The inhabitants, however, were great thieves, penetrating into the cabins of the vessels and taking every thing on which they could lay their hands. Magellan, exasperated at length, landed with forty men, burned a village and killed seven of the natives. The latter, when pierced with arrows through and through,—a weapon they had never seen before,—would draw them out by either end and stare at them till they died. Magellan gave the name of Ladrones to these islands,—a name which they retain in modern geography, though, in the time of Philip IV. of

Spain, they were called the Marianne Isles, in honor of Maria, his queen.

At another island the crew received from the inhabitants the first present of cocoanuts made to a European of which any record exists. Pigafetta describes this now world-famous fruit in a manner which shows that he considered it a most wonderful novelty. We extract a portion of his description:—"Cocoanuts," he says, "are the fruit of a species of palm-tree, which furnishes the people with bread, wine, oil, vinegar, and physic. To obtain wine, they make an incision in the top of the tree, penetrating to the pith, from which drops a liquor resembling white must, but which is rather tart. This liquor is caught in the hollow of a reed the thickness of a man's leg, which is suspended to the tree and is carefully emptied twice a day. The fruit is of the size of a man's head, and sometimes larger. Its outward rind is green and two fingers thick: it is composed of filaments of which they make cordage for their boats. Beneath this is a shell harder and thicker than that of the walnut. This they burn and pulverize, using the powder as a remedy in several distempers. Within, the shell is lined with a white kernel about as thick as a finger, which is eaten, instead of bread, with meat and fish. In the centre of the nut, encircled by the kernel, a sweet and limpid liquor is found, of a corroborative nature. This liquor, poured into a glass and suffered to stand, assumes the consistence of an apple. The kernel and liquor, if left to ferment and afterwards boiled, yield an oil as thick as butter. To obtain vinegar, the liquor itself is exposed to the sun, and the acid which results from it resembles that vinegar we make from white wine. A family of ten persons might be supported from two cocoanut-trees, by alternately tapping each every week, and letting the other rest, that a perpetual drainage of liquor may not kill the tree. We were told that a cocoanut-tree lives a century."

At another island, Pigafetta asserts that, by sifting the earth he found lumps of gold as large as walnuts and some as big as eggs even, and that all the vessels used by the king at his table were of the same precious metal. These are believed to have been gross falsehoods of Pigafetta's invention, in a view to procure for himself the command of a subsequent voyage of discovery. Magellan gratified two island-kings with the spectacle of a grand Catholic ceremony. He sprinkled them with sweet-scented water, and offered them the cross to kiss. On the elevation of the host he caused them to adore the Eucharist with joined hands. At this moment a discharge of artillery, arranged beforehand, was fired from the ships. The entertainment concluded with a hornpipe and sword-dance,—an exhibition which seemed to please the two kings highly. A large cross was then brought, garnished with nails and a crown of thorns. It was set up upon a high mountain, as a signal to all Christian navigators that they would be well treated in the island. The kings were also assured that if they prayed to it devoutly it would defend them from lightning and tempests. They had evidently suffered severely from the vagaries and violence of the electric fluid, and were delighted to be thus easily protected against its pernicious and destructive influence.

THE NATIVES OF BORNEO PREPARE TO ATTACK MAGELLAN.

CHAPTER XXIV.

DISCOVERY OF THE PHILIPPINES—THE KING OF ZUBU WISHES THE KING OF SPAIN TO PAY TRIBUTE—HE FINALLY ABANDONS THE IDEA—A WHOLE ISLAND CONVERTED TO CHRISTIANITY—MAGELLAN PERFORMS A MIRACLE—A DUMB MAN RECOVERS HIS SPEECH—MAGELLAN INVADES A REFRACTORY ISLAND—HIS DEATH—ATTEMPTS TO RECOVER HIS BODY—THE CHRISTIAN ISLAND RETURNS TO IDOLATRY—THE SHIPS ARRIVE AT BORNEO—THE SAILORS DRINK TOO FREELY OF ARRACK—FESTIVITIES AND TREACHERY—VIVID IMAGINATION OF PIGAFETTA—THE FLEET ARRIVES AT THE MOLUCCAS—THE KING OF TIDORE—A BRISK TRADE IN CLOVES—THE SPICE-TARIFF—THE VITTORIA SAILS HOMEWARD—PIGAFETTA IS AGAIN IMAGINATIVE—ARRIVAL AT THE CAPE VERDS—LOSS OF ONE DAY—COMPLETION OF THE FIRST VOYAGE OF CIRCUMNAVIGATION—PIGAFETTA'S ROMANCE BECOMES VERITABLE HISTORY.

ON the 7th of April the squadron entered the harbor of the island of Zubu, one of a group which has since been named the Philippines. Magellan sent a messenger to the king to ask an exchange of commodities. The king observed that it was customary for all ships entering his waters to pay tribute, to which the messenger replied that the Spanish admiral was the servant of so powerful a sovereign that he could pay tribute to no one. The king promised to give an answer the next day, and, in the mean time, sent fruit and wine on board the ships. Magellan had brought with him the king of Massana, a neighboring island, and this monarch soon convinced the king of Zubu that, instead of asking tribute, he would be wise to pay it. A treaty of peace and perpetual amity was soon established between his majesty of Spain and his royal brother of Zubu.

Pigafetta here introduces a ridiculous and incredible story of the conversion of these islands to Christianity by Magellan. It is as follows:—Magellan, being much displeased at learning that parents attaining a certain age in this island were treated disrespectfully by their children, told them that the Almighty, who created heaven and earth, had strictly commanded children to honor their parents and had threatened with eternal fire those who transgressed this commandment. He added other observations from Holy Writ, which afforded the islanders much pleasure, and inspired them with the desire of being instructed in the true religion. Magellan assured them that before departing he would baptize them all, if they could convince him that they accepted the boon, not through any dread with which he might have inspired them, or through any expectation of temporal advantage, but from a spontaneous emotion, and of their own will. They convinced him easily of the spontaneity of their feelings, whereupon Magellan wept for joy and embraced them all. Sunday, the 16th of April, was fixed upon for the ceremony. A scaffold was raised and covered with tapestry and branches of palm. A general salute was fired by the squadron. Magellan then told the king that one of the advantages which would accrue to him from embracing Christianity would be that he would be strengthened, and would more easily overcome his enemies. The king replied that even without this consideration he felt disposed to become a Christian. Eight hundred persons were then baptized, the queen receiving the name of Jane, after the mother of the Emperor of Spain. She begged an infant Jesus of Pigafetta, with which to replace her idols. This remarkable story concludes with a statement that one village of idolaters absolutely refused to be converted, and that Magellan therefore burned their houses, erecting a cross upon the ruins. Not content with this, Pigafetta next makes Magellan perform a miracle. The king's brother was very sick, and had totally lost his speech. The admiral said that if all the idols remaining in the island were burned, and if the prince were baptized, he would pledge his head that he would recover. Magellan then baptized the invalid, together with his two wives and ten daughters. The captain "then asked him how he found himself, and he answered, of a sudden recovering his speech, that, thanks to the Lord, he found himself very well. We were all of us ocular witnesses of this miracle. The captain then, with greater fervor than the rest of us, returned praise to God." Idols were now committed to the flames in vast numbers, and temples built upon the margin of the sea were demolished. The new Christians went about the island crying, at the top of their voice, "Viva la Castilla!" in honor of the King of Spain.

On the 26th of April, Magellan learned that a neighboring chief, named Cilapolapu, refused to acknowledge the authority of the King of Spain, and remained in open profession of paganism in the midst of a Christian community. He determined to lend his assistance to the converted chiefs to reduce and subjugate this stubborn prince. At midnight, boats left the ships, bearing sixty men armed with helmets and cuirasses. The natives followed in twenty canoes. They reached the rebellious island—Matan by name—three hours before daybreak. Cilapolapu was notified that he must obey the Christian King of Zubu or feel the strength of Christian lances. The islanders replied that they had lances too. The invaders waited for daylight, and then, jumping into the water up to their thighs, waded to shore. The enemy was fifteen hundred in number, formed into three battalions: two of these attacked them in the flank, the third in the front. The musketeers fired for half an hour without making the least impression. Trusting to the superiority of their numbers, the natives deluged the Christians with showers of bamboo lances, staves hardened in the fire, stones, and even dirt. A poisoned arrow at last struck Magellan, who at once ordered a retreat in slow and regular order. The Indians now perceived that their blows took effect when aimed at the nether limbs of their foe, and profited by this observation with telling effect. Seeing that Magellan was wounded, they twice struck his helmet from his head. He and his small band of men continued fighting for more than an hour, standing in the water up to their knees. Magellan was now evidently failing, and the islanders, perceiving his weakness, pressed upon him in crowds. One of them cut him violently across the left leg, and he fell on his face. He was immediately surrounded and belabored with sticks and stones till he died. His men, every one of whom was wounded, unable to afford him succor or avenge his death, escaped to their boats upon his fall.

"Thus," says Pigafetta, "perished our guide, our light, and our support. But his glory will survive him. He was adorned with every virtue: in the midst of the greatest adversity, he constantly possessed an immovable firmness. At sea he subjected himself to the same privations as his men. Better skilled than any one in the knowledge of nautical charts, he was a perfect master of navigation, as he proved in making the tour of the world,—an attempt on which none before him had ventured." Though Magellan only made half the circuit of the earth on this occasion, yet it may be said with reason that he was the first to circumnavigate the globe, from the fact that the way home from the Philippines was perfectly well known to the Portuguese, and that Magellan had already been at Malacca.

An attempt was made in the afternoon to recover the body of Magellan by negotiation; but the islanders sent answer that no consideration could induce them to part with the remains of a man like the admiral, which they should preserve as a monument of their victory. Two governors were elected in his stead, Odoard Barbosa and Juan Serrano. The latter, together with San Martino, the astronomer, and a number of officers, having been decoyed on shore by the converted king, were murdered by him in cold blood. He had seen the inferiority of Christians to savages in war, and, being doubtless disgusted with the boastful pretences of Christianity, had, upon Magellan's death, renounced it and returned again to idolatry. Juan Serrano was seen upon the shore, bound hand and foot: he begged the people in the ships to treat for his release; and, upon this being refused, he uttered deep imprecations, and appealed to the Almighty to call to account on the great day of judgment those who refused to succor him in his hour of need. They put to sea, leaving the unfortunate Serrano to his miserable fate.

Odoard Barbosa, now sole commander, ordered the Concepçion, one of the three ships, to be burned, transferring its men, ammunition, and provisions to the other two. After landing at various islands, he came to the rich settlement of Borneo, on the 9th of July. The king, who was a Mohammedan and kept a magnificent court, sent out to them a beautiful canoe, adorned with gold figures and peacocks' feathers. In it were musicians playing upon the bagpipe and drum. Eight officers of the island brought to the captain a vase full of betel areca to chew, a quantity of orange-flowers and jessamine, some sugarcane, and three goblets of a distilled liquor which they called arrack, and upon which the sailors became intoxicated. Permission was granted the visitors to wood and water on the island and to trade with the natives. An interview with the king was likewise accorded, which took place with every possible ceremony,—processions of elephants, presents of cinnamon, and illuminations of wax flambeaux. Notwithstanding these professions of friendship, the squadron was obliged to leave Borneo very suddenly, in consequence of the appearance of one hundred armed canoes, which they imagined to be bent upon a hostile expedition.

Among the wonders of Borneo, Pigafetta mentions two pearls as large as hens' eggs, and so round that if placed upon a polished table they never remained at rest, and cups of porcelain possessing the power to denote the presence of poison, by breaking if any were put into them. At a neighboring island where the fleet remained undergoing repairs for six weeks, Pigafetta saw a sight which he thus describes:—"We here found a tree whose leaves, as they fall, become animated and walk about. They resemble the leaves of the mulberry-tree. Upon being touched they make away, but when crushed they yield no blood. I kept one in a box for nine days, and, on opening the box, found the leaf still alive and walking round it. I am of opinion they live on air." Pigafetta's mistake here was in stating that a leaf resembled an insect: he should have spoken of the curiosity as an insect resembling a leaf. It is now known to naturalists as a species of locust.

On the 6th of November, they espied a cluster of five islands, which their pilots, obtained at their last station, declared to be the famous Moluccas. They had therefore proved the world to be round, for vessels sailing to the west from Spain had now met vessels sailing thence to the east. They returned thanks to God, and fired a round from their great guns. They had been at sea twenty-six months, and had at last, after visiting an infinity of islands, reached those in quest of which they had embarked in the expedition. On the 8th, three hours before sunset, they entered the harbor of the island of Tidore. They came to anchor in twenty fathoms' water, and discharged all their cannon. The king, shaded by a parasol of silk, came the next day to visit them, said he had dreamed of their approaching visit, had consulted the moon in reference to this dream, and was now delighted to see it confirmed. He added that he was happy in the friendship of the King of Spain, and was proud to be his vassal. This potentate, whose name was Rajah Soultan Manzour, was a Mohammedan: he was "an eminent astrologer," and had numerous wives and twenty-six children.

TIDORE.

On the 12th, a shed was erected in the town of Tidore by the Spaniards, whither they carried all the merchandise they intended to barter for cloves. A tariff of exchange was then drawn up. Ten yards of red cloth were to be worth four hundred pounds of cloves, as were also fifteen yards of inferior cloth, fifteen axes, thirty-five glass tumblers, twenty-six yards of linen, one hundred and fifty pairs of scissors, three gongs, or a hundredweight of copper. As the stock of articles brought by the strangers diminished, however, their value naturally rose, and a yard of ribbon would buy a quintal of cloves: in fact, every thing with which the ships could dispense on their return-voyage was bartered for cloves. They were soon so deeply laden that they hardly had room in which to stow their water. The Trinidada, becoming leaky, was left behind, Juan Carvajo, her pilot, and fifty-three of the crew, remaining with her. The Vittoria bade adieu to her consort on the 21st of December, the two vessels exchanging a parting salute. The number of Europeans on board of the Vittoria was now reduced to forty-six; and the fleet, which formerly consisted of five sail, was now reduced to one.

As the Vittoria made her way through the thick archipelagoes of islands which dot the seas in these latitudes, her Molucca pilot told Pigafetta amazing stories of their inhabitants. In Aracheto, he said, the men and women were but a foot and a half high; their food was the pith of a tree; their dwellings were caverns under ground; their ears were as long as their bodies, so that when they lay down one ear served as a mattress and the other as a blanket!

In order to double the Cape of Good Hope, the captain ascended as high as the forty-second degree of south latitude: he remained wind-bound for nine weeks opposite the Cape. The crew were now suffering from sickness, hunger, and thirst. After doubling the Cape, they steered northwest for two months, losing twenty-one men on the way. Pigafetta noticed that, on throwing the dead into the sea, the Christians floated with their faces turned towards heaven, while the Mohammedans they had engaged turned their faces the other way! At last, on the 9th of July, 1522, the vessel made the Cape Verds. These were in the possession of the Portuguese; and it was a very hazardous thing for the Spaniards to put themselves in their power. However, they represented themselves as coming from the west and not from the east, and made known their necessities. Their long-boat was laden twice with rice in exchange for various articles. On its third trip the crew was detained,—the Portuguese having discovered that the Vittoria was one of Magellan's fleet. She was compelled to abandon the men as prisoners, and sailed away,—her whole equipment now numbering eighteen hands, all of them, except Pigafetta, more or less disabled. The latter, to discover if his journal had been regularly kept, had inquired at the islands what day it was, and was told it was Thursday. This amazed him, as his reckoning made it Wednesday. He was soon convinced there was no mistake in his account; as, having sailed to the westward and followed the course of the sun, it was evident that, in circumnavigating the globe, he had seen it rise once less than those who had remained at home, and thus, apparently, had lost a day.

On Saturday, the 6th of September, the Vittoria entered the Bay of San Lucar, having been absent three years and twenty-seven days, and having sailed upwards of fourteen thousand six hundred leagues. On the 8th, having ascended the Guadalquivir, she anchored off the mole of Seville and discharged all her artillery. On the 9th, the whole crew repaired, in their shirts and barefooted, and carrying tapers in their hands, to the Church of Our Lady of Victory, as in hours of danger they had often vowed to do. The captain of the Vittoria, Juan Sebastian Cano, was knighted by Charles V., who gave him for his coat of arms the terrestial globe, with a motto commemorating the voyage. Pigafetta presented to Charles V. of Spain, to King John of Portugal, to the Queen Regent of France, and to Philippe, Grand Master of Rhodes, journals and narratives of the expedition. From the latter, the most complete, we have extracted the foregoing account,—taking care, however, to correct its errors, and to point out the numerous instances in which its author was indebted to his imagination for his facts.

Section IV.

FROM THE FIRST VOYAGE ROUND THE WORLD TO THE DISCOVERY OF CAPE HORN; 1519—1616.

CHAPTER XXV.

VOYAGE OF JACQUES CARTIER—MARITIME PROJECTS OF FRANCIS I. OF FRANCE —GULF OF ST. LAWRENCE—A QUICK TRIP HOME—SECOND VOYAGE—CANADA, QUEBEC, MONTREAL—A CAPTIVE KING—VOYAGE OF SIR HUGH WILLOUGHBY AND RICHARD CHANCELLOR—DISCOVERY OF NOVA ZEMBLA—DISASTROUS WINTER—FATE OF THE EXPEDITION—MARTIN FROBISHER—HIS VOYAGE IN QUEST OF A NORTHWEST PASSAGE—GREENLAND—LABRADOR—FROBISHER'S STRAITS—EXCHANGE OF CAPTIVES—SUPPOSED DISCOVERY OF GOLD—SECOND VOYAGE—A CARGO OF PRECIOUS EARTH TAKEN ON BOARD—META INCOGNITA —THIRD VOYAGE—A MORTIFYING CONCLUSION.

It would appear natural for the Spaniards to have sought to derive immediate profit from their discovery of a western passage to the South Sea. They did not do so, however; and a generation was destined to pass away before a second European vessel should enter Magellan's Strait. We must for a time, therefore, leave the Spanish and Portuguese in quiet possession of their Indian and American commerce, and turn to the several transatlantic and Arctic enterprises undertaken at this period by the French and English.

Jacques Cartier, a native of St. Malo in France, had, in 1534, finished his apprenticeship as a sailor. He conceived the idea of seeking a passage to China and the Spice Islands to the north of the Western Continent, and in the vicinity of the Pole. This was the origin of the various efforts made in

SCENE ON THE CANADIAN COAST.

quest of the renowned Northwest Passage. He also thought it incumbent upon France to assert her right to a share in the explorations and discoveries which were making Portugal and Spain both famous and rich. He caused his project to be laid before Francis I., who had long viewed with jealousy the successful expeditions of other powers, and who is said once to have exclaimed, "Where is the will and testament of our father Adam, which disinherits me of my share in these possessions in favor of Spain and Portugal?" He at once approved the proposition; and, on the 20th of April, 1534, Cartier left St. Malo with two ships of sixty tons each. No details of the outward voyage have reached us. It was rapid and prosperous, however, for the ships anchored in Bonavista Bay, upon the eastern coast of Newfoundland, on the twentieth day.

Proceeding to the north, he discovered Belle Isle Straits, and through them descended to the west into a gulf which he called St. Lawrence, having Newfoundland on his left and Labrador on his right. He thus assured himself of the insular character of Newfoundland. He discovered many of the islands and headlands in the Gulf of St. Lawrence, and some of them bear to this day the names he gave them. He had interviews with several tribes of natives, and took possession of numerous lands in the name of the King of France. In the middle of August east winds became prevalent and violent, and it was impossible to ascend the St. Lawrence River, at the mouth of which they now were. A council was held, and a return unanimously decided upon. They arrived safely at St. Malo, after a rapid and prosperous voyage.

Francis I. immediately caused three ships, respectively of one hundred and twenty, sixty, and forty tons, to be equipped, and despatched Cartier upon a second voyage of exploration, with the title of Royal Pilot. He started in May, 1535, and after a stormy voyage of two months arrived at his anchorage in Newfoundland. From thence he proceeded to the mouth of the St. Lawrence, which he calls by its Indian name of Hochelaga. Here he was told by the savages that the river led to a country called *Canada*. He ascended the stream in boats, passed a village named Stadacone,—the site of the present city of Quebec,—and arrived at the Indian city of Hochelaga, which, from a high mountain in the vicinity, he named Mont Royal,—now Montreal. He went no farther than the junction of the Ottawa and the St. Lawrence, and then returned. He remained at Stadacone through the winter, losing twenty-five of his men by a contagious distemper then very little known,—the scurvy.

Cartier returned to France in July, 1536, taking with him a Canadian king, named Donnaconna, and nine other natives, who had been captured and brought on board by compulsion. They were taken to Europe, where Donnaconna died two years afterwards: three others were baptized in 1538, Cartier standing sponsor for one of them. They seem to have all been dead in 1541, the date of Cartier's third voyage. The king ordered five ships to be prepared, with which Cartier again started for the scene of his discoveries. The narrative of this expedition is lost; but it appears to have resulted in few or no incidents of interest. Cartier was ennobled upon his return in 1542, and lived ten years to enjoy his new dignity. His descriptions of the scenery, products, and Indians of Canada are graphic and correct.

In the year 1553, "the Mystery and Company of English merchants adventurers for the discovery of regions, dominions, islands, and places unknown"—at the head of whom was Sebastian Cabot—fitted out an expedition of three vessels, and gave the chief command to Sir Hugh Willoughby, "by reason of his goodly personage, as also for his singular skill in the services of war." King Edward VI. confirmed the appointment in "a license to discover strange countries."

The fleet consisted of the Buona Speranza, of one hundred and seventy tons, commanded by Sir Hugh, with thirty-eight men, the Edward Buonaventura, of one hundred and sixty tons, commanded by Richard Chancellor, pilot-major of the expedition, with fifty-four men, and the Buona Confidentia, of ninety tons, with twenty-four men. The ships were victualled for fifteen months. On board of them were eighteen merchants interested in the discovery of a northeast passage to India,—a route, therefore, attempted by the English previous to that by the northwest, as the voyage of Sebastian Cabot can hardly be considered a serious effort. A council of twelve, in whom was vested the general direction of the voyage, was composed of the admiral, pilot-major, and other officers.

The squadron sailed from Deptford on the 10th of May, 1553, and fell in with the Norwegian coast on the 14th of July. On the 30th, while near Wardhus, the most easterly station of the Danes in Finmark, Chancellor's vessel was driven off in a storm, and was not seen again by the two others. The latter appear to have been tossed about in the North Sea for two months, in the course of which they landed at some spot on the western coast of Nova Zembla, being the first Europeans to visit that uninhabited waste. On the 18th of September they entered a harbor in Lapland formed by the mouth of the river Arzina. Here they remained a week, seeing seals, deer, bears, foxes, "with divers strange beasts, such as ellans and others, which were to us unknown and also wonderful." It was now the 1st of October, and the Arctic winter was far advanced. They resolved to winter there, first sending out parties in search of inhabitants. Three men went three days' journey to the south-southwest, but returned without having seen a human being. Others who went to the west and the southeast returned equally unsuccessful. This is the last positive intelligence we have of the fate of these hardy and unfortunate explorers. A will, however, alleged to have been made by one Gabriel Willoughby, and signed by Sir Hugh, bearing the date of January, 1554, shows, if authentic, that at least two of the party were alive at that period. Purchas, one of the oldest authorities upon navigation and travels extant, says that the Buona Speranza was discovered in the following spring by a party of Russians, who found all the crew frozen to death. In 1557, a Drontheim skipper told an Englishman, at Kegor, that he had bought the sails of the Buona Confidentia; but it is not known where she was lost, or what was the fate of the crew. The will of which we have spoken, and a fragmentary diary attributed to Sir Hugh, were found by the Russians, and were restored to the kinsmen of the adventurers in England.

The Edward Buonaventura, commanded by Chancellor, and which was separated from her consorts off Wardhus, reached Archangel, on the White Sea, in Russia, in safety, and laid the foundation of a commercial intercourse between Russia and England. On his return, his ship was lost on the coast of Scotland, and he himself, with several of his crew, drowned. Thus, of the three ships despatched, not one ever reached home; and of the officers, merchants, and men, none survived to revisit their country, except a few of the common seamen of the Edward Buonaventura. The advantages acquired at such a cost of human life were limited to the barren discovery of the ice-clad coast of Nova Zembla. Nothing had been effected towards the accomplishment of a Northeast Passage.

Martin Frobisher, a seaman of experience and enterprise, was the first Englishman to cherish the project of attempting to penetrate to Asia by the channel supposed to exist to the north of America. He communicated his design to his friends, and spent fifteen years in fruitless efforts to enlist capital and energy in the cause. Sailors, financiers, merchants, statesmen, —all regarded the scheme as visionary and hopeless. At last Lord Dudley, the favorite of Elizabeth, interested himself in Frobisher's success, and from that moment he experienced little difficulty in accomplishing his object. He formed a company, amassed the requisite sums of money, and purchased three small vessels,—two barks of twenty-five tons each, the Gabriel and the Michael, and a pinnace of ten tons. This valiant little fleet weighed anchor at Deptford on the 8th of June, 1576, and, passing the court assembled at Greenwich, discharged their ordnance, and made as imposing an appearance as their limited outfit would allow. Queen Elizabeth waved her hand at the commander from a window, and, bidding him farewell, wished him success and a happy return. On the 25th he passed the southern point of Shetland,—known as Swinborn Head. He anchored here to repair a leak and to take in fresh water. On the 10th of July, he descried the coast of Greenland, "rising like pinnacles of steeples, and all covered with snow." The crew made efforts to go ashore, but could find no anchorage for the vessels, or landing-place for the boats. On the 28th, Frobisher saw dimly, through the fog, what he supposed to be the coast of Labrador, enveloped in ice. On the 31st he saw land for the third time, and on the 11th of August entered a strait to which he gave his name.

He ascended this strait a distance of one hundred and fifty miles. It was not till the eighth day that he saw any inhabitants. He then found that the country was sparsely settled by a race resembling Tartars. He went ashore and established friendly relations with a colony of nineteen persons, to each one of whom he gave a "threaden point,"—in other words, a needle and thread. A few days afterwards, five of the crew were taken by the natives and their boat destroyed. The inlet in which this happened was called Five Men's Sound. The next morning the vessels ran in-shore, shot off a fauconet and sounded a trumpet, but heard nothing of the lost sailors. However, Frobisher caught one of the natives in return, having decoyed him by the tinkling of a bell. When he found himself in captivity, we are told that "from very choler and disdain he bit his tongue in twain within his mouth: notwithstanding, he died not thereof, but lived until he came to England, and then he died of cold which he had taken at sea." On the 26th of August, Frobisher weighed anchor and started to return to England, the snow lying a foot deep upon the decks. He arrived at Yarmouth on the 1st of October.

One of Frobisher's sailors had brought with him a bit of shining black stone, which, upon examination, was found to yield an infinitesimal quantity of gold. The Northwest Passage became now a matter of secondary interest, the mines of Frobisher's Strait promising a more speedy and abundant return. The society he had formed determined to send him out anew, in vessels better equipped and provisioned for a longer period. He left Blackwall on the 26th of May, 1577, in her Majesty's ship Aide, of one hundred and eighty tons, followed by the Gabriel and Michael, his ostensible object being to discover "America to be an island environed with the sea, wherethrough our merchants may have course and recourse with their merchandise, from these our northernmost parts of Europe to those oriental coasts of Asia, to their no little commodity and profit that do or shall frequent the same." The fleet passed the Orkneys on the 8th of June.

For a month they sailed to the westward, the season of the year being that when, in those latitudes, a bright twilight takes the place of the light of day during the few hours that the sun is below the horizon; so that the crew had "the fruition of their books and other pleasures,—a thing of no small moment to such as wander in unknown seas and long navigations, especially when both the winds and raging surges do pass their common and wonted course." Throughout the voyage they met huge fir-trees, which they supposed to have been uprooted by the winds, driven into the sea by floods, and borne away by the currents.

On the 4th of July they made the coast of Greenland. The chronicler of this voyage, who had doubtless lately visited tropical latitudes, remarks that here, "in place of odoriferous and fragrant smells of sweet gums and pleasant notes of musical birds, which other countries in more temperate zones do yield, we tasted in July the most boisterous boreal blasts." In the middle of the month they entered Frobisher's Strait. On either side the land lay locked in the embrace of winter beneath a midsummer sun. Frobisher would not believe that the cold was sufficiently severe to congeal the sea-water, the tide rising and falling a distance of twenty feet. Ten miles from the coast he had seen fresh-water icebergs, and concluded that they had been formed upon the land and by some accidental cause detached. He reconnoitred the coast in a pinnace, and penetrated some distance into the interior, returning with accounts of supposed riches which he had discovered in the bowels of barren and frozen mountains. A cargo of two hundred tons of the precious earth was taken on board of one of the vessels. On the 20th of August, says the narrative, "it was high time to leave: the men were well wearied, their shoes and clothes well worn; their basket-bottoms were torn out and their tools broken. Some, with overstraining themselves, had their bellies broken, and others their legs made lame. About this time, too, the water began to congeal and freeze about our ships' sides o' nights." The fleet, which had troubled itself very little with the Northwest Passage, at once set sail to the southeast, and arrived in England towards the end of September.

The specimens of ore were assayed and found satisfactory, and Frobisher's reports upon the route to China were received with favor. The queen gave the name of *Meta Incognita*, or Unknown Boundary, to the region explored. The Government determined to build a fort in Frobisher's Strait and send a garrison and a corps of laborers there. In the mean time, Frobisher was despatched a third time with the same three vessels, and with a convoy of twelve freight-ships which were to return laden with Labrador ore. They set sail on the 31st of May, 1578, and made Greenland on the 20th of June. In July they entered the strait, where they were in imminent danger from storms and ice. The bark Denis, being pretty well bruised and battered, became "so leaky that she would no longer tarry above the water, and sank; which sight so abashed the whole fleet, that we thought verily we should have tasted the same sauce." Boats were, however, manned, and the drowning crew were saved. The storm increased, and the ice pressed more and more upon them, so that they took down their topmasts. They cut their cables to hang overboard for fenders, "somewhat to ease the ships' sides from the great and dreary strokes of the ice. Thus we continued all that dismal and lamentable night, plunged in this perplexity, looking for instant death; but our God, who never leaveth them destitute which faithfully call upon him, although he often punisheth for amendment sake, in the morning caused the wind to cease and the fog to clear. Thus, after punishment, consolation; and we, joyful wights, being at liberty, hoisted our sails and lay beating off and on."

At last, at the close of July, such of the vessels as had not been separated from Frobisher's ship entered the Countess of Warwick's Sound, and commenced the work of mining and lading. The miners were from time to time molested by the natives, but lost no lives. They put on board of their several ships five hundred tons of ore, and, on the 1st of September, sailed with their precious freight to England, where they arrived in thirty days. The ore turned out to be utterly valueless,—a result so mortifying that it disgusted the English for many years with mining enterprises and with voyages of discovery. We shall hear of Frobisher again, in connection with Francis Drake, and in the conflict with the Spanish Armada.

The engraving upon the opposite page, which is copied from an original of the period, represents a portion of the royal fleet of England in the time of Henry VIII. The king is embarking at Dover previous to meeting Francis of France at the Field of the Cloth of Gold. This pageantry at sea was a fitting prelude to the festivities which followed upon the land.

HENRY VIII. EMBARKING AT DOVER.

FRANCIS DRAKE.

CHAPTER XXVI.

ORIGIN OF ENGLISH PIRACY—SIR JOHN HAWKINS—FRANCIS DRAKE—HIS FIRST VOYAGE TO THE SPANISH MAIN—COMMISSION GRANTED BY QUEEN ELIZABETH —EXPEDITION AGAINST THE SPANISH POSSESSIONS—EXPLOITS AT MOGADOR AND SANTIAGO—CROSSING THE LINE—ARRIVAL IN PATAGONIA—TRIAL AND EXECUTION OF DOUGHTY—PASSAGE THROUGH MAGELLAN'S STRAIT—ADVENTURES OF WILLIAM PITCHER AND SEVEN MEN—CAPE HORN—ARRIVAL AT VALPARAISO—RIFLING OF A CATHOLIC CHURCH.

WE have thus shown that, while the Spanish and Portuguese had succeeded triumphantly in their maritime expeditions, the English had disastrously failed in theirs. The tropics were held in exclusive possession by the two former nations; and the only two known routes by which ships could sail thither were also in their power. These two nations were Catholic: England was Protestant, and disinherited therefore, as it seemed, of her lawful share in the riches of the world. She had thus far wasted her means and endangered the lives of her citizens in fruitless attempts to find a route for herself, by the northwest or the northeast, to the lands of gold and gums. Baffled in these efforts, she permitted, if she did not encourage, a certain class of her subjects to engage in a system of warfare against Spain which can be characterized by no milder term than piracy. Still, those who resorted to it adduced ready arguments to prove that, so far from engaging in piratical practices, they were employed in open warfare and an honest cause. Spain and England were in a state of manifest enmity, they urged, more bitter on both sides than if they had been avowedly at war. No English subject trading in the Spanish dominions was safe unless he were a Roman Catholic, or unless, being a heretic, he succumbed to the menaces or the tortures of the Holy Inquisition. These outrages were resented by the English people before they were taken up by the British Government; and the injured parties, calling to their aid all persons of adventurous spirit or shattered fortunes, set out upon the sea, if not with the commission, at least with the connivance, of the crown, to avenge their wrongs themselves. They did not consider themselves to be pirates, because of this tacit sanction given by the Government, because of the fact that they carried on hostilities, not against all who traversed the sea, but against the Spaniards only, and because of the risk they ran,—for if taken by the enemy they had no mercy to expect. It thus became the fashion in England for men of desperate fortunes and damaged character to seek to retrieve the one and redeem the other by cruising against the Spaniards.

Among the earlier adventurers of this stamp was one Sir John Hawkins. His exploits were for a time brilliant and successful: at last, however, they were disastrous, and one of his young kinsmen, Francis Drake by name, was discreditably involved. The latter had embarked his whole means in this adventure, and lost in it all his money and no little reputation,—for he disobeyed orders and deserted his benefactor and superior in the hour of need. He brought his vessel,—the Judith, of fifty tons,—however, safely home.

Drake now resolved to engage permanently in the lawless but exciting career of which he had lately witnessed several interesting episodes. It was long before he could obtain the means of fitting out an expedition under his own command. He at last bought and equipped two vessels,—one of two hundred and fifty tons, the other of seventy,—manned them with seventy-three men, and sailed for the Spanish dominions in America. He attacked and took the town of Nombre de Dios, on the Isthmus of Darien, but was soon obliged to retreat. He afterwards took Venta Cruz, on the same isthmus, and had the good fortune to fall in with three convoys of mules laden with gold and silver, going from Panama to Nombre de Dios. He carried off the gold and buried the silver. From the summit of a mountain he obtained a sight of the Pacific Ocean or South Sea, which so kindled his enthusiasm that he uttered a fervent prayer that he might be the first Englishman who should sail upon it. He was already the first Englishman who had beheld it.

On his return to England with his treasure, he entered for a time the volunteer service against Ireland, while waiting an opportunity to execute the grand project he had formed. At last, Sir Christopher Hutton, Vice-Chamberlain and Counsellor of the Queen, presented him to Elizabeth, to whom Drake imparted his scheme of ravaging the Spanish possessions in the South Sea. The queen listened; but whether she gave him a commission, or merely assured him of her favorable sentiments, is a disputed point. It is alleged that she gave him a sword and pronounced these singular words:—"We do account that he which striketh at thee, Drake, striketh at us!" He fitted out an expedition, at his own cost and with the help of friends and partners in the enterprise, consisting of five ships,—the largest, the Pelican, his flag-ship, of one hundred tons, and the smallest of fifteen. These vessels were manned by one hundred and fifty-four men. They carried out the frames of four pinnaces, to be put together as occasion required, and, after the example of the Portuguese in their first Eastern voyages, took with them specimens of the arts and civilization of their country, with which to operate upon the minds of the people with whom they should come in contact. They sailed in November, 1577, but were driven back by a tempest. The expedition finally got to sea on the 13th of December.

At the island of Mogador, off the coast of Barbary, Drake attempted to traffic with the Moors, and in an exchange of hostages lost a man, who was taken by the natives: they then refused to trade, and Drake, after a vain effort to recover the sailor, left the island, and followed the African coast to the southward. Between Mogador and Cape Blanco he took several Spanish barks called canters,—one of which, measuring forty tons, he admitted into his fleet, sending his prisoners off in the Christopher, the pinnace of fifteen tons and one of the original five vessels. He landed on the island of Mayo, where the inhabitants salted their wells, forsook their houses, and drove away their goats. Off the island of Santiago he took a Portuguese vessel bound for Brazil, carrying numerous passengers and laden with wine. He kept the pilot, Nuno da Sylva, gave the passengers and crew a pinnace, and transferred the wine to the Pelican. The prize he made one of the fleet, having given her a crew of twenty-eight men.

At Cape Verd Drake left the African shore, and, steering steadily to the southwest, was nine weeks without seeing land. When near the equator, he prepared his men for the change of climate by bleeding them all himself. He made the coast of Brazil on the 4th of April, 1578,—the savage inhabitants making large bonfires at their approach, for the purpose, as he learned from Sylva, of inducing their devils to wreck the ships upon their coast. On the 27th he entered the Rio de la Plata, and, sailing up the stream till he found but three fathoms' water, filled his casks by the ship's side. The same night, the Portuguese prize, now named the Mary, and commanded by John Doughty, parted company, as did two days afterwards the Spanish canter, which had been named the Christopher, after the pinnace for which she had been exchanged. Drake, believing them to have concealed themselves in shoal water, built a raft and set sail in quest of them.

DRAKE AND HIS RAFT.

Early in June, Drake landed on the coast of Patagonia, where he broke up the Swan, of fifty tons, for firewood, having taken every thing out of her which could be of any use,—his object being to lessen the number of ships and the chances of separation, and to render his force more compact. His men easily killed two hundred and fifty seals in an hour, which furnished them with very tolerable eating. They entered into very pleasant relations with the natives, delighting them with the sound of their trumpets, intoxicating them with Canary wine, and dancing with them in their own savage and extravagant manner. The natives gave Drake a vexatious proof of their agility and address, by stealing his hat from his head and baffling every effort made to recover it. Shortly after sailing from this spot, named by Drake Seal Bay, the fleet fell in with the Christopher again, which Drake ordered to be unloaded and set adrift.

DRAKE AND THE PATAGONIANS.

He soon met the Portuguese Mary, and on the 20th the whole squadron anchored in the harbor named Port Julian by Magellan. Intercourse was attempted with the Indians, but was stopped on account of a fray begun by the savages, in which two of the English and one of their own party were killed. The natives made no further attempt to molest the strangers during their two months' stay in the harbor.

A very tragical event now followed. Magellan had in this place, as we have stated, quelled a dangerous mutiny, by hanging several of a disobedient and rebellious company. The gibbet was still standing, and beneath it the bones of the executed were now bleaching. Drake apprehended a similar peril, and was led to inquire into the actions of John Doughty. He found, in his investigations, that Doughty had embarked in the enterprise rather in the hope of rising to the chief command than of remaining what he started,—a gentleman volunteer: he had views, it seemed, of supplanting Drake by exciting a mutiny, and of sailing off in one of the ships upon his own account. The company were called together and made acquainted with the particulars; Doughty was tried for attempting to foment a mutiny, found guilty, and condemned to death by forty commissaries chosen from among the various crews. Doughty partook of

DRAKE CONDEMNING DOUGHTY.

the communion with Drake and several of his officers, dined at the same table with them, and, in the last glass of wine he ever raised to his lips, drank their healths and wished them farewell. He walked to the place of execution without displaying unusual emotion, embraced the general, took leave of the company, offered up a prayer for the queen and her realm, and was then beheaded near Magellan's gibbet. Drake addressed the company, exhorting them to unity and obedience, and ordered them to prepare to receive the holy communion on the following Sabbath, the first Sunday in the month.

This tragedy has been embellished by many fanciful additions on the part of Drake's apologists, and upon the part of his calumniators by many false statements. It is said by the former that Drake, after Doughty's condemnation, offered him the choice of three alternatives,—either to be executed in Patagonia, to be set ashore and left, or to be sent back to England, there to answer for his acts before the Lords of her Majesty's Council; and that Doughty replied that he would not endanger his soul by being left among savage infidels; that, as for returning to England, if any one could be found willing to accompany him on so disgraceful an errand, the shame of the return would be more grievous than death; that he therefore preferred ending his life where he was,—a choice from which no argument could persuade him. These assertions can hardly be correct, as nothing of the kind is set forth in the account of the voyage given by Fletcher, the chaplain of the expedition. It is highly improbable that Doughty, if conscious of innocence, would have rejected the offer of a trial in England; while it is unlikely that the offer was ever made, as Drake could ill spare a ship in which to send the prisoner home. Different opinions are held in the matter by different writers. Admiral Burney thought the statements too imperfect for forming, and the whole matter too delicate to express, an opinion. Dr. Johnson wrote thus on the subject:—"What designs Doughty could have formed with any hope of success, or to what actions worthy of death he could have proceeded without accomplices, it is difficult to imagine. Nor, on the other hand, does there appear any temptation, from either hope, fear, or interest, that might induce Drake, or any commander in his state, to put to death an innocent man on false pretences." Southey, in his Lives of the Admirals, is disposed to consider Drake as justified in making a severe example. Harris is of opinion that the act was "the most rash and blameworthy of the admiral's career." Sylva, Drake's Portuguese pilot, once said that Doughty was punished for attempting to abandon the expedition and return to England, and thus evidently thought that a sufficient motive existed for his execution. And it is worth remarking that the Spaniards, who never neglected an opportunity of loading Drake with obloquy, extolled him in this case for his vigilance and decision. Doughty was buried on an island in the harbor, together with the bodies of the two men slain in the fray with the savages.

The Portuguese prize, being now found leaky and troublesome, was broken up, the fleet being thus reduced to three. On the 21st of August, Drake entered Magellan's Strait,—being the second commander who ever performed the voyage through it. He cleared the channel in sixteen days, and entered the South Sea on the 6th of September. Here the Marygold was lost in a terrible storm, and the Elizabeth, being separated from Drake's vessel, wandered about in search of him for a time and then sailed for England, where her captain was disgraced for having abandoned his commander. Drake was driven from the Bay of Parting of Friends, as he named the spot in which he lost sight of the Elizabeth, and was swept southward to the coast of Terra del Fuego, where he was forced from his anchorage and obliged to abandon the pinnace, with eight men in it and one day's provisions, to the mercy of the winds.

The miseries endured by these eight men are hardly equalled in the annals of maritime disaster. They gained the shore, salted and dried penguins for food, and coasted on till they reached the Plata. Six of them landed, and, of these six, four were taken prisoners by the Indians. The other two were wounded in attempting to escape to the boat, as were the two who were left in charge. These four succeeded in reaching an island nine miles from the coast, where two of them died of their wounds. The other two lived for two months upon crabs and eels, and a fruit resembling an orange, which was the only means they had of quenching their thirst. One night their boat was dashed to pieces against the rocks. Unable longer to endure the want of water, they attempted to paddle to land upon a plank ten feet long. This was the laborious work of three days and two nights. They found a rivulet of fresh water; and one of them, William Pitcher, unable to resist the temptation of drinking to excess, died of its effects in half an hour. His companion was held in captivity for nine years by the Indians, when he was permitted to return to England.

Drake, after the loss of the pinnace, was driven again to the southward, and, in the quaint language of the times, "fell in with the uttermost part of the land towards the South Pole, where the Atlantic Ocean and the South Sea meet in a large and free scope." He saw the cape since called Cape Horn, and anchored there: he gave the name of Elizabethides to all the islands lying in the neighborhood. As he neither doubled nor named this cape, it remained for the daring navigators Schouten and Lemaire to demonstrate its importance, by passing around it from one ocean into the other, which Drake, it will be observed, had not done. He went ashore, however, and, leaning over a rock which extended the farthest into the sea, returned to the ship and told the crew that he had been farther south than any man living. He anchored at the island of Mocha on the 29th of November, having coasted for four weeks to the northward along the South American shore. He landed with ten men, and was attacked by the Indians, who took them for Spaniards. Two of his men were killed, all of them disabled, and he himself badly wounded with an arrow under the right eye. Not one of the assailants was hurt. Drake made no attempt to take vengeance for this unprovoked attack, as it was evident it was begun under the mistaken idea that they were Spaniards, whose atrocities had made every native of the country their enemy. He sailed for Peru on the same day.

Early in December he learned, from an Indian who was found fishing in his canoe, that he had passed twenty miles beyond the port of Valhario,—now Valparaiso; and that in this port lay a Spanish ship well laden. Drake sailed for this place, where he found the ship riding at anchor, with eight Spaniards and three negroes on board. These, taking the new-comers for friends,—for the Spaniards had never yet seen an enemy in this ocean,—welcomed them with drum and trumpet, and opened a jar of Chili wine in which to drink their health. Thomas Moore, the former captain of the Christopher pinnace, was the first to board the unsuspecting craft. He laid lustily about him, upon which the principal Spaniard crossed himself and jumped overboard. The rest were easily secured under the hatches. The prize was rifled, and one thousand seven hundred and seventy jars of Chili wine, sixty thousand pieces of gold, and a number of strings of pearls, were taken from her. The miserable town, consisting of nine families, who at once fled to the interior, was next ransacked. A poor little church was robbed of a silver chalice, two cruets, and a cloth with which the altar was spread. A warehouse was forced to disgorge its store of Chili wine and cedar planks. Thus did Drake, armed with the sanction of Elizabeth, Queen of England, plunder a handful of inoffensive men securely anchored in a peaceful roadstead, who saluted their coming with music and with wine. Thus did Drake commit sacrilege in a Christian church, and furnish the mess-room of his ship from the spoils of a Catholic altar. Even Southey admits that, in this affair, Drake deserves no other name than that of pirate. And we shall see that he deserved it equally well throughout his stay upon the coast.

CHAPTER XXVII.

DRAKE'S EXPLOIT WITH A SLEEPING SPANIARD—HIS ACHIEVEMENTS AT CALLAO —BATTLE WITH A TREASURE-SHIP—DRAKE GIVES A RECEIPT FOR HER CARGO —INDITES A TOUCHING EPISTLE—HIS PLANS FOR RETURNING HOME—FRESH CAPTURES—PERFORMANCES AT GUATULCO AND ACAPULCO—DRAKE DISMISSES HIS PILOT—EXCEEDING COLD WEATHER—DRAKE REGARDED AS A GOD BY THE CALIFORNIANS—SAILS FOR THE MOLUCCAS—VISITS TERNATE AND CELEBES—THE PELICAN UPON A REEF—THE RETURN VOYAGE—PROTEST OF THE SPANISH AMBASSADOR—HE STYLES DRAKE THE MASTER-THIEF OF THE UNKNOWN WORLD —QUEEN ELIZABETH ON BOARD THE PELICAN—DRAKE'S USE OF HIS FORTUNE —HIS DEATH—THE VOYAGE OF JOHN DAVIS TO THE NORTHWEST.

A FORTNIGHT after leaving Valparaiso, Drake anchored at the mouth of the Coquimbo. The watering party sent ashore had barely time to escape from a body of five hundred horse and foot. At another place, called Tarapaca, the waterers found a Spaniard lying asleep, and took from him thirteen bars of silver of the value of four thousand ducats. Southey states, as if it were a trait of magnanimity, that no personal injury was offered to the sleeping man. They next captured eight lamas, each carrying a hundred pounds of silver. At Arica they found two ships at anchor, a single negro being on board of each: from the one they took forty bars of silver, and from the other two hundred jars of wine. As the Pelican was more than a match for the two negroes, the latter wisely offered no resistance. Drake arrived at Callao, the port of Lima,—Lima being the capital of Peru,—before it was known that an enemy's ship had entered the waters of the Pacific. He immediately boarded a bark laden with silk, which he consented to leave unmolested on condition that the owner would pilot him into Callao, which he did. Here Drake found seventeen ships, twelve of which had sent their sails ashore, so that they were as helpless as logs. He rifled them of their silver, silk, and linen, and then cut their cables and let them drift out to sea. Learning that a richly-laden treasure-ship, named the Cacafuego, had lately sailed for Paita, he at once gave chase. He stopped a vessel bound for Callao; and such was his thirst for gain, that he took from it a small silver lamp, the only article of value on board. In a ship bound to Panama he found forty bars of silver, eighty pounds of gold, and a golden crucifix set with large emeralds. Soon after crossing the line, the Cacafuego was discovered ten miles to seaward, by Drake's brother John. The Pelican's sailing qualities were now improved by what Sylva, the pilot, calls a "pretty device." Empty jars were filled with water and hung with ropes over the stern, in order to lighten her bow. The Spaniard, not dreaming of an enemy, made towards her, whereupon Drake gave her three broadsides, shot her mainmast overboard, and wounded her captain. She then surrendered. Drake took possession, sailed with her two days and two nights from the coast, and then lay to to rifle her. He took from her an immense quantity of pearls and precious stones, eighty pounds of gold, twenty-six tons of silver in ingots, a large portion of which belonged to the king, and thirteen boxes of coined silver. The value of this prize was not far from one million of dollars. Then, as if he had been engaged in a legal commercial transaction, Drake asked the captain for his register of the cargo, and wrote a receipt in the margin for the whole amount!

The prize, thus lightened of her metallic cargo, was then allowed to depart. Her captain received from Drake a letter of safe conduct in case he should fall in with the Elizabeth or the Mary. This letter is remarkable for its deep and touching piety. After recommending the despoiled captain to the friendly notice of Winter and Thomas, Drake concludes thus:—"I commit you all to the tuition of Him that with his blood hath redeemed us, and am in good hope that we shall be in no more trouble, but that he will help us in adversity; desiring you, for the passion of Christ, if you fall into any danger, that you will not despair of God's mercy, for he will defend you and preserve you from all peril, and bring us to our desired haven: to whom be all honor, and praise, and glory, forever and ever. Amen.

"Your sorrowful captain,

"Whose heart is heavy for you,

"FRANCIS DRAKE."

Drake now considered his object in these seas as accomplished: the indignities offered by the Spaniards to his queen and country were avenged, and their commerce was well-nigh annihilated. He next examined the various plans of returning home with his booty. He thought it impossible to go back by the way he had come: the whole coast of Chili and Peru was in alarm, and ships had undoubtedly been despatched to intercept him. Moreover, the season (for it was now February, 1579) was unfavorable either for passing the Strait or for doubling the Cape. He might have followed the course of Magellan, and thus have circumnavigated the globe; but this seemed but a paltry imitation to his daring and inventive mind. He conceived the idea of discovering a Northwest Passage and returning to England by the North Polar Sea. He therefore sailed towards the north, making the coast of Nicaragua in the middle of March. Here he captured a small craft laden with sarsaparilla, butter, and honey. A neighboring island supplied him with wood and fish: alligators and monkeys also abounded there. A vessel from Manilla, which he captured while her crew were asleep, contributed to his stores large quantities of muslin, Chinese porcelain, and silks. A negro taken from this vessel piloted him into the haven of Guatulco, on the coast of Mexico, inhabited by seventeen Spaniards and a few negroes. Drake ransacked this place, but boasts of no other booty than a bushel of silver coins and a gold chain that Thomas

Moon took from the person of the escaping governor. At Acapulco he found a few Spaniards engaged in trying and condemning a parcel of the unhappy natives. He broke up the court, and sent both judges and prisoners on board his vessel.

DRAKE INTERRUPTING THE COURSE OF JUSTICE AT ACAPULCO.

Before leaving Acapulco, Drake put the pilot, Nuno da Sylva, whom he had taken at the Cape Verds, on board a ship in the harbor, to find his way back to Portugal as best he could. He then sailed four thousand five hundred miles in various directions, till he found himself in a piercingly cold climate, where the meat froze as soon as it was removed from the fire. This was in latitude forty-eight north. So he sailed back again ten degrees and anchored in an excellent harbor on the California coast. This harbor is considered by numerous authorities as the present Bay of San Francisco. The natives, who had been visited but once by Europeans,—under the Portuguese Cabrillo, thirty-seven years before,—had not learned to distrust them, and readily entered into relations of commerce and amity with Drake's party. From the Indians the latter obtained quantities of an herb which they called *tabak*, and which was undoubtedly tobacco. The Californians soon came to regard the strangers as gods, and did them religious honors. The king resigned to Drake all title to the surrounding country, and offered to become his subject. So he took possession of the crown and dignity of the said territory in the name and for the use of her majesty the queen. The Californians, we are told, accompanied this act of surrender with a song and dance of triumph, "because they were not only visited of gods, but the great and chief god was now become their god, their king and patron, and themselves the only happy and blessed people in all the world." Drake named the country New Albion, in honor of Old Albion or England. He set up a monument of the queen's "right and title to the same, namely, a plate nailed upon a fair great post, whereon was engraved her majesty's name, with the day and year of arrival." After remaining five weeks in the harbor, Drake weighed anchor, on the 23d of July, resolved to abandon any further attempt in northern latitudes, and to steer for the Moluccas, after the example of Magellan.

On the 13th of October he discovered several islands in latitude eight degrees north, and was soon surrounded with canoes laden with cocoanuts and fruit. These canoes were hollowed out of a single log with wonderful art, and were as smooth as polished horn, and decorated throughout with shells thickly set. The ears of the natives hung down considerably from the weight of the ornaments worn in them. Their nails were long and sharp, and were evidently used as a weapon. Their teeth were black as jet,—an effect obtained by the use of the betel-root. These people were friendly and commercially inclined. Drake visited other groups, where the principal occupation of the natives was selling cinnamon to the Portuguese. At Ternate, one of the Moluccas, the king offered the sovereignty of the isles to Drake, and sent him presents of "imperfect and liquid sugar,"—molasses, probably,—"rice, poultry, cloves, and meal which they called sagu, or bread made of the tops of certain trees, tasting in the mouth like sour curds, but melting like sugar, whereof they made certain cakes which may be kept the space of ten years, and yet then good to be eaten." Drake stayed here six days, laid in a large stock of cloves, and sailed on the 9th of November. At a small island near Celebes, where he set up his forge and caused the ship to be carefully repaired, he and his men saw sights which they have described in somewhat exaggerated terms:—"tall trees without branches except a tuft at the very top, in which swarms of fiery worms, flying in the air, made a show as if every twig had been a burning candle; bats bigger than large hens,—a very ugly poultry; cray-fish, or land-crabs, one of which was enough for four men, and which dug huge caves under the roots of trees, or, for want of better refuge, would climb trees and hide in the forks of the branches." This spot was appropriately named Crab Island.

On the 9th of January, 1580, the ship ran upon a rocky shoal and stuck fast. The crew were first summoned to prayers, and then ordered to lighten the ship. Three tons of cloves were thrown over, eight guns, and a quantity of meal and pulse. One authority says distinctly that no gold or silver was thrown into the water, though it was the heaviest part of the cargo; another authority asserts the contrary in the following passage:—"Conceiving that the best way to lighten the ship was to ease their consciences, they humbled themselves by fasting, afterwards dining on Christ in the sacrament, expecting no other than to sup with him in heaven. Then they cast out of their ship six great pieces of ordnance, threw overboard as much wealth as would break the heart of a miser to think of it, with much sugar and packs of spices, making a caudle of the sea round about." The ship was at last freed, and started again on her way. Her adventures from this point offer no very salient features: she stopped at Java, the Cape of Good Hope, and Sierra Leone. In the latter place Drake saw troops of elephants, and oysters fastened on to the twigs of trees and hanging down into the water in strings.

Drake arrived at Plymouth after a voyage of two years and ten months. Like Magellan, he found he had lost a day in his reckoning. He immediately repaired to court, where he was graciously received, his treasure, however, being placed in sequestration, to answer such demands as might be made upon it.

Drake was denounced in many quarters as a pirate, while in others collections of songs and epigrams were made, celebrating him and his ship in the highest terms. The Spanish ambassador, Bernardino de Mendoza, who called him the Master-Thief of the Unknown World, demanded that he should be punished according to the laws of nations. Elizabeth firmly asserted her right of navigating the ocean in all parts, and denied that the Pope's grant of a monopoly in the Indies to the Spaniards and Portuguese was of any binding effect upon her. She yielded, however, so far as to restore, to the agent of several of the merchants whom Drake had despoiled, large sums of money. Enough remained, however, to make the expedition a remunerating one for the captors. The queen then, in a pompous and solemn ceremony, gave to the entire affair an official and governmental ratification. She ordered Drake's ship to be drawn up in a little creek near Deptford, to be there preserved as a monument of the most memorable voyage the English had ever yet performed. She went on board of her, and partook of a banquet there with the commander, who, kneeling at her feet, rose up Sir Francis Drake. The Westminster students inscribed a Latin quatrain upon the mainmast, of which the following lines are a translation:

"Sir Drake, whom well the world's end knows, which thou didst compass round,
And whom both poles of heaven saw,—which north and south do bound,—
The stars above will make thee known, if men here silent were:
The sun himself cannot forget his fellow-traveller."

The ship remained at Deptford till she decayed and fell to pieces: a chair was made from one of her planks and presented to the University of Oxford, where it is still to be seen.

Such was the first voyage around the world accomplished by an Englishman. Drake's success awakened the spirit and genius of navigation in the English people, and may be said to have contributed in no slight degree to the naval supremacy they afterwards acquired. If, in accordance with the manner of the

QUEEN ELIZABETH KNIGHTING DRAKE.

times, he was quite as much a pirate as a navigator, and mingled plunder and piety, prayer and pillage, in pretty equal proportions, and is to be judged accordingly, he at least made a noble use of the fortune he had acquired, in aiding the queen in her wars with Spain, and in encouraging the construction of public works. He built, with his own resources, an aqueduct twenty miles in length, with which to supply Plymouth with water. He died at sea, while commanding an expedition against the Spanish West India Islands. He wrote no account of his adventures and discoveries. A volume published by Nuno da Sylva, his Portuguese pilot, whose statements were confirmed by the officers, has served as the basis of the various narratives in existence.

We may briefly allude here to an attempt made in 1585, under the auspices of the English Government, by John Davis, a seaman of acknowledged ability, with two ships,—the Sunshine and Moonshine,—to discover the Northwest Passage. After a voyage of six weeks, he saw, in north latitude 60°, a mountainous and ice-bound promontory. It was the southwestern point of Greenland, and he gave it the name of Cape Desolation, which it still retains. He now sailed to the northwest, discovered islands, coasts, and harbors, to which he gave appropriate appellations. He thus was the first to enter the strait which bears his name, and beyond which Baffin, thirty years later, was to discover the vast bay which, in its turn, was to bear his name. Davis made two subsequent voyages to these waters in search of a passage across the continent, but, with the exception of the discovery of Davis' Strait, effected nothing which needs to be chronicled here. This single discovery, however, was one of the utmost importance, as it served to stimulate research and to encourage further effort in this direction. More than two centuries were nevertheless destined to elapse before success was to be attained.

ENGLISH VESSEL OF WAR OF THE FIRST CLASS—1600.

CHAPTER XXVIII.

POLICY OF QUEEN ELIZABETH—THOMAS CAVENDISH—HIS FIRST VOYAGE—EXPLOITS UPON THE AFRICAN AND BRAZILIAN COASTS—PORT DESIRE—PORT FAMINE—BATTLES WITH THE ARAUCANIANS—CAPTURE OF PAITA—ROBBERY OF A CHURCH—REPEATED ACTS OF BRIGANDAGE—CAPTURE OF THE SANTA ANNA—THE RETURN VOYAGE—CAVENDISH'S ACCOUNT OF THE EXPEDITION—THE SPANISH ARMADA—PREPARATIONS IN ENGLAND—THE CONFLICT—TOTAL ROUT OF THE INVINCIBLES—PROCESSION IN COMMEMORATION OF THE EVENT.

Queen Elizabeth had found it to her advantage to encourage displays of public spirit in private individuals, and to excite the nobles and persons of fortune who were ambitious of distinction, as well as the indigent in search of employment, to hazard, the one their wealth, the other their lives, in the national service. She thus derived benefit from a class of people who had been of little use in any other reign. Many gentlemen of rank and position devoted a portion of their means to harassing the Spanish at sea, to prosecuting discovery in distant quarters, and to planting colonies upon savage coasts. Among the most distinguished of these was Thomas Cavendish, of Trimley, near Ipswich.

This gentleman was of an honorable family, and possessed a large estate. He equipped, in 1586, three ships of the requisite burden,—the largest, the Desire, being of one hundred and forty tons, the lesser, the Content, being of sixty, and the least, the Hugh Gallant, a bark of forty tons. He provisioned them for two years, and manned them with one hundred and twenty-three officers and men, some of whom had served under Sir Francis Drake. His patron, Lord Hunsdon, procured him a commission from Queen Elizabeth, thus assimilating his vessels to those of the navy, and rendering his contemplated piracies legitimate. Cavendish sailed from Plymouth on the 21st of July, directing his course to the south and touching upon the coasts of Guinea and Sierra Leone. Here the crew destroyed a negro town, in revenge for the death of one of their men, whom the inhabitants had killed with a poisoned arrow. Their course across the Atlantic to the Brazilian shore offers no remarkable

CAVENDISH IN BRAZIL.

features. They erected their forge upon an island, where they healed their sick and built a pinnace. Anchoring in a harbor on the Patagonian coast, Cavendish named it Port Desire, after his flag-ship,—a name which it still retains. He seems to have considered the savages to be giants, and asserts that he saw footprints eighteen inches long. He entered the Strait at the commencement of January, 1587, and soon discovered a miserable and forlorn settlement of Spaniards. These numbered twenty-three men, being all that remained of four hundred who had been left there three years before, by Sarmiento, to colonize the Strait. They had lived in destitution for the last eighteen months, being able to procure no other food than a scanty supply of shell-fish, except when they surprised a thirsty deer or seized an unsuspecting swan. They had built a fortress, in order to exclude all other nations but their own from the passage of the Strait, but had been compelled to leave it, owing to the intolerable stench proceeding from the carcasses of their unhappy companions who died of want or disease. Cavendish took the survivors on board, and named the spot upon which the fortress was built Port Famine.

PORT FAMINE.

Cavendish entered the Pacific late in February, after a tempestuous passage from the Atlantic side. Landing upon the Chilian coast, in the country of the Araucanians, he received a warm reception from the natives, who mistook his men for Spaniards, by whom the territory had been repeatedly invaded in search of gold. He afterwards undeceived them, and found them willing to satisfy his wants when convinced that they did not belong to that avaricious and cruel people. In another place, inhabited by a Spanish colony, he fought a pitched battle with two hundred horsemen, driving those who were not slain back to the mountains. At another spot farther north, the Indians brought him wood and water on their backs. In May he captured two prizes, taking out of them twenty thousand pounds' worth of sugar, molasses, calico, marmalade, and hens, and then burning them to the water's edge. He seized upon the town of Paita, which he ransacked and burned, carrying off a large quantity of household goods and twenty-five pounds' weight of pieces-of-eight, or Spanish dollars. Off the island of Puna he fell in with a ship of two hundred and fifty tons; but, being disappointed at finding her empty, he sank her out of sheer spite. The inhabitants of Puna were Christians, having followed the example of their cacique, who had married a Spanish woman and had thereupon made a profession of her religion. They were rich and industrious. Cavendish pillaged the island, burned the church, and carried off its five bells. Being attacked by the Spaniards and natives combined, he fought a long and bloody battle, after which he ravaged the fields and orchards, burned four ships on the stocks, and left the town of three hundred houses a heap of rubbish. He took a coasting-ship, rifled and scuttled her, and compelled her captain to become his pilot. He continued this course of brigandage and piracy all along the South American and Mexican coasts, destroying towns, pillaging custom-houses, and burning vessels.

Early in November, Cavendish, who had been told by the pilot he had taken that a vessel from the Philippines was expected, richly laden, at Acapulco, lay in wait for her off the headland of California. She was discovered on the 4th, bearing in for the Cape. She was the Santa Anna, of seven hundred tons, belonging to the King of Spain, and commanded by the Admiral of the South Sea. Cavendish gave chase, and, after a broadside and a volley of small-arms, boarded her. He was repulsed, but renewed the action with his guns and musketry.

The Spaniard was soon forced to surrender, and her officers, going on board the Desire, gave an account of her contents,—which they stated at thirty thousand dollars in gold, with immense quantities of damasks, silks, satins, musk, and provisions. This glorious prize was divided by Cavendish, a mutiny being very nearly the result: it was, however, prevented by the generosity of the commander. The prisoners were set on shore with sufficient means of defence against the Indians; the Santa Anna was burned, together with five hundred tons of her goods; and Cavendish then set sail for the Ladrone Islands, five thousand five hundred miles distant.

He arrived at Guam, one of the group, in forty-five days, and from thence prosecuted his homeward voyage, through the Philippine Islands and the Moluccas, to Java. He passed the months of April and May, 1588, in crossing the Indian Ocean to the Cape of Good Hope. He touched at St. Helena early in June, and, when near the Azores, in September, heard from a Flemish ship the news of the total defeat of the great Spanish Armada. He lost nearly all his sails in a storm off Finisterre, and replaced them by sails of silken grass, which he had taken from his prizes in the South Sea. The voyage of Cavendish was the third that had been performed round the world, and was the shortest of the three,—being accomplished in eight months' less time than that of Drake.

Cavendish at once wrote a letter to Lord Hunsdon, in which occurs the following brief relation of his achievements:—"It hath pleased the Almighty to suffer me to encompass all the whole globe of the world. I navigated along the coasts of Chili, Peru, and New Spain, where I made great spoils. I burned and sank nineteen sail of ships, great and small. All the towns and cities that ever I landed at I burned and spoiled, and, had I not been discovered upon the coast, I had taken a great quantity of treasure. . . . All which services, together with myself, I humbly prostrate at her majesty's feet, desiring the Almighty long to continue her reign among us; for at this day she is the most famous and victorious prince that liveth in the world. Thus, humbly desiring pardon for my tediousness, I leave your lordship to the tuition of the Almighty."

Cavendish spent his immense wealth in equipping vessels for a second voyage, which ended disastrously, and in which, after being beaten by the Portuguese off the coast of Brazil, he died of shame and grief. He ranks as one of the most enterprising, diligent, and cautious of the early English navigators, though, of course, he must be regarded as an arrant buccaneer.

From what we have said of the piracies of the English, and of their encroachments upon the domain of the Spanish, and of the ardent desire of the latter to retain the monopoly of the trade with the natives of America and to hold the exclusive right to rob and slay them at their pleasure, the reader will be prepared for the imposing but bombastic attempt made by Spain against England in 1588. Philip II. determined to put forth his strength, and his fleet was named, before it sailed, "The most Fortunate and Invincible Armada." It was described in official accounts as consisting of one hundred and thirty ships, manned by eight thousand four hundred and fifty sailors, and carrying nineteen thousand soldiers, two thousand galley-slaves, and two thousand six hundred pieces of brass. The vessels were named from Romish saints, from the various appellations of the Trinity, from animals and fabulous monsters,—the Santa Catilina, the Great Griffin, and the Holy Ghost being profanely intermixed. In the fleet were one hundred and twenty-four volunteers of noble family, and one hundred and eighty almoners, Dominicans, Franciscans, and Jesuits. Instruments of torture were placed on board in large quantities, for the purpose of assisting in the great work of reconciling England to Romanism. The Spaniards and the Pope had resolved that all who should defend the queen and withstand the invasion should, with all their families, be rooted out, and their places, their honors, their titles, their houses, and their lands, be bestowed upon the conquerors.

Elizabeth and her councillors heard these ominous denunciations undismayed, and adequate preparations were made to receive the crusaders. London alone furnished ten thousand men, and held ten thousand more in reserve: the whole land-force amounted to sixty-five thousand. The fleet numbered one hundred and eighty-one vessels,—fifty more in number than the Armada, but hardly half as powerful in tonnage. Eighteen of these vessels were volunteers, and but one of the one hundred and eighty-one was of the burden of eleven hundred tons. The Lord High-Admiral of England, Charles, Lord Howard of Effingham, commanded the fleet, with Drake, Hawkins, and Frobisher in command of the various divisions. A form of prayer was published, and the clergy were enjoined to read it on Wednesdays and Fridays in their parish churches. In this, Elizabeth was compared to Deborah, preparing to combat the pride and might of Sisera-Philip. The country awaited the arrival of the Spaniards in anxiety, and yet with confidence.

The Armada sailed from the Tagus late in May, with the solemn blessing of the Church, and patronized by every influen-

HULL OF A VESSEL OF THE ARMADA.

tial saint in the calendar. A storm drove it back with loss, and it did not sail again till the 12th of July. It was descried off Plymouth on the 20th, "with lofty turrets like castles, in front like a half-moon; the wings thereof spreading out about the length of seven miles, sailing very slowly, though with full sails, the winds being as it were weary with wafting them, and the ocean groaning under their weight." The English suffered them to pass Plymouth, that they might attack them in the rear. They commenced the fight the next day, with only forty ships. The Spaniards, during this preliminary action, found their ships "very useful to defend, but not to offend, and better fitted to stand than to move." Drake, with his usual luck, captured a galleon in which he found fifty-five thousand ducats in gold. This sum was divided among his crew. Skirmishing and detached fights continued for several days, the Spanish ships being found, from their height and thickness, inaccessible by boarding or ball. They were compared to castles pitched into the sea. The lord-admiral was consequently instructed to convert eight of his least efficient vessels into fire-ships. The order arrived as the enemy's fleet anchored off Calais, and thirty hours afterwards the eight ships selected were discharged of all that was worth removal and filled with combustibles. Their guns were heavily loaded, and their sides smeared with rosin and wild-fire. At midnight they were sent, with wind and tide, into the heart of the invincible Armada. A terrible panic seized the affrighted crews: remembering the fire-ships which had been used but lately in the Scheldt, they shouted, in agony, "The fire of Antwerp! The fire of Antwerp!" Some cut their cables, others slipped their hawsers, and all put to sea, "happiest they who could first be gone, though few could tell what course to take." Some were wrecked on the shallows of Flanders; some gained the ocean; while the remainder were attacked and terribly handled by Drake. The discomfited Spaniards resolved to return to Spain by a northern circuit around England and Scotland. The English pursued, but the exhausted state of their powder-magazines prevented another engagement. The luckless Armada never returned to Spain. A terrific storm drove the vessels upon the Irish coast and upon the inhospitable rocks of the

Orkneys. Thirty of them were stranded near Connaught: two had been cast away upon the shores of Norway. In all, eighty-one ships were lost, and but fifty-three reached home. Out of thirty thousand soldiers embarked, fourteen thousand were missing. Philip received the calamity as a dispensation of Providence, and ordered thanks to be given to God that the disaster was no greater.

A day of thanksgiving was proclaimed in England, inasmuch as "the boar had put back that sought to lay her vineyard waste." Some time afterwards, the queen repaired in public procession to St. Paul's. The streets were hung with blue cloth;

PROCESSION IN HONOR OF THE DEFEAT OF THE ARMADA.

the royal chariot was a throne with four pillars and a canopy overhead, drawn by white horses. Elizabeth knelt at the altar and audibly acknowledged the Almighty as her deliverer from the rage of the enemy. The people were exhorted to render thanks to the Most High, whose elements—fire, wind, and storm—had wrought more destruction to the foe than the valor of their navy or the strength of their wooden walls.

SIR WALTER RALEIGH.

CHAPTER XXIX.

THE FICTION OF EL DORADO—MANOA—DESCRIPTION OF ITS FABLED SPLENDORS—ATTEMPTS OF THE SPANIARDS TO DISCOVER IT—SIR WALTER RALEIGH—HIS VOYAGE TO GUIANA—HIS ACCOUNT OF THE ORINOCO—HIS DESCRIPTION OF THE SCENERY—HIS RETURN—HIS SECOND VOYAGE—EXPEDITION TO NEWFOUNDLAND—HIS DEATH—MODERN INTERPRETATION OF THE LEGEND OF EL DORADO.

THE mines of the precious metals which the Spaniards had discovered in Peru, the wealth which they annually brought home in treasure-ships to the mother-country, together with the exaggerated accounts given by Spanish authors respecting the splendor and the civilization of the empire of the Incas, had now begun to excite the cupidity and inflame the imagination of every other people in Europe. It was known that, at the time of the conquest of Peru by Pizarro, a large number of the natives escaped into the interior; and rumor added that one of the sons of the reigning Inca had withdrawn across the continent to a region situated between the Amazon and the Orinoco and called by the general name of Guiana. Here he had founded, it was added, an empire more splendid than that of Peru: its capital city, Manoa, only one European had seen. This was a Spaniard, a marine on board a man-of-war, who, according to the legend, had allowed a powder-magazine to explode and was condemned to death for his carelessness. This penalty was commuted, however, and he was placed in a boat at the mouth of the Orinoco, with orders to penetrate into the interior. He stayed seven months at Manoa, and then escaped to Porto Rico. He gave the following account of the city and kingdom, the latter being called, he said, El Dorado, or The Gilded:

The columns of the emperor's palace were of porphyry and alabaster, the galleries of ebony and cedar, and golden steps led to a throne of ivory. The palace, which was built of white marble, stood upon an island in a lake or inland sea. Two towers guarded the entrance: between them was a pillar twenty-five feet in height, upon which was a huge silver moon. Beyond was a quadrangle planted with trees, and watered by a silver fountain which spouted through four golden pipes. The gate of the palace was of copper. Within, four lamps burned day and night before an altar of silver upon which was a burnished golden sun. Three thousand workmen were employed in the Street of the Silversmiths.

The name of El Dorado, as applied to the kingdom of which Manoa was the metropolis, may refer to its wealth and splendor, or it may be derived from a habit attributed by some to the emperor, by others to the high-priests, and even to the inhabitants generally when in a state of intoxication. This custom was to cause themselves to be anointed with a precious and fragrant gum, after which gold-dust was blown upon them through tubes, till they were completely incrusted with gold. This attire was naturally considered sumptuous, and, in connection with the abundance of precious metals afforded by the country, may have given rise to the title of El Dorado. The legend, in either case, is a worthy companion to Ponce de Leon's Fountain of Youth.

No geographical fiction ever caused such an expenditure of blood and treasure as this. The Spaniards alone lost, in their attempts to discover the city of Manoa, more lives and money than in effecting any of their permanent conquests. New adventurers were always ready to start, upon the discomfiture or destruction of those who had gone before; and no disappointment suffered by the latter could daunt the hopes of those who believed the discovery reserved for them. The Spanish priests regarded the mania as a device of the Evil One to lure mankind to perdition.

The greater portion of these persons were adventurers, soldiers of fortune, and Quixotic knights-errant. The most distinguished of the converts to a belief in the existence of an El Dorado, however, it would be unjust to class among them. Sir Walter Raleigh, an Englishman of the highest talent and character, after having enjoyed the favor of Queen Elizabeth for twenty years, lost it by an intrigue with a lady of the palace. Though he repaired the injury by marrying the lady, he found he could not expect to be restored to grace except by performing some exploit which should add new lustre to his name. He had long been filled with admiration at the courage and perseverance exhibited by the Spaniards in the pursuit of their romantic and brilliant chimera. As he himself firmly believed it to be a reality, he determined to make an attempt himself. A part of his design was to colonize Guiana, and thus to extend the sphere of the industrial and commercial arts of England. He was familiar with the sea, as he had already sent out several expeditions for the colonization of Virginia in America.

He sailed from Plymouth in February, 1595, with five vessels and a hundred soldiers. In order to reach the capital city of Guiana, it was necessary to ascend the Orinoco, the navigation of which was completely unknown to the English. As the ships drew too much water, a hundred men embarked with Raleigh in boats and proceeded up the stream. In these they remained for a month, exposed to all the extremes of a tropical climate, —sometimes to the heats of a burning sun, and again to violent and torrential rains. Raleigh's account of their progress through the labyrinth of islands and channels at the river's mouths, of their precarious supplies of food and water, the appearance of the country and the manners of the natives, and, finally, of their entrance into the grand bed of the superb Orinoco, has been admired for its descriptive beauty as well as ridiculed for its extravagant credulity. Indeed, it is doubted by many whether Raleigh really believed the stories which he put in circulation. We quote a passage:

"Those who are desirous to discover and to see many nations," he writes, "may be satisfied within this river; which bringeth forth so many arms and branches leading to several countries and provinces, above two thousand miles east and west, and of these the most either rich in gold, or in other merchandises. The common soldier shall here fight for gold, and pay himself, instead of pence, with plates of gold half a foot broad, whereas he breaketh his bones in other wars for provant and penury. Those commanders and chieftains who shoot at honor and abundance shall find here more rich and beautiful cities, more temples adorned with golden images, more sepulchres filled with treasure, than either Cortez found in Mexico or Pizarro in Peru; and the shining glory of this conquest will eclipse all those so-far-extended beams of the Spanish nation. There is no country which yieldeth more pleasure to the inhabitants, for those common delights of hunting, hawking, fishing, fowling, and the rest, than Guiana does. I am resolved that, both for health, good air, pleasure, and riches, it cannot be equalled by any region in the East or West. To conclude: Guiana is a country that hath yet her maidenhead, never sacked, turned, nor wrought. The face of the earth hath not been torn, nor the virtue and salt of the soil spent; the graves have not been opened for gold, the mines not broken with sledges, nor the images pulled down out of their temples. It hath never been entered by any army of strength, nor conquered by any Christian prince. . . . I trust that He who is Lord of lords will put it into her heart who is Lady of ladies to possess it. If not, I will judge those most worthy to be kings thereof that by her grace and leave will undertake it of themselves."

Raleigh ascended the stream nearly two hundred miles, when the rapid and terrific rise of its waters compelled him to return. He took formal possession of the country, and made the caciques swear allegiance to Queen Elizabeth. He returned to England during the summer, having been but five months absent. It was then that he published the narrative from which we have quoted.

His restoration to favor precluded any further prosecution of his designs on Guiana during the reign of Elizabeth. He was imprisoned for thirteen years during the reign of James, her successor, for the crime of high-treason and supposed participation in the plot to place Lady Arabella Stuart on the throne. In 1617, he equipped a fleet of thirteen vessels in which to proceed to Guiana for the purpose of again seeking El Dorado. The fleet arrived in safety, but Raleigh was too unwell to ascend the Orinoco in person. Captain Keymis led the exploring party, and, upon being compelled to return to the ship without success, and with the news of the death in battle of Sir Walter's eldest son, committed suicide. Raleigh sailed to Newfoundland to victual and refit; but a mutiny of the crews forced him to return to England, where he was beheaded for the crime already punished by thirteen years' confinement.

Modern historians and travellers, and men of judgment and intelligence who have inhabited the regions at the mouth of the Orinoco, have not hesitated to avow their opinion that the story of El Dorado is not without some sort of foundation in fact. Humboldt accounts for it geologically, and holds the ardent imagination of the Indians to be answerable for the fable. He conjectures that there may be islands and rocks of micaslate and talc in and around Lake Parima, which, reflecting from their surfaces and angles the glowing rays of the sun, may have been transformed by the extravagant fancy of the natives into the gorgeous temples and palaces of a gilded metropolis. He attempted to penetrate to the spot, but was prevented by a tribe of Indian dwarfs. No European has ever yet visited this celebrated locality: its great distance from the sea, the trackless forests, the wild beasts and barbarian inhabitants, have repelled both the conqueror and the explorer, so that it is not known to this day what degree or what kind of authority exists for the extraordinary story in question. But, inasmuch as Cortez passed within ten miles of the wonderful city of Copan without hearing of it, the supposition that there may be aboriginal cities in the unexplored regions of South America, affording, perhaps, basis sufficient for the tale of El Dorado without its exaggerations, is neither impossible nor improbable. The magnificent ruins lately discovered in Yucatan, where they were not expected, seem to argue the existence of others in regions where positive and persistent tradition has located them.

NATIVE OF THE SOLOMON ISLANDS.

CHAPTER XXX.

DISCOVERY OF THE SOLOMON ISLANDS BY MENDANA—HE SEEKS FOR THEM AGAIN THIRTY YEARS LATER—QUIROS—THE MARQUESAS ISLANDS—THE WOMEN COMPARED WITH THOSE OF LIMA—STRANGE FRUITS—CONVERSIONS TO CHRISTIANITY—ARDUOUS VOYAGE—SANTA CRUZ—MENDANA EXCHANGES NAMES WITH MALOPÉ—HOSTILITIES—WAR, AND ITS RESULTS—DEATH OF MENDANA—QUIROS CONDUCTS THE SHIPS TO MANILLA.

THE progress of discovery now recalls us to Spain. About the year 1567, one Alvaro Mendana de Neyra, who had thus far lived in complete obscurity, followed his uncle Don Pedro de Castro to Lima, in Peru, where he had been appointed governor. Mendana, disdaining commerce, and feeling little inclination to lead a monotonous life on shore, after the taste he had had during the passage of a roving existence upon the water, resolved to undertake the discovery of new lands in the name of the King of Spain. His uncle encouraged him in his design and furnished him with the necessary funds. Mendana set sail from Callao on the 11th of January, 1568. He proceeded fourteen hundred and fifty leagues to the west, and discovered a group of islands in about 10° south latitude. One of them, to which he gave the name of Isabella, is distinguished as having been the scene of the first celebration of a Catholic mass in the Pacific Ocean. He sailed round another of the group, St. Christopher, and, after several disastrous encounters with the natives, returned to Callao. This voyage, the most important undertaken by the Spanish since the discovery of America, gave rise to multitudes of fables, with which the historians and chroniclers of Spain filled the minds of the people during the century which followed. The islands discovered by Mendana were represented as enormously rich in gold and the precious metals. The name of Solomon was given to the group,—a name which was thought to be eminently suited to so luxurious an archipelago, having formerly been that of a luxurious prince. As in those days the art of scientific navigation was in its infancy, and as latitude and longitude were not fixed with any great degree of precision, the position of the Solomon Islands was very loosely marked down by Mendana, and the question of their locality became, and for a long time remained, one of the most puzzling questions in geography.

Mendana sent home to the Spanish Government brilliant accounts of his discoveries, and solicited the means of prosecuting them still further. War and other engagements prevented the ministry from attending to his requests till the year 1595, when he obtained the command of an expedition having for its object the colonization of St. Christopher. He sailed from Callao in April with four ships carrying four hundred men: his wife, Isabel de Barretos, and three of his brothers-in-law, accompanied him. Pedro Fernandez de Quiros, of whom we shall afterwards speak more particularly, was the pilot of the fleet. They stopped at Paita, where they watered and enlisted four hundred additional men, and on the 16th of June finally started in quest of the long-lost islands. A month afterwards, being in latitude 11° south, Mendana discovered a group of three islands, to which he gave a collective name as well as individual names. He called them Las Marquesas de Mendoça, in honor of the Marquis of Mendoça, a Spaniard of distinction. They are still known as the Marquesas Islands. The natives manifested a remarkably thievish disposition, and received several rounds of grape for pilfering the jars of the watering party who had gone ashore. Though the chronicler draws a comparison in speaking of the women, he yet skilfully contrives to compliment all parties mentioned. He says, "Very fine women were seen here. Many thought them as beautiful as those of Lima, but whiter and not so rosy; and yet there are very beautiful at Lima. They have delicate hands, genteel body and waiste, exceeding much in perfection the most perfect of Lima; and yet there are very beautiful at Lima. The temperament, health, strength, and corpulency of these people tell what is the climate they live in: cloaths could well be borne with night and day; the sun did not molest much; there fell some small showers of rain. Our people never perceived lightning or dew, but great dryness, so that, without hanging up, they found dry in the morning the things which were left wet on the ground at night." A singular fruit was noticed, which the men eat green, roasted, boiled, and ripe. It had neither stone nor kernel, and the Spaniards called it blancmange. They likewise admired another fruit "inclosed in prickles like chestnuts, and which resembled chestnuts in taste, but was much bigger than six chestnuts together." Mendana ordered a grand mass to be said, during which the islanders remained on their knees with great silence and attention.

Mendana took possession of the islands in the king's name, and sowed maize in many spots which he thought favorable to its growth. The chaplain taught one of the natives to bless himself and say Jesus Maria. This being done, the shallop being refitted, three crosses erected, and wood and water having been stored, the squadron set sail again for the still-missing archipelago. The soldiers soon became despondent, and the crews were placed upon short allowance. Fourteen hundred leagues from Lima they saw a desert island, which they called St. Bernardo; and at fifteen hundred and thirty-five leagues' distance they named an island the Solitary, "as it was alone." Thus they continued their course, "many people giving their sentiments, and saying they knew not whither they were going nor what they were coming to, and other such things, which could not fail of giving pain." At last, when eighteen hundred leagues from Lima, they fell in with a large island, one hundred miles in circuit, which Mendana named Santa Cruz—since called Egmont Island by Carteret. Here was a volcano, "of a very fine-shaped hill, from the top whereof issues much fire, and which often makes a great thundering inside." Fifty small boats rigged with sails came out to the ship. The men were black, with woolly hair, dyed white, red, and blue. Their teeth were tinged red, and their faces and bodies marked with streaks. Their arms were bound round with bracelets of black rattan, while their necks were decorated with strings of beads and fishes' teeth. Mendana at once took them for the people he sought. He spoke to them in the language he had learned upon his first voyage; but they neither understood him, nor he them. Without provocation, they discharged a shower of arrows at the ship, which lodged in the sails and the rigging,—without, however, doing any mischief. The soldiers fired in return, killing one and wounding many more.

Friendly relations were soon restored, and a savage, apparently of high rank, visited the admiral in his ship. He was lean and gray-headed, and his skin was of the "color of wheat." He inquired who was the chief of the new-comers. The admiral received him with cordiality, and gave him to understand that he was. The Indian said his name was Malopé. The admiral replied that his was Mendana. Malopé at once rejoined that he would be Mendana, and that the admiral should be Malopé. He manifested much gratification at this exchange, and, whenever he was called Malopé, said, "No: Mendana;" and, pointing to the admiral, said that was Malopé. This was probably the first instance of an exchange of names—one of the most solemn acts of friendship with certain tribes of the Pacific Islanders—being effected between a European and a savage. The natives soon learned to shake hands, to embrace, to say "friend," to shave with razors, and to pare their nails with scissors. This state of amity did not last long, however, and a trivial circumstance caused suspicion, and finally hostility. The savages commenced with arrows, and the Spaniards retaliated with fire and sword. In the evening, Malopé came to the shore, and, in a loud voice, called the admiral by the name of Malopé, and, smiting his breast, declared himself to be Mendana. He said the attack had been begun by another tribe, not his, and proposed they should all sally forth against them. To this Mendana did not accede, but, landing his men, proceeded to found a colony.

At this point the details furnished by the several chroniclers of the expedition become vague and unsatisfactory. It appears that Malopé was killed in a skirmish; that the natives were not content with merely lamenting his death, but withheld all supplies from the Spaniards; that Mendana caused two mutineers to be beheaded and another to be hung. A war of extermination now commenced, and a state of sedition, misery, and want ensued, which brought Mendana rapidly to the grave. He died of disappointment and regret, in October, 1595. His successor, being wounded, died in November. The crew, worn out with fatigue and sickness, and being reduced to such an extent that twenty resolute Indians could have destroyed them, resolved to suspend the enterprise and re-embark. They took in wood and water, and sailed on the 7th of November. Quiros maintained discipline among a mutinous crew, and, after almost superhuman efforts to navigate his crazy ships upon an unknown sea, arrived with the remains of the expedition at Manilla. From thence Quiros—whose adventures and discoveries we shall soon have occasion to narrate—returned to Acapulco, in Mexico, and thence to Lima, where he petitioned the viceroy for the means of continuing the researches of Mendana. As he did not set sail till 1606, we must first attend to the various enterprises undertaken in the interval.

THE DUTCH AT WALRUS ISLAND.

CHAPTER XXXI.

ATTEMPTS OF THE DUTCH TO DISCOVER A NORTHEAST PASSAGE—VOYAGE OF WILHELM BARENTZ—ARRIVAL AT NOVA ZEMBLA—WINTER QUARTERS—BUILDING A HOUSE—FIGHTS WITH BEARS—THE SUN DISAPPEARS—THE CLOCK STOPS, AND THE BEER FREEZES—THE HOUSE IS SNOWED UP—THE HOT-ACHE—FOX-TRAPS—TWELFTH NIGHT—RETURN OF THE SUN—THE SHIPS PROVE UNSEAWORTHY—PREPARATIONS TO DEPART IN THE BOATS—DEATH OF BARENTZ—ARRIVAL AT AMSTERDAM—RESULTS OF THE VOYAGE.

In the year 1514, the Dutch resolved to seek a northeast passage by water to the Indies, across the Polar regions of Europe. Their first two attempts were attended with so little success that the States-General abandoned the undertaking, contenting themselves with promising a reward to the navigator who should find a practicable route. In 1596, the city of Amsterdam took up the matter where the Government had left it, and equipped two vessels, the chief command of which was given to Wilhelm Barentz. He started on the 10th of May, and passed the islands of Shetland and Feroë on the 22d. Not long after, the fleet saw with wonder one of the phenomena peculiar to the Arctic regions,—three mock suns, with circular rainbows connecting them by a luminous halo. On the 9th of June, they discovered two islands, to which they gave the names of Bear and Walrus Islands. They kept on, to the usual Arctic accompaniment of icebergs, seals, auroræ boreales, whales, and white bears, till they came to a land which they named Spitzbergen, or Land of Sharp-peaked Mountains.

On the 17th of July, they arrived at Nova Zembla,—discovered in 1553 by Willoughby,—and here the two ships were accidentally separated. In August, the vessel of Barentz was embayed in drifting ice, and no efforts could release her from her dangerous position. Winter was coming on, and the crew, despairing of saving the ship, which was now groaning and heaving under the pressure of the ice, resolved to build a house upon the land, "with which to defend themselves from the colde and wilde beasts." They were fortunate enough to find a large quantity of drift-wood, which had evidently floated from a distance, as the icy soil around them yielded neither tree nor herb. The work began and continued in the midst of constant fights with bears and the arduous labor of dragging stores from the ship upon hand-sleds. The cold was so extreme that their skin peeled off upon touching any iron utensil. Snow storms interrupted the progress of the house, for which they were soon obliged to obtain materials by breaking up the ship. One of the men, being pursued by a bear, was only saved by the latter's waiting to contemplate the body of one of his fellow-bears, which the sailors had killed and left to freeze stiff in an upright position.

On the 12th of October, half the crew slept in the house for the first time: they suffered greatly from cold, as they had no fire, and because, as the narrative quaintly remarks, "they were somewhat deficient in blankets." The roof was thatched, by the end of October, with sail-cloth and sea-weed. On the 2d of November, the sun raised but half his disk above the horizon: the bears disappeared with the sun, and foxes took their place. The clock having stopped, and refusing to proceed, even with increased weights, day could not be distinguished from night, except by the twelve-hour-glass. The beer, freezing in the casks, became as tasteless as water. Half a pound of bread a day was served out to each man: the provisions of dried fish and salt meat remained still abundant. The chimney would not draw, and the apartment was filled with a blinding smoke,—which the crew were obliged to endure, however, or die of cold. The surgeon made a bathing-tub from a wine-pipe, in which they bathed four at a time. They were several times snowed up, and the house was absolutely buried. Though half a league from the sea, they heard the horrible cracking and groaning of the ice as the bergs settled down one upon the other, or as the huge mountains burst asunder. On one occasion, unable to support the cold, they made a fire in their house with coal brought from the ship. It was the first moment of comfort they had enjoyed for months. They kept up the genial heat until several of the least vigorous of the men were seized with dizziness and with the peculiar pains known as the hot-ache. Gerard de Veer, the chronicler of the expedition, caught in his arms the first man that fell, and revived him by rubbing his face with vinegar. He adds, "We had now learned that to avoid one evil we should not rush into a worse one."

THE DUTCH IN WINTER QUARTERS.

They set traps all around their cabin, with which they caught on an average a fox a day. They eat the flesh, and with the skins made caps and mittens. They had the good fortune to kill a bear nine feet long, from which they obtained one hundred pounds of lard. This they found useful, not as pomatum, but as the means of burning their lamp constantly, day and night, as if it were an altar and they the vestal virgins. On the 19th of December, they congratulated themselves that the Arctic night was just one-half expired; "for," says the narrative, "it was a terrible thing to be without the light of the sun, and deprived of the most excellent creature of God, which enliveneth the entire universe." On Christmas eve it snowed so violently that they could not open the door. The next day there was a white frost in the cabin. While seated at the fire and toasting their legs, their backs were frozen stiff. They did not know by the feeling that they were burning their shoes, and were only warned by the odor of the shrivelling leather. They put a strip of linen into the air, to see which way the wind was: in an instant the linen was frozen as hard as a board, and became, of course, perfectly useless as a weathercock. Then the men said to each other, "How excessively cold it must be out of doors!"

The 5th of January was Twelfth Night, and the hut was buried under the snow. In the midst of their misery, they asked the captain's leave to celebrate the hallowed anniversary. With flour and oil they made pancakes, washing them down with wine saved from the day before and borrowed in advance from the morrow. They elected a king by lot, the master gunner being indicated by chance as the Lord of Nova Zembla. On the 8th, the twilight was observed to be slightly lengthening, and, though the cold increased with the returning sun, they bore it with cheerfulness. They noticed a tinge of red in the atmosphere, which spoke of the revival of nature. They visited the ship, and found the ice a foot high in the hold: they hardly expected ever to see her float again. The difficulty of obtaining fuel was now such, that many of the men thought it would be easier and shorter to lie down and die than make such dreadful efforts to prolong life. To save wood during the daytime, they played snow-ball, or ran, or wrestled, to keep up the circulation.

On the 24th of January, Gerard de Veer declared he had seen the edge of the sun: Barentz, who did not expect the return of the luminary for fourteen days, was incredulous, and the cloudy state of the weather during the succeeding three days prevented the bets which were made upon the subject from being settled. On the 27th, they buried one of their number in a snow grave seven feet deep, having dug it with some difficulty, the diggers being constantly obliged to return to the fire. One of the men remarking that, even were the house completely blocked up fifteen feet deep, they could yet get out by the chimney, the captain climbed up the chimney, and a sailor ran out to see if he succeeded. He rushed back, saying he had seen the sun. Everybody hastened forth and "saw him, in his entire roundness," just above the horizon. It was then decided that de Veer had seen the edge on the 24th, and they "all rejoiced together, praising God loudly for the mercy."

Another season of snow now set in, while, at the same time, the ice that bound the ship began to break up, so that the men feared she would escape and float away while they were blockaded in the house. They were obliged to make themselves shoes of worn-out fox-skin caps, as the leather was frozen as hard as horn. On the night of the 6th of April, a bear ascended to the roof of the house by means of the embankments of snow, and, attacking the chimney with great violence, was very near demolishing it. On the 1st of May, they eat their last morsel of meat, relying henceforth on what they might entrap or kill.

It was now decided that even if the ship should be disengaged she would be unfit to continue the voyage. Their only hope lay in the shallop and the long-boat, which they endeavored to prepare for the sea, in the midst of interruptions from bears, who "were very obstinate to know how Dutchmen tasted."

As late as the 5th of June, it snowed so violently that they could only work within-doors, where they got ready the sails, oars, rudder, &c. On the 12th, they set to work with axes and other tools to level a path from the ship to the water,—a distance of five hundred paces. On the 13th, Barentz wrote a brief account of their voyage and sojourn, placed it in a musket-barrel, and attached it to the fireplace in the house, for the information of future navigators. They then dragged, with infinite labor, the boats to the water, together with barrels and boxes of such stores as their now impoverished ship could yield. They bade adieu to their winter quarters on the 14th, at early morning, "with a west wind and under the protection of Heaven." Barentz, who had been a long time ill, died on the 20th, while opposite Icy Cape, the northernmost point of Nova Zembla. His loss was deeply regretted; but their "grief was assuaged by the reflection that none can resist the will of God."

The men were often obliged to drag the boats across intervening fields of ice; and sometimes, when the wind was contrary, they drew them up on a floating bank, and, making tents of the sails, camped out, as if on military service. The sentinels frequently challenged bears, and, on one occasion, three coming together and one being killed, the surviving two devoured their fallen companion. Through dangers and difficulties then unparalleled in navigation, they struggled hopefully on, descending the western coast of Nova Zembla towards the northern shores of Russia and Lapland. On the 16th of August, they met a Russian bark, which furnished them with such provisions as the captain could spare. On the 20th, they touched the coast of Lapland upon the White Sea, where they found thirteen Russians living in miserable huts upon the fish which they caught. On the 2d of September, they arrived at Kola, in Lapland, where they found three Dutch ships, one of which was their consort, which had been separated from them ten months before. Having no further use for their boats, they carried them with ceremony to the "Merchants' House," or Town-Hall, where they dedicated them to the memory of their long voyage of four hundred leagues over a tract never traversed before, and which they had accomplished in open boats. They started at once for home, and arrived on the 1st of November at Amsterdam, twelve in number. The city was greatly excited by the news of their return, for they had long since been given up for dead. The chancellor and the "ambassador of the very illustrious King of Denmark, Norway, the Goths and the Vandals" were at that moment at dinner. The voyagers were summoned to narrate their adventures before them,—which they did, "clad in white fox-skin caps."

No voyage had hitherto been so fruitful in incident, peril, and displays of persevering courage and fortitude. Though it resulted in no discovery except that of the western coast of Nova Zembla, it served the useful purpose of demonstrating the difficulty, if not the impossibility, of effecting a northeast passage.

THE FUNERAL OF MAHU AT BRAVA ISLAND.

CHAPTER XXXII.

THE FIVE SHIPS OF ROTTERDAM—BATTLE AT THE ISLAND OF BRAVA—SEBALD DE WEERT—DISASTERS IN THE STRAIT OF MAGELLAN—THE CREW EAT UNCOOKED FOOD—THE FLEET IS SCATTERED TO THE WINDS—ADVENTURES OF DE WEERT—A WRETCHED OBJECT—RETURN TO HOLLAND—VOYAGE OF OLIVER VAN NOORT—BARBAROUS PUNISHMENT—THE EMBLEM OF HOPE BECOMES A CAUSE OF DESPAIR—FIGHT WITH THE PATAGONIANS—ARREST OF THE VICE-ADMIRAL—HIS PUNISHMENT—DESCRIPTION OF A CHILIAN BEVERAGE—CAPTURE OF A SPANISH TREASURE-SHIP—A PILOT THROWN OVERBOARD—SEA-FIGHT OFF MANILLA—RETURN HOME, AFTER THE FIRST DUTCH VOYAGE OF CIRCUMNAVIGATION.

THE Dutch, who had now succeeded the Portuguese in the possession and control of the East Indies, had, up to the year 1598, made all their voyages thither by the Portuguese route,—the Cape of Good Hope. In this year, two fleets fitted out by them were directed to proceed by the Strait of Magellan and across the South Sea. The first of these expeditions is known as that of the Five Ships of Rotterdam, one of the five, however, becoming separated, and forming a distinct enterprise, under Sebald de Weert: the second was the voyage of Oliver Van Noort. We shall narrate them in order of time.

The Five Ships of Rotterdam were equipped at the charge of several merchants called the Company of Peter Verhagen. The flag-ship, commanded by Jacob Mahu, was named the Hope; another, commanded by Sebald de Weert, was the Good News, or Glad Tidings, or Merry Messenger,—all these names being given in the various translations. They sailed from Goree, in Holland, on the 27th of June, 1598.

They were off the island of Brava—one of the Cape Verds,—on the 11th of September, and sent boats ashore with empty casks in search of water. The men were accosted by some Portuguese and negroes, who told them that French and English ships were accustomed to water there, but always remained under sail. Sebald de Weert noticed four or five ruinous huts, and found them full of maize, which he at once proceeded to appropriate,—an act which the Portuguese endeavored to resent; but the Dutch flag-ship silenced their feeble resistance with her guns. The death of Mahu now caused a transfer of captains, by which Sebald de Weert left the Glad Tidings for the Good Faith. The fleet lost thirty men by the scurvy during the passage across the Atlantic. They anchored off the Rio de la Plata early in March, 1599, and observed the sea to be as red as blood. The water was examined, and found to be full of small worms, which jumped about like fleas, and which were supposed to have been shaken off by whales in their gambols, as the lion shakes dew-drops from his mane.

On the 6th of April, they entered the Strait of Magellan, and were compelled to pass the Antarctic winter there,—that is, till late in August. Gales of wind followed each other in quick succession; and the anchors and cables were so much damaged that the crews were kept in continual labor and anxiety. The scarcity of food was such that the people were sent on shore every day at low water, frequently in rain, snow, or frost, to seek for shell-fish or to gather roots for their subsistence. These they devoured in the state in which they were found, having no patience to wait to cook them. One hundred and twenty men were buried during this disastrous winter.

On the evening of September the 3d, the whole fleet, including a shallop of sixteen tons, named the Postillion, which had been put together in the Strait, entered the South Sea. A storm soon separated them, leaving the Fidelity and Faith as consorts, and scattering the rest in every direction. The adventures of the Fidelity and Faith, however, require that we should follow them in their fortunes around the world. De Weert found his ship almost unseaworthy, without a master, short of hands, and with two pilots quite too old to be efficient. After weathering another storm, which nearly sent the vessels to the bottom, both captains resolved to return to the Strait and to wait there in some safe bay for a favorable wind. On the 27th, they arrived at the mouth of the Strait, and were drifted by the current some seven leagues inland.

As the Antarctic summer was now approaching, they were in hopes of fair weather; yet during the two months of their stay they hardly had a day in which to dry their sails. The seamen began to murmur, alleging that there would not be sufficient biscuit for their return to Holland if they remained here longer. Upon this de Weert went into the bread-room, as if to examine the store, and, on coming out, declared, with a cheerful countenance, that there was biscuit enough for eight months, though in reality there was barely enough for four. On the 3d of December, they succeeded in leaving the Strait, but, by some mismanagement, anchored a league apart, with a point of land between them which intercepted the view. A gale of wind forced the Fidelity from her anchors, and she was compelled to proceed upon the voyage alone. On her arrival at the Moluccas she was attacked and captured by the Portuguese.

Sebald de Weert was thus left without a consort and almost without a crew. When leaving the Strait, and towing the only remaining boat astern, the rope broke, and the boat went adrift and was not again recovered. The next morning they saw a boat rowing towards them, which proved to belong to another Dutch fleet, under Oliver Van Noort, bound to the South Sea and the East Indies. De Weert endeavored to sail in company with them; but the reduced condition of his crew—but forty-eight men remaining out of one hundred and ten—rendered it impossible. He finally abandoned all attempts to prosecute the voyage, and, profiting by the west winds, returned through the Strait to the Atlantic. He anchored at the Penguin Islands, where a large number of birds were taken and salted. Some of the seamen who were on shore discovered a Patagonian woman among the rocks, where she had endeavored to conceal herself. The chronicle thus speaks of her:—"A state more deeply calamitous than that to which this woman was reduced, the goodness of God has not permitted to be the lot of many. The ships of Van Noort had stopped at this island about seven weeks before, where this woman was one of a numerous tribe of Patagonians; but they were savagely slaughtered by Van Noort's men. She was wounded at the same time, but lived to mourn the destruction of her race, the solitary inhabitant of a rocky, desolate island." De Weert presented her with a knife, but left her without any means of changing her situation, though she made it understood that she wished to be transported to the continent.

On the 21st of January, 1600, he left the Strait by the eastern entrance, and bent his course homewards. Six months afterwards he entered the channel of Goree, in Holland, having lost sixty-nine men during the voyage. The ship had been absent two years and sixteen days, the greater part of which had been misemployed. She had been only twenty-four days in the South Sea, and had spent nine months in the Strait of Magellan and the remainder in the passage out and back. The Faith was, nevertheless, more fortunate than her companions; for she was the only ship of the five which sailed under Jacob Mahu which ever reached home again. The Charity was abandoned at sea; the Hope was plundered by the Japanese at Bungo; the Glad Tidings was taken by the Spaniards at Valparaiso; and, as we have said, the Fidelity fell into the hands of the Portuguese at the Spice Islands. The Postillion shallop, which had been launched in the Strait, was never heard of after she entered the Pacific Ocean.

The plan of the South Sea Expedition under Oliver Van Noort was in all respects similar to that of Mahu and de Weert, and the equipment was made at the joint expense of a company of merchants. The vessels fitted out were the Mauritius, whose tonnage is not mentioned,—in which sailed, as admiral, Van Noort, who was a native of Utrecht, and an experienced seaman,—the Hendrick Frederick, and two yachts, the whole being manned by two hundred and forty-eight men. The instructions to the admiral were to sail through Magellan's Strait to the South Sea, to cruise off the coast of Chili and Peru, to cross over to the Moluccas to trade, and then, returning home, to complete the circumnavigation of the globe. He sailed on the 13th of September, three months after the departure of the Five Ships of Rotterdam.

At Prince's Island, near the coast of Guinea,—a station held by the Portuguese,—Van Noort's flag of truce was not respected by the garrison, and two Hollanders were killed and sixteen wounded. Van Noort revenged this outrage by burning all the sugar-mills which he dared to approach. He set one of his pilots ashore upon Cape Gonçalves for mutinous practices. He made the coast of Brazil early in February, 1519; but it was determined in council that, as the Southern winter was so near at hand, they would hibernate at St. Helena. They sailed eastward, and spent three months in searching for the island; but in vain. At the end of May, they unexpectedly found themselves again upon the coast of Brazil; but the Portuguese opposed their landing. On the 18th of June, the council of war sentenced two men, a constable and a gunner, "to be abandoned in any strange country where they could hereafter be of service," for mutiny; and another seaman was sentenced to be fastened, by a knife through the hand, to the mast, there to remain till he should release himself by slitting his hand through the middle. This barbarous sentence was carried into execution.

After burning one of the yachts which proved unfit for service, the fleet proceeded towards the Strait, and, on the 4th of November, anchored off Cape Virgin. Here Van Noort's ship lost three anchors, and the admiral wrote to the vice-admiral to furnish him one of his. The latter refused, saying that he was as much master as Van Noort,—a piece of impertinence which the admiral declared he would punish upon the first convenient opportunity. The vessels entered the Strait four times, and were as often forced back by the violence of the wind. On the 27th, they arrived at the two Penguin Islands. It was here that the transaction occurred to which we have alluded under Sebald de Weert. It happened as follows:

On the smallest of the islands some natives were seen, who made signs to the Dutch not to advance, and threw them some penguins from the cliffs. Seeing that the strangers continued to approach, they shot arrows at them, which the Dutch returned with bullets. The savages fled for refuge to a cavern where they had secreted their women and children. The Dutch pursued them, and used their fire-arms with unrelenting ferocity, receiving little or no damage from the feeble missiles of the natives. The latter continued to fight in defence of their women and children with undiminished courage, and not till the last man of them was killed did the Hollanders obtain an entrance.

Within they found a number of wretched mothers who had formed barricades of their own bodies to protect their children. Of these they killed several and wounded more. Seven weeks after, as has been said, Sebald de Weert found the tribe ex-

AFFRAY BETWEEN THE DUTCH AND PATAGONIANS.

terminated and but one woman surviving. Six children were taken by Van Noort on board of the fleet. One of the boys afterwards learned to speak the Dutch language, and from him were obtained several slender items of information respecting the tribe to which he had belonged, but which were far from compensating for the flagrant act of crüelty which had led to the capture of his fellow-exiles and himself.

The men went ashore near Cape Froward, and some of them ate of an herb which drove them "raging mad." During an anchorage here, the carpenters built a boat thirty-seven feet long in the keel; the blacksmith set up his forge, while the wooders made charcoal from trees which they felled. A light wind springing up, the vice-admiral, without receiving orders, fired a gun and got under way, and, though the admiral remained stationary, continued sailing on and firing guns, as if he had been commander-in-chief. Such, said Van Noort, is the effect, upon a vice-admiral, of having a larger number of anchors than his superior. He caused him to be arrested and to be tried upon the charge of exciting mutiny by insubordinate conduct, and allowed him three weeks to prepare his defence. At this period the number of deaths in the fleet had amounted to ninety-seven persons.

When the three weeks expired, the vessels were still in the Strait, and the council was assembled on board the admiral's vessel, to hear the defence of the prisoner, which proved insufficient for his acquittal, and he was condemned to be set on shore and abandoned in the Strait. This sentence was publicly read on board the different ships, and, on the 26th of January, 1600, Jacob Claesz was carried in a boat to the shore, with a small stock of bread and wine. He was thus left to shift for himself among the wild beasts and still more savage inhabitants. Van Noort ordered a prayer and exhortation to be read in the fleet during the execution of this terrible verdict.

Being still at anchor in the Strait in the middle of February, the admiral announced his determination to persevere two months longer, and, if it were still impossible to reach the Pacific by the west, to turn eastward and reach it by the Cape of Good Hope. On the 29th, the wind having veered, Van Noort, with two ships and a yacht, after a tedious navigation of a year and a half, finally entered the Great South Sea. A storm compelled the admiral to cast loose and abandon the long-boat which had been built at Cape Froward, and forced the new vice-admiral to part company. His ship was never seen again. During an anchorage upon the coast of Chili, one of the sailors whom we have already mentioned as sentenced to be abandoned upon any coast where they could be of service, was sent ashore, to open negotiations with the natives. If he succeeded and returned in safety, his sentence was to be remitted. He was favorably received, and a regular trade was established. The official narrative of the voyage thus describes the hospitality of the people:—"An elderly woman brought us an earthen vessel full of a drink of a sharp taste, of which we drank heartily. This drink is made of maize and water, and is brewed in the following manner: old women who have lost their teeth chew the maize, which, being thus mixed with their saliva, is put into a tub, and water is added to it. They have a superstitious opinion that the older the women are who chew the maize, by so much will the beverage be the better. And with this drink the natives get intoxicated and celebrate their festivals."

Soon after, Van Noort's ship gave chase to a Spaniard, which it was important to take, lest she might spread the alarm along the coast. She proved to be the Good Jesus, and to be stationed there expressly to give early notice of the arrival of strange sails. She was taken, and a prize-master placed on board to navigate her. One of the prisoners stated afterwards, that ten thousand pounds' weight of gold had been thrown overboard during her flight; and this was corroborated by the pilot, who at first denied it, but, upon being put to the torture, confessed. Van Noort now steered for the Philippines, by way of the Ladrones. On the 30th of June, the pilot of the Good Jesus, who ate at the admiral's table, was taken ill, and accused Van Noort of wishing to poison him, and maintained the charge in presence of the officers. He was sentenced to be cast head foremost into the sea,—the established Dutch mode of punishing pirates. "We therefore threw him overboard," says the journal, "and left him to sink, to the end that he should not ever again reproach us with any treachery." The Good Jesus now lost her rudder, and, being very leaky, was abandoned in mid-ocean.

While Van Noort was thus making his way towards Manilla, preparations were making at that place for defence. Cavite, the port, was fortified; two galleons were ordered to be armed and equipped. The Dutch squadron arrived off the entrance of the bay on the 24th of November, and Van Noort determined to remain there till February, to intercept all vessels bound in. He soon stopped a Japanese vessel, laden with iron and hams. He allowed her to proceed, having first purchased a wooden anchor. He remarks in the journal that he saw Japanese scimetars which could cut through three men at a blow, and that slaves were kept for the purpose of furnishing the necessary proof of their temper to purchasers. He next took a Spanish vessel laden with cocoanut wine, and a Chinese junk laden with rice. The cargoes were transferred and the vessels sunk.

Early on the morning of the 14th of December, the two galleons were seen bearing down upon the Dutch squadron, now reduced to two sails,—the Mauritius, with fifty-five men, and the Concord, with twenty-five. The Spanish ships are supposed to have had two hundred men apiece. They steered directly for the enemy, but could not return their fire, as the wind from the starboard compelled them to keep their lee ports shut. The Spanish admiral ran his ship directly upon the Dutch admiral, and his men at once overpowered the latter by the mere force of numbers. The Dutch retreated from the deck, and harassed the Spaniards from their close quarters. The colors of the Mauritius were struck, upon which the captain of the Concord, thinking his superior had surrendered, endeavored to escape, being closely pursued by the Spanish vice-admiral.

The Dutch admiral, however, was not captured yet. The Spaniards having remained masters of the open deck for six hours, Van Noort told his men they must go up and expel the enemy, or he would fire the magazine and blow up the ship. The Spanish account says that they were at this moment themselves forced to disengage their ship and withdraw their men, as the after-part of the Hollander had taken fire. At all events, the two vessels were cleared and the engagement renewed with cannon. The Spanish vessel took in water so fast that she went down not long after. The Dutch rowed about in boats among the struggling Spaniards, stabbing and knocking them on the head. In retaliation for this, the officers and crew of the Concord, which was easily taken by the Spanish vice-admiral, were conveyed to Manilla and executed as pirates and rebels. In Van

THE TWO ADMIRALS AT CLOSE QUARTERS.

Noort's ship only five men were killed, twenty-six being wounded more or less severely. He continued on his way with one vessel only, touching at Borneo, Java, and Mauritius. At the latter place, where he found other vessels at anchor, his men met with very pleasant entertainment, and on one occasion ten of them dined in an inverted tortoise-shell, the first inhabitant having withdrawn to furnish the new occupants with both soup and sitting-room.

Van Noort arrived at Rotterdam on the 26th of August, 1601, where he was received with the utmost joy, having been absent a fortnight short of three years. His was the first Dutch vessel that circumnavigated the globe, and the only one of the nine ships that sailed from Holland in 1598 in that design which succeeded in fulfilling it. The voyage contributed nothing to geography, but, in spite of the instances of barbarity with which

A DUTCH PICNIC IN THE MAURITIUS.

it abounded, added to the warlike and commercial reputation of the country, and therefore met with favor from both Government and people.

WOMAN AND CHILD OF ESPIRITU SANTO.

CHAPTER XXXIII.

QUIROS' THEORY OF A SOUTHERN CONTINENT—HIS ARGUMENTS AND MEMORIALS—HIS FIRST VOYAGE—DISCOVERIES—ENCARNAÇION—SAGITTARIA, OR TAHITI—DESCRIPTION OF THESE ISLANDS—MANICOLO—ESPIRITU SANTO—ITS PRODUCTIONS AND INHABITANTS—QUIROS BEFORE THE KING OF SPAIN—HIS BELIEF IN HIS DISCOVERY OF A CONTINENT—HIS DISAPPOINTMENT—RENEWED SOLICITATIONS—DEATH OF QUIROS—DISCOVERIES OF TORRÈS—THE MUSCOVY COMPANY OF LONDON—HENRY HUDSON—HIS VOYAGES TO SPITZBERGEN AND NOVA ZEMBLA—HIS VOYAGE TO AMERICA—CASTS ANCHOR AT SANDY HOOK—ASCENDS THE HUDSON RIVER AS FAR AS THE SITE OF ALBANY—HIS VOYAGE TO ICELAND AND HUDSON'S BAY—DISASTROUS WINTER—MUTINY—HUDSON SET ADRIFT—HIS DEATH.

WE have said, in a preceding chapter, that Pedro Fernandez de Quiros was the pilot of Mendana's second expedition. During the voyage he had reflected deeply upon the probability of the existence of a Southern continent: on his return to Peru, he asserted it, and devoted the remainder of his life to the prosecution of a plan of discovery. He was the first to bring forward scientific arguments in support of the theory,—one which, by the way, was destined to agitate and interest the world for two centuries, till its final overthrow by Cook. He presented two memorials to Don Luis de Velasco, the viceroy, praying for ships, men, and other necessaries, with which "to plough up the waters of the unknown sea, and to seek out the undiscovered lands around the Antarctic Pole, the centre of that horizon." His arguments were many of them profound, and made a deep impression upon the viceroy, who replied, however, that Quiros' desires exceeded the limits of his authority. He nevertheless despatched him with strong recommendations to the court of Spain. Philip III. gave favorable attention to his projects, and ordered that Quiros should go in person upon an expedition "among these hidden provinces and severed regions,—an expedition destined to win souls to heaven and kingdoms to the crown of Spain." Quiros returned to Lima "with the most honorable schedules which had ever passed the Council of State." He presented his papers to the viceroy, and, forgetting the obstacles and discouragements he had met with during eleven years, entered on his new and arduous labors. He built three ships, and embarked on the 20th of December, 1605, holding his course west by south.

One thousand leagues from Peru, he discovered a small island which he named Encarnaçion: to others, of little importance and uninhabited, he gave the names of Santelmo, St. Miguel, and Archangel: the tenth he called Dezena. On the 10th of February, 1606, land was seen from the topmast-head, and, to the joy of all, columns of smoke—an unmistakable sign that the land was inhabited—were perceived ascending at numerous points. A boat advanced to the surf, through which it seemed impossible to gain the shore. A young man, Francisco Ponce by name, stripped off his clothes, saying that, if they should thus turn their faces from the first danger which offered, there would be no hope of eventual success. He threw himself into the sea, and, after a fierce struggle with the receding waves, clambered up a rock to a spot where one hundred Indians were awaiting him. They seemed pleased with his resolution, and frequently kissed his forehead. Peace was made, and a safe anchorage was pointed out. The island thus discovered subsequently became, for many reasons, the most famous in the whole Pacific Ocean. Quiros called it Sagittaria; but it is now known as Tahiti or Otaheite. We shall have occasion hereafter to describe at length this lovely oasis in the desert of the waters.

SCENE IN TAHITI.

The fleet stayed here but two days, and then continued on its way. Quiros discovered several islands which have not been seen again from that time to this. To one of them he gave the name of Isla de la Gente Hermosa,—Island of Handsome People. Convinced that the mainland must be near, he kept on in search of what he called the "mother of so many islands." At one named Taumaco he seized four natives to serve him as guides and interpreters, and carried them away. He has been much blamed for this act of treachery towards a people who treated him with kindness and hospitality. Three of the four jumped overboard during the two days following, and escaped to islands in the vicinity. The chief of the island where he had taken them had informed him that, if he would change his course from the west to the south, he would come to a large tract, fertile and inhabited, named Manicolo. Following this advice, he discovered the islands of Tucopia and Nuestra Señora de la Luz. It is doubtful whether either of these has been seen by subsequent navigators. On the 26th of April, he made a land which he took to be the continent of which he was in search, and to which he gave the name of Tierra Austral del Espiritu Santo. Bougainville and Cook, who arrived here a century and a half afterwards, thought themselves justified, by acquiring the certitude that it was a group of islands and not a continent, in christening them anew,—Bougainville naming them the Grandes Cyclades, and Cook the New Hebrides.

Quiros has left an admirable picture of this fertile and delightful spot. "The rivers Jordan and Salvador," he says, "give no small beauty to their shores, for they are full of odoriferous flowers and plants. Pleasant and agreeable groves front the sea in every part: we mounted to the tops of mountains and perceived fertile valleys and rivers winding amongst green meadows. The whole is a country which, without doubt, has the advantage over those of America, and the best of the European will be well if it is equal. It is plenteous of various and delicious fruits, potatoes, yams, plantains, oranges, limes, sweet basil, nutmegs, and ebony, all of which, without the help of sickle, plough, or other artifice, it yields in every season. There are also cattle, birds of many kinds and of charming notes, honey-bees, parrots, doves, and partridges. The houses wherein the Indians live are thatched and low, and they of a black complexion. There are earthquakes,—sign of a mainland." The Spaniards found it impossible to make peace with the natives, and the few days which they spent there were passed in wrangling and bloodshed.

The achievements and discoveries of Quiros properly end here. His ships were separated, and his own crew disabled by the effects of poisonous fish which they had eaten. He called a council of his officers, and asked their opinion upon a choice of courses,—a prosecution of the voyage to China, or a return to Mexico. The latter was decided upon. Quiros arrived at Acapulco nine months after his departure from Callao.

He soon returned to Spain, where he presented a memorial to Philip III. upon the results of his voyage, and the advantage of further efforts in the same direction. His grand argument in favor of the theory that he had discovered an Austral continent was drawn from the statements of Pedro,—the only one of the four kidnapped savages of Taumaco who had remained on board. A subsequent memorial shows the fate with which all his representations to Philip met:—"I, Captain Pedro Fernandez de Quiros, say that with this I have presented to your majesty eight memorials touching the country of Australia Incognita, without to this time any resolution being taken with me, nor any reply made me, nor hope given to assure me that I shall be despatched,—having now been fourteen months in this court, and having been fourteen years engaged in this cause without pay or any other advantage in view but the success of it alone; wherewith, and through infinite contradictions, I have gone by land and sea twenty-two thousand leagues, spending all my estate and incommoding my person, suffering so many and such terrible things that even to myself they appear incredible: and all this has come to pass, that this work of so much goodness and benevolence should not be abandoned. In whose name, and all for the love of God, I beg your majesty not to neglect these innumerable benefits, which shall last as long as the world subsists, and then be eternal."

Quiros then enters into a detailed description of the islands and the continent he had seen. Their extent, he said, was as much as that of Europe, Asia Minor, England, and Ireland. They had no such turbulent neighbors as the Turks or the Moors. The people were intelligent and capable of civilization. Bread grew upon the trees. The palm yielded spirits, vinegar, honey, whey, and toddy. The green cocoanut served instead of artichoke; when ripe, for meat and cream; and, when old, for oil, wax, and balsams. The shells furnished cups and bottles. The fibres afforded oakum, cordage, and the best slow match. The leaves furnished sails, matting, and thatch. The garden-stuffs of the country were pumpkins, parsley, "with intimation of beans." The flesh was hogs, fowls, capons, partridges, geese, turkeys, ringdoves, and goats, "with intimation of cows and buffaloes." The riches were silver, pearls, and gold. The spices were nutmegs, mace, pepper, and ginger, "with intimation of cinnamon and cloves." There was ebony, and infinite woods for ship-building. At daybreak the harmony of thousands of birds trembled upon the air,—nightingales, blackbirds, larks, gold-finches, and swallows,—besides the chirping of grasshoppers and crickets. Every morning and evening the breeze was laden with fragrant scents wafted from orange-flowers and sweet basil. This enthusiastic document concludes thus:—"I can show this in a company of mathematicians, that this land will presently accommodate and sustain two hundred thousand Spaniards. None of our men fell sick from over-work, or sweating, or getting wet. Fish and flesh kept sound two or more days. I saw neither sandy ground, nor thistles, nor prickly trees, nor mangrovy swamps, nor snow on the mountains, nor crocodiles in the rivers, nor ants in the dust, nor mosquitos in the night.

"Acquire, sire, since you can with a little money, which will be required but once,—acquire heaven, eternal fame, and that new world with all its promises. Order the galleons to be ready, sire; for I have many places to go to, and much to provide and to do. Let it be observed that in all I shall be found very submissive to reason, and will give satisfaction in every thing."

These stirring appeals were disregarded by the feeble successor of Charles V.; and Quiros, who, though a Portuguese by birth, is often styled the last of the Spanish heroes, died at Panama on his way back to Lima.

We mentioned the dispersion of Quiros' fleet after leaving Espiritu Santo. We must recur for a moment to this incident, in order to follow the ship of Luis Vaez de Torrès, the second in command. He proceeded on his voyage to the southwest, and saw enough of Espiritu Santo to convince him that it was not a continent. He would have circumnavigated it had the season permitted. Standing finally to the northward, he fell in with numerous islands rich in pearls and spices, and "coasted for eight hundred leagues along the southern shore of some land to him unknown." This can have been no other shore than that of Papua or New Guinea; and it is considered positive that he was the first European to see this since famous and remarkable island. He found this whole sea to be filled with groups of islands producing spices and the usual tropical fruits. He made his way to the Philippines, where he rendered an account of his adventures since his separation from Quiros.

While these distinguished navigators were thus searching the regions lying about the equator, another adventurer, equally enterprising, was endeavoring to reach the Pole. Henry Hudson, a seaman renowned for his hardy and daring achievements, was appointed, in 1607, by the Muscovy Company of London, to the command of a vessel intended to penetrate to China by the Arctic seas to the north of Europe. His crew consisted of ten men and a boy. He advanced as far as Greenland, and returned by Spitzbergen,—being convinced that the ice formed an insurmountable barrier against farther progress. He again set out in 1608, and, keeping more to the eastward, passed to the north of Norway, Sweden, and Russia as far as Nova Zembla. The ice again stopped him, and he returned,—persuaded that the northeastern passage did not exist. The next year he was again sent upon the same errand; but, being still unsuccessful, he crossed the Atlantic to America. He coasted along the continent as far as Chesapeake Bay, and then returned to the north, entering Delaware Bay and arriving in sight of the highlands of Neversink on the 2d of September. This he pronounced a "good land to fall in with, and a pleasant land to see." The next morning he passed Sandy Hook, and came to anchor in what is now the Lower Bay of New York. "What an event," says Everett, "in the history of American population, enterprise, commerce, intelligence and power, was the dropping of that anchor at Sandy Hook!"

HUDSON'S VESSEL, THE HALF-MOON, OFF SANDY HOOK.

"Here he lingered a week," continues the same author, "in friendly intercourse with the natives of New Jersey, while a boat's company explored the waters up to Newark Bay. And now the great question:—Shall he turn back, or ascend the stream? Hudson was of a race not prone to turn back, by sea or land. On the 11th of September, he raised the anchor of the Half-Moon, and passed through the Narrows, beholding on both sides 'as beautiful a land as one could tread on;' the ship floating cautiously and slowly up the noble stream,—the first that ever rested on its bosom. He passed the Palisades, Nature's dark basaltic Malakoff; forced the iron gateway of the Highlands; anchored on the 14th near West Point; swept around and upwards the following day, by grassy meadows and tangled slopes, hereafter to be covered with smiling villages, by elevated banks and woody heights, the destined sites of towns and cities,—of Newburgh, Poughkeepsie, Catskill; on the evening of the 15th arrived 'opposite the mountains which rise from the river's side,' where he found 'a very loving people and very old men;' and, the day following, sailed by the spot hereafter to be honored by his own illustrious name. One more day wafts him up between Schodac and Castleton; and here he landed and passed a day with the natives, greeted with all sorts of barbarous hospitality, —the land 'the finest for cultivation he ever set foot on.' On the following morning, with the early flood-tide, the Half-Moon ran higher up, and came to anchor in deep water, near the site of the present city of Albany. Happy if he could have closed his gallant career on the banks of the stream which so justly bears his name, and thus have escaped the sorrowful and mysterious catastrophe which awaited him the next year."

He soon after returned to England; and, not being discouraged, nor finding it difficult to obtain the means of continuing his maritime adventures, he set sail, in 1610, in a vessel of fifty-five tons' burden, manned by twenty-three men and victualled for six months. He touched at the Orkneys and anchored at Iceland. Mount Hecla revealed to him the magnificence of a volcano in travail, and the Hot Springs obligingly cooked his food. He passed Greenland, where the sun set in the north. In the course of June and July, he passed to the northward of Labrador, and followed the strait which now bears his name. In spite of ice and disturbances among his crew, which at times assumed the character of a mutiny, he pushed on into the great inland sea known as Hudson's Bay. For a long time he did not know that it was a bay, and naturally was led to hope that he was on the point of attaining the object of all his efforts,—a passage by the northwest to China. The extent of its surface amply justified him in these expectations, for it is the largest inland sea in the world, with the exception of the Mediterranean.

On the 1st of November, after seeking winter quarters, his men found a suitable spot for beaching their vessel. Ten days afterwards, they were frozen in, with provisions hardly sufficient to last, upon the most meagre allowance, till they could expect a release from the ice. A reward was offered to those who added to the general stock by catching either birds or fish, or animals serviceable for food. A house was built; but the season was so far advanced that it could not be rendered fit to dwell in. The winter was severe, and the men lived at first upon partridges, then upon swans and teal, and finally upon moss and frogs. They assuaged the pain of their frozen limbs by applying to them a hot decoction made from buds containing a balsam-like substance resembling turpentine. Towards spring, they obtained furs from the natives, in exchange for hatchets, glass, and buttons.

When the ice broke up, they prepared to return,—the last ration of bread being exhausted on the day of their departure. A report was circulated among the crew that Hudson had concealed a quantity of bread for his own use, and a mutiny, fomented by a man named Green, broke out on the 21st of June. Hudson was seized and his hands bound. Together with the sick, and those whom the frost had deprived of the use of their limbs, he was put into the shallop and set adrift. Neither he, nor the boat, nor any of its crew, were ever heard of again, alive or dead. They undoubtedly perished in a violent storm which arose the next day, though, had they survived it, they must have soon succumbed either to hunger or exposure. Hudson died in the bay which bears his name: his name will live, however, indissolubly connected, as it is, with the American Mediterranean and the superb river and harbor which have contributed to make New York, in seventy-five years, the second commercial metropolis of the world.

The wretched mutineers made the best of their way home in the ship they had thus foully obtained. Not one of the ring-leaders lived to reach the land. The rest, after suffering the most awful extremities of famine, finally gained the shore. None of them were ever brought to trial,—probably for the reason that those who had headed the revolt had already paid the penalty of their crimes.

DUTCH VESSEL TRADING AT THE LADRONES.

CHAPTER XXXIV.

THE FLEET OF JORIS SPILBERGEN—ARRIVAL IN BRAZIL—ADVENTURES IN THE STRAIT OF MAGELLAN—TRADE AT MOCHA ISLAND—TREACHERY AT SANTA MARIA—TERRIBLE BATTLE BETWEEN THE DUTCH AND SPANISH FLEETS—RAVAGES OF THE COAST—SKIRMISHES UPON THE LAND—SPILBERGEN SAILS FOR MANILLA—ARRIVAL AT TERNATE—HIS RETURN HOME—THE VOYAGE OF SCHOUTEN AND LEMAIRE—LEMONADE AT SIERRA LEONE—A COLLISION AT SEA—DISCOVERY OF STATEN LAND—CAPE HORN—LEMAIRE'S STRAIT—ARRIVAL AT BATAVIA—CONFISCATION OF THE SHIPS—GENERAL RESULTS OF THE VOYAGE—THE VOYAGE OF WILLIAM BAFFIN—ARCTIC RESEARCHES DURING THE SEVENTEENTH CENTURY.

WE have said, in a former chapter, that the Dutch succeeded the Portuguese in the possession of the East Indies. During the struggle between these two powers for supremacy over the Spice Islands, the Dutch East India Company resolved to make a vigorous effort to reach the Moluccas by the Strait of Magellan. They equipped a fleet of six ships, for the purpose of exploring a new route. These vessels were named the Great Sun, the Half-Moon, the Morning Star, the Huntsman, and the Sea Mew, and were placed under the command of Joris Spilbergen as admiral, who had already conducted a Dutch fleet to the Indies. He received his commission from their Mightinesses the States-General. He sailed from the Texel on the 8th of August, 1614.

While upon the South American coast, a mutiny broke out in the Sea Mew, and the two ringleaders were condemned to be cast into the sea,—a sentence which was rigorously executed. They entered the Strait of Magellan on the 28th of February, 1615, but were forced out again by adverse currents. They entered again on the 2d of April, and saw men of gigantic stature upon the hills, dead bodies wrapped in the skins of penguins, and shrubs producing sweet blackberries. The mountains were covered with snow, yet the woods were filled with parrots. Water-cresses, and a tree whose bark had a biting taste, induced them to give to an inlet the name of Pepper Haven. The natives bartered ornaments of mother-of-pearl for knives and wine. The vessels entered the South Sea on the 6th of May, and on the 25th anchored off Mocha Island, half a league from the coast of Chili.

The natives were delighted to learn that the strangers were the enemies of the Spaniards their oppressors, and to see that their ships were so large and well armed. The chief of the island visited the admiral's ship and remained his guest all night. A hatchet was the price fixed upon for two fat sheep; and a hundred were obtained at this rate. The natives would not permit the Dutch to see their women, and at last, when they had disposed of all the provisions and live stock they had to spare, made signs for them to re-enter their ships and depart, with which reasonable request Spilbergen at once complied.

On the 29th, the vessels anchored off the island of Santa

Maria, and, though there were Spaniards upon it, negotiations were opened. The Dutch officers were invited by a Spaniard to dine on shore, and, having accepted and assembled for the purpose, were either led to suspect treachery, or were convinced that they were strong enough to help themselves without negotiation. They summoned soldiers from the ships, burned a number of houses, and carried off five hundred sheep. The Spaniard who was to have been their host, but who was now their prisoner, informed them that the Viceroy of Peru had been for some months aware of their approach, and that a strong force was prepared at Lima to attack them. Spilbergen determined to go in search of the Spanish fleet: the gunners were ordered to have every thing in readiness for battle, and military regulations were promulgated,—every one, from the admiral to the swabs, being determined to do or die. One of the orders was that "during the action the decks were to be continually wetted, that accidents might not happen from ignited powder."

At Concepçion, the Dutch landed and set fire to a number of houses; at Valparaiso, the Spaniards burned one of their own vessels, that she might not fall into the enemy's hands. At Arica—the seaport to which the Potosi silver was brought to be shipped to Panama—they took a small ship laden with treasure. On the evening of the 16th of July, the Spanish fleet, of eight sail, appeared in sight. The Jesu Maria, the flag-ship, had no less than four hundred and sixty men, and mounted twenty-four guns; and the whole squadron were in the same proportion better provided with men than artillery. Don Rodrigo de Mendoça was the commander. He insisted upon an immediate attack by night, saying that "any two of his ships could take all England, and much more these hens of Holland, who must be spent and wasted by so long a voyage." About ten at night, the Spanish admiral and the Dutch admiral closed,—the Jesu Maria and the Great Sun. They hailed each other, and some conversation passed before a shot was fired. The attack was then commenced by the musketry, seconded by the great guns. The ships of both fleets came up in succession and joined battle. The pomp and circumstance of war were not neglected, for the braying of the cannon was accompanied by the sounding of tambours and trumpets. The Spanish San Francisco received a broadside which the Great Sun could spare from the Jesu Maria, and soon after went to the bottom. The Sun sent out one of her boats for a rescue; but it was mistaken by the Huntsman for an enemy's boat, and was blown out of the water by a cannon-shot. The night becoming very dark, the fleets were gradually separated. The next morning five of the Spanish ships sent word to their admiral that they were going to escape if they could. The Spanish admiral and vice-admiral were lashed together for mutual support, and were, in this condition, attacked by the Great Sun and the Half-Moon. The Spanish seamen several times hung out a white flag in token of surrender, which was as often cut down by their officers, who chose rather to die than yield, especially as they had sworn to the Viceroy of Peru to bring him all the Hollanders in chains. At nightfall, the Jesu Maria cut herself loose and fled from pursuit; but her leaks and damages were so serious that she went to the bottom before dawn. This decided the victory in favor of the Dutch, who are accused of allowing many of the enemy to drown who might easily have been saved.

The victorious fleet sailed directly for Callao; but the Spanish shipping in the port was so well protected by batteries that it was not thought prudent to attack them. Soon after, a vessel laden with salt and sugar was captured and the cargo distributed. The town of Paita was plundered and burned. No money or treasure is mentioned among the booty. Keeping a sharp watch for the fleet of Panama, which the Dutch did not care to meet or engage, they proceeded to the north, and, on the 11th of October, entered the harbor of Acapulco, in Mexico or New Spain. Negotiations were entered into and a treaty was made,

CONFLICT BETWEEN THE DUTCH AND SPANISH FLEETS.

the Dutch agreeing to release all their prisoners, and the Spanish to furnish them with oxen, sheep, poultry, fruit, water, and wood. Thus the Spaniards saved their town at a small expense, and the Dutch found refreshments which they could have obtained in no other way.

On the 10th of November, they anchored at the mouth of a river reported by their prisoners to abound in fish, while its banks produced citron and other fruit trees. Boats were sent to examine it. The Dutch noticed that the footprints upon the shore were the prints of shoes, and not of feet as Nature made them. Suspecting, therefore, the presence of Spaniards, they did not disembark, but returned to the ship. The next day the admiral landed with two hundred men, and was at once attacked by a strong body of Spaniards concealed in the woods. The latter were repulsed with loss, but Spilbergen withdrew his men to the ships, as his ammunition was nearly exhausted.

THE DUTCH SURPRISED BY THE SPANIARDS.

On the 2d of December, the fleet left the American coast and directed their course west by south for the Ladrone Islands. The next year—1616—was ushered in with distempers that proved fatal to many of the seamen. On the 23d of January, they came in sight of the Ladrones, where they stopped two days to traffic with the natives for flesh, fish, fruit, and fowl. The savages were, as usual, treacherous and given to thieving, and at times required the chastisement of powder and ball. The fleet touched at the Philippines early in February, but the Indians refused to trade with them, as they were enemies of the Spaniards. They entered the Straits of Manilla, and anchored before the island of Mirabelles, remarkable for two rocks which tower to a vast height into the air. The Dutch took several barks laden with the tribute of numerous adjacent places to the city of Manilla. They gained intelligence of a fleet of twelve ships and four galleys, manned by two thousand Spaniards, besides Indians and Chinese, sent to drive their countrymen from the Moluccas and to reduce those islands to the dominion of Spain. On this news, they discharged all their prisoners, and made preparations to meet the Manilla fleet and to proceed to the assistance of their friends. They arrived on the 29th of March at Ternate, one of the principal islands of the group, where the Dutch possessed a trading-station. They were received with joy by their countrymen.

Spilbergen was now detained nine months in the Molucca and neighboring islands, in the service of the East India Company. A narrative of his transactions here would be foreign to the purpose of this work. He left the ships in which he had hitherto sailed in India, and returned to Holland in the Amsterdam. His voyage produced no new discoveries in the South Sea; but the Directors of the Company bestowed upon him the highest praise for his prudent management and timely energy. The Company may be said to have dated their grandeur from the day of his return, both as regards power and wealth,—the first resulting from his successful circumnavigation of the globe, the latter from their conquests in the Moluccas, in which he took a prominent part, and of which he brought home the first intelligence.

The Dutch East India Company held from the Government the exclusive privilege of trading in the Great South Sea,—all private citizens being prohibited from entering those waters by the Cape of Good Hope on the east or the Strait of Magellan on the west. This prohibition stimulated rather than checked the commercial ardor of the country, and it soon became the study of navigators and merchants to discover some safe means of eluding the law, it being hard, they said, that Government should close up the channels which Nature had left free. Isaac Lemaire, a rich trader of Amsterdam, was the first to whom the idea occurred of seeking another passage from the Atlantic to the Pacific than the Strait of Magellan. He imparted his views to William Cornelison Schouten, who had been three times to the East Indies in the different capacities of supercargo, pilot, and master. He too was convinced that to the south of Terra del Fuego lay another passage from one ocean to the other. Could they find this passage, they might legally trespass upon the monopoly held by the Company. They determined to attempt the discovery, and Lemaire advanced half the necessary funds, Schouten and his friends furnishing the other half. Two ships were fitted out, the larger,—the Concord,—of three hundred and sixty tons, being manned by sixty-five men, and pierced for twenty-nine guns of small calibre; the Horn, of one hundred and ten tons, carrying eight cannons, four swivels, and twenty-two men. Schouten was master and pilot of the expedition, and James Lemaire, the son of Isaac, supercargo. The object of the voyage was kept a profound secret, the officers and men being bound by their articles to go wherever they should be required, and, in compensation for this unusual condition, receiving a considerable advance upon the ordinary wages. The little fleet was equipped in the port of Horn, and left the Texel on the 14th of June, 1615, proceeding towards the coast of Africa.

On the 30th of August, they cast anchor in the roads of Sierra Leone, where they drove a brisk trade in lemons, easily purchasing a thousand for a handful of worthless glass beads. Fresh water was obtained by holding casks under a bountiful cascade, and thus easily were the materials for lemonade procured in this favored spot. They then made directly for the southwest. While in the middle of the Atlantic, the crew of the Concord were startled by her receiving a violent blow upon her bottom, although no rock was visible. The color of the sea around them changed suddenly to red, as if a fountain of blood had been discharged into it. A large horn, of a substance resembling ivory, and solid, not hollow, was subsequently found in the ship's side, having passed through three of her planks and entered the wood to the depth of a foot, leaving at least a foot more upon the outside. The vessel had evidently been in collision with a narwhal or sea-unicorn, and the broken horn and the crimsoned water plainly showed which had suffered most from the shock.

Late in October, the ships' companies were informed of the design of the voyage, and readily consented to engage in a scheme which promised both distinction and emolument. Early in December, they made the coast of Patagonia, some three hundred miles to the north of Magellan's Strait. Here the Horn, the smaller of the two vessels, caught fire by accident and was destroyed. Her iron-work, guns, and anchors were transferred to the Concord. On the 24th, the Concord passed the Strait of Magellan, and was soon in the latitude where Schouten and Lemaire hoped to make their grand discovery. While Terra del Fuego was still in sight upon their right hand, they noticed a high, rugged island upon their left, which they named Staten Land, or Land of the States. The ship passed between the two, and soon after rounded the promontory which advanced the farthest into the sea, to which, in honor of the port from which the expedition had sailed, Schouten gave the name of Cape Horn. He then launched into the South Sea, being the first who passed completely round the South American continent. Lemaire claimed the honor of giving his name to the strait which had brought them to the Cape,—one which clearly belonged to Schouten, as the leader and pilot of the expedition. The strait is still known by the name of the supercargo, geographers having consecrated, by silence, this manifest act of injustice.

Altering their course to the northward, they soon recognised the mouth of Magellan's Strait,—which rendered their discovery complete. They returned thanks to God for their success, and

CAPE HORN.

passed the wine cup three times round the company. Schouten then made for the island of Juan Fernandez, where he hoped to give rest and refreshment to his sickly and wearied crew. The currents and the winds would not permit him to land; and he was compelled to start across the Pacific in a crazy ship and with a disabled company. Like Magellan, who traversed this ocean without seeing any of the important islands which, just below the line, extend from America to Asia, forming, as it were, a girdle from shore to shore, Schouten discovered but a few insignificant rocks and reefs, passing between and at a distance from the great archipelagoes which dot the Pacific in this latitude. At one of these spots his men met an enemy more numerous and formidable than any tribe of savages. Innumerable myriads of flies followed them from the shore to the ship, so that they came on board absolutely black with the winged and buzzing infliction. The flies enveloped the vessel in a thick and melodious cloud, from which the sailors were glad to escape with the first favoring breeze. Schouten consulted geographical propriety by naming the scene of this adventure Fly Island.

THE CONCORD AT FLY ISLAND.

Early in July, 1616, they arrived at the Moluccas, and went ashore upon the island of Gilolo, where they procured poultry, tortoises, rice, and sago. They next touched at Ternate, where they were kindly entertained by the Dutch authorities. They sold their two pinnaces, still upon the deck of the Concord, together with what had been saved from the Horn; they received in return thirteen hundred and fifty reals. With this they purchased a large quantity of rice, a ton of vinegar, as much Spanish wine, and three tons of biscuit. They then sailed for Java, and cast anchor in the harbor of Jacatra—now Batavia—sixteen months after quitting the Texel, having lost but three men upon the voyage. The expedition properly terminates here; for Jan Petersen Coen, President for the Dutch East India Company at Bantam, in Java, confiscated their ship and cargo as forfeited for illegally sailing within the boundaries of the Company's charter. He sent Schouten and Lemaire to Holland, however, that they might plead their cause before a competent court. Lemaire died on his way home, overcome with grief and vexation at the disastrous end of a voyage which had been so successful till the seizure of the ship. Schouten made several subsequent voyages to the East Indies, and died, in 1625, in the island of Madagascar. His name is little known, and his memory has almost passed away, although to him clearly belongs the credit of improving upon Magellan's discovery by furnishing a safer route to the commerce of the world and substituting the doubling of Cape Horn for the threading of the Strait.

During this same year, the English made their last attempt for nearly two centuries in the Arctic waters of America. William Baffin, who had accompanied Hudson in one of his earlier voyages, embarked in the capacity of pilot on board the Discovery,—a vessel bound for the northwest and commanded by one Robert Bylot. The crew consisted of fourteen men and two boys. Passing through Davis' Strait, they came to the vast bay which now bears Baffin's name. They found it to be eight hundred miles long and three hundred wide. They ascended to the north as far as the seventy-eighth degree of latitude, where the bay seemed to taper off in a strait or sound, which they called Thomas Smith's Sound. Here Baffin observed the greatest variation of the needle known at that time,—fifty-six degrees to the west. The charts of Baffin are lost; but several of his journals are extant, and contain numerous astronomical and hydrographic observations, which have since been fully verified by the superior instruments of modern science.

Baffin saw the opening to the west which Ross, two centuries later, was to call Lancaster Sound, and through which Parry was to penetrate to Melville Island and to the Polar Sea. He was convinced that a northwest passage existed, though he never made a second voyage in search of it. For one hundred and sixty years, now, the Arctic waters of the American continent were left undisturbed by adventurers from Europe. Their icy coasts remained unvisited till the middle of the eighteenth century, when the energies of English navigators were roused into activity by the reward offered by Parliament,—twenty thousand pounds to him who should sail to China by the northwest.

EMBARKATION OF THE PILGRIMS AT DELFTHAVEN.

Section V.

FROM THE DISCOVERY OF CAPE HORN TO THE APPLICATION OF STEAM TO NAVIGATION; 1616—1807.

CHAPTER XXXV.

A FAMOUS VESSEL—THE MAYFLOWER—HER APPEARANCE—THE SPEEDWELL—DEPARTURE OF THE TWO SHIPS—ALLEGED UNSEAWORTHINESS OF THE SPEEDWELL—THE MAYFLOWER SAILS ALONE—THE EQUINOCTIAL—CONSULTATIONS—A REMEDY APPLIED—FIRST VIEW OF THE LAND—SUBSEQUENT HISTORY AND FATE OF THE MAYFLOWER.

WE have now to narrate the incidents of a voyage without precedent, in one point of view, in maritime annals, and to chronicle the adventures of a ship which may be safely said to have achieved a fame beyond that of any other that ever ploughed the ocean. When we mention the name of the Mayflower, in which the Pilgrim Fathers proceeded from Southampton Water to Plymouth Rock, we are sure that the distinction which we claim for this feeble vessel will be contested by none,—not even by those who would gladly accord the supremacy of the seas to the Nina of Columbus or the Vittoria of Magellan. The details of the voyage are few and unsatisfactory; but the vivid imagination of historians and orators has amply supplied their place.

The Mayflower was built in England, at a time when English commerce could bear no comparison with that of Holland, and when the trade with the latter power employed six hundred Dutch ships to one hundred of English build. They were picturesque in appearance, though tub-like and clumsy, the hull being broad-bottomed and capacious, while the lofty cabins, towering high both fore and aft,—a style now obsolete in Europe, but still prevailing in the Red Sea and the Levant,—caused them to roll heavily in rough water. The Mayflower was a high-sterned, quaint, but staunch little vessel of one hundred and eighty tons, and was built for one of the trading companies lately chartered by the Government. The Dutch portion of the emigration had already embarked at Delfthaven in the Speedwell, of sixty tons, and both vessels were, on the 1st of August, 1620, anchored before the old towers of Southampton. The pilgrims were then regularly organized for the voyage, being distributed according to rules laid down and accepted

THE MAYFLOWER.

by all. The larger number were of course received on board the Mayflower. On the 5th of August, both vessels weighed anchor, and sailed down the beautiful estuary of Southampton

Water: passing the Isle of Wight and the rocks known as the Needles, they entered the English Channel.

They were no sooner launched upon the fretful waters of this confined strait than their disasters began. The captain of the Speedwell, who had engaged to remain a year abroad with the vessel, actuated either by cowardice or by dissatisfaction with the enterprise, declared that his ship was leaky, and that she could not proceed to sea. Dartmouth Harbor offered an opportunity for effecting the necessary repairs, and here a week was spent: the Speedwell was then pronounced quite sound by the carpenters and surveyors. They again set sail; but the captain of the Speedwell soon profited by the vicinity of Plymouth to assert a second time that he was ready to founder. He ran into port, and the Mayflower followed. No special cause was discovered for the apprehensions of the captain; but it was decided that the Speedwell should be sent back to London as unseaworthy, with such of her passengers as were disheartened, the remainder being transferred to the larger ship. One hundred and one persons—some of them aged and infirm, and several of them women soon to become mothers—were thus imprisoned, as it were, in a vessel much too small to accommodate them; while the delays resulting from the treachery or stratagem practised by the captain of the Speedwell had already proved so serious, that it was the 6th of September before the Mayflower, with her crowd of suffering passengers, could continue the voyage thus inauspiciously commenced.

The wind was east by north, blowing, according to the journal, "a fine small gale," when the Mayflower started from Plymouth upon her lonely way. The solitude of the ocean—in this latitude almost a trackless waste—lay stretched out before them. The prosperous gale soon gave way to the equinoctial storm, and a terrible head-wind from the northwest compelled the little bark to struggle anxiously with waves which threatened to engulf her. She was soon sorely shattered: her upper works were strained, and one of the main beams amidships was bent and cracked. A consultation was held between the seamen and passengers, and the question was seriously debated whether it would not be better to put back. It was fortunately discovered, however, that one of the Dutch pilgrims had accidentally brought on board a large iron screw, and this served to rivet the defective beam. The ship proceeded on her course, struggling with westerly gales and tempestuous seas. For whole days together she was compelled to lie to, or to scud with bare poles. "Methinks," says Everett, "I see the adventurous vessel, the Mayflower of a forlorn hope, freighted with the prospects of a future State and bound across the unknown sea. I behold it pursuing, with a thousand misgivings, the uncertain, tedious voyage. Suns rise and set, weeks and months pass; and winter surprises them on the deep, but brings them not the sight of the wished-for shore. I see them now, scantily supplied with provisions, crowded almost to suffocation in their ill-stored prison, delayed by calms, pursuing a circuitous route, and now driven in fury before the raging tempest on the high and giddy waves. The awful voice of the storm howls through the rigging; the laboring masts seem straining from their base; the dismal sound of the pumps is heard; the ship leaps, as it were, madly from billow to billow; the ocean breaks and settles with engulfing floods over the floating deck, and beats, with deadening, shivering weight, against the staggered vessel." Only one death occurred during this terrible voyage,—a loss in numbers which was made good by the birth of a boy, to whom was given the name of Oceanus Hopkins.

Sixty-four days had passed, and the 9th of November had dawned. Upon this date the tempest-tossed pilgrims obtained their first view of the American coast. "To the storm-ridden voyager," writes one of their descendants, "exhausted by confinement and suffering, the sight of any shore, however wild, the aromatic fragrance that blows from the land, are inexpressibly sweet and refreshing:

> Lovely seems any object that shall sweep
> Away the vast—salt—dread—eternal deep!

And thus we find that the low sand-hills of Cape Cod, covered with scrubby woods that descended to the margin of the sea, seemed, at the first glance, a perfect paradise of verdure to the eyes of these poor sea-beaten wanderers."

The orator and statesman from whom we have already quoted thus eloquently alludes to the providential circumstances attending the arrival of the Mayflower upon the American shore:—"Let us go up in imagination to yonder hill and look out upon the November scene. That single dark speck, just discernible through the perspective glass on the waste of waters, is the fated vessel. The storm moans through her tattered canvas, as she creeps, almost sinking, to her anchorage in Provincetown Harbor; and there she lies, with all her treasures, not of silver and gold,—for of them she has none,—but of courage, of patience, of zeal, of high spiritual daring. So often as I dwell in imagination on this scene,—when I consider the condition of the Mayflower, utterly incapable as she was of living through another gale,—when I survey the terrible front presented by our coast to the navigator who, unacquainted with its channels and roadsteads, should approach it in the stormy season,—I dare not call it a mere piece of good fortune that the general north and south wall of the shore of New England should be broken by this extraordinary projection of the Cape, running out into the ocean a hundred miles, as if on purpose to receive and encircle the precious vessel. As I now see her, freighted with the destinies of a continent, barely escaped from the perils of the deep, approaching the shore precisely where the broad sweep of this most remarkable headland presents almost the only point at which, for hundreds of miles, she could with any ease have made a harbor, and this perhaps the very best on the seaboard, I feel my spirit raised above the sphere of mere natural agencies. I see the mountains of New England rising from their rocky thrones: they rush forward into the ocean, settling down as they advance; and there they range themselves, a mighty bulwark, around the Heaven-directed vessel. Yes! the everlasting God himself stretches out the arm of his mercy and his power in substantial manifestations, and gathers the meek company of his worshippers as in the hollow of his hand."

"I see the pilgrims," he continues, "escaped from their perils, landed at last, after a two months' passage, on the ice-clad rocks of Plymouth, weak and weary from the voyage,—without shelter, without means, surrounded by hostile tribes. Shut now the volume of history, and tell me, on any principle of human probability, what shall be the fate of this handful of adventurers. Tell me, man of military science, in how many months were they all swept off by the thirty savage tribes enumerated within the early limits of New England? Tell me, politician, how long did this shadow of a colony, on which your conventions and treaties had not smiled, languish on the distant coast? Student of history, compare for me the baffled projects, the deserted settlements, the abandoned adventures, of other times, and find the parallel of this. Was it the winter's storm, or disease, or labor and spare meals, or the tomahawk—that hurried this forsaken company to their melancholy fate? And is it possible that neither of these causes, that not all combined, were able to blast this bud of hope? Is it possible that from a beginning so feeble, so frail, so worthy not so much of admiration as of pity, there has gone forth a progress so steady, a growth so wonderful, an expansion so ample, a reality so important, a promise, yet to be fulfilled, so glorious?"

The Mayflower remained in Plymouth Harbor, and was the home of the women and children during the severe winter of 1620–21. She rode out the storm at her anchorage,—though she was placed in great danger by a gale upon the 4th of

February, her want of ballast—unladen as she was—rendering her light as a cockle-shell. With the opening of spring, the captain determined to return to England, and offered to carry back any of the colonists who might be disheartened by the calamities which had overtaken them,—for they had buried half their number. But their sufferings had endeared the soil to them, and not one embraced the opportunity of returning. The Mayflower left Plymouth on the 5th of April, 1621, and made the run home to London in thirty days. She seems to have performed several voyages back and forth, and, in 1630, arrived in the harbor of Charlestown, with a portion of Winthrop's company of emigrants. Her subsequent history is very uncertain; and all attempts to ascertain it have been baffled by the circumstance that several ships bore the name of Mayflower, and no reliable means exist of distinguishing her of Pilgrim celebrity from others of obscurer fame.

TASMAN'S VESSEL,—THE ZEEHAAN.

CHAPTER XXXVI.

DISCOVERY OF NEW HOLLAND—TASMAN ORDERED TO SURVEY THE ISLAND—DISCOVERY OF VAN DIEMEN'S LAND—OF NEW ZEALAND—MURDERERS' BAY—THE FRIENDLY ISLANDS—THE FEEJEES—NEW BRITAIN—AN EARTHQUAKE AT SEA—A COPIOUS LANGUAGE—CIRCUMNAVIGATION OF NEW HOLLAND—RETURN TO BATAVIA—RESULTS OF THE VOYAGE—DUTCH OPINIONS OF TASMAN'S MERIT.

THE Council of the Dutch East India Company thought proper, in 1642, to order a complete and precise survey of the lands accidentally discovered during the previous fifty years by vessels trading between Holland and Batavia, in Java. These had touched, at intervals, at numerous points upon the continental island of New Holland,—Hertog at Endracht's Land in 1616, and De Witt, Van Nuyts, and Carpenter at other points, somewhat later. It was eminently desirable that a scientific navigator should visit and render an account of this region, of which only casual glimpses had thus far been obtained. Captain Abel Jansen Tasman was intrusted with this duty by Van Diemen, Governor-General of the Company. He left Batavia in August with two vessels, the Zeehaan and the Heemskirk, and proceeded towards the south and southeast. During this portion of the voyage the needle was in such continual agitation, unwilling to remain in any of the eight points and boxing the whole compass in twenty-four hours, that Tasman was led to believe large mines of loadstone to exist in the vicinity. On the 24th of November he discovered land, and gave to it the name of Van Diemen's Land,—a name which it has retained, though in honor of its discoverer it is often, of late years, called Tasmania. He saw no inhabitants, though he fancied he heard human voices. He noticed two trees, fifteen feet in girth and sixty feet in height from the ground to the branches. Up the trunks of these trees steps, five feet apart, had been cut in the bark. By these the natives, apparently of prodigious size, had climbed into the foliage and robbed the birds' nests of their eggs. Though a sound resembling that of a trumpet had been heard, though tracks of wild beasts were fresh in the sand, and though smoke ascended from the interior in several places, no living creature was seen. Tasman set up a post, upon which every man of the company cut his name, and upon the top of which a flag was hoisted, and then set out in quest of the Solomon Islands, which he supposed to lie to the east.

On the 13th of September he discovered a high, mountainous country, to which he gave the name of Staten Land,—Land of the States, [of Holland.] Its present name is New Zealand. He coasted along the shore to the northeast, and anchored in a fine bay, though he did not disembark. The savages, who were shy at first, at last ventured on board the Heemskirk, in order to trade. Tasman, suspicious of their intentions, sent a boat with seven men from the Zeehaan, to put the crew of his consort upon their guard. These seven men, being without arms, were attacked: three of them were killed, and the other four forced to swim for their lives. The two vessels opened their fire upon the canoes of the islanders, and Tasman branded the spot with a name which still exists upon the charts,—Murderers' Bay.

MURDERERS' BAY.

On the 21st of January, 1643, he saw three islands, in latitude 21° south: he named them Amsterdam, Rotterdam, and Middlebourg. The inhabitants were peaceable and friendly, were unacquainted with the use of weapons, and very skilful in stealing. The natives called Amsterdam Tonga-Tabou; Rotterdam, Ana-Mocka; and Middlebourg, Eoa. These are now the principal members of the group known as the Friendly Islands. They remained unvisited by Europeans from the time of Tasman, in 1643, to the second voyage of Cook, in 1773,—a space of one hundred and thirty years. Cook found traditions still existing respecting Tasman's ships; and a nail was shown him which had been left by the Dutch navigator. Proceeding to the north and then to the west, Tasman discovered a group of twenty islands, girt with shoals and sands. He named them Prince William's Islands and Heemskirk's Shallows. These now form the eastern portion of the Feejee archipelago. They remained unvisited for a century and a half, until the people of the Friendly Islands spoke of them to Cook and his successors and induced them to visit them.

Tasman now feared that the currents and winds had driven him more to the westward than he had supposed; for he had not seen the sun for many weeks, and was consequently without reliable observations. He resolved to make for the north, and then for the western coast of New Guinea, in order not to be driven to the south of the island and pass it without seeing it.

NATIVES OF MURDERERS' BAY.

On the 1st of April, he saw the coast of what he supposed was New Guinea, but which was in reality New Britain. Here an earthquake terrified the seamen, for the shock caused them to fear they had struck upon a rock; but the lead did not reach the bottom. On the 20th, they passed a burning island, noticed by late navigators, and perceived flames issuing from lofty mountains. The water was full of shrubs, bamboos, and small trees, carried by the rivers to the sea. The discharge of fresh water by these rivers was such that it almost corrected the salt of the ocean. The natives showed Tasman some ginger, and sold him hogs and cocoanuts. At the island of Moa he found the inhabitants speaking a language so copious, that they could at once repeat, intelligibly, the words of any other language. Tasman did not find it so easy to speak theirs, however, as the letter *r* occurred once or more in every syllable. He purchased, for knives made of the iron hoops of water-casks, six thousand cocoanuts and a hundred bunches of bananas, or Indian figs.

On the 18th of May, Tasman reached the western extremity of New Guinea, having sailed entirely round the continent or island of Australia. He arrived at Batavia, whence he had started, after an absence of ten months. His expedition was the clearest and most precise of the several voyages which had been made for the discovery of the Terra Australis Incognita: few voyages, since that of Magellan, had contributed more to geographical science; for, by reducing the limits of the Terra Australis, as he did by circumnavigating the supposed continent, he did much to rid geography of its most important error.

Tasman made a second voyage in 1644; but his journals and his track have been completely lost,—probably by design, as the Dutch did not make geographical researches in the interest of the world, but exclusively in that of the East India Company. By his second voyage he is believed to have determined the extent of the great Gulf of Carpentaria, which so profoundly indents the northern coast of New Holland. The portion of his discoveries relative to New Zealand and the Friendly Islands has been completed by Cook; that relative to Van Diemen's Land by d'Entrecasteaux, in his voyage in search of Lapérouse. The fragments which remain of Tasman's journals attest his reasoning powers, his nautical experience, and his unerring judgment. The Dutch never published his own account of his adventures, and the few extracts which have become public crept by accident and stealth into later works and journals of discovery. A Dutch writer thus alludes to the indifference manifested by his countrymen in regard to Tasman:—"We do not know when he was born, when he went to India, or when he returned. In our grand biographical dictionaries, where you will find every puerile detail respecting such and such musty savant, only known as a professor at some university or as a quarrelsome skirmisher of the Republic of Letters, there is no room, it seems, for the first navigator of his age." The English have proposed of late to substitute a name of their own for that of Van Diemen's Land; but the appellation of Tasmania is beginning, as we have said, for evident reasons of propriety to find a place upon modern charts and maps.

A BUCCANEER.

CHAPTER XXXVII.

PIRACY—ORIGIN OF THE BUCCANEERS—THEIR MANNER OF LIFE—DRESS—OCCUPATION—THE ISLAND OF TORTUGA THEIR HEAD-QUARTERS—THEIR RELIGIOUS SCRUPLES—MANNER OF DIVIDING SPOILS—THE EXTERMINATOR—THE OBSERVANCE OF THE SABBATH—EXPLOITS OF HENRY MORGAN—IMPOTENCE OF THE SPANIARDS—CAREER OF WILLIAM DAMPIER—HIS FIRST PIRATICAL CRUISE—ADVENTURES BY LAND AND SEA—DESCRIPTION OF THE PLANTAIN-TREE—LINGERING DEATHS BY POISON—REPROACHES OF CONSCIENCE—THE NEW-HOLLANDERS—DAMPIER'S DANGEROUS VOYAGE IN AN OPEN BOAT—PIRACY UPON THE AMERICAN COAST—WILLIAM KIDD SENT AGAINST THE PIRATES—HE TURNS PIRATE HIMSELF—HIS EXPLOITS, DETECTION, AND EXECUTION—HIS BURIED TREASURES—WRECK OF THE WHIDAH PIRATE-SHIP.

It is necessary to pause at this period in our review of the grand maritime expeditions which successively left the various seaports of the world, in order to refer to a practice which was now rendering commerce hazardous and the whole highway of the seas insecure,—piracy. Besides the numerous isolated adventurers who preyed upon the vessels of any and every nation which fell in their way, a powerful association or league of robbers, who infested particularly the West India Islands and the Caribbean Sea, and who bore the name of Buccaneers, became, during the century of which we are now speaking, the peculiar dread of Spanish ships. We shall describe this fraternity in some detail. The term buccaneer is a corruption of the French word boucanier, which in its turn was made from the Caribbean noun *boucan*, being the flesh of cattle dried and preserved in a peculiar manner. The French also called them flibustiers, this word being a corruption of the English word freebooters; and this French word has been still further tortured into "Filibusters,"—a term now applied to such Americans as desire violently to extend the area of freedom.

The buccaneers were principally natives of Great Britain and France, and first attract notice in the island of St. Domingo. The Spaniards would not allow any other nation than their own to trade in the West Indies, and pursued and murdered the English and French wherever they found them. Every foreigner discovered among the islands or on the coast of the American continent was treated as a smuggler and a robber; and it was not long before they became so, and organized themselves into an association capable of returning cruelty by cruelty. The Spaniards employed coast-guards to keep off interlopers, the commanders of which were instructed to massacre all their prisoners. This tended to produce a close alliance, offensive and defensive, among the mariners of all other nations, who in their turn made descents upon the coasts and ravaged the weaker Spanish towns and settlements. A permanent state of hostilities was thus established in the West Indies, independent of peace or war at home. After the failure of the mines of St. Domingo and its abandonment by the Spaniards, it was taken possession of, early in the sixteenth century, by a number of French wanderers who had been driven out of St. Christopher; and their numbers were soon augmented by adventurers from all quarters.

As they had neither wives nor children, they generally lived together by twos for mutual protection and assistance: when one died, the survivor inherited his property, unless a will was found bequeathing it to some relative in Europe. Bolts, locks, and all kinds of fastenings were prohibited among them, the maxim of "honor among thieves" being considered a more efficient safeguard. The dress of a buccaneer consisted of a shirt dipped in the blood of an animal just slain, a leathern girdle in which hung pistols and a short sabre, a hat with feathers,—but without a rim, except a fragment in guise of a visor to pull it on and off,—and shoes of untanned hide, without stockings. Each man had a heavy musket and usually a pack of twenty or thirty dogs. Their business was, at the outset, cattle-hunting; and they sold hides to the Dutch who resorted to the island to purchase them. They possessed servants and slaves, consisting of persons decoyed to the West Indies and induced to bind themselves for a certain number of years. They treated them with great severity. The following epigrammatic conversation is reported as having taken place between an apprentice and a buccaneer. "Master," said the servant, "God has forbidden the practice of working on the Sabbath: does he not say, 'Six days shalt thou labor; and on the seventh shalt thou rest'?" "But I say unto thee," returned the buccaneer, "six days shalt thou kill cattle; and on the seventh shalt thou carry their hides to the shore."

The Spaniards inhabiting other portions of St. Domingo conceived the idea of ridding the island of the buccaneers by destroying all the wild cattle; and this was carried into execution by a general chase. The buccaneers abandoned St. Domingo and took refuge in the mountainous and well-wooded island of

Tortuga, of which they made themselves absolute lords and masters. The advantages of the situation brought swarms of adventurers and desperadoes to the spot; and from cattle-hunters the buccaneers became pirates. They made their cruises in open boats, exposed to all the inclemencies of the weather, and captured their prizes by boarding. They attacked indiscriminately the ships of every nation, feeling especial hostility and exercising peculiar cruelty towards the Spaniards. They considered themselves to be justified in this by the oppression of the Mexicans and Indians by Spanish rulers, and, quieting their consciences by thus assuming the character of avengers and dispensers of poetic justice, they never embarked upon an expedition without publicly offering up prayers for success, nor did they ever return laden with spoils without as publicly giving thanks for their good fortune.

They seldom attacked any European ships except those homeward bound,—which were usually well freighted with gold and silver. They pursued the Spanish galleons as far as the Bahamas; and if, on the way, a ship became accidentally separated from the convoy, they instantly attacked her. The Spaniards held them in such terror that they usually surrendered on coming to close quarters. The spoil was equitably divided, provision being first made for the wounded. The loss of an arm was rated at six hundred dollars, and other wounds in proportion. The commander could claim but one share,—although, when he had acquitted himself with distinction, it was usual to compliment him by the addition of several shares. When the division was effected, the buccaneers abandoned themselves to all kinds of rioting and licentiousness till their wealth was expended, when they started in pursuit of new booty.

The buccaneers now rapidly increased in strength, daring, and numbers. They sailed in larger vessels, and undertook enterprises requiring great energy and audacity. Miguel de Basco captured, under the guns of Portobello, a Spanish galleon valued at a million of dollars. In Europe, immense editions of books were published, giving accounts of the barbarities committed by the Spaniards and of the holy reprisals waged against them by the buccaneers. A Frenchman by the name of Montbars, on reading these narratives, conceived so deadly a hatred for the Spaniards, and, after becoming a buccaneer, killed so many of them, that he obtained the title of "The Exterminator." His audacity was only equalled by his love of shedding Spanish blood, by which he believed himself to be avenging the unhappy victims of Spanish colonization.

Other men joined the "Brethren of the Coast"—as they were sometimes called—from less ferocious motives. Raveneau de Lussan joined the association because he was in debt, and in consequence of a conviction entertained by him that "every honest man ought in conscience to pay his creditors." Many of the buccaneers were men of a religious temperament; or, at least, they thought that proper respect should be paid to appearances, and that due deference should be had towards the prejudices of society. It was doubtless from such sentiments as these that Captain Daniel shot one of his crew in church for behaving irreverently during mass, that Captain Sawkins threw a pair of dice overboard on finding them contributing to a game of chance on Sunday, and that Captain Watling ordered his men to regard, as the very first rule of their association, that which instructed them to keep holy the Sabbath day.

But the fame of all the buccaneer commanders was eclipsed by that of Henry Morgan, a Welshman. The boldest and most astonishing of his exploits was his forcing his way across the Isthmus of Darien from the Atlantic to the Pacific Ocean. His object was to plunder the rich city of Panama: his expedition, however, opened the way to the great Southern Sea, where the buccaneers laid the foundation of much of our geographical knowledge of that ocean. He first took the castle of San Lorenzo, at the mouth of the river Chagres, where out of three hundred and fourteen Spaniards he put two hundred to death. He left five hundred men in the castle, one hundred and fifty on board of his thirty-seven ships, and with the rest—who, after deducting the killed and wounded, amounted to about twelve hundred men—began his progress through a wild and trackless country which was then known only to the native Indians. On the tenth day, after a desperate combat with the Spaniards, he took and plundered Panama, which then consisted of about seven thousand houses. His cruelties here were abominable. He imprisoned one of his female captives, with whom he had fallen in love but who repelled his advances, causing her to be cast into a dungeon and to be insufficiently supplied with food. But his men murmured at the delay, and he was compelled to depart. He returned to the mouth of the Chagres with an enormous booty, and, after defrauding the fleet of their share of the spoils, sailed for Jamaica, which was already an English colony. He was made Deputy Governor of the island by Charles II., by whom he was also knighted. He proved an efficient officer, and gave no quarter to the buccaneers!

Morgan's expedition had pointed out a short way to the South Sea; and in 1680, some three hundred English buccaneers started from the Atlantic side to cross the isthmus. They formed an alliance with the Darien Indians, who furnished them a quantity of canoes upon the Pacific side. They launched out in these into the Bay of Panama, attacked three large armed ships, took two of them, and began cruising in them. They captured vessels and plundered towns along the coast. Some of them remained a long time in the South Sea, and made many discoveries of undoubted benefit to mankind.

The Spaniards never dared to defend themselves unless they greatly outnumbered their assailants, and even then they were usually routed with ease. They had become so enervated by luxury that they had lost all military spirit and had well-nigh forgotten the use of arms. They had acquired from the monks the idea that the buccaneers were devils, cannibals, and beings of monstrous form. They revenged themselves upon the enemy whom they dared not meet by mangling and subjecting to mimic tortures such dead bodies of the invaders as were left behind,—an exhibition of impotent rage which only excited the buccaneers to fresh cruelties.

One of the English buccaneers—William Dampier—became subsequently an eminent discoverer, author, and philosopher. After receiving a collegiate education, he went to sea in northern latitudes, which for a time disgusted him with a maritime life. A voyage to the East Indies, the superintendence of a plantation in Jamaica, and three years spent among the logwood-cutters of Campeachy, gave him a strong bias for the tropical waters. In Campeachy he became acquainted with some of the buccaneers, whose descriptions of their adventures kindled in him a fondness for a roving and piratical life. He joined an expedition under Captain John Cooke: an English pilot named Cowley was engaged as master, and embarked in complete ignorance of the nature of the voyage. They sailed in August, 1683, in the Revenge, mounting eight guns and manned by fifty-two men. Cowley was told the first day that the vessel's mission was trade and her destination St. Domingo; on the second, he was informed that piracy was her object and Guinea her market.

Stopping at the Cape Verd Islands, they resolved to go to Santiago, in the hope of finding some ship in the road, and intending to cut her cable and run away with her. They saw a ship at anchor, and approached her with hostile intent. They were not far off when her company struck her ports and ran out her lower tier of guns. Cooke bore away as fast as he could, convinced that he was unable to cope with a Dutch East Indiaman of fifty guns and four hundred men. Some time after, when off Sierra Leone, they fell in with a newly built ship of forty guns, well furnished with water, provisions, and brandy, which they boarded and captured. They named her the Revenge, and continued their voyage in her, destroying their original vessel. From here they crossed the Atlantic to the Patagonian coast. They doubled Cape Horn during a tremendous storm of rain, which furnished them with twenty-three barrels of fresh water. The weather was at this time so cold that the men could drink three quarts of burnt brandy in twenty-four hours without being intoxicated. They joined company in the Pacific with the Nicholas, of twenty-six guns, Captain John Eaton, and started together upon an attempt against the Peruvian coast. They captured three flour-ships, and learned from the prisoners that their presence was known to the Peruvian authorities. Their design upon the coast was therefore abandoned. They carried their prizes to the Gallapagos or Tortoise Islands, where they might store their captured provisions in a secure place. They arrived and anchored there on the 31st of May, 1684.

Proceeding to the northward, they descried the coast of Mexico early in July, where Cooke, who had been ill for some months, died and was buried. Edward Davis, quartermaster, was elected captain in his stead. The two ships separated on the 2d of September, the Nicholas withdrawing from the partnership. Davis and Dampier remained in the Revenge, and were soon joined by the Cygnet, a richly-loaded vessel designed for trading on this coast. Her captain lightened her by throwing his unsalable cargo overboard. They attacked Paita in the month of November, but found it evacuated. They held the town for six days, hoping the inhabitants would ransom it; but, as this hope was disappointed, they set the town on fire. On the 1st of January, 1685, they captured a package of letters sent by the President of Panama to hasten the captains of the silver-fleet from Lima, as the coast was believed to be clear. Being particularly desirous that the silver-fleet should share this belief, they suffered the letter-bearers to continue their voyage and resolved to lie in wait for the ships. In the mean time they captured several prizes, and manned them with buccaneers that they met, from time to time, engaged in small enterprises on separate accounts. By the end of May, their fleet consisted of ten sail, two of them being ships of war, carrying fifty-two guns and nine hundred and sixty men. The Spanish fleet—consisting of fourteen sail, eight of them men-of-war, and two of them fire-ships, the whole manned by three thousand men—now hove in sight. The admiral of the fleet deceived the buccaneers at night, by hoisting a light upon the topmast of an abandoned bark, by which they were decoyed into a position which gave the Spaniards the next day all the advantage of the wind. Thus was the grand scheme adroitly frustrated.

Having thus failed at sea, they agreed to try their fortune on land, and chose the city of Leon, on the coast of Nicaragua. Four hundred and seventy men were landed for this purpose. They were met and opposed by five hundred foot and two hundred horse, both of which arms of the service retreated in confusion at the first collision. As they refused to ransom the city for thirty thousand dollars, it was set on fire. A Spanish gentleman, who had been captured by the buccaneers, was released upon his promise to deliver one hundred and fifty oxen at Realejo, the next place which they intended to attack. Realejo was taken, but yielded them little of value except five hundred bags of flour, with some pitch, tar, and cordage, and the one hundred and fifty promised oxen. Captains Davis and Swan now agreed to separate,—the former wishing to return to Peru, and the latter desiring to visit the northern coasts of Mexico. Dampier remained with Swan in the Cygnet.

Towards the middle of September they came in sight of the city and volcano of Guatemala. Dampier landed at the port of Guatulco with one hundred and forty men, and marched fourteen miles to attack an Indian village, where they found nothing but vanilla beans drying in the sun. They endeavored to cut out a Lima bullion-ship lying off Acapulco, but failed. Not far from here they robbed a caravan of sixty mules, laden with flour, chocolate, cheese, and earthenware. They found and appropriated an abundance of maize, sugar, salt, and salt fish. Dampier, being afflicted with the dropsy, was cured—or, at least, much benefited—by being buried up to his neck for half an hour in the sand in California. A profuse perspiration, which was thus brought on, was the commencement of his convalescence.

Swan and Dampier were now convinced that the commerce of this region was not carried on by sea, but by land, by means of mules and caravans. They therefore resolved to try their fortune in the East Indies. They sailed from California on the 31st of March, 1686. They made the island of Guam, after a voyage of six thousand miles, in seven weeks, having but three days' provisions left, and the men having begun to talk of eating Captain Swan when these were exhausted. They found the island defended by a small fort mounting six guns, and containing a garrison of thirty men with a Spanish governor,—this being solely for the convenience of the Manilla galleons on their annual voyages from Acapulco to Manilla. The governor, being deceived as to the character of the ship, sent the captain some hogs, cocoanuts, and rice, and fifty pounds of Manilla tobacco.

They learned here, from the friar belonging to the garrison,

BOATS USED IN THE PHILIPPINE ISLANDS.

that Mindanao, one of the Philippine Islands, was very fertile and productive, and that the natives, who were Mohammedans, were at war with the Spaniards. They therefore resolved to go there, and left Guam on the 2d of June. After seeing Luzon, (Matan,) where Magellan was killed, they anchored off Mindanao, the largest of the Philippines with the exception of Luzon. Though mountainous, Dampier found its soil "deep, black, and extraordinary fat and fruitful." The valleys were moistened with pleasant brooks "and small rivers of delicate water, and in the heart of the country were mountains that yielded good gold."

Dampier's description of the plantain-tree is often quoted as a fine specimen of descriptive writing. "It is," he says, "the king of all fruit, not excepting the cocoanut. The tree is three feet round and twelve feet high: it is not raised from seed, but from the roots of old trees. As soon as the fruit is ripe the tree decays; but suckers at once spring up and bear in a twelvemonth. It comes up with two leaves, within which, by the time it is a foot high, two more spring up, and in a short time two more, and so on. When full grown, the leaves are seven or eight feet long and a foot and a half broad. The stem of the leaf is as big as a man's arm. The fruit-stem shoots out at the top of the full-grown tree,—first blossoming, and then bearing. The Spaniards give it the pre-eminence over all other fruit, as most conducive to life. It grows in a cod about seven inches long and three inches thick. The shell or rind is soft, and, when ripe, yellow. The fruit within is of the consistency of butter in winter. It has a very delicate flavor, and melts in the mouth like marmalade. It is pure pulp, without kernel, seed, or stone. A large plantation of these trees will yield fruit throughout the year, and will furnish the exclusive food of a family. The markets of Havana, Carthagena, Portobello, &c. are full of the fruit; and they are sold at the price of threepence a dozen. When used as bread, it is roasted or boiled before it is quite ripe; and sometimes a roasted plantain is, as it were, buttered with a ripe raw plantain. An English bag-pudding may be made with half a dozen ripe fruit; and, again, plantains sliced and dried in the sun taste like figs, and may be preserved in any climate. Green plantains dried and grated furnish an excellent flour for bread or puddings. The Mosquito Indians squeeze a plantain into a calabash of water and drink it: they call it mishlaw, and it re-resembles lambs'-wool made of apples and ale. It drinks brisk and cool, and is very pleasant." Such was the plantain two centuries ago.

The Sultan of Mindanao received the strangers with favor, and would gladly have induced them to settle upon the island and form the nucleus of an English trading station. Dampier would have remained, but the majority were against him. After a time, a mutiny broke out,—the principal cause being the want of active employment; and, as Captain Swan manifested no energy or address in quelling it, he and thirty-six men were left at Mindanao, the rest escaping with the ship. Dampier here remarks that they had buried sixteen men upon the island, who had died by poison,—the natives revenging the slightest dalliance with their women with a deadly, though lingering, dose or potion. Some of the mutineers that ran off with the vessel died of poison administered at Mindanao four months afterwards.

Read, the new captain, and Dampier, cruised for some time among the Philippine Islands. At one of these they saw an extraordinary display of surf-bathing on the part of the natives. The art seemed to be practised as well by the women as the men, and children in arms were taught to gambol in the water as if it were their native element, and as if they were born web-footed.

On the 4th of January, 1688, they touched at New Holland,—then known to be a vast tract of land, and by all except the Dutch supposed to be a continent. Here they found a miserable race of people, compared to whom Dampier declares the Hodmapods, though a nasty race, to be gentlemen and Christians. They lived wretchedly on cockles, muscles, and shell-fish. They were tall, straight-bodied, and thin, with small, long limbs. They had bottle noses, big lips, and wide mouths. They held their eyelids half closed, to keep the flies out. Their hair was not long and lank, like that of Indians, but black, short, and curled, like that of negroes. A bit of the rind of a tree and a handful of grass formed their only clothing. The crew landed several times, and brought the natives to some degree of familiarity by giving them a few old clothes; but they could not prevail upon them to assist them in carrying water or any other burden. When the savages found that the ragged jackets and breeches which had been given them were intended to induce them to work, they took them off and laid them down upon the shore.

Dampier was now tired of wandering about the world with this mad crew, none of whom—not even the captain—had any settled purpose or object in view. Read was afraid that Dampier would desert, and when off Sumatra executed a scheme which he hoped would render it impossible. He gave chase to a small sail which was discovered making for Acheen in Sumatra. Taking on board the four Malays who manned her and the cocoanuts with which she was laden, he cut a hole in her bottom and turned her loose. This he did in order to render Dampier and any others who might be disaffected afraid to trust themselves among a people who had been thus robbed and abused. At one of the Nicobar Islands, however, Dampier escaped, and two Englishmen and one Portuguese followed him. The four sailors of Acheen were also put ashore. The whole eight joined company, purchased a canoe, for which they gave an axe in exchange, and set off to row to Acheen. They had not proceeded half a mile before the canoe overset. They swam ashore, dragging the canoe and their chests, and spent three days in making repairs. The Acheenese fitted the canoe with that universal Polynesian apparatus,—an outrigger, or balancer, on each side,—by which capsizing is rendered impossible. They

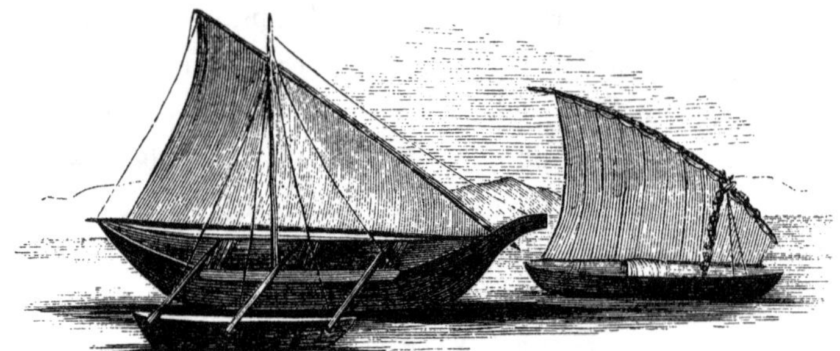

POLYNESIAN CANOE, WITH ITS OUTRIGGER.

felled a mast in the woods and made a substantial sail with mats. They put off again, following the shore for several days. At length they ventured forth upon the open sea, with one hundred and fifty miles of dangerous navigation before them. They rowed with four oars, taking their turns,—Dampier and Hall, one of the Englishmen, relieving each other at the tiller, none of the rest being able to steer. The current against them was very strong, so that, when looking in front for Sumatra, Nicobar, to their dismay, was still visible behind them. A dense halo round the sun, portending a storm, now caused great anxiety to Dampier. The wind freshened till it blew a gale, and they reefed the sail one-half of its surface. The light bamboo poles supporting the outriggers bent as if they would break; and, if they had broken, the destruction of the boat would have been inevitable. Putting away directly before the wind, they ran off their course for six hours, the outriggers being very much relieved by this change of direction.

Dampier's description of this storm is graphic and quaint. "The sky looked very black," he writes, "being covered with dark clouds. The winds blew hard and the seas ran high. The sea was already roaring in a white foam about us,—a dark night coming on, and no land in sight to shelter us, and our little ark in danger to be swallowed by every wave; and, what was worst of all, none of us thought ourselves prepared for another world. I had been in many eminent dangers before now; but the greatest of them all was but a play-game compared to this. I must confess that I was in great conflicts of mind at this time. Other dangers came not upon me with such a leisurely and dreadful solemnity: a sudden skirmish or engagement or so was nothing when one's blood was up and pushed forward with eager expectations. But here I had a lingering view of approaching death, and little or no hopes of escaping it; and I must confess that

DAMPIER'S BOAT IN THE STORM.

my courage, which I had hitherto kept up, failed me here. I had long ago repented me of my roving course of life, but never with such concern as now. I composed my mind as well as I could in the hope of God's assistance; and, as the event showed, I was not disappointed of my hopes."

The preceding representation of the storm is copied from an engraving one hundred and fifty years old, which appeared in the narrative published by Dampier himself. Were it not for this fact, we should not have reproduced it,—as it is very inaccurate, and does not give the outriggers, by which alone the canoe was maintained afloat.

About eight o'clock in the morning one of the Malays cried out, *Pulo Way*, which Dampier and Hall took to be good English, meaning "Pull away." He pointed to the horizon, where land was just appearing in sight. This was the island of Pulo Way, at the northwest end of Sumatra. It lay to the south; and, in order to make it with a strong west wind, "they trimmed their sail no bigger than an apron," and, relying upon their outriggers, made boldly for the shore, which they reached the next morning, the 21st of May. The supposed island turned out to be the Golden Mountain of Sumatra. They landed, and, after being hospitably received by the natives, arrived at Acheen early in June.

At this point the history of Dampier's adventures as a circumnavigator comes properly to an end. He published a narrative of his career, which he dedicated to Charles Montague, President of the Royal Society, and which brought him into favorable notice. His descriptions have been long admired for their graphic force; while his treatises on winds, tides, and currents show a remarkable degree of observation and science for that age of the world. His account of the Philippine Islands and of New Holland is still printed complete in the numerous collections of voyages that are constantly thrown off by the English and Continental presses. Such was the remarkable career of a man who, though without the ferocity and barbarous habits of the buccaneers, was in every sense of the word a pirate and a freebooter. We shall shortly have occasion to mention him again.

We must now refer to another species of piracy,—privateering. This did not enjoy the same repute as in the days of Drake and Hawkins; but several circumstances conspired to render it a calling permissible, if not legitimate. England and France were at war; and private armed vessels, bearing commissions from James II. and William III. against the French, roved the seas and robbed all defenceless ships which fell in their way. They attacked even the vessels of Great Britain, and from privateers became pirates. Many of the Colonial Atlantic ports of America received them and shared in their spoils. Fletcher, the Governor of New York, was bribed to befriend and protect them, while the officers under him were regular contributors to the funds with which corsairs were bought and equipped.

The English Government determined to suppress this nefarious practice, and removed Fletcher in 1695, sending the Earl of Bellamont to replace him. The latter suggested that a frigate be fitted out to assist him in the attempt; but England could spare none of her naval force from the war with France. A proposition, however, to purchase and arm a private ship for the service was received with favor, and several nobles, together with Bellamont and Colonel Richard Livingston, of New York, contributed a fund of six thousand pounds sterling. Livingston recommended, to command the vessel, one William Kidd, who had been captain of a merchant-vessel sailing between London and New York, and of a privateer against the French. Kidd was placed in command, and Livingston became his security for the share he agreed to contribute,—six hundred pounds sterling. To give character to the enterprise, a commission was issued under the great seal of England and signed by the king, William III., directed to "the trusty and well-beloved Captain Kidd, commander of the ship Adventure Galley." This vessel carried thirty guns and sixty men. Kidd departed from Plymouth in April, 1696, and arrived off the American coast in July following. He occasionally entered the port of New York, where he was cordially received, as he was considered useful in protecting its commerce. For this service the Assembly voted him the sum of two hundred and fifty pounds sterling.

He now added ninety-five men to his crew, who shipped to go to Madagascar in pursuit of pirates. He then sailed for the East Indies, and, while on his way, resolved, possessing as he did a vessel manned and equipped like a frigate, to turn pirate himself. He seems to have found ready listeners in the licentious creatures of whom he had composed his crew. He arrived off the Malabar coast, in Hindostan, where he pillaged vessels manned by Indian, Arab, and Christian crews. He lay in wait for a convoy laden with treasure, but, finding it well guarded, abandoned the attempt. He landed from time to time, burned settlements, murdered and tortured the inhabitants, and placed a price upon the heads of such persons as he thought their friends would ransom. He was once pursued by two Portuguese men-of-war, whom he fought and then contrived to elude. He captured a merchantman named the Quedagh, and, refusing the offered ransom of thirty thousand rupees, sold her and her cargo at a pirates' rendezvous for forty thousand dollars. He exchanged the Adventure for a larger vessel, and established himself at Madagascar. Here he lay in ambush, plundering the flags of every nation. He made himself dreaded, as a bloody, cruel, and remorseless bandit, from Malabar and the Red Sea across the Atlantic to the West Indies and the American coast. He arrived at New York in 1698, laden, it is asserted, with more spoil than ever fell to the lot of any other individual. He found Bellamont Governor in place of Fletcher, and deemed it necessary to conceal his treasures. He sailed along the shore of Long Island as far as Gardiner's Island, at the eastern end. He here disembarked, and, in the presence of Mr. John Gardiner, the owner of the island, whom he placed under the most solemn injunction to secrecy, buried a quantity of gold, silver, and precious stones.

After satisfying his crew by such a division of the remainder as they considered equitable, he dismissed them, and had the audacity to appear in the streets of Boston in the dress of a gentleman of leisure. Bellamont, who was Governor of Massachusetts and New Hampshire as well as of New York, met him, caused his arrest, and sent him to England for trial. He was arraigned for the murder of the gunner of his ship, whom he had killed with a bucket. Being convicted, he was hung in chains at Execution Dock on the 12th of May, 1701. The ballad which was written upon his death has survived, and is a favorable specimen of doggerel versification. We subjoin the most striking stanzas:

My name was William Kidd when I sail'd, when I sail'd;
My name was William Kidd when I sail'd;
My name was William Kidd, God's laws I did forbid,
And so wickedly I did, when I sail'd.

I cursed my father dear when I sail'd, when I sail'd;
I cursed my father dear when I sail'd;
I cursed my father dear, and her that did me bear,
And so wickedly did swear, when I sail'd.

I'd a Bible in my hand when I sail'd, when I sail'd;
I'd a Bible in my hand when I sail'd;
I'd a Bible in my hand, by my father's great command,
And I sunk it in the sand, when I sail'd.

I murder'd William Moore as I sail'd, as I sail'd;
I murder'd William Moore as I sail'd;
I murder'd William Moore, and left him in his gore,
Not many leagues from shore, as I sail'd.

And being cruel still, as I sail'd, as I sail'd,
And being cruel still, as I sail'd,
And being cruel still, my gunner I did kill,
And his precious blood did spill, as I sail'd.

My mate was sick and died as I sail'd, as I sail'd;
My mate was sick and died as I sail'd;

My mate was sick and died, which me much terrified,
When he call'd me to his bedside, as I sail'd.

And unto me he did say, See me die, see me die;
And unto me he did say, See me die ;
And unto me he did say, Take warning now by me,
There comes a reckoning day: you must die.

I thought I was undone, as I sail'd, as I sail'd;
I thought I was undone, as I sail'd;
I thought I was undone, and my wicked glass had run,
But my health did soon return, as I sail'd.

My repentance lasted not as I sail'd, as I sail'd;
My repentance lasted not as I sail'd;
My repentance lasted not; my vows I soon forgot;
Damnation's my just lot, as I sail'd.

I spied three ships of Spain as I sail'd, as I sail'd;
I spied three ships of Spain as I sail'd;
I spied three ships of Spain, I fired on them amain,
Till most of them were slain, as I sail'd.

I'd ninety bars of gold as I sail'd, as I sail'd;
I'd ninety bars of gold as I sail'd;
I'd ninety bars of gold, and dollars manifold,
With riches uncontroll'd, as I sail'd.

Then fourteen ships I saw as I sail'd, as I sail'd;
Then fourteen ships I saw as I sail'd;
Then fourteen ships I saw, and brave men they were,
Ah, they were too much for me, as I sail'd.

Thus being o'ertaken at last, I must die, I must die;
Thus being o'ertaken at last, I must die ;
Thus being o'ertaken at last, and into prison cast,
And sentence being pass'd, I must die.

Farewell the raging sea, I must die, I must die;
Farewell the raging main, I must die;
Farewell the raging main, to Turkey, France, and Spain,
I shall ne'er see you again: I must die.

To Newgate now I'm cast, and must die, and must die;
To Newgate now I'm cast, and must die;
To Newgate now I'm cast, with a sad and heavy heart,
To receive my just desert: I must die.

To Execution Dock I must go, I must go;
To Execution Dock I must go;

To Execution Dock will many thousands flock,
But I must bear the shock: I must die.

Come, all you young and old, see me die, see me die;
Come, all you young and old, see me die;
Come, all you young and old, you're welcome to my gold,
For by it I've lost my soul, and must die.

Bellamont, having in some way learned that treasure had been concealed upon Gardiner's Island, sent commissioners to secure it. They found a box containing seven hundred and thirty-eight ounces of gold, eight hundred and forty-seven ounces of silver, a bag of silver rings, a bag of unpolished stones, a quantity of agates, amethysts, and silver buttons. For this they gave a receipt to Mr. Gardiner, which is still preserved by the family. Other sums were discovered at various periods in the possession of persons who had had relations with Kidd; but the soil of Long Island never yielded up any other booty than the box which we have mentioned.

It was natural that the knowledge that Kidd had buried a portion of his spoil, that his companions had shared his good fortune according to their rank, that the vicinity of New York was the rendezvous of pirates for years,—it was natural that this knowledge should induce the prevalent belief that it was the custom among them thus to conceal their booty, and that the spot chosen by Kidd was, perhaps, the scene of the deposits of the entire gang. It was evident, too, that, unless rumor had greatly exaggerated the value of Kidd's ill-gotten gains, the box of gold and silver reckoned in ounces was but a tithe of what he had buried. It was thus that was created that feverish excitement which stimulated eager searchers for piratical store along the coasts of New York and Massachusetts, and particularly among the islets of the Sound. This search has been again and again renewed, and even now, at the distance of a century and a half, the hope of discovering the abandoned wealth of the great pirate is not altogether extinct.

Romances, ballads, and tales without number have been

written upon the adventures of Captain Kidd, his fate, and his money. The most remarkable of these is the "Gold-Bug" of Edgar A. Poe, which details the incidents of an imaginary effort made to recover the treasure the corsair had entombed.

WRECK OF THE PIRATE-SHIP WHIDAH.

Piracy did not disappear with Kidd. The coasts of the Carolinas were for a long time infested with freebooters, though at various times some fifty of them were hung in Charleston. In 1717, the famous and dreaded privateer Whidah was wrecked upon the shores of Cape Cod. This vessel carried twenty-three guns, one hundred and thirty men, and was commanded by Samuel Bellamy. The dead bodies of all but six floated ashore: these six were taken alive and executed. This was a severe loss to the pirates. But the decisive blow against them was not struck till 1723. The British man-of-war Greyhound captured a craft with twenty-five men and carried them into Rhode Island. They were tried, found guilty, and hung, at Newport, in July. This was the end of piracy in the American waters.

HOME OF ALEXANDER SELKIRK.

CHAPTER XXXVIII.

THE VOYAGE OF WOODES ROGERS—DESERTION CHECKED BY A NOVEL CIRCUMSTANCE—A LIGHT SEEN UPON THE ISLAND OF JUAN FERNANDEZ—A BOAT SENT TO RECONNOITRE—ALEXANDER SELKIRK DISCOVERED—HIS HISTORY AND ADVENTURES—HIS DRESS, FOOD, AND OCCUPATIONS—HE SHIPS WITH ROGERS AS SECOND MATE—TURTLES AND TORTOISES—FIGHT WITH A SPANISH TREASURE-SHIP—PROFITS OF THE VOYAGE—THE SOUTH SEA BUBBLE—ITS INFLATION AND COLLAPSE—MEASURES OF RELIEF.

A COMPANY of merchants of Bristol fitted out two ships in 1708—the Duke and Duchess—to cruise against the Spaniards in the South Sea. The Duke was commanded by Woodes Rogers, the Duchess by Stephen Courtney. William Dampier, whose name had long been a terror to the Spaniards, was pilot to the larger ship. They left Bristol on the 14th of July, with fifty-six guns and three hundred and thirty-three men, and with double the usual number of officers, in order to prevent the mutinies so common in privateers.

Nothing of moment occurred till the vessels anchored at Isola Grande, off the coast of Brazil. Here two men deserted, but were so frightened in the night by tigers, as they supposed, but in reality by monkeys and baboons, that they took refuge in the sea and shouted till they were taken on board. The two ships passed through Lemaire's Strait and doubled Cape Horn, and, on the 31st of January, 1709, made the island of Juan Fernandez. During the night a light was observed on shore, and Captain Rogers made up his mind that a French fleet was riding at anchor, and ordered the decks to be cleared for action. At daylight the vessels stood in towards the land; but no French fleet—not even a single sail—was to be seen. A yawl was sent forward to reconnoitre. As it drew near, a man was seen upon the shore waving a white flag; and, on its nearer approach, he directed the sailors, in the English language, to a spot where they could best effect a landing. He was clad in goat-skins, and appeared more wild and ragged than the original owners of his apparel. His name has long been known throughout the inhabited world, and his story is familiar in every language. We need hardly say that his name was Alexander Selkirk, and that his adventures furnished the basis of the romance of Robinson Crusoe.

Alexander Selkirk was a Scotchman, and had been left upon the island by Captain Stradling, of the Cinqueports, four years and four months before. During his stay he had seen several ships pass by, but only two came to anchor at the island. They were Spaniards, and fired at him; but he escaped into the woods. He said he would have surrendered to them had they been French; but he chose to run the risk of dying alone upon the island rather than fall into the hands of Spaniards, as he feared they would either put him to death or make him a slave in their mines. "He told us," says Rogers, "that he was born in Largo, in the county of Fife, and was bred a sailor from his youth.

The reason of his being left here was a difference with his captain, which, together with the fact that the ship was leaky, made him willing to stay behind; but when at last he was inclined to go with the ship the captain would not receive him. He took with him his clothes and bedding, with a firelock and some powder and bullets, some tobacco, a knife, a kettle, a Bible, with other books, and his mathematical instruments. He diverted himself and provided for his sustenance as well as he could, but had much ado to bear up against melancholy for the first eight months, and was sore distressed at being left alone in so desolate a place. He built himself two huts of pimento-trees, thatched with long grass and lined with goat-skins,—killing goats as he needed them with his gun, as long as his powder lasted. When that was all spent, he procured fire by rubbing two sticks of pimento wood together. He slept in his large hut and cooked his victuals in the smaller, and employed himself in reading, praying, and singing psalms,—so that, he said he was a better Christian during his solitude than he had ever been before, or than, he was afraid, he should ever be again.

"At first he never ate but when constrained by hunger,—partly from grief, and partly for want of bread and salt. Neither did he go to bed till he could watch no longer,—the pimento wood serving him both for fire and candle, as it burned very clear and refreshed him by its fragrant smell. His fish he sometimes boiled, and at other times broiled, as he did his goats' flesh, of which he made good broth; for they are not as rank as our goats. Having kept an account, he said he had killed five hundred goats while on the island, besides having caught as many more, which he marked on the ear and let them go. When his powder failed, he ran them down by speed of foot; for his mode of living, with continual exercise of walking and running, cleared him of all gross humors, so that he could run with wonderful swiftness through the woods and up the hills and rocks.

"He came at length to relish his meat well enough without salt. In the proper season he had plenty of good turnips, which had been sowed there by the crew of the ship and had now spread over several acres of ground. The cabbage-palm furnished him with cabbage in abundance, and the fruit of the pimento—the same as Jamaica pepper—with a pleasant seasoning for his food. He soon wore out his shoes and other clothes by running in the woods; and, being forced to shift without, his feet became so hard that he ran about everywhere without inconvenience, and could not again wear shoes without suffering from swelled feet. After he had got the better of his melan-

SELKIRK AND HIS FAMILY.

choly, he sometimes amused himself with carving his name on the trees, together with the date of his arrival and the duration of his solitude. At first he was much pestered with cats and rats, which had bred there in great numbers from some of each species which had got on shore from ships that had wooded and watered at the island. The rats gnawed his feet and clothes when he was asleep, which obliged him to cherish the cats, by feeding them with goats' flesh, so that many of them became so tame that they used to lie beside him in hundreds, and soon delivered him from the rats. He also tamed some kids, and, for his diversion, would sometimes sing and dance with them and his cats. So that by the favor of Providence and the vigor of youth—for he was now only thirty years of age—he came at length to conquer all the inconveniences of his solitude, and to be quite easy in his mind.

"When his clothes were worn out, he made himself a coat and a cap of goat-skins, which he stitched together with thongs of the same cut out with his knife,—using a nail by way of a needle or awl. When his knife was worn out, he made others as well as he could of old hoops that had been left upon the shore, which he beat out thin between two stones and grinded to an edge on a smooth stone. Having some linen cloth, he sewed himself some shirts by means of a nail for a needle, stitching them with worsted which he pulled out from his old stockings; and he had the last of his shirts on when we found him. At his first coming on board, he had so much forgotten his language, for want of use, that we could scarcely understand him, as he seemed to speak his words only by halves. We offered him a dram, which he refused, having drunk nothing but water all the time he had been upon the island; and it was some time before he could relish our provisions. He had seen no venomous or savage creature on the island, nor any other animal than goats, bred there from a few brought by Juan Fernandez, a Spaniard who settled there with a few families till the opposite continent of Chili began to submit to the Spaniards, when they removed there as more profitable."

Captain Rogers remained here a fortnight, refitting his ship. The "governor," as his men called Selkirk, never failed to procure two or three goats a day for the sick. They boiled up and refined eighty gallons of seal-oil, in order to save their candles. On the 13th of February, it was determined that two men from the Duke should sail on board the Duchess, and two from the Duchess on board the Duke, to see that justice was reciprocally done by each ship's company to the other in the division of prizes; and on the 14th the anchors were weighed, Alexander Selkirk shipping on board the Duke as second mate.

When off the Lobos Islands, they took a prize, which they named The Beginning. They learned from their prisoners that the widow of the late Viceroy of Peru was soon to embark at Callao for Acapulco, with her family and riches; and they determined to lie in wait for her. In the mean time they landed and took the town of Guayaquil, but consented to its ransom for thirty thousand dollars. They also seized thirteen small vessels, from which they took meal, onions, quinces, pomegranates, oil, indigo, pitch, sugar, gunpowder, and rice.

At the Gallapagos Islands they laid in a large stock of sea-turtles and land-tortoises, some of the former weighing four hundred pounds, while the latter laid eggs in profusion upon the decks. Some of the men affirmed that they had seen one four

feet high, that two of their party had mounted on its back, and that it easily carried them at its usual slow pace, not appearing to regard their weight. This monster was supposed to weigh seven hundred pounds at least.

Having made the coast of Mexico, and having determined to wait only eight days either for the Manilla galleon or the ship of the viceroy's widow, they were rejoiced to descry, on the morning of the 22d of December, the Spanish treasure-ship on the weather bow. Preparations were made for action, and a large kettle of chocolate was boiled for the crew in lieu of spirituous liquor. Prayers were then said, but were interrupted, before they were concluded, by a shot from the enemy. She had barrels hung at her yard-arm, which seemed to warn the English of an explosion if they attempted to board. The engagement commenced at eight, and lasted an hour, after which she struck and surrendered. She bore the imposing name of Nuestra Señora de la Encarnaçion Disenganio, and mounted twenty guns. Nine of her men were killed and nine wounded. Of the men of the Duke—the only ship of Rogers' fleet engaged—but two were wounded, Captain Rogers himself, who lost a portion of his upper jaw and two of his teeth, being one. The name of the prize was changed from Our Lady, &c. to The Bachelor, and she was equipped as a member of the squadron, which now sailed immediately for the Ladrone Islands.

They arrived at Guam on the 10th of March, 1710, where their wants were amply supplied, cocoanuts being furnished in abundance at the rate of one dollar a hundred. Captain Rogers bought one of the sailing proas of the islanders, which he had seen sail at the rate of twenty miles an hour. He carried it to England, intending to put it in the canal at St. James' Park as a curiosity. At the Cape of Good Hope they joined a number of homeward-bound ships, and sailed in company, early in April, forming a fleet of sixteen Dutch and nine English ships. Rogers and his consorts anchored at Erith, in the Thames, on the 14th of October.

This voyage is the last in which Dampier is known to have been engaged, and what became of him afterwards has never been ascertained. It would not be easy to name, before the time of Cook, a navigator to whom the merchant and mariner are so much indebted. His style was unassuming, as free from affectation as was the narrative itself from invention. Dean Swift made Captain Lemuel Gulliver hail Dampier as cousin.

The outfit of this voyage amounted to £15,000, and the gross profits to £170,000. One third of this, or £57,000, was divided among the officers and seamen. In view of this enormous return for a two years' voyage, we can hardly wonder at the fact that in this age, and during a long succeeding period, nearly all navigation was privateering, and that all ventures upon the seas appear to the reader of the present day as little better than the marauding excursions of corsairs and buccaneers.

This is the proper place for speaking of the famous Company formed for carrying on trade with the Spanish possessions in the Pacific, which received, upon its calamitous failure, the name of South Sea Bubble. This Company was formed, chartered, and prospered and fell, soon after the return of Rogers and Dampier. It originated in 1711, with Harley, the Lord Treasurer, his object being to improve public credit, and to provide for the payment of the floating debt, amounting to £10,000,000. He allured the nation's creditors by promising them the monopoly of trade with the Spanish coast in America. They greedily swallowed the glittering bait, and dreamed of El Dorado and Peruvian Golcondas. This spirit spread throughout the nation, and, in 1719, rose to a fever heat of speculation. Sir John Blunt, once a scrivener, now a prominent South Sea Director, conceived the idea of consolidating all the public funds into one, and made the proposal to the Government. The Bank of England and the South Sea Company displayed the utmost eagerness to outbid each other in the offers made for this magnificent privilege. The South Sea Company finally bid seven millions and a half, and the bill then passed the two houses of Parliament triumphantly. The Directors immediately opened a subscription of a million, and then a second, both of which were eagerly filled.

Every engine was set at work to delude the public: mysterious rumors were rife of secret treasures in America, of overtures made to Stanhope to exchange Gibraltar for a diamond-mine in Peru, and of inexhaustible piles of wealth which were only waiting to be snatched up by the fortunate subscribers to the South Sea stock. The Directors began to quote dividends of twenty, thirty, fifty per cent. They claimed that, being the only national creditor, they could soon dictate to Parliament and rule the country. The stock rose from one hundred and twenty-six to one thousand. The mania was universal,—statesmen, washer-women, Churchmen, Dissenters, ladies of high and low degree, being all smitten alike.

Other bubbles were started by other companies, some of them for the most extravagant objects, such as The Company to make Salt Water Fresh, to Build Hospitals for Bastards, to Obtain Silver from Lead, to Extract Oil from the Seeds of Sunflowers, to Import Jackasses from Spain and thus improve the Breed of English Mules, to Trade in Human Hair, and for a multitude of other equally absurd purposes. The subscriptions thus opened amounted at one period to no less than three hundred millions sterling.

These projects, which rose rapidly one after another and danced in prismatic radiance before the public view, were regarded with jealous eyes by the South Sea Directors, who wished to have a monopoly of the trade in public credulity. They therefore applied for writs of "scire facias" against their managers, and, by showing them to be frauds, suppressed them. But in thus destroying the national confidence in bubbles generally they seriously undermined that enjoyed by their own. Distrust was now excited, and every one became anxious to convert his bonds into money; and then the enormous disproportion between the promises to pay on paper and the means to redeem in coin became evident to all. The stock fell at once, as the basis which sustained it was proved to be altogether imaginary.

Thousands of families were reduced to beggary, and the rage, resentment, and disappointment were bitter and universal. The Company sank into nothingness as rapidly as it had risen to notoriety. Parliament passed a bill by which public confidence was in a measure restored, while the estates of the Directors and officers were confiscated and applied to the relief of the sufferers. The proposed commerce with the Spanish American provinces was naturally never opened, and the next expedition of the English to that quarter, so far from being a voyage for trade, was a very formidable excursion for plunder,—that of Lord Anson, in 1740. We shall refer to this at length in its proper place.

THE EAGLE AND THE PIRATE.

CHAPTER XXXIX.

THE DUTCH WEST INDIA COMPANY—RENEWED SEARCH FOR THE TERRA AUSTRALIS INCOGNITA—JACOB ROGGEWEIN—HIS VOYAGE OF DISCOVERY—BRUSH WITH PIRATES—ARRIVAL AT JUAN FERNANDEZ—EASTER ISLAND—ITS INHABITANTS—ENTERTAINMENT OF ONE ON BOARD THE SHIP—A MISUNDERSTANDING—PERNICIOUS AND RECREATION ISLANDS—GLIMPSE OF THE SOCIETY ISLANDS—A FAMINE IN THE FLEET—ARRIVAL AT NEW BRITAIN—CONFISCATION OF THE SHIP AT BATAVIA—DECISION OF THE STATES-GENERAL—VITUS BEHRING—BEHRING'S STRAIT—DESCRIPTION OF THE SCENE—DEATH OF BEHRING—SUBSEQUENT SURVEY OF THE STRAIT.

THE monopoly of the Dutch East India Company had been somewhat disturbed, as early as the year 1621, by the formation and charter of the Dutch West India Company. The latter held the exclusive commerce of the African coast from the tropic of Cancer to the Cape of Good Hope, and that of the American coast both upon the Atlantic and Pacific Oceans. In 1674, its power and influence were somewhat extended by a fresh grant of privileges and an increase of capital. It was necessary for any one proposing a new scheme of commerce within the limits under their control, to apply to the Company for permission to execute it. A mathematician by the name of Roggewein, a native of the province of Zealand, formed a project, in 1696, for the discovery of the vast continent and islands supposed to exist in the South under the name of *Terra Australis Incognita.* He died, however, before any step was taken by the Company in furtherance of his designs. His son, Jacob Roggewein, renewed the application in 1721, presenting a memorial, in accordance with which immediate orders were given for equipping three vessels,—the Eagle, of thirty-six guns, the Tienhoven, of twenty-eight, and the African galley, of fourteen. Roggewein was made admiral, and two hundred and seventy-one men were embarked upon the three ships. They sailed from the Texel on the 21st of August, 1721.

When approaching the Canaries, they saw a fleet of five sail, carrying white, red, and black colors, which caused the admiral to suspect them to be pirates. He gave the signal for action, when the enemy struck their red flag and hoisted a black one, on which was a death's-head with a powder-horn and cross-bones. A brisk encounter succeeded; and, after two hours, the pirates spread their canvas and bore away with all speed. Roggewein did not follow them,—as all ships of the West and East India Companies had strict orders to pursue their course and never to give chase. He had a long and painful passage across the Atlantic,—the crews suffering from heat, hunger, thirst, and the scurvy. Many of the men had high fevers, and some of them fits like the epilepsy.

During a terrible hurricane on the 21st of December, the Tienhoven parted company, and the Eagle and the African galley kept on together as far as the Strait of Magellan. In this latitude, Roggewein saw the group of islands which a French privateer had named Islands of St. Louis, but which some Dutch traders had subsequently called the New Islands. Roggewein baptized the group anew, and, thinking that if it should ever be inhabited the people would be the antipodes of the Dutch, gave it the name of Belgia Australis. He determined to make the passage through Lemaire's Strait, and, being propelled by a favorable wind and rapid currents, attained the western coast of

America in six days' time. Whenever the weather was clear the nights were exceedingly short; for, though it was the middle of January, the Antarctic summer was at its height. On arriving at the island of Juan Fernandez, Roggewein was surprised and rejoiced to see the Tienhoven safe at the rendezvous. The three captains dined together the next day, and made merry over their mutual convictions of each others' unhappy shipwreck.

After a considerable run to the westward, Roggewein discovered, on the 14th of April, 1722, an island sixteen leagues in extent, to which he gave the name of Easter Island, in commemoration of the day. This was one of the most important discoveries ever made in the Pacific; and Easter Island is, for many reasons, one of the most famous oases in that desert of water. Roggewein thus speaks of his first adventure there:—

"One of the inhabitants came out to us, two miles from shore, in a canoe. We gave him a piece of cloth, for he was quite naked. He was also offered beads and other toys: he hung them all, with a dried fish, about his neck. His body was all painted with every kind of figures. He was brown: his ears were extremely long and hung down to his shoulders, occasioned, doubtless, by wearing large, heavy ear-rings. He was tall, strong, robust, and of an agreeable countenance. He was gay, brisk, and easy in his behavior and manner of speaking. A glass of wine was given to him: he took it, but, instead of drinking it, threw it in his eyes, which surprised us very much. We then dressed him and put a hat upon his head; but he wore it very awkwardly. After he was regaled with food, the musicians were ordered to play on different instruments: the symphony made him very merry, and he began to leap and dance. We sent him back with presents, that the others might know in what manner we had received him. He seemed to leave us with regret, praying with great violence and uttering the word 'Odorraga! odorraga!' The next day large numbers of his countrymen came to our new anchorage, bringing us fowls and roots. At sunrise they prostrated themselves with their faces towards the east, and lighted fires as morning burnt-offerings to their idols, of which there were many upon the coast." Of these supposed idols we shall speak hereafter.

During the landing, in which one hundred and fifty of the crew took part, an islander was accidentally shot; and subsequently, as some of them touched, from curiosity, the Dutch fire-arms, a volley of bullets was discharged at them, and among the killed was the man who had first gone on board the admiral's ship. The consternation and grief of the natives was very great: they brought all kinds of provisions as ransom for the dead bodies. They threw themselves upon their knees, and offered branches of palms in sign of peace. The Dutch carried their outrages no further, but exchanged assurances of good will. They gave sixty yards of painted cloth for eight hundred fowls, some bundles of sugarcane, and a large quantity of plantains, cocoanuts, figs, and potatoes. Roggewein was of opinion that the island might be colonized to advantage, as the air was wholesome and the soil rich: the low lands seemed fitted to produce corn, and the higher grounds well adapted to vineyards. He intended to land with a sufficient force to make a general survey; but, in the mean time, a west wind forced him from his anchorage and drove him out to sea.

He soon found himself in the wide tract which had obtained the name of Bad Sea, on account of the brackish water of one of its islands. Through this region he sailed eight hundred leagues, and, by a change of wind, was driven with his consorts among a number of islands, by which they were considerably embarrassed. The Africa, which drew the least water, was sent in advance, but soon got upon the rocks and fired signals of distress. Night came on, and the natives, alarmed by the reports, kindled fires and came in crowds to the shore. The Dutch, whose confusion of mind seems to have been extreme, fired upon them without ceremony, that they might have as few dangers as possible to contend with at once. In the morning the Africa was found to be jammed between two rocks, from whence she could not be disengaged. She was therefore abandoned. The island upon which she was lost was named Pernicious Island. Five men deserted here, and were left behind. Eight leagues from Pernicious, an island, discovered at daybreak, was named Aurora; and another, seen at sunset, was called Vesper. At another, which they named the Island of Recreation, a party sent on shore for salad and scurvy-grass for the sick had so desperate an encounter with the natives, that, when a second landing was proposed, not a man could be prevailed upon to make the dangerous attempt.

Roggewein was now convinced that no Terra Incognita was to be discovered in the latitude he had kept, and therefore resolved, in accordance with his instructions, to return home by way of the East Indies. His crews were so reduced that a further loss of twenty men would compel him to abandon one of his remaining vessels. The officers regretted this decision; for they were anxious to visit the lands named Solomon's Islands by Mendana on account of their supposed wealth; but they were now compelled to return by way of New Britain, the Moluccas, and the East Indies.

Not far from Recreation Island, a group was discovered by the captain of the Tienhoven, and was named, from him, Bowman's Islands. The natives came off to the ships with fish, cocoanuts, and plantains. They were generally white, except that some were bronzed by the heat of the sun. They appeared gentle and humane: their bodies were not painted, and were clothed from the waist downward with fringes of woven silk. Around their necks they wore strings of odoriferous flowers. Roggewein describes them as altogether the most civilized and honest nation he had seen in the South Sea:—"Charmed with our arrival, they received us as divinities, and testified afterwards great regret when they perceived we were preparing to depart:

sadness was painted in their countenance as we left." These islands are supposed to have been the most northerly of the group now known as the Society Islands.

During the long run to New Britain, the frightful effects of bad provisions were made painfully manifest, for the salt meat had long been decayed, the bread was full of maggots, and the water intolerably putrid. The scurvy began to cut off four and five men a day. Cries and groans were incessantly heard in all parts of the ship: those who were well fainted at the stench of the carcasses. Some were reduced to skeletons, so that the skin cleaved to their bones, while others swelled to a monstrous and disgusting size. The journal says that "an anabaptist of twenty-five years old called out continually to be baptized, and when told, with a sneer, that there was no parson on board, became quiet, and died with great resignation." At last the high land of New Britain put an end to their miseries,—for which there was no cure on earth except fresh meat, green vegetables, and pure water.

The expedition intrusted to Roggewein having proved abortive by the failure to find a Southern continent, we shall follow his adventures no farther. It will suffice to say that his ships were confiscated at Batavia by the Dutch East India Company,—a proceeding which the West India Company resented by commencing an action for damages. After a long litigation, the States-General decreed that the former Company should furnish the latter with two ships better than those confiscated, should refund the full value of their cargoes, should pay the wages of both crews to the day of their return to Holland, together with the costs, and a heavy fine by way of punishment for having so manifestly abused their authority.

We come now to the first expedition at sea made by Russia for the purpose of extending and promoting the science of geography. Vitus Behring was a Dane in the Russian service, having been tempted by the encouragements held out to foreign mariners by Peter the Great. He had risen to the rank of captain in 1725, when the Empress Catherine, who was anxious to promote discovery in the Northeast of Asia and to settle the question, then doubtful, as to the existence of a strait between Asia and America, appointed him to the command of an expedition fitted out for that purpose. During a period of seven years, having travelled overland to Kamschatka, he explored rivers, sounded and surveyed the coasts, and sailed as far to the northward as the season and the strength of his very inferior boats would permit. In 1732, he was made captain-commander, and the next year was ordered to conduct an expedition fitted out on a very extensive scale for purposes of discovery. In 1740, he reached Okhotsk, where vessels had previously been built for him. He sailed for Awatska Bay, where he founded the settlement of Petropaulowski, known in English as the Harbor of Peter and Paul. Sailing to the northward, he landed upon the American coast, giving name to Mount St. Elias, and then, returning to the westward, struck the continent of Asia, finding a strait fifty miles wide between the two continents at the point where they approach each other the nearest. This, in honor of its discoverer, is called Behring's Strait.

The following description of this scene of desolation, as it first broke upon Behring's eye, is due to the imagination of Eugene Sue:—"The month of September," he says, "is at its close. The equinox has come with darkness, and sullen night will soon displace the short and gloomy days of the Pole. The sky, of a dark violet color, is feebly lighted by a sun which dispenses no heat, and whose white disk, scarcely elevated above the horizon, pales before the dazzling brightness of the snow. To the north, this desert is bounded by a coast bristling with black and gigantic rocks. At the foot of their Titanic piles lies motionless the vast ice-bound ocean. To the east appears a line of darkish green, whence seem to creep forth numerous white and glassy icebergs. This is the channel which now bears the name of Behring. Beyond it, and towering above it, are the vast granitic masses of Cape Prince of Wales, the extreme point of North America. These desolate latitudes are beyond the pale of the habitable world. The piercing cold rends the very stones, cleaves the trees, and bursts the ground, which groans in producing the germs of its icy herbage. A few black pines, the growth of centuries, pointing their distorted tops in different directions of the solitude, like crosses in a churchyard, have been torn up and hurled around in confusion by the storm. The raging hurricane, not content with uprooting trees, drives mountains of ice before it, and dashes them, with the crash of thunder, the one against the other.

"And now a night without twilight has succeeded to the day, —dark, dark night! The heavy cupola of the sky is of so deep a blue that it appears black, and the Polar stars are lost in the depths of an obscurity which seems palpable to the touch. Silence reigns alone. But suddenly a feeble glimmer appears in the horizon. At first it is softly brilliant, blue as the light which precedes the rising of the moon; then the effulgence increases, expands, and assumes a roseate hue. Strange and confused sounds are heard,—sounds like the flight of huge night birds as they flap their wings heavily over the plain. These are the forerunners of one of those imposing phenomena which strike with awe all animated nature. An aurora borealis, that magnificent spectacle of the Polar regions, is at hand. In the horizon there appears a semicircle of dazzling brightness. From the centre of this glowing hemisphere radiate blazing columns and jets of light, rising to measureless heights and illumining heaven, earth, and sea. They glide along the snows of the desert, empurpling the blue tops of the ice-mountains and tinging with a deepened red the tall black rocks of the two continents. Having thus reached the fulness of its splendor, the aurora grows gradually pale, and diffuses its effulgence in a luminous mist. At this moment, from the fantastic illusions of the mirage, frequent in those latitudes, the American coast,

MIRAGE AT BEHRING'S STRAITS.

though separated from that of Asia by the interposition of an arm of the sea, suddenly approaches so near it that a bridge might be thrown from one world to the other. Did human beings inhabit those regions and breathe the pale-blue vapors which pervade them, they might almost converse across the narrow inlet which serves to divide the continents. But now the aurora fades away, and the deceptive mirage sinks back into the shadowy realms from whence it came. Fifty miles of sullen waters roll again between the continents, and a three months' night settles over the ghastly and appalling scene."

It is not improbable that Behring passed to the north of East Cape, the promontory on the Asiatic side, into the Arctic Ocean beyond. He was soon compelled to return, owing to the disabled condition of his vessel, which was wrecked upon an island on the 3d of November, 1741. This island, which was little better than a naked rock, afforded neither food nor shelter; and Behring, suffering from the scurvy and sinking from disappointment, lay down in a cleft of the rock to die. The sand collected and drifted about him, half burying him alive. He would not suffer it to be removed, as it afforded him a grateful warmth. He died in this wretched condition on the 8th of December. The next summer, the few of his crew who survived the winter built a vessel from the timber of the wreck: in this they reached Kamschatka and made known the miserable fate of their commander.

Though Behring settled the fact of the existence of the strait which bears his name, it was reserved for Captain Cook to survey the entire length of both coasts. This he did with a precision and accuracy which left nothing for after-voyagers to perform, and which has made the geography of this remote and barbarous region as familiar as that of the Atlantic shores of America. The island upon which Behring died, and which was then uninhabited and without a shrub upon its surface, is now an important trading station, and affords comfortable winter quarters to vessels from Okhotsk and Kamschatka.

LORD ANSON.

CHAPTER XL.

PIRATICAL VOYAGE UNDER GEORGE ANSON—UNPARALLELED MORTALITY—ARRIVAL AND SOJOURN AT JUAN FERNANDEZ—A PRIZE—CAPTURE OF PAITA—PREPARATIONS TO ATTACK THE MANILLA GALLEON—DISAPPOINTMENT—FORTUNATE ARRIVAL AT TINIAN—ROMANTIC ACCOUNT OF THE ISLAND—A STORM—ANSON'S SHIP DRIVEN OUT TO SEA—THE ABANDONED CREW SET ABOUT BUILDING A BOAT—RETURN OF THE CENTURION—BATTLE WITH THE MANILLA GALLEON—ANSON'S ARRIVAL IN ENGLAND—THE PROCEEDS OF THE CRUISE.

THE statesmen of England had now become penetrated with the idea that, in order to consolidate their territorial supremacy, they must make their country the undisputed mistress of the seas. War was declared against Spain in 1739, and the king determined to attack that power in her distant settlements and deprive her, if possible, of her possessions in America, and especially in Peru. It was supposed that the principal resources of the enemy would be by this means cut off, and that the Spanish would be reduced to the necessity of suing for peace, deprived as they would be of the returns of that treasure by which alone they could be enabled to support the drains of a foreign war. A fleet of six vessels, manned by fourteen hundred men and accompanied by two victualling-ships, was placed under the command of George Anson, a captain in the naval service. The flag-ship was the Centurion, mounting sixty guns and carrying four hundred men. On their way out from Spithead, on the 18th of September, 1740, the fleet was joined by an immense convoy of trading ships, which were to keep them company a portion of the way,—numbering in all eleven men-of-war and one hundred and fifty sail of merchantmen.

The squadron passed through Lemaire's Strait on the 7th of March, 1741. "We could not help persuading ourselves," writes Anson, "that the greatest difficulty of our voyage was now at an end, and that our most sanguine dreams were upon the point of being realized; and hence we indulged our imaginations in those romantic schemes which the fancied possession of the Chilian gold and Peruvian silver might be conceived to inspire. Thus animated by these flattering delusions, we passed those memorable straits, ignorant of the dreadful calamities which were then impending and just ready to break upon us,—ignorant that the time drew near when the squadron would be separated never to unite again, and that this day of our passage was the last cheerful day that the greater part of us would ever live to enjoy."

The sternmost ships were no sooner clear of the Strait, than the tranquillity of the sky was suddenly disturbed, and all the presages of a threatening storm appeared in the heavens and upon the waters. The winds were let loose upon the unfortunate fleet, and for three long months blew upon them with unrelenting fury. The Severn and Pearl parted company and were never seen again. During the month of April, forty-three of the crew of the Centurion died of the scurvy; and during the passage from the Strait to the island of Juan Fernandez the flag-ship lost, by this disease, by accident, and by tempest, two hundred and fifty men; and she could not at last muster more than six foremast-men capable of doing duty. On the 22d of May, all the various disasters, fatigues, and terrors which had previously attacked the Centurion in succession now combined in a simultaneous onset, and seem to have conspired for her destruction. A terrific hurricane from the starboard quarter split all her sails and broke all her standing rigging, endangered the masts, and shifted the ballast and stores. The air was filled with fire, and the officers and men upon the decks were wounded by exploding flashes which coursed and darted from spar to spar.

Thus crippled and disabled, with five men dying every day, and not ten of the crew able to go aloft, the Centurion, separated from her consorts, and supposing them to have perished in the storm, made the best of her weary way to the island of Juan Fernandez, where she arrived at daybreak on the 9th of June, after losing eighty more men from the scurvy.

"The aspect of this diversified country would at all times," says Anson, "have been delightful; but in our distressed situation, languishing as we were for the land and its vegetable productions,—an inclination attending every stage of the sea-scurvy,—it is scarcely credible with what transport and eagerness we viewed the shore, and with how much impatience we longed for the greens and other refreshments which were then in sight, and particularly the water. Even those among the diseased who were not in the very last stages of the distemper exerted the small remains of strength which were left them, and crawled up to the deck to feast themselves with this reviving prospect. Thus we coasted the shore, fully employed in the contemplation of this enchanting landskip."

In his description of the island, Anson speaks of the former residence of Alexander Selkirk upon it, and says, "Selkirk tells us, among other things, that, as he often caught more goats than he wanted, he sometimes marked their ears and let them go. This was about thirty-two years before our arrival at the island. Now, it happened that the first goat that was killed by our people had his ears slit; whence we concluded that he had doubtless been formerly under the power of Selkirk. He was an animal of a most venerable aspect, dignified with an exceeding majestic beard and with many other symptoms of antiquity."

The Centurion was soon joined by the Tryal sloop of war, by the Gloucester, and the victualler Anna Pink: the other members of the squadron were never heard of again. Upon the island, which was entirely deserted, Anson thought he discovered appearances which indicated the recent presence there of a Spanish force; and, as they might return, every effort was made to get the ships and the men in position to cope with them on equal terms. While refitting, a sail was discovered upon the distant horizon, and the Centurion started out in pursuit of her. Anson took her for a Spanish man-of-war, and ordered the officers' cabin to be knocked down and thrown overboard, and the decks to be cleared for action. She proved, however, to be an unarmed merchantman sailing under Spanish colors. She surrendered without delay, and proved to be the Monte Carmelo, bound from Callao to Valparaiso, with a cargo of sugar and blue cloth, and, what was infinitely more acceptable to Anson and his crew, eighty thousand dollars in Spanish coin. The Centurion then returned with her prize to Juan Fernandez. The spirits of the English were greatly raised by this capture, and their despondency dissipated by so tangible an earnest of success. The repairs upon all the vessels were hastily completed, and, while they were sent to cruise in different directions in search of Spanish merchantmen, the Centurion and the Carmelo sailed, on the 19th of September, for the general rendezvous at Valparaiso.

In November, Anson determined to attack, with the force of

his two vessels, the unfortunate seaport of Paita, in Peru,—which, as may be seen from our narrative, was invariably attacked by every successive depredator. The town was taken with

BOMBARDMENT OF PAITA.

the utmost ease,—the governor, who was in bed at the time of the surprise, running away half naked in the utmost precipitation, and leaving his wife, hardly seventeen years old, and to whom he had been married but three days, to take care of herself. The custom-house, where the treasure lay, was seized upon and its contents transported to the ship. Anson, not satisfied with this, sent word to the governor, who had come to a halt on a distant hill, that he would listen to proposals for ransom. The governor, who was somewhat arrogant for a magistrate who had made so signal a display of poltroonery, did not deign to return an answer to these overtures: he collected together his people, however, and prepared to storm the city, but, upon second thoughts, prudently abstained. Pitch, tar, and other combustibles were now distributed by Anson's men among the houses of Paita; the cannon in the fort were spiked, and fire was then set to the town, which was speedily reduced to ashes. The loss of the Spaniards by the fire, in broadcloths, silks, velvets, cambrics, was represented by them to the court of Madrid as amounting to a million and a half of dollars. Anson's ships carried away with them, in plate, coin, and jewels, about one hundred and fifty thousand dollars more. Soon after leaving Paita, they fell in with a launch laden with jars of cotton. The people on board said they were very poor; but, as they were found dining on pigeon pie served up in silver dishes, it was thought advisable to search for the sources of this opulence. The jars of cotton were found to contain sixty thousand dollars in double doubloons.

Anson now determined to steer for the southern parts of California, there to cruise for the galleon due at Acapulco from Manilla towards the middle of January. He did not arrive there till the 1st of February, 1742; but, being assured by some of his Spanish prisoners that the galleon was often a month behind her average time, he stood on and off, waiting with feverish impatience for an arrival whose value he estimated in round millions. He soon learned, from some negroes whom he captured, that the galleon had arrived on the 9th of January. They added, however, that she had delivered her cargo, and that the Viceroy of Mexico had fixed her departure from Acapulco, on her return, for the 14th of March. This news was joyfully received by Anson and his men, as it was much more advantageous for them to seize the specie which she had received for her cargo than to seize the cargo itself.

It was now the 19th of February, and the galleon was not to leave port till the 14th of March, or, according to the old style followed by Anson, the 3d of March. The interval was employed in scrubbing the ships' bottoms, in bringing them into the most advantageous trim, and in regulating the orders, signals, and positions to be observed when the famous ship should appear in sight. The positions held were as follows. The squadron was stationed forty miles from shore,—an offing quite sufficient to escape observation: it consisted of the Centurion, the Gloucester, and three armed prizes: these were arranged in a circular line, and each ship was nine miles distant from the next, the two vessels at the extremes being, therefore, thirty-six miles apart. As the galleon could be easily discerned twenty miles outside of either extremity, the whole sweep of the squadron was seventy-five miles, the various vessels composing it being so connected by signals as to be readily informed of what was seen in any part of the line. The Centurion and the Gloucester were alone intended to come to close quarters, or, indeed, to engage in the action at all: they were therefore strengthened by accessions from the others.

The calls of hunger and all other duties were neglected on the 3d of March: all eyes were strained in the direction of Acapulco, and voices continually exclaimed that they saw one of the cutters returning with a signal. To their extreme vexation and dismay, both that day and the next passed without bringing news of the galleon. A fortnight went by; and Anson at last came to the melancholy conclusion that his presence upon the coast had been discovered, and that an embargo had been laid upon the object of all their hopes. He afterwards discovered that his presence was suspected, but not known, but that the wary Spaniards had frustrated his schemes by detaining the galleon till the succeeding year. With a heavy heart, the admiral gave orders for the departure of the fleet from the American coast, in prosecution of the plans drawn up previous to his leaving England. He sailed early in May with the Centurion and Gloucester only, having scuttled and destroyed his three prizes on the enemy's coast.

A terrible attack of scurvy soon reduced both vessels to half their working force, and a storm of unusual violence completely disabled the Gloucester. She held out, however, till the middle of August, when her stores, her prize-money, and her sick were with great difficulty removed to the Centurion, which was herself in a crazy and well-nigh desperate condition. The Gloucester was set on fire, lest her wreck might fall into the hands of the Spaniards: she continued burning through the night, firing her guns successively as the flames reached them: the magazine exploded at daylight.

The Centurion kept on her way, losing eight, nine, and ten

men every twenty-four hours. A leak was discovered, which all the skill of the carpenters failed to stop. The ship and men were in a condition bordering on positive despair. Under these circumstances, the sight of two distant islands revived for a time their drooping spirits. But these islands were bare and uninhabited rocks, affording neither anchorage nor fresh water. The reaction produced by this disappointment was evident in the renewed ravages of the relentless scurvy. "And now," says Anson, "the only possible circumstance which could secure the few of us which remained alive from perishing, was the accidental falling in with some other of the Ladrone Islands better prepared for our accommodation; but, as our knowledge of them was extremely imperfect, we were to trust entirely to chance for our guidance. Thus, with the most gloomy persuasion of an approaching destruction, we stood from the island-rock of Anatacan, having all of us the strongest apprehensions either of dying of the scurvy, or of being destroyed with the ship, which, for want of hands to work her pumps, might in a short time be expected to founder."

On the 27th of August, the Centurion came in sight of a fertile and, as Anson supposed, inhabited island, which he afterwards found to be one of the Ladrones and named Tinian. Fearing the inhabitants to be Spaniards, and knowing himself to be incapable of defence, Anson showed Spanish colors, and hoisted a red flag at the foretopmast head, intending by this to give his vessel the appearance of the Manilla galleon, and hoping to decoy some of the islanders on board. The trick succeeded, and a Spaniard and four Indians were easily taken, with their boat. The Spaniard said the island was uninhabited, though it was one of an inhabited group: he affirmed that there was plenty of fresh water, that cattle, hogs, and poultry ran wild over the rocks, that the woods afforded sweet and sour oranges, limes, lemons, and cocoanuts, besides a peculiar fruit which served instead of bread; that, from the quantity and goodness of the productions of the island, the Spaniards of the neighboring station of Guam used it as a storehouse and granary from whence they drew inexhaustible supplies.

A portion of this relation Anson could verify upon the spot: he discovered herds of cattle feeding in security upon the island, and it was not difficult to fill, in imagination, the rich forests which clothed it, with tropical fruits and all the varied productions of those beneficent climes. On landing, he at once converted a storehouse filled with jerked beef into an hospital for the sick: in this he deposited one hundred and twenty-eight of his invalids. The salutary effect of land-treatment and vegetable food was such that, though twenty-one died on the first day, only ten others died during the two months that the Centurion remained at anchor in the harbor.

ANSON'S ENCAMPMENT AT TINIAN.

Anson gives a romantic account of the happy island of Tinian. The vegetation was not luxuriant and rank, but resembled the clean and uniform lawns of an English estate. The turf was composed of clover intermixed with a variety of flowers. The woods consisted of tall and wide-spreading trees, imposing in their aspect or inviting in their fruit. Three thousand cattle, milk-white with the exception of their ears, which were black, grazed in a single meadow. The clamor and paradings of domestic poultry excited the idea of neighboring farms and villages. Both the cattle and the fowls were easily run down and captured, so that the Centurion husbanded her ammunition. The hogs were hunted by dogs trained to the pursuit, a number of which had been left by the Spaniards of Guam: they readily transferred their services and their allegiance to the English invaders. The island also produced in abundance the very best specifics for scorbutic disorders,—such as dandelion, mint, scurvy-grass, and sorrel. The inlets furnished fish of plethoric size and inviting taste; the lakes abounded with duck, teal, and curlew, and in the thickets the sportsmen found whole coveys of whistling plover.

On the night of the 22d of September a violent storm drove the Centurion from her anchorage, sundering her cables like packthread. Anson was on shore, down with the scurvy; several of the officers, and a large part of the crew, amounting in all to one hundred and thirteen persons, were on shore with him. This catastrophe reduced all, both at sea and on land, to the utmost despair: those in the ship were totally unprepared to struggle with the fury of the winds, and expected each moment to be their last; those on shore supposed the Centurion to be lost, and conceived that no means were left them ever to depart from the island. As no European ship had probably anchored here before, it was madness to expect that chance would send another in a hundred ages to come Besides, the Spaniards of Guam could not fail to capture them ere long, and, as their letters of marque were gone in the Centurion, they would undoubtedly be treated as pirates.

In this desperate state of things, Anson, who preserved, to all outward appearance, his usual composure, projected a scheme for extricating himself and his men from their forlorn situation. In case the Centurion did not return within a week, he said, it would be fair to conclude, not that she was wrecked, but that she had been driven too far to the leeward of the island to be able to return to it, and had doubtless borne away for Macao. Their policy, therefore, was to attempt to join her there. To effect this, they must haul the Spanish bark, which they had captured on their arrival, ashore, saw her asunder, lengthen her twelve feet,—which would give her forty tons' burden and enable her to carry them all to China. The carpenters, who had been fortunately left on the island, had been consulted, and had pronounced the proposal feasible. The men, who at first were unwilling to abandon all hope of the Centurion's return, at last saw the necessity of active co-operation, and went zealously to work.

The blacksmith, with his forge and tools, was the first to commence his task; but, unhappily, his bellows had been left on board the ship. Without his bellows he could get no fire; without fire he could mould no iron; and without iron the carpenters could not rivet a single plank. But the cattle furnished hides in plenty, and these hides were imperfectly tanned with the help of a hogshead of lime found in the jerked-beef warehouse: with this improvised leather, and with a gun-barrel for a pipe, a pair of bellows was constructed which answered the intention tolerably well. Trees were felled and sawed into planks, Anson working with axe and adze as vigorously as any of his men. The juice of the cocoanut furnished the men a natural and abundant grog, and one which had this advantage over the distilled mixture to which that name is usually applied,—that it did not intoxicate them, but kept them temperate and orderly. When the main work had been thus successfully started, it was found, on consultation, that the tent on shore, some cordage accidentally left by the Centurion, and the sails and rigging already belonging to the bark, would serve to equip her indifferently when she was lengthened. Two disheartening circumstances were now discovered: all the gunpowder which could be collected by the strictest search amounted to just ninety charges,—considerably less than one charge apiece to each member of the company: their only compass was a toy, such as are made for the amusement of school-boys. Their only quadrant was a crazy instrument which had been thrown overboard from the Centurion with other lumber belonging to the dead, and which had providentially been washed ashore. It was examined by the known latitude of the island of Tinian, and answered in a manner which convinced Anson that, though very bad, it was at least better than nothing.

On the 9th of October—the seventeenth day from the departure of the ship—matters were in such a state of forwardness that Anson was able to fix the 5th of November as the date of their putting to sea upon their voyage of two thousand miles. But a happier lot was in store for them. On the 11th, a man working upon a hill suddenly cried out, in great ecstasy, "The ship! the ship!" The commodore threw down his axe and rushed with his men—all of them in a state of mind bordering on frenzy—to the beach. By five in the afternoon the Centurion—for it was she—was visible in the offing: a boat with eighteen men to reinforce her, and with meat and refreshments for the crew, was sent off to her. She came happily to anchor in the roads the next day, and the commodore went on board, where he was received with the heartiest acclamations. The vessel had, during this interval of nineteen days, been the sport of storms, currents, leakages, and false reckonings; she had but one-fourth of her complement of men; and when, by a happy accident of driftage, she came in sight of the island, the crew were so weak they could with difficulty put the ship about. The reinforcement of eighteen men was sent at the very moment when, in sight of the long wished-for haven, the exhausted sailors were on the point of abandoning themselves to despair.

Fifty casks of water, and a large quantity of oranges, lemons, and cocoanuts were now hastily put on board the Centurion. On the 21st of October, the bark (so lately the object of all the commodore's hopes and fears) was set on fire and destroyed. The vessel then weighed anchor, and took leave of the island of Tinian,—an island which, in the language of Anson, "whether we consider the excellence of its productions, the beauty of its appearance, the elegance of its woods and lawns, the healthiness of its air, and the adventures it gave rise to, may in all these views be justly styled romantic." After a smooth run of twenty days, the Centurion came to an anchor on the 12th of November, in the roads of Macao,—thus, after a fatiguing cruise of two years, arriving at an amicable port and in a civilized country, where naval stores could be procured with ease, and, above all, where the crew expected the inexpressible satisfaction of receiving letters from their friends and families.

The Centurion remained more than five months at Macao, where she was careened, thoroughly overhauled, and refitted. The crew was reinforced by entering twenty-three men, some of them being Lascars, or Indian sailors, and some of them Dutch. On the 19th of April, the admiral got to sea, having announced that he was bound to Batavia and from thence to England, and, in order to confirm this delusion, having taken letters on board at Canton and Macao directed to dear friends in Batavia. But his real design was to cruise off the Philippine Isles for the returning Manilla galleon. Indeed, as he had the year before prevented the sailing of the annual ship, he had good reason to believe that there would this year be two. He therefore made all haste to reach Cape Espiritu Santo, the first land the galleons were accustomed to make. They were said to be stout vessels, mounting forty-four guns and carrying five hundred hands; while he himself had but two hundred and twenty-seven hands, thirty of whom were boys. But he had reason to expect that his men would exert themselves to the utmost in view of the fabulous wealth to be obtained.

The Centurion made Cape Espiritu Santo late in May, and from that moment forward her people waited in the utmost impatience for the happy crisis which was to balance the account of their past calamities. They were drilled every day in the working of the guns and in the use of their small-arms. The vessel kept at a distance from the cape, in order not to be discovered. But, in spite of all precautions, she was seen from the land, and information of her presence was sent to Manilla, where a force consisting of two ships of thirty-two guns, one of twenty guns, and two sloops of ten guns, was at once equipped: it never sailed, however, on account of the monsoon.

On the 20th of June, at sunrise, the man at the masthead of the Centurion discovered a sail in the southeast quarter. A general joy spread through the ship, and the commodore instantly stood towards her. At eight o'clock she was visible from the deck, and proved to be the famous Manilla galleon. She did not change her course, much to Anson's surprise, but continued to bear down upon him. It afterwards appeared that she recognised the hostile sail to be the Centurion, and resolved to fight her. She soon hauled up her foresail, and brought to under topsails, hoisting Spanish colors. Anson picked out thirty of his choicest hands and distributed them into the tops as marksmen. Instead of firing broadsides with intervals between them, he resolved to keep up a constant but irregular fire, thus baffling the Spaniards if they should attempt their usual tactics of falling down upon the decks during a broadside and working their guns with great briskness during the intermission. At one o'clock, the Centurion, being within gunshot of the enemy, hoisted her pennant. The Spaniard now, for the first time, began to clear her decks, and tumbled cattle, sheep, pigs, goats, and poultry promiscuously into the sea. Anson gave orders to fire with the chase-guns: the galleon retorted with her stern-chasers. During the first half-hour he lay across her bow, traversing her with nearly all his guns, while she could bring hardly half a dozen of hers to bear. The mats with which the galleon had stuffed her netting now took fire, and burned violently, terrifying the Spaniards and alarming the English, who feared lest the treasure would escape them. However, the Spaniards at last cut away the netting and tossed the blazing mass into the sea among the struggling and roaring cattle. The

Centurion swept the galleon's decks, the topmen wounding or killing every officer but one who appeared upon the quarter, and totally disabling the commander himself. The confusion of the

THE CENTURION AND THE TREASURE-SHIP.

Spaniards was now plainly visible from the Centurion. The officers could no longer bring the men up to the work; and, at about three in the afternoon, she struck her colors and surrendered.

The galleon, named the Nostra Signora de Cabadonga, proved to be worth, in hard money, one million and a quarter of dollars. She lost sixty-seven men in the action, besides eighty-four wounded; while the Centurion lost but two men, and had but seventeen wounded, all of whom recovered but one. "Of so little consequence," remarks Anson, "are the most destructive arms in untutored and unpractised hands." The seizure of the Manilla treasure caused the greatest transport to the Centurion's men, who thus, after reiterated disappointments, saw their wishes at last accomplished.

The specie was at once removed to the Centurion, the Cabadonga being appointed by Anson to be a post-ship in his majesty's service, and the command being given to Mr. Saumarez, the first lieutenant of the Centurion. The two vessels then stood for the Canton River, and arrived off Macao on the 11th of July. On the way, Anson reckoned up not only the value of the prize just captured, but the total amount of the losses his expedition had caused the crown of Spain since it left the English shores. The galleon was found to have on board one million three hundred and thirteen thousand eight hundred and forty-three dollars, and thirty-five thousand six hundred and eighty-two ounces of virgin silver, besides cochineal and other commodities. This, added to the other treasure taken in previous prizes, made the sum total of Anson's captures in money not far from two millions,—independent of the ships and merchandise which he had either burned or destroyed, and which he set down as three millions more; to which he added the expense of an expedition fitted out by the court of Spain, under one Joseph Pizarro, for his annoyance, and which, he learned from the galleon's papers, had been entirely broken up and destroyed. "The total of all these articles," he writes, "will be a most exorbitant sum, and is the strongest proof of the utility of my expedition, which, with all its numerous disadvantages, did yet prove so extremely prejudicial to the enemy."

At Macao, Anson sold the galleon for six thousand dollars, which was much less than her value. He was very anxious to get to sea at once, that he might be himself the first messenger of his good fortune and thereby prevent the enemy from forming any projects to intercept him. The Centurion weighed anchor from Macao on the 15th of December, 1743: she touched at the Cape of Good Hope on the 11th of March, 1744, where the commodore sojourned a fortnight, in a spot which he considered as not disgraced by a comparison with the valleys of Juan Fernandez or the lawns of Tinian. The fortuitous escapes and remarkable adventures which had characterized the career of his famous ship continued till she saluted the British forts. The French had espoused the cause of Spain; and a large French fleet was cruising in the Chops of the Channel at the moment when the Centurion crossed it. The log afterwards proved that she had run directly through the hostile squadron, concealed from view by a dense and friendly fog. She arrived safe at Spithead, on the 15th of June, after an absence of three years and nine months. Anson caused the captured wealth to be transported to London, upon thirty-two wagons, to the sound of drum and fife. The two millions were divided, according to the laws which regulate the distribution of prize-money, between Anson, his officers and men,—the crown abandoning every penny to those who had suffered and fought for it. Anson was now the richest man in the naval service. The sympathy and applause bestowed upon him by the public may be imagined from the fact that the narrative of his voyage went through four immense editions in a single year, was translated into seven European languages, and met with a far greater success than had ever fallen to the lot of any maritime journal.

BYRON AT KING GEORGE'S ISLAND.

CHAPTER XLI.

THE FIRST SCIENTIFIC VOYAGE OF CIRCUMNAVIGATION—THE DOLPHIN AND TAMAR—BYRON IN PATAGONIA—FALKLAND ISLANDS—ISLANDS OF DISAPPOINTMENT—ARRIVAL AT TINIAN—BYRON VERSUS ANSON—THE VOYAGE HOME—WALLIS AND CARTERET—THEIR OBSERVATIONS IN PATAGONIA—WALLIS AT TAHITI—A DESPERATE BATTLE—NAILS LOSE THEIR VALUE—A TAHITIAN ROMANCE—PITCAIRN'S ISLAND—QUEEN CHARLOTTE'S ISLANDS—NEW BRITAIN—THE VOYAGE HOME—A MAN-OF-WAR DESTROYED BY FIRE.

IN the year 1764, England was at peace with all the world, and his majesty George III. conceived an idea which till then had penetrated no royal brain,—that of sending out vessels upon voyages of discovery in the single view of extending the domain of science and contributing to the advance of geographical knowledge. Voyages had previously been undertaken for purposes either of conquest, colonization, pillage, or privateering; and discovery had usually been the result of accident, and was generally subordinate to the grand business of plunder and rapine. The king at once executed his design by giving the command of the Dolphin and Tamar—the former a man-of-war of twenty-four guns, and the latter a sloop of sixteen—to Commodore John Byron, who had been one of the wrecked captains of Anson's fleet in 1740. The vessels sailed from Plymouth on the 3d of July. Nothing of moment occurred during their passage to Rio Janeiro, if we except the fact that Byron noticed that no fish would come near his ship, though the sea was alive with them at a little distance,—a circumstance which he attributed to the Dolphin's copper sheathing. She was the first vessel upon which the experiment of coppering the bottom had been tried.

Upon the Patagonian coast, Byron saw a party of the natives on horseback, one of whom, who dismounted, he describes as follows:—"He was of a gigantic stature, and seemed to realize the tales of monsters in human shape: he had the skin of some wild beast thrown over his shoulders, as a Scotch Highlander wears his plaid. Round one eye was a large circle of white; a circle of black surrounded the other, and the rest of his face was streaked with paint of different colors. His height could not be less than seven feet. This frightful Colossus and his whole company conducted themselves in a peaceable and orderly manner which certainly did them honor." Byron entered Magellan's Strait in December. During an anchorage here, a part of the men slept on shore: they were always awakened from their first slumber by the roaring of wild beasts, which the darkness of the night and the loneliness of their situation rendered horrible beyond description. The animals were prevented from invading the tent by the kindling of large fires.

Having determined to await the arrival of the Florida,—a store-ship which was to follow him,—Byron returned into the

Atlantic and discovered a group of islands, of which he took possession for King George III. by the name of the Falkland Islands. Here the seals and penguins were so numerous that it was impossible to walk upon the beach without first driving them away. The men were also compelled to do battle and fight hand-to-hand encounters with enormous and formidable sea-lions, and with animals as large as a mastiff and as fierce as a wolf. On returning to Port Desire, in February, 1765, the whales about the ship rendered the navigation dangerous, and one of them blew a jet of water over the quarterdeck. The Florida arrived about the same time, and the Dolphin and Tamar took from her all the provisions they could store. They then entered the Strait, and, for seven weeks and two days, struggled with the terrible weather which at the period of the spring equinox prevails in that tempestuous region. They made Cape Deseado on the 8th of April, and soon after entered the South Sea.

Turning to the north as far as Juan Fernandez, and then making a long stretch to the west, Byron discovered, on the 7th of June, in 14° 5′ south latitude and in 145° west longitude, a group of islands covered with delightful groves and evidently producing cocoanuts and bananas in abundance. Turtles were seen upon the shore; and the whole aspect of the island was tropical and attractive in the extreme. But a violent surge broke upon every point of the coast, and the steep coral rocks which formed the shore rendered it unsafe to anchor. The sailors, prostrated with scurvy, stood gazing at this little paradise with sensations of bitter regret; and Byron accordingly named the group the Islands of Disappointment. Two days later, however, he discovered another group, to which he gave the name of King George's Islands. Here the savages, in attempting to repel an invasion of their domain, provoked reprisals, and two or three of them were killed: one, being pierced by three balls which went quite through his body, took up a large stone and died in the act of throwing it. Byron obtained several boatloads of cocoanuts and a large quantity of scurvy-grass. After discovering and naming Prince of Wales' and Duke of York's Islands, Byron bore away for the Ladrones, a month's sail to the west.

In due time, and after a voyage accomplished without incident, the two vessels arrived at the Ladrone island of Tinian, already famous from the glowing description given of it by Lord Anson. They anchored not far from the spot where the Centurion had lain, and in water so clear that they could see the bottom at the depth of one hundred and forty-four feet. Byron gives a very different account of the island from that furnished by Anson,—a fact attributable to the circumstance that he visited it during the rainy season. The undergrowth in the woods was so thick, he says, that they could not see three yards before them: the meadows were covered with stubborn reeds higher than their heads, and which cut their legs like whipcord. Every time they spoke they inhaled a mouthful of flies. In the Centurion's well they found water that was brackish and full of worms. Centipedes bit and scorpions bled. The ships rolled at anchor as never ships rolled before. The rains were incessant. The heat was suffocating, being only nine degrees less than the heat of the blood at the heart. Anson's cattle were very shy; for it took six men three days and three nights to capture and kill a bullock, whose flesh, when dragged home to the tents, invariably proved to be fly-blown and useless.

After a stay of nine weeks at Tinian, Byron weighed anchor on the 30th of September, with a cargo of two thousand cocoanuts. On the 5th of October, he touched at the Malay island of Timoan. The inhabitants were inclined to drive hard bargains and to part with as few provisions as possible. They were even offended at the sailors hauling the seine and taking fish upon their coast. Leaving this ungenerous island, they met with a fortnight of light winds, dead calms, and violent tornadoes, accompanied with rain, thunder, and lightning. On the

19th of October, they hailed an English craft belonging to the East India Company and bound from Bencoolen to Bengal. The master sent them a sheep, a turtle, a dozen fowls, and two gallons of arrack. With this assistance Byron easily reached Java, where he took in stores of rice and arrack. Nothing of moment occurred during the run home, except the incident of a collision between the Dolphin and a whale, in which the latter appeared to be the greatest sufferer, as the water was deeply tinged with blood. Byron arrived at Deal on the 7th of May, 1766. Each ship had lost six men, including those that were drowned. This number was so inconsiderable that it was deemed probable that more of them would have died had they remained on shore. Byron, having discharged all the duties devolving on him during this voyage with prudence and energy, could not be held responsible for the poverty of the scientific results obtained, —a circumstance owing to the absence of scientific men, naturalists, mathematicians, astronomers, &c. The Government resolved to make another effort, and to equip the expedition in a style more adequate to its necessities. The Dolphin was immediately refitted and furnished for a voyage to be made in the same seas under Captain Samuel Wallis. The Swallow, a sloop of fourteen guns, was appointed to be her consort, instead of the lumbering Tamar, and Captain Carteret, who had accompanied Byron, was ordered to command her. The Prince Frederick was appointed to accompany them as store-ship. They left Plymouth in company on the 22d of August, 1766.

The run to Magellan's Strait offers no points of interest. They entered into amicable relations with the Patagonians. These people, who, from Magellan's and Byron's accounts, had obtained the reputation of being giants of seven feet, were measured with a rod by Wallis. The tallest were six feet six, while their average height was from five feet ten to six feet. He invited several of them on board, where, following the example of Magellan, he showed one of them a looking-glass. "This, however," he says, "excited little astonishment, but afforded them infinite diversion." The Prince Frederick took on board, by Wallis' order, several thousand young trees, which had been carefully removed with their roots and the earth about them, and transported them to the Falkland Islands, where there was no growth of wood. Captain Carteret climbed a mountain in the hope of obtaining a view of the South Sea: he erected a pyramid, in which he deposited a bottle containing a shilling and a paper,—a memorial which, he remarked, might possibly remain there as long as the world endured. At other points the land was bare, covered with snow, or piled to the clouds with rocks, looking like the ruins of nature doomed to everlasting sterility and desolation.

A storm now disabled both ships, and Carteret found the Swallow to be almost unmanageable. From this time forward, during the passage of the Strait, the inhabitants they met seemed to be the most miserable of human beings,—half frozen, half fed, half clothed. After four months' dangerous and tedious navigation, they issued from the Strait into the ocean on the 11th of April, 1767, bidding farewell to a region where in the midst of summer the weather was tempestuous, "where the prospect had more the appearance of chaos than of nature, and where, for the most part, the valleys were without herbage and the hills without wood." A storm here separated the Dolphin and the Swallow, and from this point the adventures of Wallis and Carteret form two distinct narratives. We shall follow the course of the Dolphin, and then return to that of the Swallow.

Wallis sailed to the northwest for two months without incident, discovering Whitsun Island and Queen Charlotte's Island in mid-ocean. At last, on the 19th of June, he touched at Quiros' island of Sagittaria: it had been lost for a century and a half, and its existence even was doubted. The Dolphin was soon surrounded by hundreds of canoes, containing at least eight hundred peoole. They did not manifest hostile intentions, however, contenting themselves with petty thefts. Wallis sent his boats to sound for an anchorage, and, observing the canoes gather around them, fired a nine-pounder over their heads. A skirmish followed, which resulted in the wounding of several on both sides. But, on Wallis' attempting to enter the Bay of Matavai, the islanders offered a determined resistance: three hundred canoes, manned by two thousand warriors, surrounded him and attacked him with a hail of stones. Repulsed for a time, they twice rallied, and hurled stones weighing two pounds on board, by means of slings. At last a cannon-ball cut the canoe bearing the chief in halves, whereupon canoes and warriors disappeared with the utmost precipitation. The ship was now warped up to the shore, and the boats landed without opposition. Mr. Furneaux, the lieutenant, took possession of the island for his majesty, in honor of whom he called it King George the Third's Island. The water proving to be excellent, rum was mixed with it, and every man drank his majesty's health. The natives choosing to make a demonstration at midnight, Wallis cleared the coast with his guns, and sent the carpenters ashore with their axes, to destroy all the canoes which in their precipitation they had left. Fifty canoes, some of them sixty feet long, were thus broken up. These measures brought the savages to terms, and boughs of plantains were soon exchanged and vows of friendship pantomimically expressed. Trade was established, and a tent erected at the watering place. The crew now lived sumptuously upon fruits and poultry, and in a fortnight the commander hardly knew them for the same people. This, as we have said, was the island which Cook was to render famous under the name of Tahiti.

It was not long before it was discovered that nails, the principal medium of exchange, seemed to have lost their value with the islanders. Bringing forth large spikes from their pockets, they intimated that they desired nails of a similar size and strength. It was now ascertained that the sailors, having no nails of their own, had drawn all the stout hammock-pins, and had ripped out the belaying cleats. Every artifice was practised to discover the thieves, but without success.

On the 11th of July, a tall woman of pleasing countenance and majestic deportment came on board. She proved to be Oberea, sovereign of the island. She seemed quite fascinated by Wallis, who was recovering from a severe illness, and invited him to go on shore and perfect his convalescence. He accepted the invitation, and the next day called upon her at her residence,—an immense thatched roof raised upon pillars. She ordered four young girls to take off his shoes and stockings and gently chafe his skin with their hands. While they were doing this, the English surgeon who accompanied Wallis took off his wig to cool himself. Every eye was at once fixed upon this prodigy of nature. The whole assembly stood motionless in silent astonishment. They would not have been more amazed, says Wallis, had they discovered that the surgeon's limbs had been screwed on to the trunk. Oberea accompanied Wallis on his way back to the shore, and whenever they came to a little puddle of water she lifted him over it.

It was now discovered that one Francis Pinckney, a seaman, had drawn the cleats to which the main-sheet was belayed, and had then removed and bargained away the spikes. Wallis called the men together, explained the heinousness of the offence, and ordered Pinckney to be whipped with nettles while he ran the gauntlet three times round the deck. To prevent the ship from being pulled to pieces and the price of provisions from being disproportionately raised, he directed that no man should go ashore except the wooders and waterers.

Oberea now became romantic and tender. She tied wreaths of plaited hair around Wallis' hat, giving him to understand that both the hair and workmanship were her own. She made him presents of baskets of cocoanuts, and of sows big with young. She said he must stay twenty days more; and, when he replied that he should depart in seven days, she burst into tears, and was with great difficulty pacified. When the fatal hour arrived, she threw herself down upon the arm-chest and wept passionately. She was with difficulty got over the side into her canoe, where she sat the picture of helpless, unutterable woe. Wallis tossed her articles of use and ornament, which she silently accepted without looking at them. He subsequently bade her adieu more privately on shore. A fresh breeze sprang up, and the Dolphin left the island on the 27th of July.

PARTING OF WALLIS AND OBEREA.

On his way to Tinian he discovered several islands, one of which the officers did their commander the honor of calling Wallis' Island. At Tinian they found every article mentioned by Lord Anson, though it required no little time and labor to noose a bullock or bag a banana. When they left, each man had laid in five hundred limes. On the passage to Batavia, and thence to Table Bay, the sick-list was very large, and several men were lost by disease and accident. At the Cape, the crew were attacked by the small-pox, and a pest-tent was erected upon a spacious plain. The infection was not fatal in any instance. The Dolphin anchored in the Downs on the 20th of May, 1768. Wallis was enabled to communicate a paper to the Royal Society in time for that body to give to Lieutenant Cook, then preparing for his first voyage, more complete instructions by which to govern his movements.

We must now return to the Swallow, commanded by Philip Carteret, and, as far as the Strait of Magellan, the consort of the Dolphin. A storm, as we have said, separated them; and, while Wallis sailed to the northwest, Carteret was driven due north. He was surprised to find Juan Fernandez fortified by the Spanish, and did not think it prudent to attempt a landing. Sailing now due west, he discovered an island to which he gave the name of Pitcairn, in honor of the young man who first saw it. This island we shall have occasion to mention more particularly hereafter, as it became the scene of the romantic adventures of the mutineers of the Bounty. The vessel had now become crazy, and leaked constantly. The sails were worn, and split with every breeze. The men were attacked by the scurvy; and Carteret began to fear that he should get neither ship nor crew in safety back to England.

At last, on the 12th of August, land was discovered at daybreak, which proved to be a cluster of islands, of which Carteret counted seven. Ignorant that Mendana had discovered them in 1595, nearly two centuries previously, and had given them the name of Santa Cruz, Carteret took possession of them, naming them Queen Charlotte's Islands and giving a distinctive appellation to each member of the archipelago. Cocoanuts, bananas, hogs, and poultry were seen in abundance as they sailed along the shore; but every attempt to land ended in bloodshed and repulse. They now steered to the northwest, and, on the 26th of August, saw New Britain and St. George's Bay, discovered and named by Dampier. Anchoring temporarily, and again wishing to weigh anchor, Carteret found, to his dismay, that the united strength of the whole ship's company was insufficient to perform the labor. They spent thirty-six hours in fruitless attempts, but, having recruited their strength by sleep, finally succeeded. They had neither the strength to chase turtle nor the address to hook fish. Cocoanut-milk gradually revived the men, who also received benefit from a fruit resembling a plum.

The wind not allowing Carteret to follow Dampier's track around New Britain, the idea struck him that St. George's Bay might in reality be a channel dividing the island in twain. This the event proved to be correct. On his way through, he noticed three remarkable hills, which he called the Mother and Daughters, the Mother being the middlemost and largest. Leaving the southern portion of the island in possession of its old name, New Britain, he called the northern portion New Ireland. On leaving the channel, the vessel was in such a state that no time or labor could be any longer devoted to science or geography: the essential point was to reach some European settlement. Carteret discovered numerous islands and groups, and, after touching at Mindanao, arrived at Macassar, on the island of Celebes, in March, 1768. He had buried thirteen of his men, and thirty more were at the point of death: all the officers were ill, and Carteret and his lieutenant almost unfit for duty. The Dutch refused him permission to land, and Carteret determined to run the ship ashore and fight for the necessaries of life, to which their situation entitled them, and which they must either obtain or perish. A boat, bearing several persons in authority, put out to them, and commanded them to leave at once, at the same time giving them two sheep and some fowls and fruit. Carteret showed them the corpse of a man who had died that morning, and whose life would probably have been saved had provisions been at once afforded him. This somewhat shocked them; and they inquired very particularly whether he had been among the Spice Islands, and, upon receiving a negative reply, which they appeared to believe, directed him to proceed to a bay not far distant, where he would find shelter from the monsoon and provisions in abundance. He proceeded, therefore, to Bonthain, where he altered his reckoning, having lost about eighteen hours in coming by the west, while the vessels that had come by the east had gained about six. He stayed here two months, with difficulty obtaining natives to replace the many seamen he had lost. On the passage from Bonthain to Batavia, the ship leaked so fast that the pumps, which were kept constantly at work, were hardly able to keep her free. He arrived at Batavia on the 2d of June. Here the Dutch authorities again placed every obstacle in his way; and it was the last week in July before he could heave down the ship for repairs. These being completed, he set sail for England.

On the 30th of January, 1769, he touched at Ascension, where it was the custom, as the island was uninhabited, for every ship to leave a letter in a bottle, with the date, name, destination, &c. With this custom Carteret of course complied. Three weeks afterwards, he was overhauled by a ship bearing French colors and sailing in the same direction as himself. Carteret was very much surprised to hear the French captain call him and his ship by name: he was still more surprised to hear that the Dolphin had already returned to England, and had reported his—Carteret's—probable loss in Magellan's Strait. "How did you learn the name of my ship?" shouted Carteret through his trumpet. "From the bottle at Ascension," was the reply. "And how did you hear of the opinion formed in England of our fate?" "From the French gazette at the Cape of Good Hope." "And who may you be, pray?" "A French East Indiaman, Captain Bougainville." The vessel was La Boudeuse, whose voyage round the world we shall narrate in the following chapter. The Swallow anchored at Spithead on Saturday, the 20th of March, having been absent three years wanting two days. No navigator had yet done so much with resources so insufficient: Carteret's discoveries were of the highest interest in a geographical point of view. He was a worthy predecessor of Cook; and his achievements with a crazy ship and a disabled crew prepared the public mind for the researches which his already distinguished successor would be enabled to make with the carefully equipped expedition which had lately started under his command.

A harrowing incident which occurred at sea about this time produced a painful sensation throughout Europe. The French man-of-war Le Prince, being on her way from Lorient to Pondicherry by way of Cape Horn, was discovered to be on fire. Smoke was noticed ascending almost imperceptibly from one of the hatchways. The usual measures were promptly taken, eighty marines being placed on duty with loaded muskets to enforce obedience from the crew. The pumps and buckets were totally inadequate to master the now raging flames; while the fresh water, set running from the casks, was of equally little service. The yawl, by the captain's orders, had been lowered: seven men seized it and rowed rapidly away. Of the other boats, two were burned, and one was swamped as it touched the water. The consternation now became general; and the despairing shrieks of the dying, mingled with the cries of the affrighted animals on board, rendered the scene one of terrible confusion. The chaplain went about, granting a general absolution, and extending the remission of their sins even to those who, to avoid death by fire, committed suicide by leaping into the sea. There were six women on board, two of them the cousins of the captain. They were lowered into the water upon hen-coops, the captain bidding them an eternal farewell, as it was his duty and his determination to perish with the ship.

The water was now alive with human beings, clinging to spars, oars, barrels, and other floating materials. Upon one spar were nine men, who had escaped the fury of one element, and were calmly awaiting the fate which they were expecting from another. They were destined to die by neither, but in a manner, if any thing, more horrible. The flames, reaching the cannon, which by some fatal coincidence were loaded, discharged them

one by one. A ball, striking the spar by which these nine devoted men were kept afloat, ploughed its way through them all, killing several outright and mortally wounding the rest. Not one escaped. The mast now fell into the sea, making terrible havoc among those within its reach; while at every moment a gun launched its reckless metal upon the water. The chaplain, clinging to a bit of charred wood, edified all who heard him by his piety and resignation. Once he tried to sink, but was brought back by the first lieutenant. "Let me go," said he; "I am full of water, and it cannot avail to prolong my sufferings." "In his holy company," says the lieutenant, in his narrative, "I passed three hours: during which time I saw one of the captain's cousins give up the effort to keep herself afloat, and fall back and drown." This lieutenant, surviving the rest, hailed the seven men in the yawl, by whom he was taken in, as were also the pilot and the quartermaster. These ten persons were all that were saved out of the three hundred who composed the vessel's crew. The frigate soon blew up; and, after this frightful scene of her expiring agony, all relapsed into silence.

The lieutenant assumed the command of the boat, and, rowing to the remains of the wreck, ordered a search for stores and other articles of which they had pressing need. They found a keg of brandy, fifteen pounds of salt pork, a piece of scarlet cloth, twenty yards of coarse linen, and a quantity of staves and ropes. With the scarlet and an oar they made a mast and sail, with a key they made a pulley, and with a stave a rudder. With this equipment, and without astronomical instruments, they started upon their adventurous voyage, being six hundred miles distant from the coast of Brazil.

Favored by a brisk breeze, they sailed during eight days, making seventy-five miles every twenty-four hours. They were nearly naked, and suffered terribly from exposure to the rays of a tropical July sun. On the sixth day, a light rain gave them the hope of satisfying their devouring thirst. They licked the drops from the sail, but found them already bitterly impregnated with salt. They suffered as much from hunger as thirst; for the salt pork, which had been found to cause blood-spitting, had been abandoned on the fourth day. A draught of brandy from time to time revived them somewhat, but burned their stomachs without moistening them, causing them pain rather than satisfaction. On the eighth night, the lieutenant passed ten hours at the helm, not one of the remaining nine having the strength to relieve him. It was not possible they could survive another day. The dawn of the 3d of August brought with it the blessed sight of land, and, collecting all their strength, to avoid being wrecked by the currents, tides, and reefs, they landed in safety late in the afternoon. The men rushed upon the beach, and, in their joy, rolled in the sand, and mingled thanksgivings with their shouts of joy. They no longer appeared like human beings, suffering having rendered their faces frightful to behold. The lieutenant twisted a piece of red cloth about his loins to show his rank to such inhabitants as they might fall in with. A rapidly-flowing stream being discovered, they all rushed into it, and lapped, rather than drank, its beneficent waters.

The place where they were was a Portuguese settlement, and they were hospitably received by the colonists, who gave them shirts and manioc in abundance. Proceeding to Pernambuco, where a Portuguese fleet was stationed, they were welcomed with kindness by the officers, the lieutenant being admitted to the admiral's mess, and the men being distributed among the ships and placed on full pay. They were soon restored to their country, and the lieutenant communicated to the Government an official account of the disaster.

BOUGAINVILLE.

CHAPTER XLII.

COLONIZATION OF THE FALKLAND ISLANDS—ANTOINE DE BOUGAINVILLE—HIS VOYAGE AROUND THE WORLD—ADVENTURE AT MONTEVIDEO—THE PATAGONIANS—TAKING POSSESSION OF TAHITI—FRENCH GALLANTRY—CEREMONIES OF RECEPTION—SOJOURN AT THE ISLAND—AOTOUROU—THE FIRST FEMALE CIRCUMNAVIGATOR—FAMINE ON BOARD—REMARKABLE CASCADE—ARRIVAL AT THE MOLUCCAS—INCIDENTS THERE—RETURN HOME.

SEVERAL years before the period of which we are speaking, the French Government had colonized the Falkland Islands, lying off the eastern coast of Patagonia. The establishment lasted barely three years, and, in an agricultural point of view, was a complete and disastrous failure. The Spanish crown subsequently claimed these islands as belonging to the continent of South America, and the King of France was easily induced to abandon them. Captain Louis-Antoine de Bougainville was instructed, in 1766, to proceed to the islands, and there, in the name of his French majesty, cede them to the Spanish authorities who would be sent out for the purpose. He was then to continue on, by the Strait of Magellan and the Pacific, to the East Indies, and thence to return home. Should he accomplish this task, he would be the first French circumnavigator of the globe.

Bougainville received the command of the frigate La Boudeuse, carrying twenty-six twelve-pounders, and was to be joined at the Falklands by the store-ship l'Étoile. He sailed from Brest on the 5th of December, the Prince of Nassau-Singhen, who had been allowed to accompany the expedition, being on board. They arrived at Montevideo early in February, 1767, and found there the two Spanish frigates to whose commander Bougainville was to surrender the Falkland Islands, and with whom he sailed in company on the 28th of the month. They met with severe weather, but arrived safely at their destination towards the close of March. The settlement was made over to the Spaniards on the 1st of April: the Spanish colors were planted and saluted at sunrise and sunset. The French inhabitants were informed they might either remain or return: a portion embarked with the garrison for Montevideo, on their way back to France.

Bougainville waited at the islands till the end of May for the store-ship, which was to join him at this point, and then returned to Rio Janeiro, where he hoped to get tidings of her. She had but just arrived, bringing salt meat and liquor sufficient for fifteen months, but no bread or vegetables. So he was forced to go, in quest of these provisions, back to Montevideo. From here he went to Buenos Ayres, on the opposite side of the bay formed by the mouths of the La Plata, making the journey, however, overland, as a contrary wind prevented his proceeding by water. At night, he and his party slept in leathern tents, while tigers howled around them on every side. Coming to the river St. Lucia, which is wide, deep, and rapid, they were at a loss how to cross it. At last their guide procured a hollow canoe, the master of which fastened a horse on each side of the bow, and then boldly assumed the reins. He sup-

A FERRY BOAT AT BUENOS AYRES.

ported the heads of the horses above the water and drove them safely across it. The Frenchmen landed on the opposite side dryshod.

It was not till the 14th of November that the Boudeuse and Étoile, having taken in supplies of biscuit and bread, sailed, for the last time, from Montevideo. They made the entrance of the Strait of Magellan a fortnight afterwards. On the 8th of December, they saw a number of Patagonians, who had kept up fires all night, hoisting a white flag on an eminence,—a flag which some European ship had evidently given them as a pledge of alliance. Bougainville went on shore, where some thirty natives received him with every mark of good will. They embraced him and his party, shook hands with them, and imitated the report of muskets with their mouths, showing that they were accustomed to fire-arms. They aided the botanist in collecting plants and simples, and one of them applied to the .physician for a prescription for his inflamed eye. They asked for tobacco, and swallowed small draughts of brandy, blowing with their mouths after the draught and uttering a tremulous inarticulate sound. They begged them to remain over night, and, upon the invitation being politely declined, accompanied them with ceremony to the shore.

Bougainville, with three of his officers, spent some hours in taking soundings near Cape Froward. Perceiving a small flat rock, which barely afforded them standing-room, they mounted

BOUGAINVILLE IN MAGELLAN'S STRAIT.

upon it, hoisted their colors, and shouted Vive le Roi! The coast now resounded for the first time, says Bougainville, with this compliment to his majesty. Upon which an English commentator remarks "that it is a striking instance of the vanity by which the French nation is distinguished." The vessels, being retarded by constant head-winds and harassed by violent storms, occupied fifty-two days in threading the channel, and the month of January, 1768, was well advanced before they discovered the boundless expanse of the Pacific.

Sailing to the northwest, they passed several low, half-drowned islands, one of which Bougainville called Harp Island. A cluster of reefs he called the Dangerous Archipelago. Sore throats now troubling the crew, he attributed them to the snow-water of the Strait, and cured them by putting a pint of vinegar and a dozen red-hot bullets into the daily water-cask. He combated the scurvy by employing lemonade prepared from a concentration in the form of powder. He made fresh water from salt water by means of a distilling apparatus which furnished a barrelful every night. In order to economize their drinking-water, their bread was kneaded with water dipped up from the sea. On the 4th of April, they discovered land; and fires burning during the night over a wide extent of coast showed them that it was inhabited and populous. In the morning a canoe propelled by twelve naked men approached. The chief, with a prodigious growth of hair which stood like bristles divergent on his head, offered the commander a cluster of bananas, indicating that this was the olive-branch in use in Tahiti,—the island at which the ships had now arrived. Presents were exchanged and an alliance effected.

The vessels were now surrounded with canoes laden with cocoanuts and bananas, and a brisk and tolerably honest trade was driven by the natives and the strangers. The aspect of the coast—the mountains covered with foliage to their very summits, the lowlands interspersed with meadows and with plantations of tropical fruit, cascades pouring down from the rocks into the sea, streams flowing among lovely clusters of huts situated upon the shore—offered an enchanting scene to the wearied crews. While the Boudeuse was casting her anchor, canoes filled with women came around her. "These," adds Bougainville, with characteristic French gallantry, "are not inferior for agreeable features to most European women. It was very difficult, amidst such a sight, to keep at their work four hundred young sailors who had seen none of the fair sex for six months. The capstan was never hove with more alacrity than on this occasion."

The captain and several officers now went on shore, where they were received with high glee by all, with the exception of a venerable man, apparently a philosopher, "whose thoughtful and suspicious air seemed to show that he feared the arrival of a new race of men would trouble those happy days which he had spent in peace." A poet, reclining beneath a tree, sang them a song to the accompaniment of a flute which a musician blew, not with his mouth, but with one of his nostrils. In return for this entertainment, the strangers gave, at night, an exhibition of sky-rockets, witch-quills, and other pyrotechnics. The chief, learning that the Prince of Nassau was a man of royal blood, offered him a wife; but, as the lady was advanced in years and correspondingly mature in appearance, the prince plead a previous union and escaped.

The vessels stayed here a fortnight, cutting wood and drawing water. They lost six anchors during their sojourn, and twice narrowly missed utter shipwreck,—"the worst consequence of which would have been to pass the remainder of their days on an isle adorned with all the gifts of nature, and to exchange the sweets of the mother-country for a peaceable life exempt from cares." The islanders expressed infinite regret at their departure,—one of them, Aotourou by name, being unable to endure the separation, and asking permission to go with them. He gave his young wife three pearls which he had in his ears, kissed her, and went on board the ship. Bougainville quitted the island on the 16th of April, no less surprised at the sorrow the inhabitants testified at his departure than at their affectionate confidence on his arrival.

He directed his course so as to avoid the Pernicious Isles, warned by the disasters of Roggewein to avoid them. Aotourou pointed at night to the bright star in Orion's shoulder, indicating that they should guide their course by it, and that in two days it would bring them to a fertile island where he had friends and children. Being vexed that no attention was paid to his advice, he rushed to the helm, seized the wheel, and endeavored to put the ship about. In the morning he climbed to the mast-head, and sought, in the distant horizon, the favored land of which he had spoken.

The vessels kept on steadily to the westward, passing through Navigator's Islands and the group which Quiros had named Espiritu Santo. To the latter Bougainville gave the name of Grandes Cyclades,—one, however, not destined to be long retained. He was at this time informed that Baré, the servant of M. de Commerçon, the botanist of the Étoile, was a woman. He went on board the store-ship to make investigations. He thought the report incredible, as Baré was already an expert botanist, and had acquired the name, during his excursions with his master among the snows of Magellan's Strait,—where he carried provisions, fire-arms, and bundles of plants,—of being his beast of burden. The first suspicion of him occurred at Tahiti, where the natives, with the keen intuition of savages, cried out in their dialect, "It is a woman!" and insisted on paying her the attentions due to her sex. When Bougainville went on board the Étoile, Baré, bathed in tears, admitted that she was a woman. She said she was an orphan, had served before in men's clothes, and that the idea of a voyage around the world had inflamed her curiosity. Bougainville does her the justice to state that she always behaved on board with the most scrupulous modesty. She was not handsome, and was twenty-seven years of age. She was the first woman that ever circumnavigated the globe.

It was not long before the provisions began to give out, and the crew were put upon half rations. The commander was soon obliged to forbid the eating of old leather, as it was becoming as scarce as biscuit and was quite as necessary. The butcher shed tears upon sacrificing a favorite goat, and Bougainville turned away his head as that sanguinary personage, with equally cruel intent, whistled to a young Patagonian dog. Breakers, reefs, and channels, where the tide ran fast and dangerously, indicated the presence of land, to which was given the name of Louisiade. This is a group of islands inhabited by Papuans.

On the coast of New Britain, at an uninhabited spot which Bougainville named Port Praslin, he obtained a supply of inferior provisions, such as thatch-palms, cabbage-trees, and mangle apples. A species of aromatic ivy was likewise found, in which the physicians discovered anti-scorbutic properties; and a store of it was therefore laid in. An immense cascade, which furnished the vessels with fresh water, is enthusiastically described by Bougainville. After a stay of eight days at Port Praslin,

CASCADE AT PORT PRASLIN.

during which time the heavens were black with continual tempests, the vessels profited by a change of wind and continued their westerly course. The field-tents were cut up, and trousers made from them were distributed to the two ships' companies. Another ounce was taken from the daily allowance of bread. From time to time canoes would shoot out from the coast of New Britain; but the hostility and treachery of the natives rendered all efforts to obtain food from them unavailing.

On the 1st of September, Bougainville made the island of Boero, one of the Moluccas, where he knew the Dutch had a small factory and a weak garrison. All his men were now sick, without exception. The provisions remaining were so nauseous that, as he says, "the hardest moments of the sad days we passed were those when the bell gave us notice to take in this disgusting and unwholesome food. But now our misery was to have an end. Ever since midnight a pleasant scent exhaled from the aromatic plants with which the Moluccas abound; the aspect of a considerable town, situated in the bottom of the gulf, of ships at anchor there, and of cattle rambling through the meadows, caused transports which I have doubtless felt, but which I can not here describe."

It was found that the Dutch East India Company reigned supreme, and that the governor was disposed to keep to the letter of his instructions, which forbade him to receive any ships but those of the monopoly. Bougainville was obliged to plead the claims of hunger and considerations of humanity before the authorities would listen to him. They then furnished him with rice, poultry, sago, goats, fish, eggs, fruit, and venison, the latter being the flesh of stags introduced and acclimated by the Dutch. Henry Inman, the Dutch governor, though placed in a critical position by this arrival, behaved as became an honorable and generous man. He first did his duty towards his superiors, and then towards fellow-creatures in distress. Aotourou, the Tahitian, not being taken ashore by the commander on his first visit, imagined that it was because he was bow-legged and knock-kneed, and begged some of the sailors to stand upon his legs and straighten them out.

During the run back to France, by way of the Cape of Good Hope, St. Helena, and the Cape Verd Islands, nothing happened which requires mention here. Bougainville entered the port of St. Malo on the 16th of March, 1769, having been absent two years and four months, and having lost but seven men during the voyage. He was the first Frenchman who ever went round the world in one ship,—one Gentil de la Barbinais, a pirate, having accomplished a voyage of circumnavigation in several ships, some fifty years before. He sustained his claim to this honor by publishing, two years afterwards, a narrative of his expedition, written in an animated and graceful style, and which established his reputation as a sailor and explorer.

CAPTAIN JAMES COOK.

CHAPTER XLIII.

EXPEDITION DESPATCHED AT THE INSTANCE OF THE ROYAL SOCIETY—LIEUTENANT JAMES COOK—INCIDENTS OF THE VOYAGE—A NIGHT ON SHORE IN TERRA DEL FUEGO—ARRIVAL AT TAHITI—THE NATIVES PICK THEIR POCKETS—THE OBSERVATORY—A NATIVE CHEWS A QUID OF TOBACCO—THE TRANSIT OF VENUS—TWO OF THE MARINES TAKE UNTO THEMSELVES WIVES—NEW ZEALAND—ADVENTURES THERE—REMARKABLE WAR-CANOE—CANNIBALISM DEMONSTRATED—THEORY OF A SOUTHERN CONTINENT SUBVERTED—NEW HOLLAND—BOTANY BAY—THE ENDEAVOR ON THE ROCKS—EXPEDIENT TO STOP THE LEAK—A CONFLAGRATION—PASSAGE THROUGH A REEF—ARRIVAL AT BATAVIA—MORTALITY ON THE VOYAGE HOME—COOK PROMOTED TO THE RANK OF COMMANDER.

In the year 1768, the Royal Society of England induced the Government to equip and despatch a vessel to the South Seas. The reader may perhaps imagine—and, from what has preceded in this volume, he would be amply justified in so doing—that its purpose was plunder, and its object either the capture of the Manilla galleon or the sack and pillage of the luckless town of

Paita. Thirty years, however, have elapsed since the voyage of Anson,—the last of the royal buccaneers. The vessel whose career we are now to chronicle sought neither capture, nor spoil, nor prize-money. It was a peaceful ship, with a peaceful name, —the Endeavor: her commander bore a name to be rendered illustrious by peaceful deeds, and he was bound upon a peaceful errand. James Cook, an officer of forty years of age, who had rendered efficient service in America, at the capture of Quebec, and who had shown himself a capable astronomer, was instructed to proceed to the island named Sagittaria by Quiros, and King George the Third's Island by Wallis, there to observe and record the transit of the planet Venus over the disk of the sun. The position of the island as reported by Wallis was deemed to be exceedingly favorable for such an observation. Cook was promoted to the rank of lieutenant; Charles Green was attached to the ship in the capacity of astronomer, Joseph Banks and Solander —the latter a Swede and a pupil of Linnæus—in that of naturalists, Buchan as draughtsman, and Parkinson as painter. The vessel sailed from Plymouth Sound, with a fair wind, on the 25th of August.

The voyage to Rio Janeiro was enlivened by many incidents now of quite ordinary occurrence, but novel and interesting to navigators one hundred years ago. They saw flying-fish whose scales had the color and brightness of burnished silver. They caught a specimen of that species of mollusk which sailors call a Portuguese Man-of-War,—a creature ornamented with exquisite pink veins, and which spreads before the wind a membrane which it uses as a sail. They observed that luminous appearance of the sea now familiar to all, but then a startling novelty. They were of opinion that it proceeded from some light-emitting animal: they threw over their casting-net, and drew up vast numbers of medusæ, which had the appearance of metal heated to a glow and gave forth a white and silvery effulgence. At Rio Janeiro the viceroy regarded them with strong suspicion, and refused to allow Mr. Banks to collect plants upon the shore. He could not understand the transit of Venus over the sun, which he was told was an astronomical phenomenon of great importance,—having gathered the idea from his interpreter that it was the passage of the North Star through the South Pole. On Wednesday, the 7th of December, they again weighed anchor, and left the American dominions of the King of Portugal, the air at the time being laden with butterflies, and several thousands of them hovering playfully about the mast-head.

Towards the 1st of January, 1769, the sailors began to complain of cold, and each of them received a Magellanic jacket. On the 11th, in the midst of penguins, albatrosses, sheer-waters, seals, whales, and porpoises, they descried the Falkland Islands, and, soon after, the coast of Terra del Fuego. On the 15th, ten or twelve of the company went on shore, and were met by thirty or forty of the natives. Each of the latter had a small stick in his hand, which he threw away, seeming to indicate by this pantomime a renunciation of weapons in token of peace. Acquaintance was then speedily made: beads and ribbons were distributed, and a mutual confidence and good-will produced. Conversation ensued,—if speaking without conveying a meaning, and listening without comprehending, can be called so. Three Indians accompanied the strangers back to the ship. One of them, apparently a priest, performed a ceremony of exorcism, vociferating with all his force at each new portion of the vessel which met his gaze, seemingly for the purpose of dispelling the influence of magic which he supposed to prevail there.

A botanical party under Solander and Banks attempted an excursion into the interior, for the purpose of obtaining specimens of the plants of the country. The snow lay deep upon the ground, and the weather was very severe. An accident rendered it impossible for them to return to the ship; and they were compelled to pass the night, without shelter, among the mountains. Solander well knew that extreme cold, when joined with fatigue, produces a torpor and sleepiness which are almost irresistible: he therefore conjured the company to keep moving, whatever pain it might cost them. "Whoever sits down," said he, "will sleep; and whoever sleeps will wake no more." He was the first to find the inclination, against which he had warned others, unconquerable, and he insisted upon being suffered to lie down upon the snow. He declared that he must obtain some sleep, though he had but just spoken of the perils with which sleep was attended. He soon fell into a profound slumber, in which he remained five minutes. He was then awakened, upon the reception of the news that a fire had been kindled. He was roused with great difficulty, and found that he had almost lost the use of his limbs, his muscles being so shrunk that his shoes fell from his feet. Richmond, a black servant, slept and never woke: two others, overcome with languor, made their bed and shroud in the snow. Such are the terrible effects of cold in the Land of Fire.

On the 22d of January, Cook weighed anchor and commenced the passage through the Straits of Lemaire; on the 26th, he doubled Cape Horn and entered the Pacific Ocean. He sailed for many weeks to the westward, making many of the islands which had been discovered the year before by the French navigator Bougainville, and himself discovering others. On the 11th of April, he arrived at King George's Island, his destination, and the next morning came to anchor in Port Royal Bay, in thirteen fathoms' water. The natives brought branches of a tree, which seemed to be their emblem of peace, and indicated by their gestures that they should be placed in some conspicuous part of the ship's rigging. They then brought fish, cocoanuts, and bread-fruit, which they exchanged for beads and glass. The ship's company went on shore, and mingled in various ceremonies instituted for the purpose of promoting fellowship and good-will. During one of these, Dr. Solander and Mr. Markhouse—the latter a midshipman—suddenly complained that their pockets had been picked. Dr. Solander had lost an opera-glass in a shagreen case, and Mr. Markhouse had been relieved of a valuable snuff-box. A hue and cry was raised, and the chief of the tribe informed of the theft. After great effort and a long delay, the shagreen case was recovered; but the opera-glass was not in it. After another search, however, it was found and restored. The savages, upon being asked the name of their island, replied, O-Tahiti,—"It is Tahiti." The present mode of writing it, therefore,—Otaheite,—is erroneous: Tahiti is the proper spelling.

Cook now made preparations for observing the transit of Venus. He laid out a tract of land on shore, and received from the chief of the natives a present of the roof of a house, as his contribution to science. He erected his observatory under the protection of the guns of his vessel, being somewhat suspicious of the object of such constant offerings of branches as the inhabitants insisted upon making. Mr. Parkinson, the painter, found it difficult to prosecute his labors; for the flies covered his paper to such a depth that he could not see it, and eat off the color as fast as he applied it. The music of the country, as the party gathered from a serenade played in their honor, was at once eccentric and laborious. The favorite instrument was a sort of German flute, which sounded but four semitones. The performer did not apply this apparatus to his mouth, but, stopping up one of his nostrils with his thumb, blew into it with the other, as Bougainville had already had occasion to observe.

One day Mr. Banks was informed that an Indian friend of his, Tubourai by name, was dying, in consequence of something which the sailors had given him to eat. He hastened to his hut, and found the invalid leaning his head against a post in an attitude of the utmost despondency. The islanders about him intimated that he had been vomiting, and produced a leaf folded up with great care, which they said contained some of the poison from the fatal effects of which he was now expiring. He had chewed the portion he had taken to powder, and had swallowed the spittle. During Mr. Banks's examination of the leaf and its contents, he looked up with the most piteous aspect, intimating that he had but a short time to live. The deadly substance proved to be a quid of tobacco. Mr. Banks prescribed a plentiful dose of cocoanut-milk, which speedily dispelled Tubourai's sickness and apprehensions.

On the 1st of May, the astronomical quadrant was taken on shore for the first time and deposited in Cook's tent. The next morning it was missing, and a vigorous search was instituted. It had been stolen by the natives and carried seven miles into the interior. Through the intervention of Tubourai it was recovered and replaced in the observatory.

Thus far the integrity of Tubourai had been proof against every temptation. He had withstood the allurements of beads, hatchets, colored cloth, and quadrants, but was finally led astray by the fascinations of a basket of nails. The basket was known to have contained seven nails of unusual length, and out of these seven five were missing. One was found upon his person; and he was told that if he would bring back the other four to the fort the affair should be forgotten. He promised to do so, but, instead of fulfilling his promise, removed with his family to the interior, taking the nails and all his furniture with him.

The transit of Venus was observed, with perfect success, on the 3d of June, by means of three telescopes of different magnifying powers, by Cook, Dr. Solander, and Mr. Green. Not a cloud passed over the sky from the rising to the setting of the sun. A party of natives contemplated the process in solemn silence, and were made to understand that the strangers had visited their island for the express purpose of witnessing the immersion of the planet.

The ship was to leave Tahiti on the 10th of June, and the time was now spent in preparations for departure. On the evening of the 9th, it was discovered that two marines, Webb and Gibson, had gone ashore, and were not to be found. It was ascertained that they had married two young girls of the island, with whom they had been in the habit of having stolen interviews, and to whom they were very much attached. They were recovered with much difficulty, and compelled, by the stern laws of the naval service, to leave their wives behind them. The vessel sailed on the 13th, an Indian named Tupia having been gratified in his desire to accompany Cook upon his voyage. As the anchor was weighed, he ascended to the mast-head, weeping, and waving a handkerchief to his friends in the canoe. The latter vied with each other in the violence of their lamentations, which was considered by the English as more affected than genuine.

Lieutenant Cook now discovered, successively, the various islands which he regarded as forming an archipelago, and to which he gave the name of Society Islands. He left the last of them on the 15th of August, and on the 25th celebrated the anniversary of their leaving England by taking a Cheshire cheese from a locker and tapping a cask of porter. On the 30th, they saw the comet of that year, Tupia remarking with some agitation that it would foment dissensions between the inhabitants of the two islands of Bolabola and Ulieta, who would seem, from this, to have been peculiarly susceptible to meteorological influences. On the 7th of October, they discovered land, and anchored in an inlet to which they gave the name of Poverty Bay. This was the northeast coast of New Zealand,—an island discovered in 1642 by Tasman, and which had not been seen since, a space of one hundred and twenty-seven years. The natives received them with distrust, and several of them were somewhat unnecessarily killed by musket-shots. All efforts to enter into amicable relations with them failed, and Cook determined to make another attempt at some other point of the coast. Here a bloody fight took place, which resulted in the capture of three young savages by Cook's men. They expected to be put to death, and, when relieved from their apprehension by the kindness with which they were treated, were suddenly seized with a voracious appetite, and seemed to be in the highest possible spirits. During the night, however, they gave way to grief, sighed often and deeply, and sang low and solemn tunes like psalms. The next morning they were brilliantly decorated with beads, bracelets, and necklaces, and displayed in this guise to their countrymen on shore. The negotiation totally failed: the boys were sent home, and the ship stood away from the inhospitable shore on Wednesday, the 11th.

Cook coasted along the island to the south, now alarming the natives by a single musket-shot, now dispersing a hostile fleet of a dozen well-armed canoes by a discharge of a four-pounder loaded with grape-shot, but aimed wide of the mark. At another time Tupia would be ordered to acquaint a party of shouting and dancing savages that the strangers had weapons which, like thunder, would instantaneously destroy them. Cook was badly worsted in a bargain he made with a species of New Zealand confidence-man, who came under the stern and proposed to trade. Cook offered him a piece of red baize for his bear-skin coat. The savage accepted. Cook passed over the article, upon which the islander paddled rapidly away, taking with him the baize and the bear-skin. An attempt made by a party of the natives to kidnap Tupia's servant, Tayeto,—a Tahitian like himself,—and which was near being successful, induced Cook to name the deep indentation of the sea at this point of the coast, Kidnapper's Bay.

Somewhat farther to the south they found the natives more disposed to be friendly, and Mr. Banks and Dr. Solander went ashore and shot several birds of exquisite beauty. Some of the ship's company returned at night with their noses besmeared with red ochre and oil,—a circumstance which Cook explains by saying that "the ladies paint their faces with substances which are generally fresh and wet upon their cheeks and were easily transferred to the noses of those who chose to salute them. These ladies," he goes on to say, "were as great coquettes as any of the most fashionable dames in Europe, and the young ones as skittish as an unbroken filly. Each of them wore a petticoat, under which was a girdle made of the blades of highly-perfumed grass."

At another point they set up the armorer's forge, to repair the braces of the tiller. They here met an old man who insisted on showing them the military exercises of the country, with a lance twelve feet long, and a battle-axe made of bone and called a patoo-patoo. An upright stake was made to represent the enemy, upon which he advanced with great fury: when he was supposed to have pierced the adversary, he split his skull with his axe. From this final act it was inferred that in the battles of this country there was no quarter. It was also ascertained that cannibalism was a constant and favorite practice. They here saw the largest canoe they had yet met with. She was sixty-eight feet and a half long, five broad, and three deep: she had a sharp keel, consisting of three trunks of trees hollowed out: the

A NEW ZEALAND CANOE.

side-planks were sixty-two feet long in one piece, and quite elaborately carved in bas-relief: the figure-head was also a masterpiece of sculpture.

The expedition had thus far been sailing to the southward. Dissatisfied with the results, and finding it difficult to procure water in sufficient quantities, Cook put about, determining to follow the coast to the northward. He named a promontory in the neighborhood Cape Turnagain. Another promontory, more to the north, where a huge canoe made a hasty retreat, he called Cape Runaway. On the 9th of November, the transit of Mercury was successfully observed, and the name of Mercury Bay given to the inlet where the observation was made. Two localities, for reasons which will be obvious, were called Oyster Bay and Mangrove River. Before leaving Mercury Bay, Cook caused to be cut, upon one of the trees near the watering-place, the ship's name, and his own, with the date of their arrival there, and, after displaying the English colors, took formal possession of it in the name of his Britannic Majesty King George the Third.

On the 17th of December, they doubled North Cape, which is the northern extremity of the island, and commenced descending its western side. The weather now became stormy and the coast dangerous, so that the vessel was obliged to stand off to great distances, and intercourse with the natives was very much interrupted. At one point, however, the English satisfied themselves that the inhabitants ate human flesh,—the flesh, at least, of enemies who had been killed in battle. An Indian, to convince Mr. Banks of the truth of this, seized the bone of a human fore-arm divested of its flesh, bit and gnawed it, drawing it through his mouth, and indicating by signs that it afforded him a delicious repast. The bone was then returned to Mr. Banks, who took it on board ship with him as a trophy and a souvenir. He was afterwards told that the New Zealanders ate no portion of the heads of their enemies but the seat of the intellect, and was assured that as soon as a fight should take place they would treat him to the sight of a banquet of brains.

By the end of March, 1770, the ship had circumnavigated the two islands forming what is now known as New Zealand, and had therefore proved—what was before uncertain—that it was insular, and not a portion of any grand Southern mainland. The whole voyage, in fact, had been unfavorable to the notion of a Southern continent, for it had swept away at least three-quarters of the positions upon which it had been founded. It had also totally subverted the theory according to which the existence of a Southern continent was necessary to preserve an equilibrium between the Northern and Southern hemispheres; for it had already proved the presence of sufficient water to render the Southern hemisphere too light, even if all the rest should be land.

The vessel left New Zealand on the 31st of March, sailing due west, and, on the 18th of April, Mr. Hicks, the first lieutenant, discovered land directly in the ship's path. This was the most southerly point of New Holland, and was called, from its discoverer, Point Hicks. Cook followed the coast for many days to the northward; and it was only on the third that he learned, from ascending smoke, that the country was inhabited. On the thirteenth, he saw a party of natives walking briskly upon the shore. These subsequently retired, leaving the defence of the coast to two persons of very singular appearance. Their faces had been dusted with a white powder, and their bodies painted with broad streaks of the same color, which, passing obliquely over their breasts and backs, looked not unlike the cross-belts worn by civilized soldiers: the same kind of streaks were also drawn round their legs and thighs, like broad garters. Each of them held in his hand a weapon two feet and a half long. The landing party detached by Cook numbered forty men; and one of the musketeers was ordered to show the two champions the folly of resistance, by lodging a charge of small shot in their legs. The wooders and waterers then went ashore, and with some difficulty obtained the necessary supplies.

Early in May, Cook landed at a spot to which, from a casual circumstance, he gave the name of BOTANY BAY,—a name now famous the world over. Mr. Banks and Dr. Solander collected here large quantities of plants, flowers, and branches of unknown trees; and it was this incident that furnished the pastoral appellation to the Retreat for Transported Criminals. They found the woods filled with birds of the most exquisite beauty; the shallow coasts were haunted with flocks of waterfowl resembling swans and pelicans; the mud-banks harbored vast quantities of oysters, muscles, cockles, and other shell-fish. The inhabitants went totally naked, would never parley with the strangers, and did not seem to understand the Tahitian dialect of Tupia.

At a place which, in consequence of the difficulty of procuring fresh water, received the name of Thirsty Sound, the watering party met with singular adventures. They found walking exceedingly difficult, owing to the ground being covered with a kind of grass, the seeds of which were very sharp and bearded backwards, so that when they stuck into their clothes they worked forward by means of the beard till they pierced the flesh. Mosquitos stung them at every pore. The air was so filled with butterflies that they saw, smelt, tasted, and breathed butterflies. Black ants swarmed upon the trees, eating out the pith from the small branches and then inhabiting the pipe which had contained it; and yet the branches, thus deprived of their marrow and occupied by millions of insects, bore leaves, flowers, and even fruit. They saw a species of fish resembling a minnow, which appeared to prefer land to water: it leaped before them, by means of its breast-fins, as nimbly as a frog; when found in the water it frequently jumped out and pursued its way upon the dry ground; in places where small stones were standing above the surface of the water at a little distance from each other, it chose rather to leap from stone to stone than to pass through the water. They saw several of them proceed dry-shod over large puddles in this ingenious and unusual manner. The ship left Thirsty Sound on the 31st of May.

On the night of Sunday, the 10th of June, the vessel struck at high tide upon a rock which lay concealed in seventeen fathoms' water, and beat so violently against it that there seemed little hope of saving her. Land was twenty-five miles off, with no intervening island in sight. The sheathing-boards were soon seen to be floating away all around, and the false keel was finally torn off. The six deck-guns, all the iron and stone ballast, casks, staves, oil-jars, decayed stores, to the weight of fifty tons, were thrown overboard with the utmost expedition. To Cook's dismay, the vessel, thus lightened, did not float by a foot and a half at high tide,—so much did the day tide fall short of that of the night. They again threw overboard every thing which it was possible to spare; but the vessel now began to leak, and it was feared she must go to the bottom as soon as she ceased to be supported by the rock,—so that the floating of the ship was anticipated not as a means of deliverance, but as an event that would precipitate her destruction. The ship floated at ten o'clock, and was heaved into deep water: there were nearly four feet of water in the hold. The leak was held at bay for a time; but the men were finally exhausted, and threw themselves down upon the deck, flooded as it was to the depth of three inches by water from the pumps. The vessel was finally saved by the following expedient, proposed and executed by Mr. Markhouse. He took a lower studding-sail, and having mixed together a large quantity of oakum and wool, chopped pretty small, stitched it down in handfuls upon the sail as tightly as possible. The sail was then hauled under the ship's bottom by ropes; and, when it came under the leak, the suction which carried in the water carried in with it the oakum and the wool. The leak was so far reduced that it was easily kept under by one pump. The vessel was finally got ashore and beached in Endeavor River: the surrounding localities were fitly named Tribulation Bay, Weary Point, and the Islands of Hope.

The repairs of the vessel occupied many weeks,—the officers and crew occupying themselves in the mean time in fishing, in endeavors to obtain interviews with the natives, and in excursions for botanical or geological purposes. On the 14th of July, Mr. Gore killed an animal which had excited the interest and curiosity of the English in the highest degree, being totally unlike any animal then known. The name given by the natives to this creature was "kangaroo." He was dressed the next day for dinner, and proved most excellent fare.

A party of natives in the neighborhood having been rendered hostile by the refusal of a pair of fat turtle belonging to the ship, they snatched a brand from under a pitch-kettle which was boiling, and, making a circuit to the windward of the few articles on shore, set fire to the grass in their way. This grass, which was five or six feet high and as dry as stubble, burned with amazing fury. The fire made rapid progress towards a tent where the unhappy Tupia was lying sick of the scurvy, scorching in its course a sow and two pigs. Tupia and the tent were saved in the nick of time: the armorer's forge, or such parts of it as would burn, was consumed. The powder, which had been taken ashore, had been transported back to the magazine but two days before. At night, the hills on every side were discovered to be on fire,—the conflagration having spread with wonderful celerity. On the 3d of August, the ship sailed from Endeavor River, the carpenter having at last completed the necessary repairs.

The ship now coasted along the edge of a reef which stretched out some twenty miles from the shore. This became suddenly of so formidable an aspect, and the winds and waves rolled them towards it with such sure and fatal speed, that the boats were got out and sent ahead to tow, and finally succeeded in getting the ship's head round. The surf was now breaking to a tremendous height within two hundred yards: the water beneath them was unfathomable. An opening in the reef was now discovered, and the dangerous expedient of forcing the ship through it was successfully tried. They anchored in nineteen fathoms' water, over a bottom of coral and shells. The opening through the reef received the name of Providential Channel.

They sailed to the northward many days within the reef, till they at last found a safe passage out. Cook then for the last time hoisted English colors upon the eastern coast, which he was confident no European had seen before, and took possession of its whole extent, from south latitude thirty-eight to latitude ten. He claimed it, in behalf of his Majesty King George the Third, by the name of New South Wales, with all its bays, rivers, harbors, and islands. Three volleys of small-arms were then fired, and the spot upon which the ceremony was performed was named Possession Island. The ship passed out to the westward, finding open sea to the north of New Holland,—a circumstance which gave great satisfaction to all on board, as it showed that New Holland and New Guinea were separate islands, and not, as had been imagined, different parts of the supposed Southern continent. On Thursday, the 24th of August, the ship left New Holland, steering towards the northwest, with the intention of making the coast of New Guinea.

Early in September they arrived among a group of islands which they supposed to lie along the coast of New Guinea. As they attempted to land, Indians rushed out of the thickets upon them, with hideous shouts, one of them throwing something from his hand which burned like gunpowder but made no report. Their numbers soon increased, and they discharged these noiseless flashes by four and five at a time. The smoke resembled that of a musket; and, as they held long hollow canes in their hands, the illusion would have been perfect had the combustion been accompanied by concussion. Those on board the ship were convinced the natives possessed fire-arms, supposing that the direction of the wind prevented the sound of the discharge from reaching them. Cook determined to lose no time in this latitude, having accomplished what he considered as of paramount importance; that is, he had sailed between the two lands of New Holland and New Guinea, and had thus established their insular character beyond any possibility of controversy.

He now sailed to the west, and anchored, on the 8th of October, at Batavia, in Java. Here he laid up the ship for repairs. "What anxieties we had escaped," he writes, "in our ignorance that a large portion of the keel had been diminished to the thickness of the under leather of a shoe!" But the ship's company, which had been so wonderfully preserved from the perils of the sea, were destined to undergo the rude attacks of disease upon land. Markhouse, the surgeon, Tupia and Tayeto, the Tahitians, and four sailors, were rapidly carried off by fever. On the 27th of December, the ship weighed anchor, the sick-list including forty names. Before doubling the Cape of Good Hope, she lost Sporing, one of the assistant naturalists, Parkinson, the artist, Green, the astronomer, Molineux, the master, besides the second lieutenant, four carpenters, and ten sailors. Cook was forced to wait a month at the Cape; and on the 12th of July, 1771, he cast anchor in the Downs, after a cruise of three eventful years. His crew was decimated and his ship no longer sea-worthy. The skill and enterprise displayed by Cook, and the important results attained by the voyage, induced the Government to raise him to the rank of commander. We shall follow him upon his second voyage, in the next chapter.

COOK'S SHIP BESET BY WATER-SPOUTS.

CHAPTER XLIV.

COOK'S SECOND VOYAGE—A STORM—SEPARATION OF THE SHIPS—AURORA AUSTRALIS—NEW ZEALAND—SIX WATER-SPOUTS AT ONCE—TAHITI AGAIN—PETTY THEFTS OF THE NATIVES—COOK VISITS THE TAHITIAN THEATRE—OMAI—ARRIVAL AT THE FRIENDLY ISLANDS—THE FLEET WITNESS A FEAST OF HUMAN FLESH—THE NEW HEBRIDES—NEW CALEDONIA—RETURN HOME—HONORS BESTOWED UPON COOK.

THE English Government now determined to despatch an expedition in search of the supposed Southern or Austral continent. A Frenchman, by the name of Benoit, had seen in 1709, to the south of the Cape of Good Hope, in latitude 54° and in longitude 11° East, what he believed to be land, naming it Cape Circumcision. Cook was placed in command of the Resolution and Adventure, and instructed to endeavor to find this cape and satisfy himself whether it formed part of the great continent in question. He left Plymouth on the 13th of July, 1772, and the Cape of Good Hope on the 22d of November.

A terrific gale soon drove both vessels from their course, washed overboard their live-stock, and well-nigh disabled the Resolution. The cold increased suddenly, and drawers and fearnaughts were served in abundance to the crew. Immense ice-islands now occupied the horizon, and the sea, dashing over them to the height of sixty feet, filled the air with its ceaseless roar. On Sunday, the 13th of December, they were in the latitude of Cape Circumcision, but ten degrees east of it. For weeks they kept in high Southern latitudes, now menaced by towering peaks of ice, now enclosed by immense fields and floating masses, till, towards the 1st of February, 1773, Cook came to the unwelcome conclusion that the cape discovered by Benoit was nothing more than a huge tract of ice, which, being chained to no anchorage and subject to no latitude, he had no reason to expect to find in the spot where the credulous Frenchman had discovered it sixty years before.

On the 8th of February, the Resolution lost sight of the Adventure, and cruised three days in search of her, firing guns and burning false fires, but without success. On the 17th, between midnight and three in the morning, Cook saw lights in the sky similar to those seen in high Northern latitudes and known by the name of Aurora Borealis: the Aurora Australis had never been seen before. It sometimes broke out in spiral rays and in a circular form; its colors were brilliant, and it diffused its light throughout the heavens. On the 24th, a tremendous gale, accompanied with snow and sleet, made great havoc among the ice-islands, breaking them up, and largely increasing the number of floating and insidious enemies the ship had to contend with. These dangers were now, however, so familiar to the crew, that the apprehensions they caused were never of long duration, and were in some measure compensated by the seasonable supplies of water the ice-islands afforded them, and without which they would have been greatly distressed.

On the 16th of March, Cook found himself in latitude 59°, longitude 146° East. He now determined to quit this quarter, where he was convinced he should find no land, and proceed to New Zealand to look for the Adventure and to refresh his crew. On the 26th, he anchored in Dusky Bay, New Zealand, after having been one hundred and seventeen days at sea, and having sailed eleven thousand miles without once seeing land. This point, the most southerly of New Zealand, had never been visited by a European before.

While coasting to the northward, towards Queen Charlotte's Sound, where he expected to find the Adventure, Cook suddenly observed six water-spouts between his vessel and the land. Five of them soon spent themselves; the sixth started from a point three miles distant, and passed within fifty yards of the stern of the Resolution, though she felt no shock. The diameter of its base was about sixty feet: within this space the sea was much agitated and foamed up to a great height. From this a tube was formed, by which the water and air were carried up in a spiral stream to the clouds, from whence the water did not descend again, being dispersed in the upper regions of the atmosphere. "I have been told," says Cook, "that the firing of a gun will dissipate water-spouts; and I am sorry that we did not try the experiment, as we were near enough and had a gun ready for the purpose; but as soon as the danger was past I thought no more about it."

On the 18th of May, the Resolution discovered the Adventure in Queen Charlotte's Sound: the crews of the two ships were overjoyed at meeting each other after a separation of fourteen weeks. The captain of the latter had seen upon the coast some natives of the tribe which had furnished Tupia to Cook's vessel upon his first voyage. They seemed quite concerned when informed that he had died at Batavia, and were anxious to know whether he had been killed, and whether he had been buried or eaten.

Before leaving the island, potatoes, turnips, carrots, and parsnips were planted in spots favorable to their growth, and the natives were made to understand their value as esculent roots. A ewe and ram were sent ashore from the Resolution,—the last pair of the large stock put on board at the Cape of Good Hope; but they probably ate a poisonous plant during the night, for they were found dead in the morning. The Adventure put ashore a boar and two sows, in the hope that they would multiply and replenish the island.

The two ships sailed in company from New Zealand on the 7th of June, their purpose being to proceed to the eastward in search of land as far as longitude 140° West, between the latitudes of 41° and 46° South. During a long cruise, Cook saw nothing which induced in him the belief that they were in the neighborhood of any continent between the meridian of New Zealand and America. A fact which militated against it was, that they had, as is usual in all great oceans, large billows from every direction in which the wind blew a fresh gale. These billows never ceased with the cause which first put them in motion, —a sure indication that no land was near. They constantly passed low and half-submerged islands,—now consisting of coral shoals fretting the waves into foam, and now of islets clothed with verdure. On the 17th of August they arrived at Tahiti, after an entirely fruitless voyage.

The thieving and cheating propensities of the natives appeared in bold relief during the sojourn of the English upon their coast. The latter sometimes paid in advance for promised supplies of hogs and fowls, in which case they were sure never to get them,—the wary trader making off with his axe, shirt, or nails, and dispensing with the necessity of fulfilling his engagement. The practice of overreaching was not confined to the underlings of society, but extended even to the chiefs. A potentate of high warlike renown came one day to the side of the Resolution, and offered for sale a superb bundle of cocoanuts, which was readily bought by one of the officers. On untying it, it was found to consist of fruit which they had already once bought, and which had been tapped, emptied of the milk, and thrown overboard. The dishonest dignitary sat in his canoe at a distance, indicating by the glee and vigor of his pantomime that he enjoyed in a supreme degree the brilliant success of this mercantile fraud.

At another part of the coast, Cook and his officers were invited by Otoo, the king, to visit the theatre, where a play was to be enacted with music and dancing. The performers were five men and one woman, who was no less a personage than the king's sister. The instruments consisted of three drums only,

and the music lasted about an hour and a half. The meaning of the play was not apparent to the English, except that it abounded in local allusions,—the name of Cook constantly re-

RECEPTION OF COOK AT THE FRIENDLY ISLANDS.

curring. The dancing-dress of the lady was very elegant, being ornamented with long tassels made of feathers, hanging from the waist downwards.

Cook left Tahiti early in September, taking with him a young savage named Poreo, who was smitten with a desire to visit foreign parts. At the neighboring island of Huaheine, a native named Omai, belonging to the middle class, was also taken on board. Cook thus speaks of him two years later:—"Omai has most certainly a good understanding, quick parts, and honest principles: he has a natural good behavior, which renders him acceptable to the best company, and a proper degree of pride, which teaches him to avoid the society of persons of inferior rank. He has passions of the same kind as other young men, but has judgment enough not to indulge them to an improper excess." Omai was taken back to Huaheine by Cook when he started upon his third voyage of discovery, in 1776. We shall have occasion hereafter to chronicle the incidents of this restoration.

Cook arrived at Middlebourg, one of the Friendly Islands, early in October. Two canoes, rowed by three men each, came boldly alongside; and some of them entered the ship without hesitation. One of them seemed to be a chief, by the authority he exerted, and accordingly received a present of a hatchet and five nails. Tioony—such was this potentate's name—was thus cheaply conciliated. Cook and a party soon embarked in a boat, accompanied by Tioony, who conducted them to a little creek, where a landing was easily effected. Tioony brandished a branch of the tree of peace in his right hand, extending his left towards an immense crowd of natives, who welcomed the English on shore with loud acclamations. Not one of them carried a weapon of any sort: they thronged so thickly around the boat that it was difficult to get room to land. They seemed more desirous to give than receive; and many threw whole bales of cloth and armfuls of fruit into the boat, and then retired without either asking or waiting for an equivalent. Tioony then conducted the strangers to his house, which was situated upon a fine plantation beneath the shade of shaddock-trees. The floor was laid with mats. Bananas and cocoanuts were set before them to eat, and a beverage was prepared for them to drink. This was done in the following manner:—Pieces of a highly-scented root were vigorously masticated by the natives; the chewed product was then deposited in a large wooden bowl and mixed with water. As soon as it was properly strained, cups were made of green leaves which held nearly half a pint, and presented to the English. No one tasted the contents but Cook,—the manner of brewing it having quenched the thirst of every one else. In this island, as well as in the neighboring one of Amsterdam, the people—both men and women—were observed to have lost one or both of their little fingers. Cook endeavored in vain to discover the reason of this mutilation; but no one would take any pains to inform him.

Cook noticed with interest the sailing canoes of these islands. A remarkable feature was the sail,—which, being suspended by its spar from a forked mast, could be so turned that the prow

CANOES OF THE FRIENDLY ISLANDS.

of the boat became its stern, and *vice versâ*. They sailed with equal rapidity in either direction.

On his return to New Zealand in November, Cook found that his efforts to introduce new plants and animals had been frustrated by the natives. One of the sows had been incapacitated by a severe cut in one of her hind-legs; the other sow and the boar had been sedulously kept separate. The two goats had been killed by a fellow named Gobiah, and the potatoes had been dug up. Cook here had the satisfaction of beholding a feast of human flesh. A portion of the body of a young man of twenty years was broiled and eaten by one of the natives with evident relish. Several of the ship's crew were rendered sick by the disgusting sight.

The Adventure separated from her consort at this point; nor was she again seen during the remainder of the voyage. Cook left New Zealand early in December for a last attempt in the Southern Ocean. On the 12th he saw the first ice, and on the 23d, in latitude 67°, found his passage obstructed by such quantities that he abandoned all hopes of proceeding any farther in that direction, and resolved to return to the north. As he was in the longitude of 137°, it was clear that there must be a vast space of sea to the north unexplored,—a space of twenty-four degrees, in which a large tract of land might possibly lie.

Late in February, 1774, Cook was taken ill of bilious colic, and for some days his life was despaired of. The crew suffered severely from scurvy. On the 11th of March, they fell in with Roggewein's Easter Island, which they recognised by the gigantic statues which lined the coast. They noticed a singular disproportion in the number of the males and females, having counted in the island some seven hundred men and only thirty women.

Early in April, Cook arrived among the Marquesas Islands, discovered in 1595 by Mendana. On the 22d, he arrived at Point Venus, in Tahiti, where he had observed the transit in 1769, and of which the longitude was known: he was able, therefore, to determine the error of his watch, and to fix anew its rate of going. The natives, and especially Otoo, the king, expressed no little joy at seeing him again. On leaving Tahiti, Cook visited in detail the islands named Espiritu Santo by Quiros and Grandes Cyclades by Bougainville. As he determined their extent and position, he took the liberty of changing their name to that of the New Hebrides.

Cook now discovered the large island of New Caledonia, whose inhabitants he mentions as possessing an excellent character. Subsequent navigators, however, ascertained them to be cannibals. They were much lower in the scale of intelligence than the Tahitians. Their canoes were of the most clumsy

NEW CALEDONIAN DOUBLE CANOE.

description, and were generally propelled in pairs by poles. Cook was unable to obtain provisions; and, as his crew were now suffering from famine, he returned to New Zealand, where he arrived on the 18th of October. He left again on the 10th of November, and anchored on the 21st of December in Christmas Sound, in Terra del Fuego. He doubled Cape Horn, discovered numerous islands of little importance, and finally headed the vessel for the Cape of Good Hope. He anchored in Table Bay on the 19th of March, 1775. He here found news of the Adventure, which had already passed the Cape on her way home. On the 30th of July, Cook landed at Plymouth, after an absence of three years and eighteen days. During this space of time he had lost but four men, and only one of these four by sickness. He was promoted to the rank of captain, was elected a member of the Royal Society of London, and received the Godfrey Copley gold medal in testimony of the appreciation in which his efforts to preserve the health of his crew were held by the Government. He was now forty-seven years of age.

A SANDWICH ISLAND KING PROCEEDING TO VISIT COOK.

CHAPTER XLV.

COOK'S THIRD VOYAGE—THE NORTHWEST PASSAGE—OMAI—HIS RECEPTION AT HOME—THE CREW FOREGO THEIR GROG—DISCOVERY OF THE SANDWICH ISLANDS—NOOTKA SOUND—THE NATIVES—CAPE PRINCE OF WALES—TWO CONTINENTS IN SIGHT—ICY CAPE—RETURN TO THE SANDWICH ISLANDS—COOK IS DEIFIED—INTERVIEW WITH TEREOBOO—SUBSEQUENT DIFFICULTIES—A SKIRMISH—PITCHED BATTLE AND DEATH OF COOK—RECOVERY OF A PORTION OF HIS REMAINS—FUNERAL CEREMONIES—LIFE AND SERVICES OF COOK.

Cook might justly have retired at this period to private life, to enjoy his well-earned reputation. But the grand question of the Northwest Passage, now agitated by the press and the public, induced him once more to tempt the perils of foreign adventure. As every effort to force a passage through Baffin's or Hudson's Bay had signally failed, it was determined to make the experiment through Behring's Straits. On the 9th of February, 1776, Cook received the command of the sloop-of-war Resolution,—the vessel in which he had made his last voyage,—the Discovery, of three hundred tons, being appointed to accompany the expedition. Both ships were equipped in a manner befitting the nature of their mission: they were well supplied with European animals and plants, which they were to introduce into the islands of the Pacific. Omai, the young Tahitian whom Cook had brought to England, was placed on board the Resolution, as it was not likely another opportunity would occur of sending him home. He left London with regret; but the consciousness that the treasures he carried with him would raise him to an enviable rank among his countrymen operated by degrees to alleviate his sorrow. The Resolution sailed from Plymouth on the 12th of July, and was followed, on the 10th of August, by the Discovery: both vessels joined company, early in November, at the Cape of Good Hope.

As we have already been frequently over the track now for the third time traversed by Cook, we shall merely give his route, without detailing his adventures, which did not materially differ from those of his former voyages. He arrived at Van Diemen's Land in December, and passed a fortnight of the month of February, 1777, in Queen Charlotte's Sound, New Zealand. Soon after he discovered an island which the natives called Mangya: he noticed that the inhabitants, for want of a better pocket, slit the lobe of their ear and carried their knife in it. At another island of the same group, Omai extricated himself and a party of English from a position of great danger by giving the natives an exaggerated account of the instruments of war used on board the two ships anchored in the offing. "These instruments," he said, "were so huge that several people could sit conveniently within them; and one of them was sufficient to crush the whole island at a shot." Had it not been for this formidable story, Omai thought the party would have been detained on shore all night. At one of the Society Islands

Cook planted a pineapple and sowed some melon-seeds. He was somewhat encouraged to hope that endeavors of this kind would not be fruitless, for upon the same day the natives served up at his dinner a dish of turnips, being the produce of the seeds he had left there during his last voyage.

The Resolution soon anchored off Tahiti, and Cook noticed particularly the conduct of Omai, now about to be restored to his home and his friends. A chief named Ootu, and Omai's brother-in-law, came on board. There was nothing either tender or striking in their meeting. On the contrary, there seemed to be a perfect indifference on both sides, till Omai, having taken his brother down into the cabin, opened the drawer where he kept his red feathers and gave him three of them. Ootu, who would hardly speak to Omai before, now begged that they might be friends. Omai assented, and ratified the bargain with a present of feathers; and Ootu, by way of return, sent ashore for a hog. But it was evident to the English that it was not the man, but his property, they were in love with. "Such," says Cook, "was Omai's first reception among his countrymen. Had he not shown to them his treasure of red feathers, I question much whether they would have bestowed even a cocoanut upon him. I own I never expected it would be otherwise."

The important news of the arrival of red feathers was conveyed on shore by Omai's friends, and the ships were surrounded early the next morning by a multitude of canoes crowded with people bringing hogs and fruit to market. At first a quantity of feathers not greater than might be plucked from a tomtit would purchase a hog weighing fifty pounds; but such was the quantity of this precious article on board that its value fell five hundred per cent. before night. Omai was now visited by his sister; and, much to the credit of them both, their meeting was marked by expressions of the tenderest affection. Cook foresaw, however, that Omai would soon be despoiled of every thing he had if left among his relatives: so it was determined to establish him at the neighboring island of Huaheine. A large lot of land was obtained there from the chief, and the carpenters of the two ships set about building him a house fit to contain the European commodities that were his property. Cook told the natives that if Omai were disturbed or harassed he should upon his next visit make them feel the weight of his resentment. Omai took possession of his mansion late in October, and on Sunday, November 2, bade adieu to the officers of the ship. He sustained himself in this trying ordeal till he came to Cook, and then gave way to a passionate burst of tears. He wept abundantly while being conveyed on shore. "It was no small satisfaction to reflect," writes Cook, "that we had brought him back safe to the spot from which he was taken. And yet such is the strange nature of human affairs that it is probable we left him in a less desirable situation than he was in before his connection with us. He had tasted the sweets of civilized life, and must now become more miserable from being obliged to abandon all thoughts of continuing them." The career and destiny of Omai were perhaps more remarkable than those of any other savage: he was cherished by Cook, painted by Reynolds, and apostrophized by Cowper.

During the stay of the vessels at the Society Islands, Cook induced the crews to give up their grog and use the milk of cocoanuts instead. He submitted it to them whether it would not be injudicious, by drinking their spirits now, to run the risk of having none left in a cold climate, where cordials would be most needed, and whether they would not be content to dispense with their grog now, when they had so excellent a liquor as that of cocoanuts to substitute in its place. The proposal was unanimously agreed to, and the grog was stopped except on Saturday nights.

Early in February, 1778, Cook made a most important discovery,—that of the archipelago now known as the Sandwich Islands, so named by Cook in honor of the Earl of Sandwich,

OMAI.

First Lord of the Admiralty. He visited five of these islands, one of which was Oahu. He found a remarkable similarity of manners and coincidence of language with those of the Society Islands, and in his journal asks the following question:—"How shall we account for this nation having spread itself in so many detached islands, so widely separated from each other, in every quarter of the Pacific Ocean? We find it from New Zealand in the south to the Sandwich Islands in the north! And, in another direction, from Easter Island to the New Hebrides! That is, over an extent of three thousand six hundred miles north and south, and five thousand miles east and west!"

From the Sandwich Islands Cook sailed to the northeast, and on the 7th of March struck the coast of America, upon the shores of the tract named New Albion by Sir Francis Drake. The skies being very threatening, he gave the name of Cape Foulweather to a promontory forming the northern extremity. Late in March the two vessels entered a broad inlet, to which Cook gave the name of King George's Sound; but it is better known now by its original name of Nootka Sound. Cook found the natives friendly and willing to sell and buy. They were under the common stature, their persons being full and plump without corpulence, their faces round, with high prominent cheeks, noses flattened at the base with wide nostrils, low forehead, small black eyes, thick round lips, and well-set though not remarkably white teeth. The color of their skin, when not incrusted with paint or dirt, was nearly as white as that of Europeans, and of that pale effete cast which distinguishes the Southern nations of Europe. A remarkable sameness characterized the countenances of the whole nation, the expression of all being dull and phlegmatic. It was not easy to distinguish the women from the men; and not a female was seen, even among those in the prime of life, who had the least pretensions to being called handsome.

Cook gives a very long and detailed account of the manners

and customs of these people, their habitations, weapons, food, domestic animals, language, and religious views, and concludes by remarking that they differ so essentially in every respect from the inhabitants of the various Pacific islands that it is

HABITATIONS IN NOOTKA SOUND.

impossible to suppose their respective progenitors were united in the same tribe, or had any intimate connection when they emigrated from their original settlements into the places where their descendants were now found.

Cook left Nootka Sound on the 26th of April, and early in May entered a deep inlet, to which he gave the name of Prince William's Sound. Proceeding on his course, as he supposed, toward Behring's Strait, he was surprised to find various indications that he was no longer in the sea, but ascending a wide and rapidly-flowing river. He was, however, encouraged to proceed by finding the water as salt as that of the ocean. Having traced the stream a distance of two hundred miles from its entrance, without seeing the least appearance of its source, and despairing of finding a passage through it to the Northern seas, Cook determined to return. Mr. King, one of the officers, was sent on shore to display the flag and take possession of the country and river in his majesty's name, and to bury in the ground a bottle containing some pieces of English coin of the year 1772. The vessels left the river—afterward named, by order of Lord Sandwich, Cook's River—on the 5th of June.

On the 9th of August, Cook arrived at a point of land, in north latitude 66°, which he called Cape Prince of Wales, and which is the western extremity of North America. Had he sailed directly north from this spot, he would have passed through Behring's Straits. But the attraction of two small islands drew him to the westward, and by nightfall he anchored in a bay on the coast of Asia, having in the course of twenty-four hours been in sight of the two continents. On the 12th, while sailing to the north, both continents were in sight at the same moment. On the 17th, a brightness was perceived in the northern horizon, like that reflected from ice, commonly called the blink. But it was thought very improbable that they should meet with ice so soon. Still, the sharpness of the air and gloominess of the weather seemed to indicate some sudden change. The sight of a large field of ice soon left no doubt as to the cause of the brightness of the horizon. At half-past two, being in latitude 71° and in twenty-two fathoms water, Cook found himself close to the edge of the ice, which was as compact as a wall and twelve feet out of water. It extended to the north as far as the eye could reach. A point of land upon the American coast obtained the name of Icy Cape.

The season was now so far advanced that Cook abandoned all attempts to find a passage through to the Atlantic this year, and directed his attention to the subject of winter quarters. Discovering a deep inlet upon the American side, he named it Norton's Sound, in honor of Sir Fletcher Norton, Speaker of the House of Commons. At Oonalaska, an island some distance to the south, he fell in with three Russian carriers, who had some store-houses and a sloop of thirty tons' burden. They appeared to have a thorough knowledge of the attempts which had been made by their countrymen, Kamschatka, Behring, and others, to navigate the Frozen Ocean.

On the 26th of October, Cook left Oonalaska for the Sandwich Islands, intending to spend the winter months there, and then to

MAN OF THE SANDWICH ISLANDS.

direct his course to Kamschatka, arriving there by the middle of May in the ensuing year. On the 26th of November, the two ships anchored at the archipelago of the Sandwich Islands and discovered several new members of the group. At Owhyhee, Cook found the natives more free from reserve and suspicion than any other tribe he had met; nor did they even once attempt a fraud or a theft. Cook's confidence, already great, was still further augmented by a singular, if not grotesque, incident.

The priests of the island resolved to deify the captain, under the name of Orono. One evening, as he landed upon the beach, he was received by four men, who immediately swathed him in red cloth, and then conducted him to a sort of sacrificial altar, where, by means of an indescribable ceremony, consisting of rapid speeches, offerings of putrid hogs and sugarcanes, invo-

WOMAN OF THE SANDWICH ISLANDS.

cations, processions, chants, and prostrations, they conferred upon him a celestial character and the right to claim adoration. At the conclusion, a priest named Kaireekeea took part of the kernel of a cocoanut, which he chewed, and with which he then rubbed the captain's face, head, hands, arms, and shoulders. Ever after this, when Cook went ashore, a priest preceded him, shouting that Orono was walking the earth, and calling upon the people to humble themselves before him. Presents of pigs, cocoanuts, and bread-fruit were constantly made to him, and an incessant supply of vegetables sent to his two ships: no return was ever demanded or even hinted at. The offerings seemed to be made in discharge of a religious duty, and had much the nature of tribute. When Cook inquired at whose charge all this munificence was displayed, he was told that the expense was borne by a great man, named Kaoo, the chief of the priests, and grandfather of Kaireekeea: this Kaoo was now absent, attending Tereoboo, the king of the island.

The king, upon his return, set out from the village in a large canoe, followed by two others, and paddled toward the ships in great state. Tereoboo gave Cook a fan, in return for which Cook gave Tereoboo a clean shirt. Heaps of sugarcane and bread-fruit were then given to the ship's crew, and the ceremonies were concluded by an exchange of names between the captain and the king,—the strongest pledge of friendship among the inhabitants of the Pacific islands.

It was not long before Tereoboo and his chiefs became very anxious that the English should bid them adieu. They imagined the strangers to have come from some country where provisions had failed, and that their visit to their island was merely for the purpose of filling their stomachs. "It was ridiculous enough to see them stroke the sides and pat the bellies of our sailors," says King, the continuator of Cook's journal, "and telling them that it was time for them to go, but that if they would come again the next bread-fruit season they should be better able to supply their wants. We had now been sixteen days in the bay; and, considering our enormous consumption of hogs and vegetables, it need not be wondered that they should wish to see us take our leave." When Tereoboo learned that the ships were to sail on the next day but one, he ordered a proclamation to be made through the villages, requiring the people to bring in presents to Orono, who was soon to take his departure.

On the 4th of February, 1779, the vessels unmoored and sailed out of the harbor, after having received on board a present of vegetables and live stock which far exceeded any that had been made them either at the Friendly or Society Islands. The weather being, however, extremely unfavorable, they were compelled to return for shelter, and on the 11th dropped anchor in nearly the same spot as before. The foremast was found to be much damaged, the heel being exceedingly rotten, having a large hole up the middle of it capable of holding four or five cocoanuts. The reception of the ships was very different from what it had been on their first arrival: there were no shouts, no bustle, no confusion. The bay seemed deserted, though from time to time a solitary canoe stole stealthily along the shore.

Toward the evening of the 13th, a theft committed by a party of the islanders on board the Discovery gave rise to a disturbance of a very serious nature. Pareea, a personage of some authority, was accused of the theft, and a scuffle ensued, in which

Pareea was knocked down by a violent blow on the head with an oar. The natives immediately attacked the crew of the pinnace with a furious shower of stones and other missiles, and forced them to swim off with great precipitation to a rock at some distance from the shore. The pinnace was immediately ransacked by the islanders, and would have been demolished, but for the interposition of Pareea, who, upon the recognition of his innocence, joined noses with the officers and seemed to have forgotten the blow he had received.

When Captain Cook heard of what had happened, he expressed some anxiety, and said that it would not do to allow the islanders to imagine that they had gained an advantage. It was too late to take any steps that evening, however. A double guard was posted at the observatory, and at midnight one of the sentinels, observing five savages creeping toward him, fired over their heads and put them to flight. The cutter of the Discovery was stolen, toward morning, from the buoy where it was moored. At daylight, Cook loaded his double-barrelled gun and ordered the marines to prepare for action. It had been his practice, when any thing of consequence was lost, to get the king or several of the principal men on board, and to keep them as hostages till it was restored. His purpose was to pursue the same plan now. He gave orders to seize and stop all canoes that should attempt to leave the bay. The boats of both ships, well manned and armed, were therefore stationed across the mouth of the harbor. Cook went ashore in the pinnace, obtained an interview with the king, satisfied himself that he was in no wise privy to the theft committed, and invited him to return in the boat and spend the day on board the Resolution. Tereoboo readily consented, and, having placed his two sons in the pinnace, was on the point of following them, when an elderly woman, the mother of the boys, and a younger woman, the king's favorite wife, besought him with tears and entreaties not to go on board. Two chiefs laid hold of him, insisting that he should go no farther. The natives now collected in prodigious numbers and began to throng around Captain Cook and their king. Cook, finding that the alarm had spread too generally, and that it was in vain to think of kidnapping the king without bloodshed, at last gave up the point.

Thus far, the person and life of Cook do not appear to have been in danger. An accident now happened which gave a fatal turn to the affair. The ships' boats, in firing at canoes attempting to escape, had unfortunately killed a chief of the first rank. The news of his death arrived just at the moment when Cook, after leaving the king, was walking slowly toward the shore. It caused an immediate and violent ferment: the women and children were at once sent off: the warriors put on their breast-

DEATH OF CAPTAIN COOK.

mats and armed themselves with spears and stones. One of the natives went up to Cook, flourishing a long iron spike by way of defiance, and threatening him with a large stone. Cook ordered him to desist, but, as the man persisted in his insolence, was at length provoked to fire a load of small shot. As the shot did not penetrate the matting, the natives were encouraged, by seeing the discharge to be harmless, to further aggression. Several stones were thrown at the marines: their lieutenant, Mr. Phillips, narrowly escaped being stabbed by knocking down the assailant with the butt end of his musket. Cook now fired his second barrel, loaded with ball, and killed one of the foremost of the natives. A general attack with stones and a discharge of musketry immediately followed. The islanders, contrary to the expectations of the English, stood the fire with great firmness, and, before the marines had time to reload, broke in upon them with demoniacal shouts. Four marines were instantly killed; three others were dangerously wounded; Phillips received a stab between the shoulders, but, having fortunately reserved his fire, shot the man who had wounded him just as he was going to repeat the blow.

The last time that Cook was seen distinctly, he was standing at the water's edge, calling out to the people in the boats to cease firing. It is supposed that he was desirous of stopping further bloodshed, and wished the example of desisting to proceed from his side. His humanity proved fatal to him; and he lost his life in attempting to save the lives of others. It was noticed that while he faced the natives none of them offered him any violence, deterred, perhaps, by the sacred character he bore as an Orono; but the moment he turned round to give his orders to the men in the boats, he was stabbed in the back and fell, face foremost, into the water. The islanders set up a deafening yell and dragged his body on shore, where the dagger with which he had been killed was eagerly snatched by the savages from each others' hands, each one manifesting a brutal eagerness to have a share in his destruction.

"Thus fell," writes King, "our great and excellent commander. After a life of so much distinguished and successful enterprise, his death, as regards himself, cannot be reckoned premature, since he lived to finish the work for which he seemed designed, and was rather removed from the enjoyment than cut off from the acquisition of glory. How sincerely his loss was felt and lamented by those who had so long found their general security in his skill and conduct, and every consolation in their hardships in his tenderness and humanity, it is neither necessary nor possible for me to describe: much less shall I attempt to paint the horror with which we were struck, and the universal dejection and dismay which followed so dreadful and unexpected a calamity."

When the consternation consequent upon the loss of their commander had in some measure subsided, Clarke, the captain of the Discovery, assumed the chief command of the expedition. The ships were in such a bad condition, and the discipline became so relaxed upon the withdrawal of the master-mind, that it was decided to employ pacific measures, rather than a display of vigorous resentment, to obtain the restitution of the remains of Cook and of the four massacred soldiers. The moderation of the English produced no effect, however, the natives using the bodies of the marines in sacrificial burnt-offerings to their divinities. As they considered that of Cook as of a higher order, they cut it carefully in pieces, sending bits of it to different parts of the island. Upon the evening of the 15th, two priests brought clandestinely to the ship the portion they had received for religious purposes,—flesh without bone, and weighing about nine pounds. They said that this was all that remained of the body, the rest having been cut to pieces and burned: the head, however, and all the bones, except what belonged to the trunk, were in the possession of Tereoboo.

The natives on shore passed the night in feasts and rejoicings, seeking evidently to animate and inflame their courage previous to the expected collision. The next day, about noon, finding the English persist in their inactivity, great bodies of them, blowing their conch-shells and strutting about upon the shore in a blustering and defiant manner, marched off over the hills and never appeared again. Those who remained compensated for the paucity of their numbers by the insolence of their conduct. One man came within musket-shot of the Resolution and waved Cook's hat over his head, his countrymen upon the water's edge exulting in his taunts and jeers. The watering-party sent upon their daily duty were annoyed to such an extent that they only obtained one cask of water in an afternoon. An attack upon the village was in consequence decided upon, and was executed by the marines in a vigorous and effective manner. A sanguinary revenge was taken for the death of their commander: many of the islanders were slain, and their huts were burned to the ground. This severe lesson was necessary, for the natives were strongly of opinion that the English tolerated their provocations because they were unable to suppress them, and not from motives of humanity. At last, a chief named Eappo, a man of the very first consequence, came with presents from Tereoboo to sue for peace. The presents were received, but answer was returned that, until the remains of Captain Cook were restored, no peace would be granted.

On Saturday, the 20th, a long procession was seen to descend the hill toward the beach. Each man carried a sugarcane or two upon his shoulders, with bread-fruit and plantains in his hand. They were preceded by two drummers, who planted a staff with a white flag upon it by the water's edge and drummed vigorously, while the rest advanced one by one and deposited their presents upon the ground. Eappo, in a long feathered cloak, and with a bearing of deep solemnity, mounted upon a rock and made signs for a boat. Captain Clarke went ashore in the pinnace, ordering Lieutenant King to attend him in the cutter. Eappo went into the pinnace and delivered to the captain a quantity of bones wrapped up in a large quantity of fine new cloth and covered with a spotted cloak of black and white feathers. The bundle contained the hands of the unfortunate commander entire; the skull, deprived of the scalp and the bones that form the face; the scalp, detached, with the hair cut short, and the ears adhering to it; the bones of both arms, the thigh and leg bones, but without the feet. The whole bore evident marks of having been in the fire, with the exception of the hands, the flesh of which was left upon them,—with several large gashes crammed with salt, apparently for the purpose of preventing decomposition. The lower jaw and feet, which were wanting, had been seized by different chiefs, Eappo said, and Tereoboo was using every means to recover them.

The next morning Eappo came on board, bringing with him the missing bones, together with the barrels of Cook's gun, his shoes, and several other trifles that had belonged to him. Eappo was dismissed with orders to "taboo" the bay—that is, to place it under interdict—during the performance of the funeral ceremonies. This was done: not a canoe ventured out upon the water during the remainder of the day, and, in the midst of the silence and solemnity of the scene, the bones were placed in a coffin and the service of the Church of England read over them. They were then committed to the deep, beneath the booming thunders of the artillery of both vessels. "What our feelings were on this occasion," says King, "I leave the world to conceive: those who were present know that it is not in my power to express them."

No one man ever contributed more to any science than did Captain Cook to that of geography. We have seen that on his first voyage he discovered the Society Islands, determined the insular character of New Zealand, discovered the straits which cut that island in halves, and made a complete survey of both portions. He explored the eastern coast of New Holland, gave Botany Bay its name, and surveyed an extent of upward of two thousand miles. In his second voyage he resolved the problem of a Southern continent, having traversed that hemisphere in such a manner as to leave no probability of its existence, unless near the Pole, out of the reach of navigation and beyond the habitable limits of the globe. He discovered New Caledonia, the largest island in the South Pacific except New Zealand; he settled the situations of numerous old discoveries, rectifying their longitude and remodelling all the charts. On his third voyage he discovered, to the north of the equator, the group called the Sandwich Islands,—a discovery which, all things considered, and from their situation and products, may be said to be the most important acquisition ever made in the Pacific. He explored what had hitherto remained unknown of the western coast of America,—an extent of three thousand five hundred miles,—and ascertained the proximity of the two great continents of Asia and America. "In short," says King, "if we except the Sea of Amur, and the Japanese Archipelago, which still remain imperfectly known to the Europeans, he has completed the hydrography of the habitable globe." After Christopher Columbus, Cook acquired, and now, at a distance of nearly a century, still enjoys, the highest degree of popularity which ever fell to the lot of a navigator and discoverer.

LAPÉROUSE.

CHAPTER XLVI.

LOUIS XVI. AND THE SCIENCE OF NAVIGATION—VOYAGE OF LAPÉROUSE—ARRIVAL AT EASTER ISLAND—ADDRESS OF THE NATIVES—OWHYHEE—TRADE AT MOWEE—SURVEY OF THE AMERICAN COAST—A REMARKABLE INLET—DISTRESSING CALAMITY—SOJOURN AT MONTEREY—RUN ACROSS THE PACIFIC—THE JAPANESE WATERS—ARRIVAL AT PETROPAULOWSKI—AFFRAY AT NAVIGATORS' ISLES—LAPÉROUSE ARRIVES AT BOTANY BAY, AND IS NEVER SEEN AGAIN, ALIVE OR DEAD—VOYAGES MADE IN SEARCH OF HIM—D'ENTRECASTEAUX—DILLON—D'URVILLE—DISCOVERY OF NUMEROUS RELICS OF THE SHIPS AT MANICOLO—THEORY OF THE FATE OF LAPÉROUSE—ERECTION OF A MONUMENT TO HIS MEMORY.

LOUIS XVI., King of France, became at this period deeply interested in the study of the science of geography and navigation. Upon the perusal of the voyages, discoveries, and services of Cook, he conceived the idea of admitting the French nation to a share in the glory which the English were reaping from maritime adventure and exploration. He drew up a plan of campaign with his own hand, ordered the two frigates Boussole and Astrolabe to be prepared for sea, and gave the command of the expedition to Jean-François Galaup de la Pérouse,—better known as Lapérouse. The vessels were supplied with every accessory of which they could possibly have need. The instructions and recommendations received from the Academy of Sciences fill a quarto volume of four hundred pages. The fleet sailed from Brest on the 1st of August, 1785, and arrived at Concepçion, in Chili, late in February, 1786.

After a short stay here, the two frigates again put to sea, and, early in April, anchored in Cook's Bay, in Easter Island. Here the two commanders landed, accompanied by about seventy persons, twelve of whom were marines armed to the teeth. Five hundred Indians awaited them at the shore, the greater part of them naked, painted, and tattooed, others wearing pendent bunches of odoriferous herbs about their loins, and others still being covered with pieces of white and yellow cloth. None of them were armed, and, as the boats touched the land, they advanced with the utmost alacrity to aid the strangers in their disembarkation. The latter marked out a circular space, where they set up a tent, and enjoined it strongly upon the islanders not to intrude upon this enclosure. The number of the natives had now increased to eight hundred, one hundred and fifty of whom were women. While the latter would seek, by caresses and agreeable pantomime, to withdraw the attention of the Frenchmen from passing events, the men would slyly pick their pockets. Innumerable handkerchiefs were pilfered in this way; and the thieves, emboldened by success, at last seized their caps from their heads and rushed off with them. It was noticed that the chiefs were the most adroit and successful plunderers, and that though, for appearance' sake, they sometimes ran after an offender, promising to bring him back, it was evident that they were running as slowly as they could, and that their object was rather to facilitate than to prevent their escape. Lapérouse was not saved from spoliation by his rank: a polite savage, having assisted him over an obstruction in the path, removed his chapeau and fled with the utmost rapidity. On re-embarking to return to the ships, only three persons had handkerchiefs, and only two had caps. Lapérouse stayed but a day on this island, having nothing to gain and every thing to lose. There was no fresh water to be found, the natives drinking sea-water, like the albatrosses of Cape Horn. In return for the hospitality with which they had been received, Lapérouse caused several fertile spots to be sown with beets, cabbages, wheat, carrots, and squashes, and even with orange, lemon, and cotton seeds. "In short," says Lapérouse, "we loaded them with presents, overwhelmed with caresses the young and children at the breast; we sowed their fields with useful grains; we left kids, sheep, and hogs to multiply upon their island; we asked nothing in exchange; and yet they robbed us of our hats and handkerchiefs, and threw stones at us when we left." The following reflection, which concludes Lapérouse's account of Easter Island, could only have proceeded from a Frenchman:—"I decided to depart during the night, flattering myself that when, upon the return of day, they should find our vessels gone, they would attribute our departure to our just resentment at their conduct, and that this conclusion might render them better members of society."

Lapérouse now sailed to the northeast, intending to touch at the Sandwich Islands,—a distance of five thousand miles. He hoped to make some discovery during this long stretch, and placed sailors in the tops, animated by the promise of a prize to discover as many islands as possible. In the furtherance of this design, the two frigates sailed ten miles apart,—by which the visible horizon was considerably extended. Lapérouse was destined, however, to owe his celebrity to his misfortunes and not to his discoveries: he arrived, on the 28th of May, at Owhyhee, without once making land. "The aspect of the island," he writes, "was charming. But the sea beat with such violence upon the coast, that, like Tantalus, we could only long for and devour with our eyes that which it was impossible for us to reach." This prospect was aggravated by the sight of one hundred and fifty canoes laden with pigs and fruit which put out from the shore: forty of them were capsized in attempting to come alongside while the frigates were under full sail. The water was full of swimming savages, struggling pigs, and tempting cocoanuts; but the necessity of making an anchorage before nightfall compelled them to seek another portion of the island.

On the 30th of May, Lapérouse landed upon the island of Mowee, where he found the savages mild, polite, and commercially inclined. Exchanges of pigs and medals were made with great success. Lapérouse abstained from taking possession of the island in the name of the King of France,—Cook not having visited Mowee,—inasmuch as he considered European usages in this respect extremely ridiculous. "Philosophers must often have wept," he writes, "at seeing men, simply because they have cannon and bayonets, count sixty thousand of their fellow-creatures as nothing, and look upon a land which its inhabitants have moistened with their sweat and fertilized with the bones of their ancestors for centuries as an object of legitimate conquest."

On the 23d of June, in latitude 60° north, Lapérouse struck the American coast: he recognised at once Behring's Mount St. Elias, whose summit pierced the clouds. From this point southward as far as Monterey, in Mexico, lay an extent of coast which Cook had seen but not surveyed. The exploration of this coast was a work essential to the interests of navigation and of commerce; and, though the season only allowed him three months, he undertook and executed it in a manner creditable to the navy of France. He discovered a harbor that had escaped the notice of preceding navigators. This harbor or bay seems to have been a remarkable place. The water is unfathomable, and is surrounded by precipices which rise perpendicularly from the water's edge into the regions of eternal snow. Not a blade of grass, not a green leaf, grows in this desolate and sterile spot. No breeze blows upon the surface of the bay: its tranquillity is never troubled except by the fall of enormous masses of ice from numerous overhanging peaks. The air is so still and the silence so profound that the noise made by a bird in laying an egg in the hollow of a rock is distinctly heard at the distance of a mile and a half. To this wonderful bay Lapérouse gave the name of Frenchport.

A painful accident occurred as the vessels, after a somewhat prolonged stay, were about departing from the spot. Three boats, manned by twenty-seven men and officers, were sent to make soundings in the bay, in order to complete the chart of the survey. They had strict orders to avoid a certain dangerous current, but became involved in it unawares. Two boats' crews perished, consisting of twenty-one men, the greater part of them under twenty-five years of age. Two brothers, by the name of Laborde, whom their superior officers never separated, but always sent together on missions of peril, were among the victims of the disaster. A monument was erected to their memory, and a record buried in a bottle beneath it. The inscription was thus conceived:—

> "At the entrance of this bay twenty-one brave sailors perish'd:
> Whoever you may be, mingle your tears with ours."

On the 13th of September, Lapérouse arrived at Monterey, after a cursory examination of the coast, determining its directions, but without exploring its sinuosities and inlets. The Spanish commander of the fort and of the two Californias had received orders from Mexico to extend all possible hospitality to the adventurers. He executed his instructions to the

LAPEROUSE'S DISASTER AT FRENCHPORT.

letter, sending immense quantities of fresh beef, eggs, milk, vegetables, and poultry on board, and then declining to hand in the bill. On the 24th, every thing being in readiness, the vessels started upon their route across the Pacific, the intention of Lapérouse being to make for Macao, on the Chinese coast. He hoped on his way to make many discoveries of islands upon this unknown sea,—the Spaniards, in their single beaten track from Acapulco to Manilla, never varying more than thirty miles to the north or south of their usual and average latitude. He also hoped not to find, in the longitude marked against it, a very doubtful island named Nostra Señora de la Gorta, that he might erase it from the charts. This he was unable to do, for the winds did not allow him to pass within a hundred miles of its supposed position. When half-way across the Pacific, he discovered a naked, barren rock, to which he gave the name of Necker, after the French Minister of Finance. He arrived at Macao on the 3d of January, 1787, after a voyage entirely free from incident or adventure. He spent three months here and at Manilla, and finally, on the 10th of April, started for the scene of the most important portion of his mission,—the coasts of Tartary and of Japan,—the waters which separate the mainland of the former from the islands of the latter being very imperfectly known to Europeans.

Early in June, Lapérouse entered a sea never before ploughed by a European keel; and, as it was only known from Japanese or Corean charts, published by the Jesuits, it was his first object either to verify their surveys or to correct their errors. As the Jesuits travelled and made their calculations by land, Lapérouse added hydrographic details and observations to their data, which he found quite generally correct. His voyage in these latitudes set many doubts at rest. After several months spent in these labors, the expedition arrived at Petropaulowski in September of the same year. The officers were grievously disappointed in not finding letters and despatches from France, but one evening, during a Kamschatka gala ball, the arrival of a courier from Okhotsk was announced, and the ball was interrupted that the mail might be opened and delivered. The news was favorable for all, though, after so long an absence, it was natural that there should be evil tidings for some among so many. Lapérouse learned that he had been promoted in rank; and the Governor of Okhotsk caused this event to be celebrated by a grand discharge of artillery. M. de Lesseps, the interpreter attached to the expedition, was detached from it at this point by Lapérouse and sent across the continent by way of Okhotsk, Irkoutsk, and Tobolsk to St. Petersburg, and thence to Paris, with the ships' letters and Lapérouse's journal. It is from this journal, published at Paris, that we have obtained the details of the expedition as we have thus far chronicled them.

The track of Lapérouse was now directly south, through the heart of the Pacific Ocean. He touched, on the 9th of December, at Maouna, one of Navigator's Isles. The vessels were at once surrounded by a hundred or more canoes filled with pigs and fruit, which the natives would only exchange for glass beads, which in their eyes were what diamonds are to Europeans. Delangle, the captain of the Astrolabe, went ashore with the watering party. The islanders made no objection to their landing their casks; but as the tide receded, leaving the boats high and dry upon the beach, they became troublesome, and finally forced Delangle to a trial of his muskets. For this they took a sanguinary vengeance. Delangle was killed by a single blow from a club, as was Lamanon, the naturalist. Eleven marines were savagely murdered, either with stones or heavy sticks, while twenty were seriously wounded. The rest escaped by swimming. Lapérouse did not feel himself sufficiently strong to attempt reprisals. The natives hurled stones with such force and accuracy that they were more than a match for as many musketeers. Besides, he had lost thirty-two men and two boats, and his situation generally was such that the slightest mischance would now compel him to disarm one frigate in order to refit the other. It was late in January, 1788, that he arrived at Botany Bay, in New Holland,—the last place in which he was ever seen, alive or dead.

His last letter to the Minister of Marine was dated at Botany Bay, the 7th of February. In this he stated the route by which he intended to return home, and the dates of his anticipated arrivals at various points. His plan was to visit the Friendly Islands, New Guinea, and Van Diemen's Land, and to be at the Isle of France, near Madagascar, at the beginning of December. His letter arrived in due course at Paris, where the public mind was too much agitated by the throes of revolution to pay much heed to matters of such remote interest. At last, in the year 1791, the Society of Natural History called the attention of the Constituent Assembly to the fate of Lapérouse and his companions. The hope of recovering at least some wreck of an expedition undertaken to promote the sciences induced the Assembly to send two other ships to Botany Bay, with orders to steer the same course from that place that Lapérouse had traced out for himself. Some of his followers, it was thought, might have escaped from the wreck, and might be confined on a desert island or thrown upon some savage coast. Two ships were therefore fitted out, and placed under the command of Rear-Admiral d'Entrecasteaux.

The ships returned in two years, without having obtained the slightest clue to the fate of Lapérouse: their commander had died of scurvy at Java. At the Friendly Islands, the first landing that Lapérouse was to make after leaving Botany Bay, the inhabitants, who remembered Cook perfectly, and who knew the difference between French and English, declared that Lapérouse had not visited them. As they were the most civilized and hospitable of all the Pacific islanders, it was thought improbable that he had ever sailed as far as the very first station of his route,—an opinion which was confirmed by finding no trace of him at any subsequent point of his intended track. No floating remnants of wood or iron work were anywhere discovered; and the public mind gradually settled into the conviction that the two unfortunate vessels were lost upon their passage from Botany Bay to the Friendly Islands. The cause was supposed to be neither fire, nor leakage, nor the effects of a stress of weather,—causes which could hardly be fatal at the same moment to two vessels. It was generally believed that, as the Boussole and Astrolabe were accustomed to keep as near each other as possible during the night, they both simultaneously dashed upon a hidden quicksand. In this manner, one vessel would not have been able to take warning in time by the disaster of the other.

In the year 1813, one Captain Dillon, in the service of the British East India Company, putting in at one of the Feejee Islands, found there two foreign sailors, one of whom was a Prussian, the other a Lascar. At their request he transported them to the neighboring island of Tucopia, where he left them, the natives expressing no hostility toward them nor objections to their stay. In 1826,—thirteen years afterward,—Captain Dillon again touched at Tucopia, where he found them comfortable and contented. The Lascar sold the armorer a silver sword-hilt of French manufacture and bearing a cipher engraved upon it. It resulted from Dillon's inquiries that the natives had obtained many articles of iron and other metals from a distant island named Manicolo, where, as they said, two European ships had been wrecked forty years before. It immediately occurred to Dillon that this circumstance was connected with the loss of the vessel of Lapérouse, whose fate still remained involved in uncertainty. Aware of the interest felt in Europe in the fate of the unfortunate navigator, he sailed with the Prussian to Manicolo, but, being prevented from landing by the surf and the coral reef, bore away to New Zealand and proceeded on his voyage.

In 1827, Dumont d'Urville was sent out by the French Government in the sloop-of-war Astrolabe to explore the great archipelagoes of the Pacific, with incidental authority to follow up any clue he might discover to the fate of Lapérouse. At Hobart Town, in Van Diemen's Land, he heard some account of the efforts made by Dillon, and determined to conclude what he had begun. He sailed at once for Manicolo, and, after examining the eastern coast of the island without success, proceeded to the western. Here he found numerous articles of European manufacture in possession of the savages, who steadfastly refused to say whence they had obtained them or to point out the scene of any catastrophe or shipwreck. At last, the offer of a piece of red cloth induced a painted islander to conduct a boat's crew to the spot which is now regarded as that at which the lamented commander and his vessels met their untimely fate. Scattered

about in the bed of the sea, at the depth of about twenty feet, lay anchors, cannon, and sheets of lead and copper sheathing, completely corroded and disfigured by rust. They succeeded in recovering many of them from the water,—an anchor of fourteen hundred pounds, a small cannon coated with coral, and two brass swivels, in a good state of preservation. Thus possessed of evidence which after the lapse of forty years must be considered as conclusive, d'Urville erected near the anchorage a cenotaph to the memory of the hapless navigator. It was placed in a small grove, and consecrated by a salute of twenty-one guns and three volleys of musketry.

The islanders were now profuse in their explanations of the circumstances attending the calamity. As far as d'Urville

CONSECRATION OF THE CENOTAPH.

could interpret their language and their pantomime, the ships struck upon the reef during a gale in the night. One speedily sank, only thirty of her crew escaping; the other remained for a time entire, but afterwards went to pieces, her whole crew having been saved. From her timbers they constructed a schooner, in which labor they occupied seven moons or months, and then sailed away and never returned. What befell them after their second embarkation, what was the fate of their daring little vessel,—if indeed any such was ever built,—no one has survived to tell. It is safe to believe that both vessels were lost upon the island of Vanikoro, now one of the archipelago of the New Hebrides. It is supposed that Lapérouse was the first European navigator that visited it, Dillon the second, and d'Urville the third.

SCENE IN TERRA DEL FUEGO.

CHAPTER XLVII.

THE TRANSPLANTATION OF THE BREAD-FRUIT TREE — THE VOYAGE OF THE BOUNTY—A MUTINY—BLIGH, THE CAPTAIN, WITH EIGHTEEN MEN, CAST ADRIFT IN THE LAUNCH — INCIDENTS OF THE VOYAGE FROM TAHITI TO TIMOR — TERRIBLE SUFFERINGS AND A MARVELLOUS ESCAPE — ARRIVAL OF THE MUTINEERS AT TAHITI — THEIR REMOVAL TO PITCAIRN'S ISLAND — SUBSEQUENT HISTORY—VOYAGE OF VANCOUVER—ALGERINE PIRACY—BURNING OF THE PHILADELPHIA—PROUD POSITION OF THE UNITED STATES.

In the year 1787, the merchants and planters of England, interested in his Majesty's West India possessions, petitioned the king to cause the bread-fruit tree to be introduced into these islands; and, in accordance with this request, the armed transport Bounty, of two hundred and fifteen tons, was purchased and docked at Deptford to be furnished with the proper fixtures. Lieutenant William Bligh, who had been round the world with Cook, was appointed to command her. Her cabin was fitted with a false floor cut full of holes sufficient to receive one thousand or more garden-pots. She was victualled for fifteen months, and laden with trinkets for the South Sea Islanders. Her destination was Tahiti by way of Cape Horn. She sailed late in December, 1787.

After a three months' tempestuous passage, she made the eastern coast of Terra del Fuego. She contended thirty days here with violent westerly gales, seeking either to thread the strait or double the cape. Finding either course impossible, Bligh ordered the helm to be put a-weather, having resolved to cross the South Atlantic and approach Tahiti from the westward,—a determination which was successfully executed.

Bligh gave directions to all on board not to inform the natives of the object of their visit, lest, by the natural law of supply and demand, the price-current of bread-fruit trees should suddenly rise. He contrived to make the chiefs believe that he was doing them a favor in conveying specimens of their plants to the great King of England. A tent was erected on shore to receive the trees, some thirty of which were potted every day. On the 4th of April, 1789, the vessel set sail, with one thousand and fifteen roots in pots, tubs, and boxes.

It was now that an event took place which rendered the cruise of the Bounty one of the most extraordinary in the annals of the sea. A mutiny, which had been planned in secrecy, broke out on the 27th. The whole crew were engaged in it, with the exception of eighteen men. Bligh, with these eighteen,—most of them officers,—was hurried into the launch, which was cut loose, with one hundred and fifty pounds of bread, twenty-eight gallons of water, a little rum and wine, with a quadrant and compass. A few pieces of pork, some cocoanuts, and four cutlasses, were thrown at them as they were cast adrift. Some of the mutineers laughed at the helpless condition of the launch; while others expressed their confidence in Bligh's resources by exclaiming, with oaths, "Pshaw! he'll find his way home if you give him pencil and paper!" "Blast him! he'll have a vessel built in a month!"

Bligh was convinced that, defenceless and unarmed as they were, they had nothing to hope from the inhabited islands of the surrounding waters. He told the crew that no chance of relief remained except at Timor, where there was a Dutch colony, at a distance of three thousand five hundred miles. They all agreed, and bound themselves by a solemn promise, to live upon one ounce of bread and a gill of water a day. They then bore away across this unknown and barbarous sea, in a boat twenty-three feet long from stem to stern, deep-laden with nineteen men, and barely supplied with food for two. There is nothing in maritime annals more worthy of a place in a work treating of "Man upon the Sea" than is this marvellous voyage from Tahiti to Timor.

The first thing done was to return thanks to God for their preservation and to invoke His protection during the perils they were to encounter. The sun now rose fiery and red, foreboding a severe gale, which, before long, blew with extreme severity. The sea curled over the stern, obliging them to bale without cessation. The bread was in bags, and in danger of being soaked and spoiled. Unless this could be prevented, starvation was inevitable. Every thing was thrown overboard that could be spared,—even to suits of clothes: the bread was then secured in the carpenter's chest. A teaspoonful of rum and a fragment of bread-fruit—collected from the floor of the boat, where it had been crushed in the confusion of departure—was now served to each man.

They constantly passed in sight of islands, upon which they did not dare to land. They kept on, alternately performing prayers, dining on damaged bread, and sipping infinitesimal quantities of rum or other cordial. On grand occasions, Bligh served out as the day's allowance a quarter of a pint of cocoanut-milk and two ounces of the meat. One half of the men watched while the other half slept with nothing to cover them but the heavens. They could not stretch out their limbs, for there was not room: they became dreadfully cramped, and at last the dangers and pains of sleep were such that it became an additional misery in their catalogue of sorrows. A heavy thunder-shower enabled them to quench their thirst for the first time and to increase their stock of water to thirty-four gallons; but, in compensation, it wet them through and caused them to pass a cold and shivering night. The next day the sun came out, and they stripped and dried their clothes. Bligh thought the men needed additional creature comfort under these dismal circumstances, and issued to each an ounce and a half of pork, an ounce of bread, a teaspoonful of rum, and half a pint of cocoanut-milk. They kept a fishing-line towing from the stern; but in no one instance did they catch a fish.

Bligh now became convinced that in serving ounces of bread by guess-work he was dealing out overmeasure, and that if he continued to do so his stores would not last the eight weeks he had intended they should. So he made a pair of scales of two cocoanut-shells, and, having accidentally found a pistol-ball, twenty-five of which were known to weigh a pound, or sixteen ounces, he adopted it as the measure of one ration of bread. The men were thus reduced from one ounce to two hundred and seventy-two grains. Another thunder-shower now came on, and they caught twenty gallons of water. The usual consolation of a thimbleful of rum was served when the storm was over, together with one mouthful of pork. The men soon began to complain of pains in the bowels; and nearly all had lost in a measure the use of their limbs. Their clothes would not dry when taken off and hung upon the rigging, so impregnated was the atmosphere with moisture. On the fifteenth day they discovered a number of islands, which, though forming part of the group of the New Hebrides, had been seen neither by Cook nor Bougainville, and thus, in the midst of their agonies, the barren satisfaction of contributing to geographical science was, as it were in derision, awarded to them. The men now clamored for extra allowances of pork and rum,—which Bligh sternly refused, administering his bullet-weight of bread with the severest ceremony.

"At dawn of the twenty-second day," says Bligh, "some of my people seemed half dead: our appearances were horrible, and I could look no way but I caught the eye of some one in distress. Extreme hunger was now too evident; but no one suffered from thirst, nor had we much inclination to drink,—that desire, perhaps, being satisfied through the skin. Every one dreaded the approach of night. Sleep, though we longed for it, afforded no comfort: for my own part, I almost lived without it." Bligh now examined the remaining bread, and found sufficient to last for twenty-nine days; but, as he might be compelled to avoid Timor and go to Java, it became necessary to make the stock hold out for forty days. He therefore announced that supper would hereafter be served without bread!

A great event happened on the twenty-seventh day. A noddy—a bird as large as a small pigeon—was caught as it flew past the boat. Bligh divided it, with the entrails, into nineteen portions, and distributed it by lots. It was eaten, bones and all, with salt water for sauce. The next day a booby—which is as large as a duck—was caught, and was divided and devoured like the noddy, even to the entrails, beak, and feet. The blood was given to three of the men who were the most distressed for want of food. On the thirtieth day they landed upon the northern shore of New Holland, and gave thanks to God for his gracious protection through a series of disasters and calamities then almost unparalleled.

They found oysters upon the rocks, which they opened without detaching them. A fire was made by the help of a magnifying-glass; and then, with the aid of a copper pot found in the boat, a delicious stew of oysters, pork, bread, and cocoanut was cooked, of which every man received a full pint. Spring water was obtained by digging where a growth of wire grass indicated a moist situation. The soft tops of palm-trees and fern-roots furnished them a very palatable addition to their mess. After laying in sixty gallons of water and as many oysters as they could collect, they re-embarked, after having slept two nights on land and having been greatly benefited thereby. Keeping to the northwestward, and coasting along the shore, they landed from time to time in search of food. On the 2d of June, the watch of the gunner, which had been the only one in the company successfully to resist the influences of the weather, finally stopped, so that sunrise, noon, and sunset were now the only definite points in the twenty-four hours. On the next day, having followed the northeastern shore of New Holland as far as it lay in their route, they once more launched into the open sea.

On Thursday, the 11th, they passed, as Bligh supposed, the meridian of the eastern point of Timor,—a fact which diffused universal joy and satisfaction. On Friday, at three in the morning, the island was faintly visible in the west, and by daylight it lay but five miles to the leeward. They had run three thousand six hundred and eighteen miles in an open boat in forty-one days, with provisions barely sufficient for five. Though life had never been sustained upon so little nourishment for so long a time, and under equal circumstances of exposure and suffering, not a man perished during the voyage. Their wants were most kindly supplied by the Dutch at Coupang, and every necessary and comfort administered with a most liberal hand.

On his return to England, Bligh published a narrative of his voyage and of the mutiny, which was soon translated into all the languages of Europe. He ascribed the revolt to the desire of the crew to lead an idle and luxurious life at Tahiti, though subsequent developments, and his own outrageous and brutal conduct when Governor of New South Wales, proved quite conclusively that his cruelties and tyranny had rendered him odious and intolerable. The British Government could not allow such a transaction upon the high seas to pass unpunished, and despatched the frigate Pandora, Captain Edwards, to Tahiti in the month of August. Only ten of the mutineers were found, the rest having withdrawn to another island through fear of discovery, as we shall now relate, merely stating that the ten persons taken were conveyed to England, where they were tried and executed.

John Adams, one of the mutineers, being apprehensive that the English Government would make an attempt to punish the revolt, resolved to escape to some neighboring and uninhabited island, and there establish a colony. With eight Englishmen, one of whom was Christian, the ringleader in the mutiny, their Tahitian wives, and a few islanders of both sexes, he sailed in the Bounty to Pitcairn's Island, which had been lately seen by Carteret. They arrived there in 1790, and, having unladen the vessel, burned her. A settlement was formed, which prospered in spite of the continual quarrels between the males of the two races. This hostility resulted, in three years, in the extinction of the

COLONISTS OF PITCAIRN'S ISLAND.

savages, leaving upon the island Adams, three Englishmen, ten women of Tahiti, and the children, some twenty in number. One of the Englishmen, having succeeded in distilling brandy from a root which grew in abundance, drank to excess and threw himself headlong from a rock into the sea. Another was slain for entertaining designs upon the wife of the only remaining Englishman except Adams. Thus, in 1799, Adams and Young were the only males of the original colony surviving. They began to reflect upon their duties toward their children and those of their companions: they commenced holding religious services morning and evening, and instructed the rising generation in such rudimental branches of education as their own learning would permit. Young died in 1801, and Adams became the administrator and patriarch of the colony. He was assisted by the Tahitian women, who showed a remarkable capacity for civilization and aptitude for refinement. An English frigate, the Briton, touched at Pitcairn in 1814, and her captain offered to take Adams back to England, promising him to procure his pardon from the king. But the forty-seven persons, women and children, forming the settlement, besought their patriarch not to leave them. In 1825, Captain Beechey visited the island, and found the population increased to sixty-six. Adams was sixty years old, but still vigorous and active. He begged Beechey to marry him, according to the rites of the English Church, to the woman with whom he had lived, and who was now infirm and blind. Beechey gladly acceded to the request. Soon after, an English missionary, named Buffet, went out to Pitcairn to assist Adams in the discharge of his duties and to succeed him upon his death. The latter event occurred in 1829. Vessels occasionally stopped at Pitcairn, and the English Government was thus kept informed of the progress of its interesting colony.

In 1856, the descendants of the original settlers, having increased so much as to outgrow the resources of their sea-girt home, abandoned Pitcairn's Island, and transferred themselves, with their goods and chattels, to Norfolk Island, directly west and toward New South Wales. They numbered one hundred and ninety-nine in all, the oldest man being sixty-two, and the oldest woman eighty. Charles Christian is the grandson of Christian the ringleader. Their new home contains about fourteen thousand acres, and is well watered, fertile, and healthy, the soil producing abundantly both European and tropical fruits, vegetables, grains, and spices. The history of the present colony, the offspring in the third generation of European fathers and Tahitian mothers, is as remarkable as any tale in romance or any legend in mythology.

In the year 1790,—to return to chronological order,—the British Government determined to make one more attempt to discover a channel of communication between the Atlantic and Pacific to the north of the American continent, and selected to command the expedition Lieutenant George Vancouver, who had accompanied Cook on his second and third voyages. He was raised to the rank of captain and placed at the head of an expedition consisting of the sloop-of-war Discovery and the armed tender Chatham. He left Falmouth on the 1st of April, 1791; and, as the Admiralty had designated no route by which to proceed to the Pacific, he decided to go by way of the Cape of Good Hope. He arrived here without adventure in July, and, late in September, struck the southern coast of New Holland at a cape to which he gave the name of Chatham, from the President of the Board of Admiralty.

The two vessels coasted to the eastward, surveying the indentations and giving names to all points of interest. A harbor being discovered, it received the name of King George the Third's Sound, and Vancouver took possession of the land in the name of his Gracious Majesty. A wretched hovel, three feet high, in the form of a bee-hive cut through the centre from the apex to the base, and constructed of slender twigs, here revealed the presence of inhabitants; while the singular appearance of the trees and the vegetation, which had evidently undergone the action of fire,—the shrubs being completely charred and the grass having been shrivelled by the heat,—showed that, miserable as they certainly were, they were acquainted with the uses and abuses of fire. At last they discovered a deserted village, consisting of some two dozen huts or hives, which had

apparently been the residence of a considerable tribe. They gratified their curiosity by contemplating and investigating these humiliating efforts of human ingenuity.

Continuing to the eastward, Vancouver touched at New Zealand, and arrived at a spot where he had been with Cook eighteen years before. An inlet which Cook had been unable to explore, and which he had named in consequence "NOBODY KNOWS WHAT," was explored by Vancouver and called by him "SOMEBODY KNOWS WHAT." Running to the north, he discovered an island whose inhabitants spoke the language of the great South Sea nation and who seemed perfectly acquainted with the uses of iron, though they had little or none of that metal. A Sandwich Islander, whom Vancouver had brought from London as an interpreter, and who was named Towerezoo, was of very little assistance; for he had been so long absent that he now spoke English much better than his mother-tongue, and spoke the latter no better than Vancouver. The island appeared to go by the name of Oparo, by which Vancouver thought fit to distinguish it till it should be found more properly entitled to another. The two vessels arrived in December at Tahiti, and anchored in Matavai Bay. The chronometers were landed, in order to correct them by the known longitude of the island; the sails were unbent, the topmasts struck, for a thorough examination of the rigging. The Discovery went by accident upon a rock, and was for a while in great danger. On

Sunday, the 1st of January, 1792, every one had as much fresh pork and plum-pudding as he could eat, and a double allowance of grog was served in which to drink the time-honored toast. The formula, however, was slightly altered to suit the state of the case: the gunner of the Discovery being the only married man of the party, the toast given was SWEETHEARTS AND WIFE!

On the 24th of January, the two ships turned their head to the northward, now for the first time commencing the voyage in view of which the expedition had been equipped. They ran the two thousand five hundred miles that lay between them and the Sandwich Islands in the space of five weeks, and anchored off Owhyhee on the 1st of March. They touched the American coast, or that part of it known as New Albion, in 39° north latitude, which Vancouver now explored and surveyed. In August he entered Nootka, where, in accordance with his instructions, he was to receive from the Spanish authorities the formal cession of the colony they had established. He found his Catholic Majesty's brig Active already there, commanded by Señor Don Juan Francisco de la Rodega y Quadra. The two commanders agreed to honor each other by a mutual salute of thirteen guns, which was done; while other courtesies were cordially exchanged. The ceremony then took place. Vancouver now returned to Owhyhee, and the king, smitten by a sudden and vehement attachment for the English, proposed to make over the island to the dominion of the King of England. All the insular dignitaries assembled on the decks of the Discovery, and the surrender was made in the midst of speeches and cannonades. Vancouver did not seem to have been deeply impressed with the importance of this event. The solemnity of the transaction was not increased by the circumstance that it took place upon the spot where Cook had so recently been massacred.

Returning to the north, Vancouver continued his surveys and explorations of the American coast as far as the fifty-sixth degree of latitude. He terminated his operations on the 22d of August, at Port Conclusion, where an additional allowance of grog was served, that the day might be celebrated with proper festivity. He returned to Europe with the certitude that no passage existed from the North Pacific across the American continent into the Atlantic. His surveys remain as a monument of his activity, skill, and perseverance. The present charts of the coast of North America upon the Pacific are based upon them. More than nine thousand miles of shore, with its headlands, capes, rivers, bays, promontories, and labyrinths of islands, had been carefully explored by surveying parties in boats, in superintending which Vancouver injured his health and brought on the decline which terminated in his death, in the year 1798, at the early age of forty-eight.

We have now to record the remarkable series of acts by which the United States of America, in the twenty-fifth year of their existence as a nation, put an end to a humiliation to which the commercial powers of Europe had submitted for centuries. From the time when the Spanish Moors, driven out of Granada by Ferdinand the Catholic, settled on the opposite coast and commenced the practice of piracy, the Barbary States, Tunis, Tripoli, and Algiers, had been united against all Christian commerce in the Mediterranean. Emboldened by impunity, they extended their operations into the Atlantic, seizing the vessels of all nations who did not pay them tribute. England under Cromwell, and France under Louis XIV., however, caused their flags to be respected. The Dutch, Danes, and Swedes, by paying an annual tax, purchased exemption from seizure,—thus giving the sanction of a treaty to the outrage and consenting to wear an odious badge of servitude. Russia and Austria were protected by special agreements.

During the early years of the American Republic, Tripoli intimated to the Government the propriety of paying tribute. Jefferson replied, in 1800, by declaring war against Tripoli, and sent out an armed naval force under Commodore Dale. This officer, with two frigates and a sloop-of-war, blockaded Tripoli, preventing the cruisers from getting to sea, and thus protecting our commerce. Commodore Preble followed with seven vessels in 1803. In October, one of his ships,—the Philadelphia, Captain Bainbridge,—engaged in reconnoitring the harbor of Tripoli, grounded and was forced to surrender. The officers were treated as prisoners of war, the sailors as slaves. The vessel was floated and moored in the harbor, strongly manned by Tripolitans, whose naval force was thus unexpectedly augmented.

The American squadron rendezvoused at Syracuse, in Sicily, —somewhat over a day's sail from Tripoli. A young lieutenant under Preble, named Decatur, formed a plan for destroying the Philadelphia and thus reducing the Tripolitans again to their ordinary naval strength. Preble consented to the scheme, and Decatur armed a ketch which he had captured, and with it entered, in February, 1804, under cover of the night, the harbor of Tripoli. He had with him an old pilot who spoke the Tripolitan language. On approaching the Philadelphia, they were challenged; but the pilot replied that he had lost his anchor and merely wished to fasten his vessel to the frigate till morning. A boat was sent ashore by the Tripolitans to ask permission, and then Decatur and his men leaped upon the deck. They rushed upon the affrighted corsairs, fifty in number, and drove them into the sea. They set fire to the Philadelphia, and, by the light of the blaze, escaped without the loss of a single man. One sailor was wounded by receiving upon his arm a blow from a sabre with which the turbaned pirate meant to decapitate Decatur.

The Tripolitans were enraged at the loss of their prize, and treated Bainbridge and his enslaved crew with greater severity than ever. Three times did Preble enter the harbor of Tripoli with his fleet and open his broadsides against the town, destroying some of the shipping, but making no material impression. At last, a series of brilliant actions upon land under General Eaton, whose army consisted of nine Americans, twenty Greeks, and five hundred Egyptians, and the arrival of the frigate Constitution in June, 1805, forced the Bashaw of Tripoli to come to terms; and he released his prisoners and abandoned forever the levying of tribute upon American ships. Peace was at once concluded.

In 1812, the United States being at war with England, the Dey of Algiers thought our Government would be unable to cope with two enemies upon the ocean, and determined to resume piracy on our vessels. He pretexted the unsatisfactory quality of a cargo of military stores furnished by our Government, and ordered the American agent to leave the capital. Depredations were immediately recommenced: our vessels were plundered and confiscated and their crews enslaved. The President suggested the importance of taking measures of prevention, in his message to Congress in December, 1814, and, after the signing of the treaty of peace with England, despatched two squadrons to the Mediterranean, under Decatur and Bainbridge,

BURNING OF THE PHILADELPHIA.

both now commodores. The former captured, in June, an Algerine frigate of forty-four guns and a brig of twenty-two. He then sailed for Algiers. The American navy had earned an enviable distinction in the war with England, and the sight of our gallant fleet inspired the dey with a salutary terror. He consented to the terms imposed by Decatur, which were to give up all captured men and property, to pay six million dollars for previous exactions, and to exempt our commerce from tribute for all time to come. A treaty was signed on the 4th of July, —an auspicious date for so honorable an achievement.

The proud position thus attained by the United States attracted the attention of Europe. Our Government had extorted expressions of submission from the corsairs such as no other power had ever obtained. The Congress of Vienna discussed the subject, and it was resolved that from that time forward Christian slavery in Algiers was suppressed. The English sent Lord Exmouth to bombard that city, and compelled the dey to submit to conditions like those imposed by Decatur. The Algerines were not yet broken, however. They placed their city in a formidable state of defence, and then proceeded to intercept the trade of the French. The French Government declared war,—a measure which resulted in the capture of Algiers in 1830 and in the seizure of Abd-el-Kader in the winter of 1847–48. These events have led to the colonization of the territory by the French and to the partial extinction of the Algerine people. Piracy in the Mediterranean may safely be said to be at an end forever.

THE CLERMONT: THE FIRST STEAMBOAT.

CHAPTER XLVIII.

APPLICATION OF STEAM TO NAVIGATION—ROBERT FULTON—CHANCELLOR LIVINGSTON—LAUNCH OF THE CLERMONT—SHE CROSSES THE HUDSON RIVER—HER VOYAGE TO ALBANY—DESCRIPTION OF THE SCENE—FULTON'S OWN ACCOUNT—LEGISLATIVE PROTECTION GRANTED TO FULTON—THE PENDULUM-ENGINE—CONSTRUCTION OF OTHER STEAMBOATS—THE STEAM-FRIGATE FULTON THE FIRST—THE FIRST OCEAN-STEAMER, THE SAVANNAH—ACCOUNT OF HER VOYAGE—MISAPPREHENSIONS UPON THE SUBJECT.

In the year 1807, a new agent was introduced into the science of navigation,—one which was destined to effect as great a change in the duration of a voyage at sea as the compass had effected in its practicability. Steam was applied to a boat upon the Hudson, and the Clermont, propelled by wheels, steamed from Jersey City to Albany. Though this was an event that immediately concerned river-navigation, and though twelve years were to elapse before the accomplishment of the first ocean steam-voyage, we cannot with propriety omit an account of the conception, construction, and success of the first river-steamboat.

Robert Fulton was born in Lancaster county, Pennsylvania, in the year 1765. He manifested a genius for mechanics at an early age, though portrait-painting was his first profession. He spent many years in England and France, and conceived the idea of a vessel propelled by steam in 1793. He received no countenance from Napoleon, and returned to the United States in December, 1806. His mind was now occupied with two projects,—the invention of submarine explosives and the construction of a steamboat. He published a work entitled "Torpedo War," with the motto, "The liberty of the seas will be the happiness of the earth." He renewed his acquaintance with Chancellor Livingston, whom he had known when ambassador to Paris. This gentleman had long had entire faith in the practicability of steam-navigation, and as early as 1798 had obtained from the Legislature of New York a monopoly of all such navigation upon the waters of the State, provided he would within twelve months build a boat which should go four miles an hour by steam. When they met in America, in 1806, the two entered into a partnership and commenced the construction of a boat. Finding the expenses unexpectedly heavy, they offered to sell one-third of their patent; but no one would invest in an enterprise universally deemed hopeless. The boat was nevertheless launched, in the spring of 1807, from the shipyard of Charles Brown, on the East River. She was supplied with an engine built in England, and was driven by steam, in August, from the New York side to the Jersey shore. The incredulous crowd who had assembled to laugh stayed to wonder and applaud.

The Clermont soon after sailed for Albany, her departure having been announced in the newspapers as a grand and unequalled curiosity. "She excited," says Colden, in his Life of Fulton, "the astonishment of the inhabitants of the shores of the Hudson, many of whom had not heard even of an engine, much less of a steamboat. There were many descriptions of the effects of her first appearance upon the people of the bank of the river: some of these were ridiculous, but some of them were of such a character as nothing but an object of real grandeur could have excited. She was described, by some who had indistinctly seen her passing in the night, as a monster moving on the waters, defying the winds and tide, and breathing flames and smoke. She had the most terrific appearance from other vessels which were navigating the river when she was making her passage. The first steamboat—as others yet do—used dry pine wood for fuel, which sends forth a column of ignited vapor many feet above the flue, and whenever the fire is stirred a galaxy of sparks fly off, and in the night have a very brilliant and beautiful appearance. This uncommon light first attracted the attention of the crews of other vessels. Notwithstanding the wind and tide, which were adverse to its approach, they saw with astonishment that it was rapidly coming toward them; and when it came so near that the noise of the machinery and paddles was heard, the crews—if what was said in the newspapers of the time be true—in some instances shrunk beneath their decks from the terrific sight and left their vessels to go on shore, whilst others prostrated themselves and besought Providence to protect them from the approaches of the horrible monster which was marching on the tide and lighting its path by the fires which it vomited."

Fulton himself wrote the following account of the trip up the river and back, and published it in the American Citizen:—"I left New York on Monday at one o'clock, and arrived at Clermont, the seat of Chancellor Livingston, at one o'clock on Tuesday: time, twenty-four hours; distance, one hundred and ten miles. On Wednesday, I departed from the chancellor's at nine in the morning, and arrived at Albany at five in the afternoon: time, eight hours; distance, forty miles. The sum is one hundred and fifty miles in thirty-two hours,—equal to near five miles an hour.

"On Thursday, at nine o'clock in the morning, I left Albany, and arrived at the chancellor's at six in the evening: I started from thence at seven, and arrived at New York at four in the afternoon; time, thirty hours; space run through, one hundred and fifty miles,—equal to five miles an hour. Throughout my whole way, both going and returning, the wind was ahead: no advantage could be derived from my sail: the whole has therefore been performed by the power of the steam-engine."

In a letter to one of his friends, Fulton wrote:—"I overtook many sloops and schooners beating to windward, and parted with them as if they had been at anchor. The power of propelling boats by steam is now fully proved. The morning I left New York there were not perhaps thirty persons who believed that the boat would even move one mile an hour, or be of the least utility; and while we were putting off from the wharf, which was crowded with spectators, I heard a number of sarcastic remarks. This is the way in which ignorant men compliment what they call philosophers and projectors. . . . Although the prospect of personal emolument has been some inducement to me, yet I feel infinitely more pleasure in reflecting on the immense advantage that my country will derive from the invention."

The Clermont was now advertised as a regular passenger-boat upon the Hudson. She met with numerous accidents during the season; and her obvious defects would have been remedied by the application of as obvious improvements by Fulton himself, had not other persons anticipated him by taking out patents for improvements which they themselves proposed. They thus caused him infinite annoyance, and even contested his right as an inventor. Shipmasters, too, who looked upon his boat as an intruder upon their domain, ran their vessels purposely foul of her on more than one occasion. The Legislature saw fit to counteract the effects of this hostility by passing an act prolonging Livingston and Fulton's privilege five years for every additional boat established,—the whole time, however, not to exceed thirty years. It also made all combinations to destroy the Clermont offences punishable by fine and imprisonment.

Thus protected, the Clermont ran throughout the season, always well laden with passengers. In the winter she was enlarged and improved. The wheel-guards were strengthened, and became a prominent and essential feature of the boat. The rudder was replaced by one of much larger dimensions, and a steering-wheel towards the bow was substituted for the ordinary tiller. The accommodations for passengers were made much more comfortable,—luxurious even,—and the public taste was consulted in the application of numerous coats of rather gaudy paint. She then commenced her trips for the season of 1808. She started regularly at the appointed hour,—at first much to the discontent of travellers who had before been waited for by both sloops and stages. At the end of the season the Clermont was altogether too small for the crowds who thronged to take passage. Two boats, the Car of Neptune and the Paragon, were therefore soon added to the line.

Fulton, menaced by constant contestation of his rights, took out a patent in 1809 from the General Government, and another, for improvements, in 1811. His system was so simple—the adaptation of paddle-wheels to the axle of the crank of Watt's engine—that it seemed then, as it has proved since, almost impossible by any specifications effectually to protect it. The famous Pendulum Company caused Fulton for a time much trouble. They built a boat the wheels of which were to be moved by a pendulum. While she was upon the stocks and the wheels were resisted only by the air, the labor of a few men made them turn regularly and rapidly; but when she was launched, and the pendulum encountered the resistance of the water, neither pendulum, wheels, nor boat would stir. The Pendulum Company were aghast at this phenomenon, and clearly saw that if the boat was to be moved by the wheels, and the wheels by the pendulum, something must be devised of sufficient power to move the pendulum. There was nothing, evidently, but the steam-engine; and so they copied Fulton's. Lawsuits followed;

and in his argument in behalf of Fulton Mr. Emmet thus spoke of the Pendulum gentlemen:—"They are men who never waste health and life in midnight vigils and painful study; who never dream of science in the broken slumbers of an exhausted mind; who bestow upon the construction of a steamboat just as much mathematical calculation and philosophical research as on the purchase of a sack of wheat or a barrel of ashes." Fulton gained his cause, and the boat which was to go by clock-work was prohibited from going even by steam.

In 1812, Fulton built the Fire-Fly; and, as the town of Newburgh, half-way to Albany, offered sufficient traffic to support at least one boat, she was placed upon that route. In the same year he constructed two ferry-boats for crossing the Hudson, making them with rudder and bow at either end. He also contrived floating docks for their reception, and a method of stopping them without concussion. In 1813, he built a steam-vessel of four hundred tons and unusual strength, to ply in Long Island Sound between New York and New Haven. She was the first steamboat constructed with a round bottom. We quote a passage referring to her from a work published in 1817:—"During a great part of her route she would be as much exposed as she could be on the ocean: it was therefore necessary to make her a perfect sea-boat. She passes daily, and at all times of the tide, the dangerous strait of Hell-Gate, where for the distance of nearly a mile she often encounters a current running at the rate of at least six miles an hour. For some distance she has within a few yards of her, on each side, rocks and whirlpools which rival Scylla and Charybdis even as they are poetically described. This passage, previously to its being navigated by this vessel, was always supposed to be impassable except at certain stages of the tide; and many a shipwreck has been occasioned by a small mistake in the time. The boat passing through these whirlpools with rapidity, while the angry waters are foaming against her bows and appear to raise themselves in obstinate resistance to her passage, is a proud triumph of human ingenuity. The owners, as the highest tribute they had in their power to offer to his genius, and as an evidence of the gratitude they owed him, called her the Fulton."

Early in 1814, the United States and England being at war, Fulton conceived the idea of a steam vessel-of-war, capable of carrying a strong battery, with furnaces for redhot shot, and sailing four miles an hour. Congress authorized the construction of such a floating battery, and the keel was laid on the 18th of June. The vessel was launched on the 27th of October the same year, in the midst of excited and applauding throngs. Before she sailed, however, her engineer and builder had been removed to another sphere: Fulton died on the 24th of February, 1815. The Legislature paid an unusual tribute to his memory: they resolved to wear mourning for three weeks. This manifestation of regret for the loss of a man who had never held office nor served his country in any public capacity was entirely unprecedented.

On the 4th of July, the steam-frigate made a trial trip, and, with her engines alone, sailed fifty-three miles in eight hours and twenty minutes. The following description of the Fulton the First, as she was called, is given by the committee appointed to examine her in behalf of Congress:—"She is a structure resting on two boats and keels separated from end to end by a channel fifteen feet wide and sixty-six feet long. One boat contains the caldrons of copper to prepare her steam; the cylinder of iron, its piston, lever, and wheels, occupy part of the other. The water-wheel revolves in the space between them. The main or gun deck supports the armament, and is protected by a parapet, four feet ten inches thick, of solid timber, pierced by embrasures. Through thirty port-holes as many thirty-two pounders are intended to fire redhot shot, which can be heated with great safety and convenience. Her upper or spar deck, upon which several thousand men might parade, is encompassed by a bulwark, which affords safe quarters: she is rigged with two stout masts, each of which supports a large lateen yard and sails: she has two bowsprits and jibs, and four rudders, one at each extremity of each boat, so that she can be steered with either end foremost: her machinery is calculated for the addition of an engine which will discharge an immense column of water, which it is intended to throw upon the decks and through the port-holes of an enemy and thereby deluge her armament and ammunition. If in addition to all this we suppose her to be furnished, according to Mr. Fulton's intention, with hundred-pound Columbiads, two suspended from each bow so as to discharge a ball of that size into an enemy's ship ten or twelve feet below her water-line, it must be allowed that she has the appearance, at least, of being the most formidable engine for warfare that human ingenuity has contrived."

Such was the first step towards the establishment of a steam-navy. Forty years afterwards, George Steers built the propeller-frigate Niagara; and the reader, by comparing the two vessels, will have an adequate idea of the immense strides made in naval mechanics and engineering during the lapse of less than half a century. In Europe the size and qualities of the Fulton the First were at the time ludicrously exaggerated, as will be seen from the following passage from a Scotch treatise on steamships. After magnifying her proportions threefold, the author continues:—"The thickness of her sides is thirteen feet of alternate oak plank and cork wood: she carries forty-four guns, four of which are hundred-pounders; quarter-deck and forecastle guns, forty-four-pounders; and, further to annoy an enemy attempting to board, can discharge one hundred gallons of boiling water in a minute, and, by mechanism, brandishes three hundred cutlasses with the utmost regularity over her gunwales, works also an equal number of heavy iron spikes of great length, darting them from her sides with prodigious force and withdrawing them every quarter of a minute!"

The frigate made a second experimental trip, on the 11th of September, with her armament and stores on board, her draught of water being eleven feet. She changed her course by reversing the motion of her wheels. She fired salutes as she passed the forts, and performed manœuvres around the United States frigate Java. The machinery was not affected in the slightest degree by the detonation of her guns. Her average speed was five and a half miles an hour,—Fulton having contracted to obtain three miles an hour only. The city of New York now felt itself invulnerable; but the cessation of hostilities, which occurred soon after, precluded the necessity of employing her as a means of defence. It is probable that such a contrivance, even in the present advanced state of naval warfare, would be found useful in protecting the mouths of harbors,—not as a frigate, but as a floating battery or movable fortress. The fact that this vessel was built by Fulton makes him the father not only of steam-navigation, but of the steam-navies of the world as well. We shall have occasion to chronicle at intervals, as we progress in our record, the successive steps of improvement in the science, till we arrive at the era of steam floating palaces upon American rivers, of steam pleasure-yachts owned by American merchants, of commercial steam-leviathans, American and English, bearing the names of continents and oceans, and of the peerless steam-frigate to which we have already alluded,—" a noble ship with a noble name, bound, in 1857, upon the noblest of missions."

The history of the first ocean-steamer is very incompletely and unsatisfactorily told in the annals of the time. The following is the substance of all that has been preserved of the first transatlantic steam-voyage on record:

The Savannah, a steamer of three hundred and fifty tons, intended to ply between New York and Liverpool, under the command of Captain Moses Rodgers, was launched at New York on the 22d of August, 1818. She made a preliminary voyage to the city whose name she bore, in April, 1819, where she arrived in seven days, after a very boisterous passage. She was several times compelled to take in her wheels—having machinery for the purpose—and rely upon her sails, which was done with all the promptitude and safety anticipated. This trial trip left no doubt that she would successfully accomplish the object for which she was built. She left Savannah for Liverpool soon after, and the New York newspapers of the second week in June announced that she had been spoken at sea, all well. In the log-book of the Pluto, which arrived soon after at Baltimore from Bremen, occurred the following passage:

"June 2.—Clear weather and smooth sea: lat. 42°, long. 59°, spoke and passed the elegant steamship Savannah, eight

THE SAVANNAH: THE FIRST OCEAN-STEAMER.

days out from Savannah to St. Petersburg by way of Liverpool. She passed us at the rate of nine or ten knots; and the captain informed us she worked remarkably well, and the greatest compliment we could bestow was to give her three cheers, as the happiest effort of mechanical genius that ever appeared on the Western ocean. She returned the compliment."

Niles' New York Register of the 21st of August contains the following paragraph in italics at the head of its column of foreign news:—"The steamship Savannah, Captain Moses

Rodgers,—the first that ever crossed the Atlantic,—arrived at Liverpool in twenty-five days from Savannah, all well, to the great astonishment of the people of that place. She worked her engine eighteen days." The next record of her movements is that she sailed in August for St. Petersburg, passing Elsinore on the 13th, and that the British "*wisely* supposed her visit to be *somehow* connected with the ambitious views of the United States." She arrived back at Savannah in November, in fifty days from St. Petersburg *viâ* Copenhagen and Arendal in Norway, all well, and, in the language of Captain Rodgers, "with neither a screw, bolt, or a rope-yarn parted, though she encountered a very heavy gale in the North Sea." She left Savannah for Washington on the 4th of December, losing her boats and anchors off Cape Hatteras.

It is a singular fact, and one not creditable to the English, that many of their works treating of inventions and the progress of the arts and sciences entirely overlook this voyage out and back of the Savannah, and uniformly make the British steamers Sirius and Great Western the pioneers, in 1837, in the great work of ocean steam-navigation. The authors of these works err either through design or ignorance, and in either case display a marked unfitness for their vocation. Were they to consult the London and Liverpool newspapers of the time, they would find ample record of the accomplishment of a steam-voyage nearly twenty years before the period to which they assign it. We have said enough, however, to prove that the first steam-vessel that crossed the ocean was built in New York, and that Moses Rodgers, her captain, was an American citizen. When we arrive at the year in which the two British steamers inaugurated steam commercial intercourse between the hemispheres, we shall record it, with due acknowledgment of its importance; but we repeat the assertion that, as the first river-steamer was the Clermont, the first Atlantic steamer was the Savannah: both one and the other were built in New York.

Section VI.

FROM THE APPLICATION OF STEAM TO NAVIGATION TO THE LAYING OF THE ATLANTIC CABLE: 1807–1857.

CHAPTER XLIX.

ARCTIC EXPLORATIONS — RUSSIAN RESEARCHES UNDER KRUSENSTERN AND KOTZEBUE — FREYCINET—ROSS—THE CRIMSON CLIFFS—LANCASTER SOUND—BUCHAN AND FRANKLIN — PARRY — THE POLAR SEA — WINTER QUARTERS — RETURN HOME — DUPERREY — EPISODES IN THE WHALE-FISHERY — PARRY'S POLAR VOYAGE—BOAT-SLEDGES—METHOD OF TRAVEL—DISHEARTENING DISCOVERY—82° 43′ NORTH.

WE have now entered the nineteenth century. From this time forward we shall find little or no romantic interest attaching to the history of the sea, with the single exception of that of the Arctic waters. The epoch of adventure stimulated by the thirst for gold has long since passed: there are no more continents to be pursued, and few islands to be unbosomed from the deep. There was once a harvest to be reaped; but there remain henceforward but scanty leavings to be gleaned. The navigator of the present century cannot hope to acquire a rapid fame by brilliant discoveries: he must be content if he obtain a tardy distinction by patient observation and minute surveys,—a task far more useful than showy, and, while less attractive, much more arduous. Our narrative, therefore, of the remaining maritime enterprises will be correspondingly succinct. The reader's interest, as we have said, will attach almost exclusively to the Polar adventures of the heroes of the Northwest

Passage: of Ross, who saw the Crimson Cliffs; of Parry, who discovered the Polar Sea; of James Clarke Ross, who stood upon the North Magnetic Pole; of McClure, who threaded the Northwest Passage; of Franklin and of Kane, the martyrs to Arctic science. Though we shall dwell more particularly upon these voyages, we shall nevertheless mention in due order those undertaken for other purposes in all quarters of the globe.

In 1803, Alexander of Russia determined to enter the career of maritime discovery and geographical research. He sent Captain Krusenstern upon a voyage round the world, in the London-built ship Nadeshda. Nothing resulted from this voyage except the augmented probability that Saghalien was not an island, but a peninsula joined to the mainland of China by an isthmus of sand.

In 1815, the Russian Count Romanzoff fitted out an expedition at his own expense for the advancement of geographical science. The specific object of the voyage was to explore the American coast both to the north and south of Behring's Straits, and to seek a connection thence with Baffin's Bay. The command was given to Otto Von Kotzebue, a son of the distinguished German dramatist Kotzebue. In Oceanica he discovered an uninhabited archipelago, which he named Rurick's Chain,

RECEPTION OF KOTZEBUE AT OTDIA.

from one of his vessels. In Kotzebue Gulf, northeast of Behring's Straits, he discovered an island which was supposed to contain immense quantities of iron, from the violent oscillations of the needle. Upon a second visit to Otdia, one of the Rurick Islands, in 1824, the inhabitants remembered him upon his shouting the syllables *Totobu,*—their manner of pronouncing his name. They received him with great joy, rushing into the water up to their hips: they then lifted him out of his boat and carried him dry-shod to the shore.

In 1817, Louis XVIII. sent Captain Freycinet upon the first voyage which, though undertaken for the advancement of science, had neither hydrography nor geography for its object. Its purpose was to determine the form of the globe at the South Pole, the observation of magnetic and atmospheric phenomena, the study of the three kingdoms of nature, and the investigation of the resources and languages of such indigenous people as the vessel should visit. The expedition was conducted with skill; but its results, being purely scientific, do not require mention here.

In the winter of 1816, the whalers returning from the Greenland seas to England reported the ice to be clearer than they had ever known it before. The period seemed favorable for a renewal of Arctic exploration; and in 1818 the Admiralty fitted out two vessels—the Isabella and Alexander—for the purpose. Captain John Ross was sent in the first to discover a northwest passage, and Lieutenant Edward Parry in the second, to penetrate if possible to the Pole. Their instructions required them to examine with especial care the openings at the head of Baffin's Bay. Sailing on the 18th of April, they reached the coast of Greenland on the 17th of June. They saw tribes of Esquimaux who had never seen men of any race but their own, and who felt and testified an indescribable alarm at the sight of the adventurers. It was subsequently proved that what they feared was contagion. Quite at the northern extremity of the bay, Ross observed the phenomenon which has given so romantic, almost legendary, a character to his voyage, —that of red snow. He saw a range of peaks clothed in a garb which appeared as if borrowed from the looms and dyes of Tyre. The spot is marked upon the maps as "The Crimson Cliffs." The color was at the time supposed to be a quality inherent in the snow itself; but subsequent investigations have established its vegetable origin.

The ships were now at the northern point of Baffin's Bay, among the numerous inlets which Baffin had failed to explore. They all appeared to be blocked up with ice, and none of them held out any flattering promise of concealing within itself the long-sought Northwest Passage. Smith's Strait, where the bay ends, was carefully examined; but it proved to be enclosed by ice. Returning towards the south by the western coast of the bay, they arrived at the entrance of Lancaster Sound on the 30th of August, just as the sun, after shining unceasingly for nearly three months, was beginning to dip under the horizon. The vessels sailed up the sound some fifty miles, through a sea clear from ice, the channel being surrounded on either hand by mountains of imposing elevation. It was here that Ross committed the fatal mistake which was to cloud his own reputation and to put Parry, his second, forward as the first of Arctic navigators. He asserted, and certainly believed, that he saw a high ridge of mountains stretching directly across the passage. This, he thought, rendered farther progress impracticable, and the order was given to put the ships about. Ross returned to England, convinced that Baffin was correct in regarding Lancaster Bay as a bay only, without any strait beyond. It was destined that Parry should thread this strait and find the Polar Sea beyond.

In the same year the British Government sent an expedition under Captain Buchan and Lieutenant—afterwards Sir John—Franklin, to endeavor to reach the Pole. The objects were to make experiments on the elliptical figure of the earth, on magnetic and meteorological phenomena, and on the refraction of the atmosphere in high latitudes. The two vessels—the Dorothea and Trent—sailed in April, 1818, and made their way towards Magdalena Bay, in Spitzbergen. In latitude 74° north, near an island frequented by herds of walruses, a boat's crew was attacked by a number of these animals, and only escaped destruction by the presence of mind of the purser. He seized a loaded musket, and, plunging the muzzle into the throat of the leader of the school, discharged its contents into his bowels. As the walrus sinks as soon as he is dead, the mortally-wounded animal at once began to disappear beneath the water. His

companions abandoned the combat to support their chief with their tusks, whom they hastily bore away from the scene of action.

The climate here was mild, the atmosphere pure and brilliant, and the blue of the sky as intense as that of Naples. Alpine plants, grasses, moss, and lichens, flourished in abundance, and afforded browsing pasturage to reindeer at the height of fifteen hundred feet above the sea. The shores were alive with awks, divers, cormorants, gulls, walruses, and seals. Eider-ducks, foxes, and bears preyed and prowled upon the ice; and the sea furnished a home to jaggers, kittiwakes, and whales. Having ascended as high as 80° 34′ N., and finding it impossible to penetrate farther to the north, Buchan resolved to quit the waters of Spitzbergen and stand away for those of Greenland. A pack of floating icebergs, upon which the waves were beating furiously, beset the ships. The Trent came violently in collision with a mass many hundred times her size. Every man on board lost his footing; the masts bent at the shock, while the timbers cracked beneath the pressure. This accident rendered a prosecution of the voyage impracticable, and the two ships returned to England, where they arrived in October. The expedition thus failed of the main object it was intended to accomplish.

As we have already remarked, Ross neglected the opportunity afforded him of penetrating to the interior of Lancaster Sound,—thus leaving for another the glory of attaching his name to the discoveries to be made there. The Government, being dissatisfied with his management, and being encouraged by Lieutenant Parry to believe that the supposed chain of mountains barring the passage had no existence but in Ross's imagination, gave him the command of two ships, strongly manned and amply stored, for the prosecution of discovery in that direction. He left England on the 11th of May, 1819, with the ship Hecla and the gun-brig Griper. On the 15th of June he unexpectedly saw land,—which proved to be Cape Farewell, the southern point of Greenland, though at a distance of more than a hundred miles. The ships were immovably "beset" by ice on the 25th: their situation was utterly helpless, all the power that could be applied not availing to turn their heads a single degree of the compass.

The officers and men occupied themselves in various manners during this period of inaction. Observations were made on the dip and variation of the magnetic needle, and lunar distances were calculated. White bears were enticed within rifle-distance by the odor of fried red-herrings, and then easily shot. On the 30th the ice slackened, and, after eight hours' incessant labor, both ships were moved into the open sea. On the 12th, Parry obtained a supply of pure water which was flowing from an ice-berg, and the sailors shook from the ropes and rigging several tons' weight of congealed fog. The passage to Lancaster Sound was laborious, and was only effected by the most persevering efforts on the part of all.

An entrance into the sound was effected on the 1st of August; and Parry felt, as did the officers and men, that this was the point of the voyage which was to determine the success or failure of the expedition. Reports, all more or less favorable, were constantly passed down from the crow's nest to the quarter-deck. The weather was clear, and the ships sailed in perfect safety through the night. Towards morning all anxiety respecting the alleged chain of mountains across the inlet was at an end; for the two shores were still forty miles apart, at a distance of one hundred and fifty miles from the mouth of the channel. The water was now as free from ice as the Atlantic; and they began to flatter themselves that they had fairly entered the Polar Sea. A heavy swell and the familiar ocean-like color which was now thought to characterize the water were also encouraging circumstances. The compasses became so sluggish and irregular that the usual observations upon the variation of the needle were abandoned. The singular phenomenon was soon for the first time witnessed of the needle becoming so weak as to be completely controlled by local attraction, so that it really pointed to the north pole of the ship,—that is, to the point where there was the largest quantity of iron.

Ice for a time prevented the farther western progress of the vessels, and they sailed one hundred and twenty miles to the south, in a sound which they called Prince Regent's Inlet. Parry suspected, though incorrectly, that this inlet communicated with Hudson's Bay. Returning to the mouth of the inlet, he found the sea to the westward still encumbered with ice; but a heavy blow, accompanied with rain, soon broke it up and dispersed it. They proceeded slowly on, naming every cape and bay which they passed: an inlet of large size they called Wellington, "after his Grace the Master of the Ordnance." Being now convinced that the passage through which they had thus far ascended was a strait connecting two seas, Parry gave it the name of Barrow's Strait, after Mr. Barrow, Secretary of the Admiralty. The prospects of success during the coming six weeks were now felt by the commander of the expedition to be "truly exhilarating."

An island—by far the largest Parry had seen in these waters—appeared early in September, and the men worked their arduous way along its southern coast, till, on the 4th, they reached the longitude of 110° west. The two ships then became entitled to the sum of £5000,—the reward offered by Parliament to the first of his Majesty's subjects that should penetrate thus far to the westward within the Arctic Circle. The island was called Melville Island, from the First Lord of the Admiralty. In a bay named The Bay of the Hecla and Griper, the anchor was dropped for the first time since leaving England; the ensigns and pennants were hoisted, and the British flag waved in a region believed to be without the pale of the habitable world.

The summer was now at its close, and it became necessary to make a selection of winter quarters. A harbor was found, a passage-way cut through two miles of ice, and the ships settled in five fathoms' water: they were soon firmly frozen in at a cable's-length from the shore. Hunting, botanizing, excursions upon the island, experiments in an observatory erected on shore, and amateur theatricals, afforded some relief from the unavoidable inactivity to which officers and crew were now condemned. Parry had named the group of islands of which Melville is the largest, the North Georgian Islands, in honor of King George; and during the days of constant darkness a weekly news-

CUTTING IN.

paper, entitled "The North Georgia Gazette and Winter Chronicle," was edited by Captain Sabine, the astronomer.

The sun reappeared on the 3d of February, 1820, after an absence of ninety-one days. The theatre was soon closed and the newspaper discontinued. The ice around the ships was seven feet thick, though by the middle of May the crews had cut it away so as to allow the ships to float, and had sawed a channel for their boats. On the 1st of August, there was not

CUTTING OUT.

the slightest symptom of a thaw; on the 2d, the ice broke up and disappeared with a suddenness altogether inexplicable. Parry determined to return home at once, and arrived at Leith, in Scotland, towards the close of October. He was received with great favor, and was rewarded for his signal services by promotion to the rank of captain.

Parry made a second voyage in 1821, with instructions to seek a passage by Hudson's Strait instead of by Lancaster Sound. It was totally unsuccessful. He made a third attempt, in 1824, with the Fury and the Hecla. The Fury was lost in Lancaster Sound, and Parry returned baffled and for a time disheartened.

In 1822, a French captain, named Duperrey, made a voyage, under the orders of the Government, which is in many respects the most remarkable on record. He sailed seventy-five thousand miles in thirty-one months, without losing a man or having a single name upon the sick-list; nor did the ship once need repairs. The discoveries made were not important, but the surveys effected and the observations upon terrestrial magnetism recorded were interesting and valuable.

At about this period, the perils incident to the whale-fishery were strangely augmented by a circumstance which we cannot forbear mentioning. The whale, whose intellectual faculties had been sharpened by the warfare waged against him for two hundred years, was suddenly found to be animated by a new and vehement passion,—that of revenge. "Mocha Dick," who earned a terrible reputation for ferocity, only succumbed after many years of successful resistance. His body proved to be covered with scars, his flesh bristled with harpoons, and his head was declared to be wonderfully expressive of "old age, cunning, and rapacity." Not long after this, a sperm-whale was wounded by a boat's crew from the Essex. A brother leviathan, eighty-five feet long, approached the ship within twenty rods, eyed it steadfastly for a moment, and then withdrew, as if satisfied with his observations. He soon returned at full speed: he struck the ship with his head, throwing the men flat upon their faces. Gnashing his jaws together as if wild with rage, he made another onset, and, with every appearance of an avenger of his race, stove in the vessel's bows. This was the first example on record of the whale's displaying positive design in seeking an encounter. He certainly acted from

THE WHALE OF CAPTAIN DEBLOIS.

the promptings of revenge, and, moreover, directed his attacks upon the weakest part of the ship.

The whale of Captain Deblois, of the ship Ann Alexander, was a still more remarkable animal. When harpooned, instead of seeking to escape, he turned upon the boat, and, in the language of an eye-witness, "chawed it to flinders." The second boat met the same fate. The whale then dashed upon the ship, and broke through her timbers, letting the water in in torrents. In an hour the vessel lay a wreck upon the ocean. Four months afterwards, the crew of the Rebecca Sims captured a whale of large size but of enfeebled energies. He was found to have a damaged head, with large fragments of a ship's fore-timbers buried in his flesh; while two harpoons, sunk almost to his vitals, and labelled "Ann Alexander," designated him as the fierce but now exhausted antagonist of Captain Deblois, of New Bedford.

In 1827—to return to the Arctic explorations—a new idea was broached with reference to the Pole and the most likely method of reaching it. Captain Parry, despairing of getting there in ships, conceived the plan of constructing boats with runners, which might be dragged upon the ice, or, in case of need, be rowed through the water. The Government approved of the idea, and two boats were specially constructed for the service: each one, with its furniture and stores, weighed three thousand seven hundred and fifty-three pounds. They were placed on board the sloop-of-war Hecla; and the expedition left the Nore on the 4th of April, 1827, for Spitzbergen. At Hammersfeld, in Norway, they took on board eight reindeer and a quantity of moss for their fodder.

After experiencing a series of tremendous gales, being beset in the ice till the 8th of June, the Hecla was safely anchored on the northern coast of Spitzbergen, in Hecla Cove. Parry gave his instructions to his lieutenants, Foster and Crozier, and on the 22d left the ship in the two boats, having named them the Enterprise and Endeavor, with provisions for seventy-one days. The ice appeared so rugged that the reindeer promised to be of little assistance, and were consequently left behind. The following is an abridged account of the extraordinary method of travelling adopted upon this singular voyage:

"It was my intention," says Parry, "to travel by night and rest by day, thus avoiding the glare resulting from the sun shining from his highest altitudes upon the snow; and proceeding during the milder light shed during his vicinity to the horizon,—for of course, during the summer, he never set at all. This practice so completely inverted the natural order of things that the officers, though possessing chronometers, did not know night from day. When we rose in the evening, we commenced our day by prayers; after which we took off our raccoon-skin sleeping-dresses, and put on our box-cloth travelling-suits. We breakfasted upon warm cocoa heated with spirits of wine—our only fuel—and biscuit: we then travelled five hours, and stopped to dine, and again travelled four, five, or six hours, according to circumstances. It then being early in the morning, we halted for the night, selecting the largest surface of ice we happened to be near for hauling the boat on. Every man then put on dry stockings and fur boots, leaving the wet ones—which were rarely found dry in the morning—to be resumed after their slumbers. After supper the officers and men smoked their pipes, which served to dry the boat and awnings, and often raised the temperature ten degrees. A watch was set to look out for bears, each man alternately doing this duty for one hour. It now being bright day, the evening was ushered in with prayers. After seven hours' sleep, the man appointed to boil the cocoa blew a reveillé upon the bugle, and thus at nightfall the day was recommenced."

The difficulty of travelling was much greater than had been anticipated. The ice, instead of being solid, was composed of small, loose, and rugged masses, with pools of water between them. In their first eight days they made but eight miles' northing. At one time the men dragged the boats only one hundred and fifty yards in two hours. On the 17th of July they reached the latitude of 82° 14′ 28″,—the highest yet attained. On the 18th, after eleven hours' exhausting labor, they advanced but two miles; and on the 20th, having apparently accomplished twelve miles in three days, an observation revealed the alarming fact that they had really advanced but five. The terrible truth burst upon Parry and his officers: the ice over which they were with such effort forcing their weary way *was actually drifting to the south!* This intelligence was concealed from the men, who had no suspicion of it, though they often laughingly remarked that they were a long time getting to this eighty-third degree. They were at this time in 82° 43′ 5″. The next observation extinguished the last ray of hope: after two days' labor, they found themselves in 82° 40′. The drift was carrying them to the south faster than their own exertions took them to the north! In fact, the drift ran four miles a day. It was evidently hopeless to pursue the journey any farther. The floe upon which they slept at night rolled them back to the point they had quitted in the morning. Parry acquainted the men with the disheartening news, and granted them one day's rest.

The ensigns and pennants were now displayed, the party feeling a legitimate pride in having advanced to a point never before reached by human beings, though they had failed in an enterprise now proved beyond the pale of possibility. They returned without incident of moment to England. Parry did not totally abandon the idea of eventually reaching the Pole over the ice, and as late as 1847 was of the opinion that at a different season of the year, before drifting comes on, the project may yet be realized. Still, no mortal man has ever yet set foot upon the pivot of the axis of the globe; and it is not venturing too much to predict that no man ever will.

CHAPTER L.

ROSS'S SECOND VOYAGE—THE NORTH MAGNETIC POLE—D'URVILLE—ENDERBY'S LAND—BACK'S VOYAGE IN THE TERROR—THE GREAT WESTERN AND SIRIUS—UNITED STATES' EXPLORING EXPEDITION—THE ANTARCTIC CONTINENT—SIR JOHN FRANKLIN'S LAST VOYAGE IN THE EREBUS AND TERROR—ETFORTS MADE TO RELIEVE HIM—DISCOVERY OF THE SCENE OF HIS FIRST WINTER QUARTERS—THE GRINNELL EXPEDITION—THE ADVANCE AND RESCUE—LIEUTENANT DE HAVEN—DR. KANE—RETURN OF THE EXPEDITION.

In the year 1828, Sir John Ross applied to the Government for the means of making a second voyage to the Arctic waters of America, and was refused. The next year, Mr. Sheriff Booth, a gentleman of liberal spirit, offered to assume the pecuniary responsibilities of the expedition, and empowered Ross to make what outlay he thought proper. He bought and equipped the Victory, a packet-ship plying between Liverpool and the Isle of Man. She had a small high-pressure engine, and paddle-wheels which could be lifted out of the water. She sailed in May, 1829. We shall give but a brief account of the incidents of the voyage till we arrive at the event which has made James Clarke Ross, the nephew of Sir John, illustrious,—the discovery of the North Magnetic Pole,—that mysterious spot towards which forever points the needle of the mariner's compass.

While in Baffin's Bay, in June, the Victory lost her foretopmast in a gale; two of the sailors who were reefing the topsails had barely time to escape with their lives. Proceeding

through Lancaster Sound, and then descending to the south into Prince Regent's Inlet, Ross arrived, after coasting three hundred miles of undiscovered shore, at a spot which he thought would furnish commodious winter quarters. The whole territory received the name of Boothia, in honor of the patron of the expedition. Here they remained eleven months, beset by ice; not even during the months of July and August, 1830, did the ship stir from the position in which she was held fast. At last, on the 17th of September, she was found to be free, and the delighted crew prepared for a speedy deliverance. The unfortunate vessel sailed only three miles, however, when she was again firmly frozen in. The engine, which had proved a wretched and most inefficient contrivance, was taken out and carried ashore,—an event which was hailed with pleasure by all. "I believe," says Ross, "that there was not a man who ever again wished to see its minutest fragment." Another year of monotony and silence now stared the weather-bound navigators in the face. Six months elapsed before even a land-excursion could be attempted; but in May, 1831, occurred the great discovery to which we have referred.

Commander James Clarke Ross was the second officer of the ship. He started in April, with a party, to make explorations inland. The dipping-needle had long varied from 88° to 89°,

—thus pointing nearly downwards,—90° being, of course, the amount of variation from the horizontal line of the ordinary compass which would have made it directly vertical. Commander Ross was extremely desirous to stand upon the wonderful spot where such an effect would be observed, and joined a number of Esquimaux who were proceeding in the direction where he imagined it lay. He determined, if possible, so to set his foot that the Magnetic Pole should lie between him and the centre of the earth. Arriving at a place where the dipping-needle pointed to 89° 46′, and being therefore but fourteen miles from its calculated position, he could no longer brook the delay attendant upon the transportation of the baggage, and set forward upon a rapid march, taking only such articles as were strictly necessary. The tremendous spot was reached at eight in the morning of the 1st of June. The needle marked 89° 59′,—one minute from the vertical,—a variation almost imperceptible. We give the particulars of this most interesting event in the words of the discoverer himself:

"I believe I must leave it to others to imagine the elation of mind with which we found ourselves now at length arrived at this great object of our ambition: it almost seemed as if we had accomplished every thing we had come so far to see and do,—as if our voyage and all its labors were at an end, and that nothing now remained for us but to return home and be happy for the remainder of our days.

"We could have wished that a place so important had possessed more of mark or note. It was scarcely censurable to regret that there was not a mountain to indicate a spot to which so much of interest must ever be attached; and I could even have pardoned any one among us who had been so romantic or absurd as to expect that the Magnetic Pole was an object as conspicuous and mysterious as the fabled mountain of Sinbad,—that it even was a mountain of iron or a magnet as large as Mont Blanc. But Nature had here erected no monument to denote the spot which she had chosen as the centre of one of her greatest powers.

"As soon as I had satisfied my own mind, I made known to the party the gratifying result of all our joint labor; and it was then that, amidst mutual congratulations, we fixed the British flag on the spot and took possession of the North Magnetic Pole and its adjoining territory in the name of Great Britain and King William the Fourth. We had abundance of materials for building, in the fragments of limestone which covered the beach; and we therefore erected a cairn of some magnitude, under which we buried a canister containing a record of the interesting fact,—only regretting that we had not the means of constructing a pyramid of more importance and of strength sufficient to withstand the assaults of time and the Esquimaux. Had it been a pyramid as large as that of Cheops, I am not sure that it would have done more than satisfy our ambition under the feelings of that exciting day. The latitude of this spot is 70° 5′ 17″, and its longitude 96° 46′ 45″ west from Greenwich."

We must remark in this connection that the fixation of the *latitude* of the Magnetic Pole was the only important element of this discovery; for, as the Magnetic Pole revolves about the North Pole at the rate of 11′ 4″ a year, it consequently changes its annual *longitude* by that amount. A quarter of a century has elapsed since its longitude was settled for the year 1831; and this lapse of time involves a change of place of between four and five degrees. It requires no less than eighteen hundred and ninety years to accomplish the cycle of revolution. The latitude of the Pole of course remains unchanged. It will always be sufficient glory for Ross to have stood upon the spot where the Pole then was: the fact that the spot then so marvellous has since ceased to be so is assuredly no cause for detracting from his merit. After this discovery the party returned to the ship.

In September the ice broke up, and the Victory, which had the previous year sailed three miles, this year sailed four. She was again immediately frozen in: the men's courage gave way, and the scurvy began to appear. Their only hope of a final deliverance seemed to be to proceed overland to the spot where the Fury had been lost under Parry in 1824, and to get her supplies and boats. The distance was one hundred and eighty miles to the north. They drank a parting glass to the Victory on the 29th of May, 1832, and nailed her colors to the mast. After a laborious journey of one month, they reached Fury Beach, where they found three of the boats washed away, but several still left. These were ready for sea on the 1st of August, when the whole party embarked. They were compelled to return in October, and made preparations for their fourth Polar winter. The season was one of great severity: in February, 1833, the first death by scurvy took place. Ross himself and several of the seamen were attacked by the disease. It was not till August that the boats were again able to move. They reached Barrow's Strait on the 17th, and on the morning of the 26th descried a sail. They made signals by burning wet powder, and succeeded in attracting the stranger's attention. She was a whaler, and had been formerly commanded by Ross himself. Thus they were rescued. After a month's delay, the vessel, now filled to its utmost capacity with blubber, sailed for Hull, in England. There Ross and his officers received a public entertainment from the mayor and corporation. The former then repaired to London, reported himself to the Secretary of the Admiralty, and obtained an audience of the king. His Majesty accepted the dedication of his journal, and allowed him to add the name of William the Fourth to the Magnetic Pole. He learned that he had been given up for lost long since, and that parties had been sent out in search of him.

All concerned in this interesting expedition were rewarded by Parliament. Mr. Booth was shortly after knighted; Commander Ross was made post-captain; the other officers received speedy promotion; and Government paid the crew the wages which had accrued beyond the period of fifteen months for which they were engaged,—amounting in all to £4580. A select committee of the House of Commons was appointed to consider the claims of Captain Ross himself, and concluded its labors by recommending that a sum of £5000 be voted to him by Parliament.

In 1825, Captain d'Urville was sent by Charles X. of France upon a voyage similar to those performed by Freycinet and Duperrey. As we have already had occasion to say, this officer was fortunate enough to return to France with the positive proofs of the destruction of the vessels of Lapérouse upon the island of Vanikoro. He surveyed the whole of the Feejee archipelago, and restored upon French maps its native name of Viti. The results of d'Urville's labors are comprised in twelve octavo volumes, sixty-three charts, twelve plans, eight hundred and sixty-six designs representing the various island nations, their arms, dwellings, &c., and four hundred landscapes and marine views. Admiral d'Urville ranks as the first French navigator of this century.

In 1830, two rich shipping-merchants of London, by the name of Enderby, sent Captain Biscoe to the Antarctic Ocean to fish for seals, in the brig Tula and the cutter Lively, giving him directions to seek for land in high southern latitudes. In February, 1831,—being then as far south as the sixty-ninth parallel and in 12° west,—he saw distinct and positive signs of land. On the 27th, in 66° of latitude and 47° of longitude, he convinced himself of the existence of a long reach of land; but huge islands of ice prevented his approaching it. The magnificence of the aurora australis, appearing now under the forms of grand architectural columns and now as the fringes of tapestry, drew the attention of the sailors so constantly towards the heavens that they neglected to watch the ship's track amid mountains of floating and tumbling ice. Captain Biscoe gave to the discovery the name of Enderby's Land. Farther to the west he discovered an island, which he named Adelaide, in honor of the Queen of England. It presents an imposing appearance,—a tall peak burying itself in the clouds and often peering out above them. Its base is surrounded with a dazzling girdle of snow and ice, which extends, though sapped and excavated by the action of the waves, some nine hundred feet into the sea.

In 1836, the English Government appointed Captain George Back — who had lately been upon a land-expedition in the American Arctic regions in search of Captain and Commander Ross—to the since celebrated ship Terror, for the purpose of determining the western coast-line of Prince Regent's Inlet. The voyage, though entirely unsuccessful, is one of the most remarkable on record,—showing as it did a power of resistance and endurance in a ship which till then was not believed to belong either to iron or heart of oak. Back proceeded no farther than Baffin's Bay, the Terror remaining for ten months fast in the gripe of its "cradle" or "ice-wagon," as the men called the huge floating berg upon which she rested. He was knighted on his return, and his sturdy ship was put out of commission and docked. It is a subject of regret that so splendid a specimen of marine architecture, as far as strength and solidity are concerned, should have met the fate which she has encountered. Where she is no mortal knows, except perhaps a few inaccessible Esquimaux; for she has perished with her lost consort, the Erebus, and their hapless commander, Sir John Franklin.

In the year 1838, on the 23d of April, two ocean-steamers—the first with the exception of the Savannah—entered the harbor of New York. They were the Sirius and the Great Western. They had been expected, and their arrival was the signal for general rejoicings and the theme of universal congratulation. Crowds of people—men, women, and children—assembled along the wharves to view the unwonted spectacle. The Sirius was a vessel of seven hundred tons and three hundred and twenty horse-power, and had previously plied between Liverpool and Cork. She had left the latter port on the 4th of April, and had therefore been nineteen days upon the passage. The Great Western was a new ship: she was of thirteen hundred and forty tons; her extreme length was two hundred and thirty-six feet; her depth of hold, twenty-three feet; breadth of beam, thirty-five feet; diameter of wheels, twenty-eight feet; length of paddle-boards, ten feet; diameter of cylinder, six feet; length of stroke, seven feet. She had four boilers, and could carry eight hundred tons of coal,—sufficient for twenty-six days' consumption. She had left Bristol on the 8th of April, and had accomplished the voyage in fifteen days and five hours. Her mean daily rate was two hundred and forty miles, or nine miles an hour, with unfavorable weather and strong head-winds. She was expected to stop either at the Azores or at Halifax, but succeeded in making the passage direct. She consumed but four hundred and fifty tons of coal out of six hundred. This event was looked upon by all as an earnest of the complete triumph of ocean steam-navigation; and the Great Western is regarded by the people of the two countries as the pioneer ship among the many noble vessels that have plied upon the great Atlantic ferry. The Britannia—the first vessel of the Cunard line to cross the ocean—arrived at Boston on the 18th of July, 1840, after a passage of fourteen days and eight hours.

In this same year, (1838,) the United States' Exploring Expedition,—consisting of the Vincennes, a sloop-of-war of twenty guns, Lieutenant Charles Wilkes, commander-in-chief; the Peacock, eighteen-gun sloop-of-war, William L. Hudson, commanding; the Porpoise, ten-gun brig; the Relief, exploring vessel; and the schooners Flying-Fish and Sea-Gull,—sailed from Hampton Roads. Its objects were to explore the Southern and Pacific Oceans; to ascertain, if possible, the situation of that part of the Antarctic continent supposed to lie to the south of New Holland, and to make researches and surveys of importance to ships navigating the Polynesian seas. The squadron was absent four years, and accomplished a vast amount of arduous labor interesting to science and invaluable to commerce. We propose to speak only of what became afterwards its prominent feature,—the supposed discovery of an Antarctic continent.

On the 15th of February, 1840, land was seen in longitude 106° 40′ E. and latitude 65° 57′ S. The next day the ships were within seven miles of it, and, "by measurement, the extent of the coast of the Antarctic continent then in sight was made seventy-five miles." The men landed on an ice-island, where they found stones, boulders, gravel, sand, and clay. Everybody wished to possess a piece of the Antarctic continent; and many fragments of red sandstone and basalt were carried away. The island was believed to have been detached from the neighboring land. Subsequent voyages, however, have thrown great doubts upon the accuracy of these assertions. James Clarke Ross, who was sent with the Erebus and Terror, in 1839, to the South Pole, was informed at Van Diemen's Land of Wilkes' alleged discovery. He reached the spot in January, 1841, and, instead of an Antarctic continent, found water five hundred fathoms deep. The existence of such a continent, therefore, must be regarded as altogether hypothetical. "It is natural," says the London Athenæum, "that a commander of his country's first scientific expedition should wish to make the most of it; but Science is so august in her nature and so severe in her rules that she declines recording in her archives any sentence as truth on which there rests the slightest liability of doubt: in all such cases she prefers the Scotch verdict,—'Not proven.'"

Though at this period the discovery of a Northwest Passage—if one existed—was no longer expected to afford a short and commodious commercial route to the Indies and to China, yet the scientific and romantic interest of the subject still exerted a powerful effect on both nations and Governments. Great Britain resolved to make one last attempt, and, selecting two vessels whose fame was now world-wide, appointed Sir John Franklin to their command,—the Erebus being his flag-ship, with Captain Crozier, as his second, in the Terror. The officers and crew, all told, numbered one hundred and thirty-eight picked and resolute men. The instructions given to Franklin were to proceed, with a store-ship ordered to accompany him, as far up Davis' Straits as that vessel could safely go, there to transfer her provisions and send her home. He was then to get into Baffin's Bay, enter Lancaster Sound, thread Barrow's Straits, and follow Parry's track due west to Melville Island, in the Polar Sea. Here the instructions, with an assurance which seems incredible now, begged the whole question of a Northwest Passage, and directed him to proceed the remaining nine hundred miles which separate that point from Behring's Strait,—a region which it was hoped would be found free from obstruction. He was not to stop to examine any opening to the northward, but to push resolutely on to Behring's Strait, and return home by the Sandwich Islands and Panama. He sailed from the Thames on the 19th of May, 1845. He received the store-ship's cargo in Davis' Straits, and then despatched her home. His two ships were seen by a whaler named the Prince of Wales on the 26th of July: they were in the very middle of Baffin's Bay, moored to an iceberg and waiting for open water.

Two years passed away, and, nothing being heard from them, the public anxiety respecting them became very great. The Government determined to attempt their rescue, and sent out three several expeditions in 1848. The two first—one overland to the Polar Sea, under Richardson and Rae, another by Behring's Strait, in the ships Herald and Plover — totally failed of success, as they were founded upon the supposition that Franklin had advanced farther westward than Parry in

1820,—a supposition altogether unlikely. The third—consisting of the Enterprise and Investigator, under Captain Sir James Clarke Ross—was equally unsuccessful, though conducted in a quarter where success was at least possible. At Port Leopold, at the mouth of Prince Regent's Inlet, Ross formed a large depôt of provisions,—the locality having been admirably chosen, being upon Parry's route to the Polar Sea, and upon any track Franklin would be likely to take on his way back, in case he had already advanced beyond it. His men built a house upon shore of their spare spars, and covered it with such canvas as they could dispense with. They lengthened the Investigator's steam-launch, so that it would be capable of carrying Franklin and his crew safely to the whalers' rendezvous, and left it. They then made their way through the ice to Davis' Straits, and arrived in England early in November, 1849.

The probable fate of Franklin now absorbed all minds, and the Admiralty, Parliament, the public, and the press eagerly discussed every theory which would account for his prolonged absence, and every means by which succor could be sent to him. The Admiralty offered a reward of one hundred guineas for accurate information concerning him. Lady Franklin offered the stimulus of £2000, and a second of £3000, to successful search; and the British Government sought to enlist the services of the whalers by announcing a bonus of £20,000. A vessel was sent to land provisions and coal at the entrance to Lancaster Sound. Three new expeditions were sent out in 1850 by the Government, besides one by public subscription, assisted by the Hudson Bay Company, under Sir John Ross, and another by Lady Franklin. They accomplished wonders of seamanship, and their crews endured the most harassing trials; but we have no space to chronicle any thing beyond the finding of a few distinct but unproductive traces of the missing adventurers, which occurred in the following manner:

Captain Ommaney, of the Assistance and Intrepid, landed on Cape Riley, in Wellington Channel, late in August. There he observed sledge-tracks and a pavement of small stones which had evidently been the floor of a tent. Around were a number of birds' bones and fragments of meat-tins. Upon Beechey Island, three miles distant, were found a cairn or mound constructed of layers of meat-tins filled with gravel, the embankment of a house, the remains of a carpenter's shop and an armorer's forge, with remnants of rope and clothing; a pair of gloves laid out to dry, with stones upon them to prevent their blowing away. The oval outline of a garden was still distinguishable. But the most interesting and valuable result of these investigations was the finding of three graves with inscriptions, one of which will show the tenor of the whole:

"Sacred to the memory of William Braine, R.M., of H.M.S. Erebus, who died April 3, 1846, aged thirty-two years. *Choose ye this day whom ye will serve.*—Josh. xxiv. 15."

This and one of the other inscriptions, dated in January, seemed to fix at this spot the first winter quarters of Franklin,—for 1845–46. They also show that but three men died during the winter; and three out of one hundred and thirty-eight is not a high proportion of mortality. The seven hundred empty meat-tins seemed to show that the consumption of meat had been moderate; for the ships started with twenty-four thousand canisters. This was the substance of the intelligence obtained during this year of the fate of the wanderers; and it was, as will be noticed, already five years old.

An expedition was also fitted out for the search in 1850, under the combined auspices of Henry Grinnell, Esq., a merchant of New York, and the United States Navy Department,—the former furnishing the ships and the means, the latter the men and the discipline. Two hermaphrodite brigs,—the Advance and Rescue,—of one hundred and forty-four and ninety tons respectively, manned by thirty-eight men, all told, and strengthened for Arctic duty beyond all precedent, were prepared for the service. They were placed under the command of Lieutenant De Haven,—Dr. E. K. Kane, of the Navy, being

DR. KANE.

appointed surgeon and naturalist to the squadron. They sailed from New York on the 23d of May, and in less than a month descried the gaunt coast of Greenland at the moment when the distinction between day and night began to be lost. The Danish inhabitants of the settlement at Lievely made them such presents of furs as their own scanty wardrobes permitted. Two sailors, complaining of sickness, were landed at Disco Island, thence to make the best of their way home.

Thus far the weather had been favorable, and they passed the seventy-fourth degree without meeting ice. On the 7th of

July, being still in Baffin's Bay, they encountered the pack. It was summer-ice, consisting of closely-set but separate floes. They could not make over three miles a day headway through it,—which they considered a useless expenditure of labor. They remained beset for twenty-one days, when the pack opened in various directions. The ships now reached Melville Bay, on the east side of Baffin's Bay,—Lancaster Sound, through which they were to pass, being upon the west. Melville Bay, from the fact that it is always crowded with icebergs, and presents in a bird's-eye view all the combined horrors and perils of Arctic navigation, has received the appellation of the "Devil's Nip." Across this formidable indentation the two vessels made their weary way, occupying five weeks in the transit. A steam-tug would have towed them across in forty-eight hours. In the middle of August the vessels entered Lancaster Sound, and, on the morning of the 21st, overhauled the Felix, engaged in the search, under the veteran Sir John Ross. The next day, the Prince Albert, one of Lady Franklin's ships, was seen, and, soon after, the intelligence was received of the discovery of traces of Franklin and his men. The navigators of both nations visited Beechey Island and saw there the evidences which we have already mentioned. The Advance and Rescue now strove in vain to urge their way to Wellington Channel. The sun travelled far to the south, and the brief summer was rapidly coming to a close. The cold increased, and the fires were not yet lighted below. On the 12th of September the Rescue was swept from her moorings by the ice and partially disabled. The pack in which they were enveloped, though not yet beset, was evidently drifting they knew not whither. The commander, convinced that all westward progress was vain for the season, resolved to return homeward. The vessels' heads were turned eastward, and slowly forced a passage through the reluctant ice. On the evening of the 14th of September, Dr. Kane was endeavoring, with the thermometer far below zero, to commit a few words to his journal, when he heard De Haven's voice. "Doctor," he said, "the ice has caught us: we are frozen up."

The Advance was now destined to undergo treatment similar to that suffered by the Terror under Captain Back. For eight mortal months she was carried, cradled in the ice, backwards and forwards in Wellington Channel, wherever the winds and currents listed. At first, before the ice around them had become solid, they were exposed to constant peril from "nips" of floating and besieging floes; but these huge tablets soon became a protection by themselves receiving and warding off subsequent attacks. Early in October, the vessels were more firmly fixed than a jewel in its setting.

They now made preparations for passing the winter. The two crews were collected in the Advance. Until the stoves could be got up, a lard-lamp was burned in the cabin, by which the temperature was raised to 12° above zero. The condensed moisture upon the beams from so many breaths caused them to drip perpetually, till canvas gutters were fitted up, which carried off a gallon of water a day. The three stoves were soon ready, and these, together with the cooking-galley, diffused warmth through the common room formed by knocking the forecastle and cabin into one. Light was furnished by four argand and three bear's-fat lamps. The entire deck of the Advance was covered with a housing of thick felt. On the 9th of November their preparations were fairly completed.

The sun ceased to rise after the 15th of November: after that, the east was as dark at nine in the morning as at midnight; at eleven there was a faint twilight, and at noon a streak of brown far away to the south. The store-room would have furnished an amateur geologist with an admirable cabinet, so totally were the eatables and drinkables changed in appearance by the cold. "Dried apples and peaches assumed the appearance of chalcedony; sour-krout was mica, the laminæ of which were with difficulty separated by a chisel; butter and lard were passable marble; pork and beef were rare specimens of Florentine mosaic; while a barrel of lamp-oil, stripped of the staves, resembled a sandstone garden-roller."

The crews soon began to suffer in health and spirits: their faces became white, like celery kept from the light. They had strange dreams and heard strange sounds. The scurvy appeared, and old wounds bled afresh. Dr. Kane endeavored to combat the disease by acting upon the imagination of the sufferers. He ordered an old tar with a stiff knee to place the member in front of a strong magnet and let it vibrate to and fro like a pendulum. A wonderful and complete cure was thus effected. He practised all sorts of amiable deceptions upon his patients,—making them take medicine in salad and gargles in beer. Not a man was lost during the voyage.

From time to time fissures would open in the ice around them with an explosion like that of heavy artillery. It became necessary to make preparations for abandoning the vessel, and sledges, boats, and provisions were gotten ready for an emergency. The men were drilled to leave the ship in a mass at the word of command. The crisis seemed to be upon them many a time and oft; but the Advance held firmly together, and the ice around her gradually became solid as granite again. Dr. Kane lectured at intervals on scientific subjects, till the return of light brought with it a return of hope and animal spirits. On the 29th of January, 1851, the sun rose above the horizon, after an absence of eighty-six days. "Never," says Dr. Kane, "till the grave-clod or the ice covers me may I forego this blessing of blessings again! I looked at him thankfully, with a great globus in my throat."

The ice-pack did not open till the close of March. Previous to this, all the successive symptoms of the coming thaw presented themselves. The ice began to smoke, and the surface became first moist and then soft. It was soon too warm to skate, and the cabin-lamps, that had burned for four months without cessation, were extinguished. The mercury rose to 32°; the housings were removed from the Advance, and the Rescue's men returned to their deserted ship. The saw was put in motion early in May; but the grand disruption of the ice, which was either to free the ships or crush them, did not occur till the 5th of June. It was five o'clock in the afternoon when the first crack was heard, and the water, spirting up, was seen following the track of the fissure. In half an hour the ice was seamed with cracks in every direction, some of them spreading into rivers twenty feet across. The Rescue was released at once: the coating of the Advance held on for three days more, parting at last under the weight of a single man. The liberated ships soon made the Greenland coast, at Godhavn, where they spent five days in reposing, in celebrating the Fourth of July, and in splicing the main-brace,—this latter being a convivial, and not a mechanical, operation. The vessels arrived safely at the Brooklyn Navy-Yard on the 1st of October, 1851. The vessels were restored to Mr. Grinnell, with the stipulation that the Secretary of the Navy might claim them, in case of need, for further search in the spring.

CHAPTER LI.

KENNEDY'S EXPEDITION—SIR EDWARD BELCHER—McCLURE—DISCOVERY OF THE NORTHWEST PASSAGE—JUNCTION OF McCLURE AND KELLETT—EPISODE OF THE RESOLUTE—COMMODORE PERRY'S EXPEDITION—DECISIVE TRACES OF THE FATE OF SIR JOHN FRANKLIN—THE LEVIATHAN.

ENCOURAGED by the discovery of traces of her husband, Lady Franklin caused the Prince Albert, upon her return with the intelligence, to be at once refitted for another Arctic voyage. The expedition, though conducted with consummate skill by William Kennedy, late of the Hudson's Bay Company, and Lieutenant Bellot, of the French Navy, his second, totally failed of success. It returned in October, 1853. In the mean time, another and more imposing expedition—that under Sir Edward Belcher—had sailed for the Polar regions. The squadron consisted of five vessels,—the Assistance, with the steamer Pioneer, the Resolute, with the steamer Intrepid, and the North Star storeship. They sailed on the 28th of April, 1852, and arrived at their head-quarters at Beechey Island—the scene of Franklin's hibernation in 1846—on the 10th of August. The North Star remained here with the stores, while the two ships, with their respective tugs, started upon distinct voyages of exploration,—Sir Edward Belcher, in the Assistance, standing up Wellington Channel, and Captain Kellett, in the Resolute, proceeding to Melville Island. The latter was instructed to seek at this point for intelligence of Captains McClure and Collinson, who had been sent to Behring's Strait in 1850, in order to force their way eastward from thence, and who had not since been heard of. As the interest of Sir Edward Belcher's expedition centres entirely in the junction effected by Kellett with McClure, we revert to the adventures of the latter explorer, now distinguished as the discoverer of the Northwest Passage.

Collinson and McClure sailed in the Enterprise and Investigator for Behring's Strait *viâ* Cape Horn on the 20th of January, 1850. They arrived at the strait in July. The Enterprise, being foiled in her efforts to get through the ice, turned about and wintered at Hong-Kong. McClure, in the Investigator, kept gallantly on through the strait, and, during the month of August, advanced to the southeast, into the heart of the Polar Sea, along a coast never yet visited by a ship, and on the 21st of August arrived at the mouth of Mackenzie River, discovered by Mackenzie in his land-expedition in 1789 to determine the northern coast-line of America. He had now passed the region visited and surveyed in former years by Franklin, Back, Rae, and others, in overland explorations, and on the 6th of September arrived at a point considerably to the east of any land marked upon the charts. He now began to name the islands, headlands, and indentations. On the 9th, the ship was found to be but sixty miles to the west of the spot to which Parry, sailing westward, had carried his ship in 1820. Could he but sail these sixty miles his name would be immortal. "I cannot," he writes, "describe my anxious feelings. Can it be possible that this water communicates with Barrow's Straits and shall prove to be the long-sought Northwest Passage? Can it be that so humble a creature as I am will be permitted to perform what has baffled the talented and wise for hundreds of years?" On the 17th, the Investigator reached the longitude of 117° 10′ west,—thirty miles from the waters in which Parry wintered with the Hecla and Griper in a harbor of Melville Island. Alas! the vessel went no farther east: the ice drifted perceptibly to the west, and it was fated that these thirty miles should remain, as they had remained for ages, as impassable to ships as the Isthmus of Suez.

The Investigator passed the winter heeled four degrees to port and elevated a foot out of water by a "nip," in which position she rested quietly for months. Late in October, a sledge-party of six men, headed by McClure, started to traverse on foot the distance which it was forbidden their ship to cross. On the 25th, they saw the Polar Ocean ice. The next morning, before daybreak, they ascended a hill six hundred feet high, convinced that the dawn would reveal them the previous surveys of Sir Edward, and make them the discoverers of the Northwest Passage, by connecting their voyage from the west with his from the east. The return of day showed their anticipations to be correct: Melville Strait was visible to the north, and between it and them, though there was plenty of ice, there was no intervening land. They had discovered the Passage,—that is, an ice-passage, which of course involved a water-passage when the state of the atmosphere permitted it. Though they regretted bitterly that they could not get their ship through, their only remaining course was to send one of their party home by the well-known route through Barrow's Straits, and thus prove the existence of the passage by the return of one who had made it. They erected a cairn and left a record of their visit, and then commenced their homeward journey to the ship. McClure became separated from his companions, and nearly perished in the snow. He arrived in safety, however, and the grand discovery was duly celebrated and the main-brace properly spliced. Numerous searching-parties were now from time to time sent out, and in the middle of July the ice broke up and the Investigator was released. She drifted five miles more to the east,—thus reducing the distance of separation to twenty-five miles. Here she was again firmly and inextricably frozen in. Another and another winter passed; and it was not till the spring of 1853 that relief reached them. In order to make a consecutive story, we must return to that portion of Sir Edward Belcher's squadron which, under Captain Kellett, was sent to Melville Island, and which arrived there late in 1852. At this period, Kellett, in the Resolute, and McClure, in the Investigator, were about one hundred and seventy miles apart.

A sledge-party sent out by Kellett discovered, with the wildest delight, in October, 1852, a cairn in which McClure had deposited, the April previous, a chart of his discoveries. They were compelled to wait the winter through; and it was not till the 10th of March that Kellett ventured to send a travelling-party in quest of the Investigator. The communication was effected on the 6th of April, 1853. McClure thus describes it:

"While walking near the ship, in conversation with the first lieutenant, we perceived a figure coming rapidly towards us from the rough ice at the entrance of the bay. He was certainly unlike any of our men; but, recollecting that it was possible some one might be trying a new travelling-dress preparatory to the departure of our sledges, and certain that no one else was near, we continued to advance. The stranger came quietly on: had the skies fallen upon us we could hardly have been more astonished than when he called out, 'I'm Lieutenant Pim, late of the Herald, now of the Resolute. Captain Kellett is in her, at Dealy Island.'

"To rush at and seize him by the hand was the first impulse; for the heart was too full for the tongue to speak. The news flew with lightning rapidity: the ship was all in commotion; the sick, forgetful of their maladies, leaped from their hammocks; the artificers dropped their tools, and the lower deck was cleared of men; for they all rushed for the hatchway, to be assured that a stranger was actually among them and that his tale was true. Despondency fled the ship, and Lieutenant Pim received a welcome—pure, hearty, and grateful—that he will surely remember and cherish to the end of his days."

It was now decided to abandon the Investigator, immovably fixed as she was in the ice. Her colors were hoisted on the 3d of June, and she was left alone in Mercy Bay. The officers and crew arrived on board the Resolute on the 17th. McClure sent Lieutenant Gurney Cresswell, with despatches for the Admiralty, by sledges, down to Beechey Island, where he found a Government vessel and at once sailed for England. Though he had not made the Northwest Passage, he had at least crossed the American continent within the Arctic Circle; and this had yet been done by no mortal man.

Kellett and McClure remained for many months in the Resolute and Intrepid, beset in the ice. They received instructions from Belcher, in April, 1854, to abandon their ships. The latter were placed in a condition to be occupied by any Arctic searching-party,—the furnaces of the steamer being left ready to be lighted. Sir Edward Belcher had also been compelled to abandon his vessels, the Assistance and Pioneer: the four crews met at Beechey Island, and embarked on board their storeship, the North Star, which had been laid up for two years. They arrived in England late in September. The reader will at once recognise the Resolute as the ship which was found in Baffin's Bay, in 1855, by Captain Buddington, of the New London whaler George Henry. She had forced her way, unaided by man, through twelve hundred miles of Arctic ice. The incidents of her arrival at New London, of the abandonment to the American sailors of all claim upon her by the British Government, of her purchase by the United States Congress from her new owners, her re-equipment at the Brooklyn Navy-Yard, and her restoration to the English Navy by Captain Hartstene, U.S.N., are still fresh in the minds of all.

In the year 1853, an expedition sent by the United States under Commodore Perry ventured into waters never before ploughed by vessels of a Christian nation. On the 8th of

July, the precipitous southern coast of Niphon — the largest island of the Japanese group — loomed up through the fog.

JAPANESE VESSEL.

The American steamers entered the Bay of Jeddo, eight miles wide at the mouth but spreading to a width of twelve beyond. They were now land-bound, with the shores of an empire almost fabulous enclosing them on every side. Though peremptorily forbidden to anchor, though surrounded by myriads of boats filled with men eager for a conflict, though menaced by forts which seemed formidable till examined through the glass, the fleet kept on, and finally, by dint of persistence and several salutary displays of power, the commodore, having at his disposal the national steamers Susquehanna, Mississippi, and Powhatan, the frigate Saratoga, and the ships Macedonian, Vandalia, Lexington, and Southampton, wrung from the sullen monopolists a treaty opening to American trade the port of Simoda, in Niphon, and that of Hakodadi, in Jesso. It now remains for the Americans to lead the Japanese, by

THE LEVIATHAN.

judicious and honorable treatment, to experience and acknowledge the benefits of commerce and intercourse with the nations of Christendom.

To return once more to the Arctic researches. Soon after the return of Belcher and McClure to England, decisive intelligence of Franklin and his party was received in England. Dr. Rae, who had been engaged for a year past in a search by land, had met a party of Esquimaux who were in possession of numerous articles which had belonged to Franklin and his men. They stated that in the spring of 1850 they had seen forty white men, near King William's Land, dragging a boat and sledges over the ice. They were thin and short of provisions: their officer was a tall, stout, middle-aged man. Some months later the natives found the corpses of thirty persons upon the mainland, and five dead bodies upon a neighboring island. They described the bodies as mutilated; whence Dr. Rae inferred that the party had been driven to the horrible resource of cannibalism. The presence of the bones and feathers of geese, however, showed that some had survived till the arrival of wild-fowl, about the end of May. Dr. Rae purchased such articles of the natives as would best serve to identify their late possessors. All furnished decisive testimony; but a round silver plate gave peculiarly strong evidence, bearing as it did the following inscription:—"Sir John Franklin, K.C.B." The slight clue thus yielded of his fate was the last which has thus far been obtained; and it will doubtless be the only one till the Arctic seas give up their dead. The expedition of Dr. Kane had, however, already sailed from New York.

It was while these events were transpiring that the keel of the mammoth steam-vessel—known at first as the Great Eastern, and afterwards as the Leviathan—was laid, at Milwall, on the Thames. We refer the reader to the engraving on the opposite page for a view of this "village adrift."

CAPE ALEXANDER: THE ARCTIC GIBRALTAR.

CHAPTER LII.

THE SECOND GRINNELL EXPEDITION—THE ADVANCE IN WINTER QUARTERS—TOTAL DARKNESS — SLEDGE-PARTIES — ADVENTURES — THE FIRST DEATH — TENNYSON'S MONUMENT—HUMBOLDT GLACIER—THE OPEN POLAR SEA—SECOND WINTER — ABANDONMENT OF THE BRIG — THE WATER AGAIN — UPERNAVIK—RESCUE BY CAPTAIN HARTSTENE — DEATH AND SERVICES OF DR. KANE—ATTEMPT TO LAY THE ATLANTIC CABLE—CONCLUSION.

THE Government of the United States forwarded to Dr. Kane, in the month of December, 1852, an order "to conduct an expedition to the Arctic Seas in search of Sir John Franklin." The brig Advance was again placed at his disposal by Mr. Grinnell, and manned by eighteen picked men. Dr. Kane's plan was to enter Smith's Sound at the top of Baffin's Bay,—into which, alone of the Arctic explorers, Captain Inglefield had penetrated in August, 1852, in the Isabel,—to reach, if possible, the supposed northerly open sea, where he hoped to find traces of the missing navigators. He sailed from New York on the 30th of May, 1853, touched at Fiskernaes, in Greenland, on the 1st of July, where he engaged the services of Hans Cristian, a native Esquimaux of nineteen years. Through ice and fog the vessel forced her way, and on the 7th of August doubled Cape Alexander, a promontory opposite another named Cape Isabella,—the two being the headlands of Smith's Strait, and styled by Dr. Kane the Arctic Pillars of Hercules.

The vessel closed with the ice again the next day, and was forced into a landlocked cove. Every effort to force her through the floes was tried, without success, and, after undergoing the most appalling treatment from the wind, waves, and ice combined, the brig was warped into winter quarters, in Rensselaer Bay, on the 22d of August, and was frozen in on September 10. There she lies to this hour,—"to her a long resting-place indeed," writes Kane; "for the same ice is around her still." This was in latitude 78° 37′ N.,—the most northerly winter quarters ever taken by Christians, except in Spitzbergen, which has the advantage of an insular climate. An observatory was erected, a thermal register kept hourly, and magnetic observations recorded. Parties were sent out to establish provision-depôts to the north, to facilitate researches in the spring. Three depôts or "caches" were made, the most distant being in latitude 79° 12′: in this they deposited six hundred and seventy pounds of pemmican and forty of meat-biscuit. These operations were arrested by darkness in November, and the crew prepared to spend one hundred and forty days without the light of the sun. The first number of the Arctic newspaper, "The Ice-Blink," appeared on the 21st. The thermometer fell to 67° below zero. Chloroform froze, and chloric ether became solid. The air had a perceptible pungency upon inspiration: all inhaled it guardedly and with compressed lips. The 22d of December brought with it the midnight of the year: the fingers could not be counted a foot from the eyes. Nothing remained to indicate that the Arctic world had a sun. The men during this their first winter kept up their spirits wonderfully; but most of the dogs died of diseases of the brain brought on by the depressing influences of the darkness.

The first traces of returning light were observed on the 21st of January, when the southern horizon had a distinct orange tint. Towards the close of February the sun silvered the tall icebergs between the headlands of the bay: his rays reached the deck on the 28th, and perpetual day returned with the month of March. The men found their faces badly mottled by scurvy-spots, and they were nearly all disabled for active work. But

"CHAOS."

six dogs remained out of forty-four. "No language can describe," says Kane, "the chaos at the base of the rock on which the storehouse had been built. Fragments of ice had been tossed into every possible confusion, rearing up in fantastic equilibrium, surging in long inclined planes, dipping into dark valleys, and piling in contorted hills." A sledge-party was sent out on the 19th to deposit a relief cargo of provisions; on the 31st, three of its members returned, swollen, haggard, and almost dumb. They had left four of their number in a tent, disabled and frozen. Dr. Kane at once started with a rescue of nine men, and, after an unbroken march of twenty-one hours, came in sight of a small American flag floating upon a hummock. They were received with an explosion of welcome. The return with the sledge laden with the weight of eleven hundred pounds was effected at the expense of tremendous efforts of energy and endurance.

While still nine miles from their half-way tent, they felt the peculiar lethargic sensation of extreme cold,—symptoms which Kane compares to the diffused paralysis of the electro-galvanic shock. Bonsall and Morton asked permission to go to sleep, at the same time denying that they were cold. Hans lay down under a drift, and in a few moments was stiff. An immediate halt was necessary. The tent was pitched, but no one had the strength to light a fire. They could neither eat nor drink. The whiskey froze at the men's feet. Kane gave orders to them to take four hours' rest and then follow him to the half-way tent, where he would have ready a fire and some thawed pemmican. He then pushed on with William Godfrey. They were both in a state of stupor, and kept themselves awake by a continued articulation of incoherent words. Kane describes these hours as the most wretched he ever went through. On arriving at the tent, they found that a bear had overturned it, tossing the pemmican into the snow. They crawled into their reindeer sleeping-bags and slept for three hours in a dreamy but intense slumber. On awaking, they melted snow-water and cooked some soup; and on the arrival of the rest of the party they all took the refreshment and pushed on towards the brig. Their strength soon failed them again, and they began to lose their self-control. Kane tried the experiment of a three minutes' sleep, and, finding that it refreshed him, timed the men in their turns. Doses of brandy, and, finally, the distant sight of the brig, revived and encouraged them. The last mile was accomplished by instinct, as none of the men remembered it afterwards: they staggered into the cabin delirious and muttering with agony.

Death now entered the devoted camp: Jefferson Baker died of lockjaw on the 7th of April. A meeting with a party of Esquimaux now enabled Kane to reinforce his dog-team, and

WILD DOG TEAM.

encouraged him to start, late in April, upon his grand sledge-excursion to the north. It failed, however, completely. Kane became delirious on the 5th of May, and fainted every time he was taken from the tent to the sledge. He was conveyed back to the brig, and from the 14th to the 20th lay hovering between life and death. Short as the expedition was, however, several remarkable discoveries were made. "Tennyson's Monument" was the name given to a solitary column of greenstone, four hundred and eighty feet high, rising from a pedestal two hundred and eighty feet high,—both as sharply finished as if they had been cast for the Place Vendôme. But the most wonderful feature was the Great Glacier of Humboldt,—an ice-ocean of boundless dimensions, in which a complete substitution had been effected of ice for water. "Imagine," Kane writes, "the centre of the continent of Greenland occupied through nearly its whole extent by a deep unbroken sea of ice that gathers perennial increase from the water-shed of vast snow-covered mountains and all the precipitations of the atmosphere upon its own surface. Imagine this moving onward like a great glacial river, seeking outlets at every fiord and valley, rolling icy cataracts into the Atlantic and Greenland seas, and, having at last reached the northern limit of the land that has borne it up, pouring out a mighty frozen torrent into unknown Arctic space. . . . Here was a plastic, moving, semi-solid mass, obliterating life, swallowing rocks and islands, and ploughing its way with irresistible march through the crust of an investing sea."

Other sledge-parties were from time to time sent out. One of six men left the brig on the 3d of June, keeping to the north and reaching Humboldt Glacier on the 15th. Four returned to the ship on the 27th, one of them entirely blind. Hans Christian and William Morton kept on, and finally, in north latitude 81° 22′, sighted open water,—an open Polar sea. To the cape at which the land terminated Morton gave the name of Cape Constitution. A lofty peak on the opposite side of the channel, but a little farther to the north, and the most remote northern land known upon our globe, was named Mount Edward Parry, from the great pioneer of Arctic travel.

A second winter now stared the explorers in the face. "It is horrible," says Kane, "to look forward to another year of disease and darkness, without fresh food or fuel." Still, preparations were made for the direful extremity. Willow-stems and sorrel were collected as antiscorbutics. Lumps of turf, frozen solid, were quarried with crowbars, and with them the ship's sides were embanked. During the early months a communication was kept up with the nearest Esquimaux station, seventy-five miles distant, and thus scanty supplies of fox, walrus, seal, and bear meat were occasionally obtained. These failed, however, during the months of total darkness. Early in February, Kane wrote in his journal:—"We are contending at odds with angry forces close around us, without one agent or influence within eighteen hundred miles whose sympathy is on our side." On the 4th of March, the last fragment of fresh meat was served, and the whole crew would have perished miserably of starvation, had it not been for the successful issue of a forlorn-hope excursion to the Etah Esquimaux station undertaken by Hans and two dogs. Dr. Kane ate rats, and thereby escaped the scurvy. The bunks were warmed by oil-lamps, after the Esquimaux fashion: the beds and the men's faces became in consequence black and greasy with soot. The sufferings endured by the party were perhaps the most dreadful to which Arctic adventurers have ever been subjected.

The abandonment of the brig had been resolved upon before the setting in of winter, and the misery of the hours of darkness had been in some measure alleviated by the progress of the preparations for that event,—in making clothing, canvas moccasins, seal-hide boots, and in cutting water-tight shoes from the gutta-percha speaking-tube. Provision-bags were made of sail-cloth rendered impervious by coats of tar. Into these the bread was pressed by beating it to powder with a capstan-bar. Pork-fat and tallow were melted down and poured into other bags to freeze. The three boats—none of them sea-worthy—

were strengthened, housed, and mounted on sledges rigged with shoulder-belts to drag by: one of them they expected to burn for fuel on reaching water. The powder and shot, upon which their lives depended, were distributed in canisters: Kane took the percussion-caps into his own possession, as more precious than gold. The 17th of May was fixed upon for the departure.

The farewell to the brig was made with due solemnity. The day was Sunday, and prayers and a chapter of the Bible were read. Kane then stated in an address the necessities under which the ship was abandoned and the dangers that still awaited them. He believed, however, that the thirteen hundred miles of ice and water which lay between them and North Greenland could be traversed with safety for most and hope for all. A brief memorial of the reasons compelling the desertion of the vessel was fastened to a stanchion near the gangway, to serve as their vindication in case they were lost and the brig was ever visited. The flags were hoisted and hauled down again, and the men scrambled off over the ice to the boats, no one thinking of the mockery of cheers.

We have not space to detail the perils, adventures, and narrow escapes from starvation of this hardy party in their romantically dangerous escape to the south. On the 16th of June, the boats and sledges approached the open water. "We see its deep-indigo horizon," writes Kane, "and hear its roar against the icy beach. Its scent is in our nostrils and our hearts." The boats, which were split with frost and warped by sunshine, had to be calked and swelled before they were fit for use. The embarkation was effected on the 19th: the Red Eric, the smallest of the three boats, swamped the first day. They spent their first night in an inlet in the ice. Sometimes they would sail through creeks of water for many successive hours: then would follow days of weary tracking through alternate ice and water. During a violent storm, they dragged the boats upon a narrow shelf of ice, and found themselves within a cave which myriads of eider had made their breeding-ground. They remained three days in this crystal retreat, and gathered three thousand eggs. They doubled Cape Dudley Digges on the 11th of June, and spent a week at Providence Halt, luxuriating on a dish composed of birds sweeter and juicier than canvas-backs and a salad made of raw eggs and cochlearia. The coast now trended to the east; the wide expanse of Melville Bay lay between them and Upernavik,—that Danish outpost of civilization. The party was at one moment in the actual agonies of starvation, when a lucky shot at a sleeping seal saved them from the dreaded extremity. They soon saw a kayak—a native boat—in which one Paul Zacharias was seeking eider-down

among the islands. Not long after, the single mast of a small shallop—the Upernavik oil-boat—loomed up through the fog. They landed the next day in the midst of a crowd of children, and drank coffee that night before hospitable Danish firesides.

THE TELEGRAPHIC FLEET.

A Danish vessel—the Mariane—was to return to Denmark on the 4th of September, and at that date Kane and his party embarked on board of her, the captain engaging to drop them at the Shetland Islands. On the 11th they arrived at Godhavn, and there, at the very moment of their final departure, Captain Hartstene's relief-squadron was sighted in the offing. With the rescue of the adventurers closes our record of Arctic peril and discovery.

Dr. Kane fell a victim to his zeal in the arduous paths of science. He died, on the 16th of February, 1857, at Havana, where he was seeking to recuperate his debilitated system beneath a tropical sun. His loss was sincerely lamented by the whole country. No commander was ever better fitted by nature for the task confided to him; and no historian ever chronicled the results of his own labors in language more enthralling or in a style more commanding and picturesque.*

In the summer of 1857, an attempt to unite the two hemispheres by means of a submerged electric cable was made under the auspices of the New York, Newfoundland, and London Telegraph Company, assisted by vessels furnished by the Governments of Great Britain and the United States. Of this undertaking—unsuccessful as it was, and fresh as it is in the minds of all—our account will properly be brief. The idea was first conceived in the year 1853, in America, and was earnestly pursued in defiance of all obstacles,—Cyrus H. Field, Esq., Vice-President of the Company, being one of its most zealous and indefatigable champions. Surveys and deep-sea explorations, made by Captain Berryman, U.S.N., in the Dolphin and Arctic, in 1853 and 1856, resulted in the discovery of a submarine ledge or prairie, at a depth varying from two to two and a half miles, extending

* We have to acknowledge our indebtedness to Messrs. Childs & Peterson, the publishers of Dr. Kane's narrative, for the use of the spirited engravings which thus far illustrate this chapter.

HAULING THE CABLE ASHORE.

from Cape Race, in Newfoundland, to Cape Clear, in Ireland. This tract received the name of the Telegraphic Plateau. Lieutenant Maury, of the National Observatory, inferred, from observations made in the Atlantic during a long series of years, that both sea and air would be in the most favorable condition for laying the wire between the 20th of July and the 10th of August. The telegraphic fleet consisted of the U.S. steam-frigate Niagara, Captain Hudson, to lay the first half of the cable from Valentia Bay, in Ireland, of H.B.M. steamer Agamemnon, to lay the second half of the cable, and of six other auxiliary steamers of both nations.

The Niagara commenced shipping the cable from the factory at Birkenhead, near Liverpool, late in June, and completed the work in somewhat less than a month. The share of each of the two vessels was twelve hundred and fifty miles of wire,—the wire itself being an elaborate combination of fine copper strands and gutta-percha coatings. The whole fleet was assembled in Valentia Bay on the 4th of August. The Lord-Lieutenant of

LANDING THE CABLE.

Ireland was already upon the ground, the guest of the Knight of Kerry. The next evening, the shore-end of the cable was hauled from the stern of the Niagara to shallow water by an attendant tug named the Willing Mind, and from thence taken ashore, in the midst of the cheers of the spectators, by a boat's crew of American sailors. The expedition set sail on Thursday, the 6th. It was understood that the first message was to be the following, from Queen Victoria to President Buchanan:— "Glory be to God on high, and on earth peace and good-will towards men."

All went on favorably for several days: a constant communication was kept up between the Niagara and the shore. At four o'clock on the following Tuesday, the signals suddenly ceased. The return of the squadron confirmed the fears entertained: the cable had broken in deep water. Three hundred and thirty-five nautical miles had been laid, and the last half of it in water over two miles in depth. The Niagara was making at the time four miles an hour, and the cable running out at a greater speed,—from five to six miles an hour. This was more than could be afforded, and the retard strain upon the brakes was increased to three thousand pounds. The cable bore the augmented pressure for a time, but finally parted, to the dismay of the whole fleet. The vessels returned to England; and the enterprise was abandoned for another year. Though thus postponed, little or no doubt existed upon its ultimate success. The exhilarating triumph which eventually attended the efforts of the Company will form the subject of the next chapter.

THE CABLE IN THE BED OF THE OCEAN.

CHAPTER LIII.

SECOND AND THIRD ATTEMPTS TO LAY THE ATLANTIC CABLE—THE FAILURE IN THE MONTH OF JUNE—DESCRIPTION OF THE CABLE—THE VOYAGE OF THE NIAGARA—THE CONTINUITY—ALL RIGHT AGAIN—CHANGE FROM ONE COIL TO ANOTHER—THE KNIGHTS OF THE BLACK HAND—UNFAVORABLE SYMPTOMS—THE INSULATION BROKEN—THE THIRD OF AUGUST—AN ANXIOUS MOMENT—LAND DISCOVERED—TRINITY BAY—MR. FIELD VISITS THE TELEGRAPH STATION—THE OPERATORS TAKEN BY SURPRISE—LANDING OF THE CABLE—IMPRESSIVE CEREMONY—CAPTAIN HUDSON RETURNS THANKS TO HEAVEN—THE VOYAGE OF THE AGAMEMNON—THE QUEEN'S MESSAGE—THE SIXTEENTH OF AUGUST—DEEP-SEA TELEGRAPHING—THE EQUATOR AND THE CABLE—CONCLUSION.

THE Atlantic Telegraph Company, undeterred by their failure to lay the cable in 1857, resolved to make another attempt in the summer of the following year, the American and English Governments again placing the Niagara and the Agamemnon at their disposal. It was decided, however, in order to lessen the chances of unfavorable weather, that the two vessels should proceed to mid-ocean, should there splice their respective ends of the wire, and that the Agamemnon should then steam to Valentia Harbor and the Niagara to Trinity Bay. They were each furnished with an ingenious contrivance for paying out the cable,—the invention of Mr. Everett, of the United States Navy. June was the month selected, and the ships departed upon their errand. They were absent much longer than was expected, in the event of a successful accomplishment of their purpose. When they returned to Queenstown, it was to tell of storm, disaster, and failure. Still undaunted, the Company again despatched the ships. The Niagara and Agamemnon met in mid-ocean on the 28th of July: the splice was effected, and the task began. The Niagara had eight hundred and eighty-two miles to sail, and eleven hundred miles of cable; the Agamemnon, with the same quantity of cable, had but eight hundred and thirteen miles to sail. The Niagara had three hundred tons of coal, the Agamemnon five hundred. At one o'clock the wire began to reel over the stern of the Niagara, westward and homeward bound.

The following engraving will give a correct idea of the manner in which the cable is formed. The core, or conductor, is composed of seven copper wires wound tightly together.

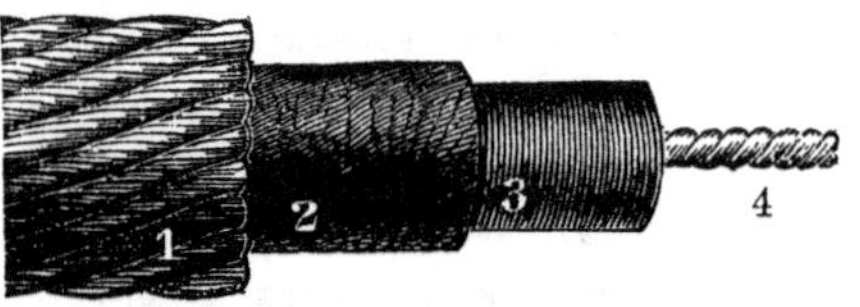

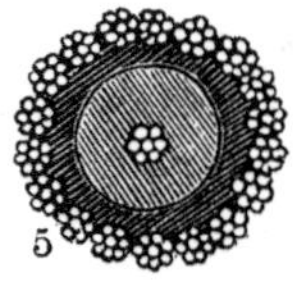

1. Wire—eighteen strands, seven to an inch.
2. Six strands of yarn.
3. Gutta percha, three coats.
4. Conducting wires, seven in number.
5. Section of the cable, eleven-sixteenths of an inch in diameter.

The flexibility of this cable is so great that it may be tied in a knot round the arm without injury. Its weight is eighteen hundred and sixty pounds to the mile, and its strength such that six miles of it may be suspended vertically in water of that depth without breaking.

"The sea is smooth,"—we quote the extremely interesting journal of an eye-witness*, writing upon the first day,—"the barometer well up; and, if we can only do for the next seven days as well as we have done since one o'clock, we shall be at Newfoundland by the 5th of August, and in New York some time between the 15th and 20th of the same month. But we have been somewhat too hasty in our calculations, for our ship has just slowed down, and the propeller has ceased working for the last ten minutes. There must be something wrong to cause this interruption. Let us take a look at the machine. The cable still goes out, which certainly would not be the case if it had parted. Ah! the continuity! That's it: there's where the difficulty lies; and, as the electricians are the only parties who can inform us on that point, we at once go in search of them. A visit to their office explains the whole matter. The continuity is not gone altogether, but is defective,—so defective that it is impossible to get a signal through the cable. Still, there is not 'dead earth' upon it, and all hope, therefore, is not lost. When dead earth, as it is termed, is on the conductor, then, indeed, the difficulty is beyond remedy; for it shows that the conductor must be broken and is thrown under the influence of terrestrial magnetism. But the continuity is not gone; and, although with darkening prospects, we are still safe while it remains, imperfect as it is. It would be absurd to say that the occurrence was not discouraging: it was painfully so; for the hopes of some of us had really begun to revive, and we were gaining confidence every hour. Now nothing could be done. We must wait until the continuity should return or take its final departure. And it did return, and with greater strength than ever. At ten minutes past nine P.M., the electrician on duty observed its failing, and at half-past eleven he had the

* Mr. John Mullaly.

gratifying intelligence for us that it was 'all right again.' The machinery was once more set in motion, the cable was soon going out at the rate of six miles an hour, and the electrical signals were passing between the ships as regularly as if nothing had occurred to interfere with or interrupt the continuity."

The change of the wire from the forward main-deck coil to that on the deck immediately below, on the third day, is thus described, the operation being a most delicate and perilous one:—"At least an hour before the change was made, the outer boundaries of the circle in which the cable lay was literally crowded with men; and never was greater interest manifested in any spectacle than that which they exhibited in the proceedings before them. There were serious doubts and misgivings as to the successful performance of this important part of the work; and these only served to increase the feeling of anxiety and suspense with which they silently and breathlessly await the critical moment. The last flake has been reached, and as turn after turn leaves the circle every eye is intently fixed on the cable. Now there are but thirty turns remaining; and, as the first of these is unwound, Mr. Everett, who has been in the circle during the last half-hour, gives the order to the engineer on duty to 'slow down.' In a few moments there is a perceptible diminution in the speed, which continues diminishing till it has reached the rate of about two miles an hour.

"'Look out now, men,' says Mr. Everett, in his usual quiet, self-possessed way. The men are as thoroughly wide-awake as they can be, and are waiting eagerly for the moment when they shall lift the bight, or bend, of the cable and deliver it out safely. One of the planks in the side of the cone has been loosened, and, just as they are about taking the cable in their hands, it is removed altogether; so that, as the last yard passes out of the now empty circle, the line commences paying out from the circle below, or the 'orlop' deck, as it is called. The men—who are no other than the coilers, or 'Knights of the Black

Hand,' as they have not inappropriately been termed—have done their work well; and the applause with which they have been greeted by the crowd of admiring spectators is the most gratifying testimony they can receive of the fact. They have hardly passed the cable out of the circle before they are received with as enthusiastic a demonstration of approval as the rules of the navy will permit.

"Confidence is growing stronger,"—this is the fourth day,—"and there is considerable speculation as to the time we shall reach Newfoundland. The pilot who is to bring us into Trinity Bay is now in great repute, and is becoming a more important personage every day. We are really beginning to have strong hopes that his services will be called into requisition and that in the course of a few days more we will be in sight of land. But the sea is not at all so smooth as it was the day before: it is, in fact, so rough as to favor the belief that there must have been a severe gale a short time since in these latitudes. The condition of the vessel is such as to alarm us greatly for the safety of the cable should it come on to blow very hard, as the large amount already paid out and the quantity of coal consumed have lightened her so much as to render her rather uneasy in a heavy sea. The wind is increasing, and, although it has not yet attained the magnitude of a gale, it is blowing rather fresh for us in the present unsettled state of our minds. Both wind and sea are nearly abeam; and the rolling motion which the latter creates brings a strain upon the cable which gives rise to the most unpleasant feelings. The sea, too, seems to be getting worse every minute, and strikes the slender wire with all its force. Every surge of the ship affects it; and as it cuts through each wave it makes a small white line of foam to mark its track. The sight of that thread-like wire battling with the sea produces a feeling somewhat akin to that with which you would watch the struggles of a drowning man whom you have not the power of assisting.

You can only look on and trust either that the sea will go down or that the cable may be able to resist the force of the waves successfully. Of the former there is very little prospect, but of the latter there is every reason for hope. The contest has been going on now for several hours, and there is no more sign of the cable parting than when it commenced. The electricians report the continuity perfect; and the signals which are received at intervals from the Agamemnon show that that vessel is getting along with her part of the work in admirable style. What more can we desire?"

An incident occurring upon the fifth day is thus described:—

"I have said that, despite the bad weather and heavy sea, the paying-out process was going on well; but during the night the continuity was again affected; and although it was restored and became as strong as ever, yet it was for about three hours a very unpleasant affair. It was subsequently found that the difficulty was caused by a defect of insulation in a part of the wardroom coil, which was cut out in time to prevent any serious consequences. There were only a few on board the ship, however, aware of the occurrence until after the defect was removed and the electrical communication was re-established between the two ships. Both Mr. Laws and Mr. De Santy—the two electricians on the Niagara—were of the opinion that the insulation was broken in some part of the wardroom coil; and, on using the tests for the purpose of ascertaining the precise point, they found that it was about sixty miles from the bottom of that coil, and between three or four hundred from the part which was then paying out. The cable was immediately cut at this point and spliced to a deck coil of ninety miles, which it was intended to reserve for laying in shallow water and was therefore kept for Trinity Bay. About four o'clock in the morning the continuity was finally restored, and all was going on as well as if nothing had occurred to disturb the confidence we felt in the success of the expedition."

Upon the sixth day—the 3d of August, the anniversary of the day upon which Columbus sailed from Palos—the great work took place of the change from "the fore-hold coil to that in the wardroom, which are at least two hundred feet apart. This occurred at eight o'clock in the morning; and, as the time was known to all on board, there was even a larger crowd assembled to witness it than I observed at any of the other changes. It was considered a most critical time; and, although the operation turned out to be very simple, it was anticipated by some with considerable uneasiness. The splice between the two coils had been made some hours in advance, and men were stationed all along the line of its course from the hold to the wardroom. Mr. Everett and Mr. Woodhouse were both on hand; the best men had been picked out to pass up the bight, when the last turn should be reached; and one man, named Henry Paine, a splicer, was specially appointed to walk forward with the bight to the after or wardroom coil. As the last flake was about to be paid out the ship was slowed down, and by the time the last three or four turns came to be paid out she could hardly be said to be moving through the water. The line came up more slowly from the hold, until we were nearing the bight, where it could not have been going out faster than half a mile an hour. One more turn and the bight comes up. There is not a sound to be heard from the crowd who are watching it with eager and anxious faces from every point of view. No one speaks, or has ventured to speak for the last minute, except the engineers, and they have very little to say, for their orders are conveyed in the most laconic style; and the quick 'ay, ay!' of the men show that they understand the full value of time. 'Now, men,' says Mr. Everett, 'look out for the bight,' as those in the hold hand it up to the men on the orlop deck, and it is passed from hand to hand till it reaches the platform and long passage which has been built upon the spar-deck for this part of the work. Here the bight arrives at last, and Paine takes it in his hand, paying out as he follows the line of the cable to the wardroom coil. How anxiously the men watch him as he walks that terrible distance of two hundred feet, and think that if he should happen to trip or stumble while he holds that bight in his hand the great enterprise may end in disaster! It is not a difficult task; but how often have things that are so easily performed been defeated by want of coolness! There is, however, such an easy self-possession about the man, as he comes slowly aft with the long black line, that inspires confidence. All hands have deserted the decks below, and follow him as he walks aft, and one, in his impatience to get a glimpse of him, has nearly fallen through the skylight of the engine-room, in which he has smashed several panes of glass in the effort to save himself. 'Pick up the pieces,' says Paine, in a vein of quiet humor, as he proceeds on his course without interruption, and, coming up to the wheel, which is immediately above the wardroom, he straightens the bight, and the cable begins to run out from the top of the coil on the deck beneath. His work is done; and, as the line passes out of his hands, he receives a round of applause from the hands of the spectators, who, but for those terrible navy rules, would have greeted him with a cheer that would have done his heart good. As it is, they must give vent to their feelings in some way; and the exclamations of 'Well done!' 'That's the fellow!' 'Good boy, Paine!' are not a bad compromise, after all. Besides, it might be rather premature at this time to indulge in any triumphant expression of feeling before we are even in sight of land."

Upon the seventh day land was discovered from the masthead. "It is now half-past two o'clock, and we are entering Trinity Bay at a speed of seven and a half knots an hour, paying out the cable at a very slight increase on the same rate. The curve which it forms between the ship and the water proves that there is little or no strain upon it, and proves also another thing,—that it can be run out at eight, nine, and, I believe, ten

Trinity Bay
Gorgon
Niagara
Agamemnon
Valorous
Valentia Bay
Average depth two miles

TELEGRAPHIC PLATEAU.

miles with the greatest safety. This, however, as I have previously stated, cannot be done with old cable that has been coiled so often as to have a tendency to kink; and there is—as has been already intimated—some of this kind which we shall be obliged to pay out before landing. A signal signifying 'all well' has been received from the Agamemnon, which must now be on the point of landing her cable at Valentia Bay, Ireland, which is about sixteen hundred and forty miles from our present position."

At eight o'clock in the evening, while the Niagara was proceeding up Trinity Bay and was yet some eighteen miles distant from the landing-place, Mr. Field left the ship for the purpose of visiting the telegraph station and sending a despatch to the United States. "It was near two o'clock in the morning before he arrived at the beach; and, as it was quite dark, he had considerable difficulty in finding the path that led up to the station. There was no house in sight, and the whole scene was as dreary and as desolate as a wilderness at night could be. A silence as of the grave reigned over every thing before him; while behind, at a distance of a mile, he could see the huge hull of the Niagara looming up indistinctly through the gloom of night, and the light of the lamps on her deck making the darkness still darker and blacker by the contrast. He entered the narrow road, and after a journey of what appeared to be twenty miles he came in sight of the station, which stands about half a mile from the beach. There was, however, no sign of life there; and the house in its stillness looked strangely in unison with every thing around. It had a deserted look, as if it had long since ceased to be the habitation of man. In vain he looked for a door in the front; but there was no entrance there. He looked up at the windows, in the hope, perhaps, of being able to enter by that way; but the windows in the lower story were beyond his reach; and the house, having been partly built on piles, had the appearance of being raised on stilts. A detour of the establishment, however, led to the discovery of a door in the side; and through this he finally succeeded in effecting an entrance. The noise he made in getting in, it was natural to expect, would arouse the inmates; but there seemed either to be no inmates to arouse, or those inmates were not easily disturbed. He stopped for a moment to listen, and as he listened he heard the breathing of sleepers in an apartment near him. The door was immediately thrown open, and in a few seconds the sleepers were awake,—wide awake, and opening their eyes wider and wider as the wonderful news fell upon their astonished and delighted ears. They could hardly believe the evidence of their senses, and were bewildered at what they heard. The cable laid, when, but a few short weeks before, they had received the news of disaster and defeat, and they had looked only to the far-distant future for the accomplishment of the great work! The cable laid, and they unconscious of it!—they, who had waited and watched so many weary days and weeks for the ships they had begun to believe would never come! And they were now in the bay, —those same ships,—within a mile of them! Can they be dreaming? Dreaming! No. What they have heard is true,—all true; and there is the living witness before them.

"'What do you want?' was the exclamation of the first who was awakened, as he endeavored to rub the sleep out of his eyes.

"'I want you to get up,' said Mr. Field, 'and help us to take the cable ashore.'

"'To take the cable ashore?' re-echoed the others, who were now just awakening, and who heard the words with a dim, dreamy idea of their meaning; 'to take the cable ashore?'

"'Yes,' said Mr. Field; 'and we want you at once.'

"They were now thoroughly aroused; and, directing Mr. Field to the bedrooms of the other sleepers,—for there were four or five others in the house,—they prepared themselves with all haste to assist in landing the cable. Mr. Field found that the telegraph office would not be open till nine o'clock that morning, and that the operator of the New York, Newfoundland, and London telegraph was absent at the time. He also ascertained that the nearest station at which he could find an operator was fifteen miles distant, and that the only way of getting there was on foot. Now, fifteen miles in Newfoundland is about equal to twice the distance in a civilized country, and is a tolerably long walk; but it was something to be the bearer of such news to a whole continent, and so two of the young men willingly volunteered for the journey, bearing with them, for transmission to New York and the whole United States, the despatch which contained the first announcement of the successful accomplishment of the work."

Upon the eighth day the cable was landed, the ships being dressed with flags in honor of the occasion. Sixty men from the Niagara, and forty from the British ships Gorgon and Porcupine, took part in this task and the attendant ceremonies. "The landing-place for the cable is a very picturesque little beach, on which a wharf has been constructed. A road, about the dimensions of a bridle-path, has been cut through the forest, and up this road, through bog and mire, you find your way to the telegraph station, about half a mile distant. Alongside of this road a trench has been dug for the cable, to preserve it from accidents to which it might otherwise be liable.

"When the boats arrived at the landing, the officers and men jumped ashore, and Mr. North, first lieutenant of the Niagara, presented Captain Hudson with the end of the cable. Captain Otter, of the Porcupine, and Commander Dayman, of the Gorgon, now took hold of it, and, all the officers and men following their example, a procession was formed along the line. The road or path over which we had to take the cable was a most primitive affair. It led up the side of a hill a couple of hundred feet high, and had been cut out of the thick forest of pines and other evergreens. In some places the turf—which is to be found here on the top of the highest mountains—was so soft with recent rains that you would sink to your ankles in it. Well, it was up this road we had to march with the cable; and a splendid time we had. It was but reasonable to suppose that the three captains who headed the procession would certainly pick out the best parts and give us the advantage of the stepping-stones; but it appeared all the same to them; and they plunged into the boggiest and dirtiest parts with a recklessness and indifference that satisfied us they were about the worst pilots we could have had on land, despite their well-known abilities as navigators.

"This memorable procession started at a quarter to six o'clock, and arrived at the telegraph station about twenty minutes after. The ascent of the hill was the worst part of the journey; but when we got to the top the scene which opened before us would have repaid us for a journey of twenty miles over a still worse road. There beneath us lay the harbor, shut in by mountains, except at the entrance from Trinity Bay; and there, too, lay the steamers of the two greatest maritime nations of the world. On every side lies an unbroken wilderness, and, if we except the telegraph station, at which we will soon arrive, not a single habitation to tell that man has ever lived here.

"Never was such a remarkable scene presented since the world began. Even now, at the very point of its realization, it does not seem as if the work in which we have been engaged has been accomplished. The continuity, however, without which the cable would be utterly valueless, is as perfect now as it ever was. Mr. Laws and Mr. De Santy, the two chief electricians who have accompanied us from England, have 'tasted' the current, and about a dozen others at the head of the procession have done the same thing. The writer himself is a witness on this point, and will never forget the singular acid taste which it had. Some received a pretty strong shock,—so strong that they willingly resigned the chance of repeating the experiment.

"On the arrival of the procession the cable is brought up to the house and the end placed in connection with the instrument. The deflection of the needle on the galvanometer gives incontrovertible evidence that the electrical condition of the cable is satisfactory. The question now is, How shall we properly celebrate the consummation of the great event? How, but by an acknowledgment to that Providence without whose favor the enterprise must have ended in disaster and defeat? Captain Hudson took up his position on a pile of boards, the officers and men standing round amid shavings, stumps of trees, pieces of broken furniture, sheets of copper, telegraph-batteries, little mounds of lime and mortar, branches of trees, huge boulders, and a long catalogue of other things equally incongruous.

"'We have,' said the captain, 'just accomplished a work which has attracted the attention and enlisted the interest of the whole world. That work,' he continued, 'has been performed not by ourselves: there has been an Almighty Hand over us and aiding us; and, without the divine assistance thus extended us, success was impossible. With this conviction firmly impressed upon our minds, it becomes our duty to acknowledge our indebtedness to that overruling Providence who holds the sea in the hollow of his hand. "Not unto us, O Lord, not unto us, but to thy name, be all the glory." I hope the day will never come when, in all our works, we shall refuse to acknowledge the overruling hand of a divine and almighty Power. . . . There are none here, I am sure, whose hearts are not overflowing with feelings of the liveliest gratitude to God in view of the great work which has been accomplished through his permission, and who are not willing to join in a prayer of thanksgiving for its successful termination. I will therefore ask you to join me in the following prayer, which is the same, with a few necessary alterations, that was offered for the laying of the cable.'"

This prayer was then offered at the throne of grace by the captain, the auditors responding at its close with an "Amen" which showed with what profound emotion they regarded the scene in which they were such prominent actors.

THE AGAMEMNON IN A GALE.

In regard to the voyage of the Agamemnon we find little to say which would not be a repetition of that of the Niagara, with the exception that she experienced much less favorable weather, and that the admirable paying-out machine invented by our countryman, Mr. Everett, performed its delicate duty under more trying circumstances than those to which it had been subjected on the American frigate. The Queen's Message was transmitted over the wire on the 16th of August; and, intelligence of the fact being made known the same evening throughout the Northern and Western States, the people gave themselves up to the wildest demonstrations of joy. Few persons of an age to appreciate the significance of the triumph will forget that memorable night.

With the laying of the cable our duty as a chronicler ends.

We have not to follow the inventors, electricians, and commanders to the land, and detail the ovations of which they were the honored objects. The public will long remember the eloquence of the orators who dilated upon the theme, the inspired language in which the newspapers held forth to their amazed subscribers, and the prophetic vein in which the clergy felt justly entitled to indulge. Fifty years from now, those who were boys on the 16th of August will tell, with undiminished interest, of the tar-barrels and bonfires, the salutes and fireworks, the illuminations and torchlight processions, which, from one end of the country to the other, welcomed the inspiring tidings and made the summer night gorgeous with flames and clamorous with artillery. The cable is at length laid through the bed of the Atlantic Ocean. Over what jagged mountain-ranges is that slender filament carried! In what deep oceanic valleys does it rest! Through what strange and unknown regions, among things how uncouth and wild, must it thread its way! Still, in spite of this first magnificent success, deep-sea telegraphing must be regarded as in its very infancy; and doubtless many new and even more marvellous feats will yet be performed claiming admission among the achievements of Man upon—or rather beneath—the Sea.

Perhaps the best among the numerous good things suggested by the happy return of the Telegraphic Fleet was the following sentiment:—"THE EQUATOR AND THE CABLE: the former an imaginary line which divides the poles, the latter a veritable line which connects the hemispheres!"

"Far, far below ocean's heaving breast,
Where the storm-spirit ever is hush'd to rest,
The cable now lies on its snowy bed,—
The glittering ashes of ocean's dead;
And storms shall not break nor tempests sever
This arch of promise, for ever and ever,
Till an angel shall stand with one foot on the sea
And swear that time no longer shall be."

Thus conclude the chronicles of the sea. It is a thought eminently calculated to teach a lesson of humility, that the sea, after centuries of submission to man and of ministration to his necessities and his pleasures, is positively and absolutely the same, in its physical aspects, as when, after the subsidence of the waters of the Deluge, it took its place in the great hollows and valleys of our globe. Man has often made the wilderness to blossom as the rose; but not one iota of change has he wrought upon the investing desert of waters. With that splendid stanza upon a splendid theme, and which will be as immortal as its subject, we close our record of the achievements of Man upon the Sea:

Thy shores are empires, changed in all save thee:
  Assyria, Greece, Rome, Carthage, what are they?
Thy waters wasted them while they were free,
  And many a tyrant since: their shores obey
  The stranger, slave, or savage: their decay
Has dried up realms to deserts: NOT SO THOU,
  UNCHANGEABLE SAVE TO THY WILD WAVES' PLAY:
TIME WRITES NO WRINKLE ON THINE AZURE BROW:
SUCH AS CREATION'S DAWN BEHELD, THOU ROLLEST NOW.

THE END.

www.ingramcontent.com/pod-product-compliance
Lightning Source LLC
LaVergne TN
LVHW021104110826
845150LV00001B/160

9781425565176